Daryl Douglas Mowat received his honours B.Sc. degree in kinesiology from the University of Waterloo. He worked as a paraprofessional habilitation counsellor with various target groups; however, his career was cut short by bouts of oversensitivity, which required his hospitalization on a few occasions.

By meditating on his inner world, Daryl realized that his oversensitivity was his overreaction to his sensations of excitement and anxiety. In learning to control his reactions, Daryl realized that entities from realms of the after-death were occasionally stimulating sensations in his body. The knowledge he gained by interacting with these entities resulted in this book.

To my late mother, Grace, my late father, Jim, my late brother, Maynard, my sister Arden, my brother, Myles, and my sister, Shelley, because all the members of my parent's nuclear family supported me unfailingly in my effort to write this book. Shelley was especially involved in relating her understanding of metaphysics to me so that we could discuss our different viewpoints upon it and work towards a mutual understanding of it.

Daryl Douglas Mowat

NATURALISM

The Freedom of a Self's Harmony within Nature's Harmony

AUSTIN MACAULEY PUBLISHERS™
LONDON • CAMBRIDGE • NEW YORK • SHARJAH

Copyright © Daryl Douglas Mowat 2024

The right of Daryl Douglas Mowat to be identified as author of this work has been asserted by the author in accordance with sections 77 and 78 of the Copyright, Designs and Patents Act 1988.

All rights reserved. No part of this publication may be reproduced, stored in a retrieval system, or transmitted in any form or by any means, electronic, mechanical, photocopying, recording, or otherwise, without the prior permission of the publishers.

Any person who commits any unauthorised act in relation to this publication may be liable to criminal prosecution and civil claims for damages.

The story, the experiences, and the words are the author's alone.

A CIP catalogue record for this title is available from the British Library.

ISBN 9781528916325 (Paperback)
ISBN 9781528916332 (Hardback)
ISBN 9781528961523 (ePub-e-book)

www.austinmacauley.com

First Published 2024
Austin Macauley Publishers Ltd®
1 Canada Square
Canary Wharf
London
E14 5AA

I would like to thank, first and foremost, Douglas Wayne Boyd, my best friend, for the patience and the interest he showed in relation to my occasionally outlandish ideas that I explored with him during the writing of this book. His contribution to this book was invaluable because he contributed the sanity of his loving attitude which he gives to all whom he meets.

Secondly, I would like to thank my former wife Carol Dengis for her insightful comments in regards to my ideas about the disciplines of computer science, physics, and psychology. It is satisfying to know that we have both transformed the psychological baggage that we brought to our marriage which was the cause of our divorce so that we can, once again, relate lovingly to each other without feeling the need to re-establish the bond of marriage.

Thirdly, I would like to thank all the atheists, agnostics, Jews, Christians, Muslims, Baha'is, Hindus, Taoists, and Buddhists with whom I discussed frankly the drawbacks and merits of their metaphysical or religious viewpoints. Contrary to the popular belief that these viewpoints should not be discussed because such discussions supposedly lead to enmity (and thus enemies), my discussions with these people only led to my deepened understanding of the Truth because our discussions were carried out with the mutual respect that only a loving attitude can produce. As a consequence, I did not develop enemies; I developed friends.

Fourthly, I would like to thank you, the reader of this book, for reading this book because, by reading it, you will be in a position to help others cultivate their attitudes of love so that it is more likely that they will develop their understanding and become enlightened, that is, if they are not already enlightened.

Fifthly, I would like to thank the staff at the Ontario Disability Support Program (ODSP) and the MPPs of the Ontario Province for granting me the funds to buy a laptop computer so that I could write my book. I would also like to express my gratitude to the people of Ontario for paying the taxes they do so that I can receive a disability pension from ODSP.

Finally, I would like to thank all the people at Austin Macauley Publishers who worked together so well to produce my book. These people were unfailingly professional and helpful and did not complain at all about the numerous mistakes I made—and continue to make—in my endeavour to be a helpful professional too. I would especially like to express my thanks to the people with whom I was in direct contact through the internet, by mail, or by telephone. These people are Shannon Bourne, Office Assistant, Nathan Kerslake, Junior Editor, Rebecca Ponting, Managing Editor, James Amstell, Executive Board Member, Dr Rosalind Lyons, Associate Editor, Eden Moas, Editorial Assistant, Jamie Yardley, Junior Production Coordinator, Alfie Fisher, Accountants Assistant, Matthew Smith, Accountants Assistant, Amanda Harrison, Accounts Executive, Kurt David, Executive Editor, Egle Jeffery, Executive Editor, Norma Clarke, Publishing Coordinator, and James Morris, Publishing Coordinator.

Table of Contents

Preliminary Notes — 11
- *First Note* — 11
- *Second Note* — 12
- *Third Note* — 13
- *Fourth Note* — 14
- *The Twenty-Five Fundamental Truths of Selfism* — 36

Chapter One: The Reality of Images, — 48
Apparitions and Appearances — 48
- *Conclusion* — 69

Chapter Two: A Self's Development of Harmony — 74
- *A Self's Harmonious Contentment Between Its Disharmonious Discontentments* — 74

Chapter Three: The Empirical Basis for a Self's Understanding and Wisdom — 84

Chapter Four: Continuity in Immediacy Versus Time in Eternity — 123
- *The Truths of Continualists and the Falsehoods of Temporalists* — 148
- *Conclusion* — 158

Chapter Five: Nature and Deoxyribonucleic Acid (DNA) — 170
- *Individuals Are Inclusive While Communities Are Exclusive* — 203

Chapter Six: The Myth of the Big Bang and the Reality of the Harmonious Infiniverse — 205

Chapter Seven: Ontology Versus Scientism   **238**

   Conclusion   *275*

Chapter Eight: The Character Types and Personality Roles of a Self   **282**

   Conclusion   *305*

Chapter Nine: The Implications of Naturalism for Society   **322**

   The Facts of Naturalists and the Fictions of Creationists   *324*

Final Note   **332**

Glossary   **334**

References   **359**

Preliminary Notes

First Note

Selfology is the ontological study of the self, its selfological qualities, how it uses its needs to activate its sensor, and how it uses its cognition to sense by way of its sensor. I developed selfology because I realised that the ego, psyche and mind, the being, soul and consciousness, and the ipsum, anima, and animus are all religious fictions because they're based on the fantasy of principles, rather than the reality of Nature's harmony. Martin Buber, who wrote the book, *I and Thou*, failed to understand that "I" and "Thou" refer to "its" or selves of Nature, not fictional "non-its" of a fictional God, like egos, beings, or ipsa.

A self is the guide of its senses, not the controller of its senses, because a self is inevitably influenced by its sense oof what's happening in, to, and around it; therefore, a realistic self is a *self-guider who self-guides*, not a "self-controller who self-controls", its senses. The assumption that a self is able to act and react without being influence is entirely mistaken.. A self often attempts to control its sensor because the self delusionally mistakes control for reality, rather than the illusion it is.

Unfortunately, many religions are based on the notion that a self is a center of command, rather than a center of guidance which gives rise to the philosophy of authority and the doctrine of authoritarianism, rather than the philosophy of liberty and the doctrine of libertarianism. Authoritarianism is the denial of guidance because an authoritarian wants to control every self as well as the self it is, instead of just guide its selfological qualities. An authoritarian self is stupid because it doesn't understand that it's unable to control the self it is. An authoritarian self doesn't understand that it's unable to "get hold" of the self it is which is why self-control is impossible. An authoritarian self's ignorance of this fact is its ignorance of its Freedom which is The Ultimate Truth of every self's existence and Nature's Existence.

Second Note

I appreciate the art of knowledgeably, meaningfully, and factually expressing my words as my philosophy. My words are the way I express my wisdom as my philosophy. My words express my knowledge, not my understanding. Happily, my understanding will always remain a mystery to you just as your understanding will always remain a mystery to me.

A self's uses its intelligence to perceive a symbolised fact which has been derived from an unsymbolised meaning, while *wisdom* is a self's understanding of how the facts it has perceived are related. A self usually labels its meanings as a symbolisation of its facts and uses these symbolisations to define each other. A sensation which is known, rather than hypothesised as a fact, takes on a certain, rather than an uncertain, meaning. A sensation is my experience of an impulse of energy occurring in my sensable organism. A sensable organism is a self's sensibly sensed organic body which the self lives as well as inhabits.

My understanding of a sensation I experience is not sharable. I'm only able to share facts, not my sensations or the meanings of these sensations. My facts are my symbolisations of my meanings, not the understanding with which I express them; therefore, we only understand each other's symbolic facts, not each other's inner understanding.

There is also a danger to symbols because some symbols are unrelated to our sensations. Many of the words we develop aren't based on our experience; therefore, these words are only nominal (words without a referent). The words "God", "Creator", and "destiny" confused me because they're words without referents; however, I realised that the word "I" refers to a *reality* which I am unable to sense because I am the inhabiter of my "objects" and my "subjectives", e.g., my objective sensor and my objective sensable organism as well as my subjective faculty of cognition and my subjective ability of knowing.

I am not an object to sense; I am also unable to use my cognition to sense what "I" am because I can only realise that I exist as a subject we call a "self". My book, Naturalism: The Freedom of a Self's Harmony within Nature's Harmony, is based on the fact that I realise the self I am as I cognise my use of Nature's Will, even though I'm unable to experience the self I am.

Third Note

I value my integrity because my integrity is my uncompromising respect for the natures of Nature (the realities of Reality). My integrity is not based on morality because morality is selfpathic. Selfpathy is the tendency of a self to suffer. My integrity is based on harmony. My harmony is selfkomic. Selfkomy is the tendency of a self to enjoy.

Nature's willing expresses Its harmony because Nature is free of the desire to end Its use of Its Will. A selfkom has learned the futility of its desire to end its use of Nature's Will.

A selfpath is a self who suffers from its expression of who and how it's pretending to be and leads others to suffer from its pretensions because it chooses disharmonious actions. A selfpath's *expression* of disharmony is the result of its *impulsive desire to restrict its own and others' Freedom.*

A "selfkom" is a self who enjoys its expression of who it's expressing as well as how it expresses who it's expressing because it chooses to express harmonious actions and reactions. A selfkom's *expression* of harmony is the result of its *spontaneous Freedom.*

My religious acceptance of other religions and religious views is my respect for the Freedom of selves, not my "tolerance" of them and their Freedom. As the founder of my own verbal religion (my spoken or written account of my religion in signs, like words), I know my Freedom to agreeably disagree with your verbal religion is essential, especially if I find your verbal religion is inadequate. You may interpret my criticisms to be unacceptably sinful, rather than acceptably sinless, but my criticisms are always meant to help you develop.

My verbal religion of signs is in accord with my *nonverbal* religion of harmony. I'm asking you to discern this book with your nonverbal religion of harmony. I welcome your criticisms of my verbal religion because I'm able to learn from your criticisms (if they're constructive); however, your verbosity is only critically constructive if it issues from your nonverbal religion of harmony which is why I only accept learning from the critiques of a self whose verbosity is harmonious, instead of captivating.

Fourth Note

The words, italicised below, describe Nature, Its natures other than Its selves, Its natural selves, as well as the results of Its willing or driving.

1. Nature is *Reality, Activity, Ether, Quality, Energy, Matter, or Thingness. Nature is the Source of everything.*
2. Nature's natures are Its infinite *mortal realities, activities, phenomena, qualities, condensed energies, materialised matters, or things* which are the existents of the realms of the before-death (the Infiniverse). Some natures have structures which are evolved, grown, and developed from Nature by Its willing, deteriorated by Its willing, and devolved by Its willing. Vibrations deteriorate these natural structures; therefore, evolved and grown natural structures are instable because Nature is continually willing these natural structures to vibrate.
3. Selves are Nature's *immortal centers, activities, things, phenomena, qualities, energies, or matters*, like you and I. Selves are generated by and developed from Nature; therefore, Nature is the Origin of selves. Nature also generates a self's *sensor or objective large uncondensed energy form* (objective luef) as It's generating and developing the self. A self generates its cognition's *knowing or cognising* by instinctively and nondeliberately or noninstinctively and deliberately using Nature's Will in tandem with Nature's use of Its Will.

A self uses Nature's Will in its sensor or "luef" to drive Nature's will waves or vitalities which are Nature's results of gravity-antigravity, magnetism, electromagnetism, electro-weak nuclearity, weak nuclearity, and strong nuclearity. Nature's vitalities are not forces because Nature has no need to force. Nature's Will is in every self as the Non-Individual basis of the self's individual needs; therefore, every self uses Nature's Will or drive in its individual needs so it can use Nature's Will to fulfil these needs Introduction

This book is about Nature as well as natures, like you.

You are a self. You are who you are because the word "who" refers to your genuine, sincere, and authentic expression of you from what you are, instead of the person, role or false self you pretend to be..

You are what you are because what you are is the self you are. The word "what" refers to the reality you are. You're able to express your selfological qualities, like your needs, desires, abilities, and emotions, from what you are, genuinely, sincerely, and authentically. I'm anticipating that you're asking the question "What am I as a self?" The answer to your question is that you are a *center* of Nature. As a center of Nature, you are a relative uncondensed energy or a relative unmaterialised matter because Nature is unbounded uncondensed Energy or unbounded unmaterialised Matter.

The word "how" refers to your way or manner of expressing either who you are or what you are; therefore, how you are is either a phony expression of who you aren't (the person you aren't) or a genuine, sincere, and authentic expression of who you are from what you are (the self you are).

The word "why" refers to the cause, purpose, or reason for which a happening is exists and is volitioned or willed. Why you use Nature's Volition or Will to volition or will who you are or aren't is due to your fear of revealing your genuine, sincere, and authentic selfological qualities to other selves because you don't want to suffer their cruel responses. Ironically, they are cruel because, like you, they are afraid to genuinely, sincerely, and authentically reveal their selfological qualities, which means that you are as cruel as they are if you are pretending to be who you aren't.

There is no cause, purpose, or reason for what you are because Nature has no cause, purpose, or reason for Its volitioning or willing of phenomena, natures, or realities, like you. Nature evolves, grows, develops, deteriorates, and devolves without being caused, purposed, or reasoned by another reality to evolve, grow, develop, deteriorate, or devolve.

There is no God controlling Nature. Nature's Freedom is absolute in Its volitioning or willing because Nature is uncontrolled. Selves' Ultimate Truth of Freedom is also absolute or uncontrolled in their use of Nature's Volition or Will; therefore, it's impossible for a self to have self-control. A self relatively guides, rather than controls, its selfological qualities, and a self never guides the self it is.

The word "where" refers to your place, relation, respect, or situation in Nature. As a center of Nature, you are always here, just as your selfological qualities are "in here" or are in you as your inherencies, while your sensor, you sensable organism (your organic body), and your outer world are "out there" as your externalisations.

The word "when" refers to what is happening as a current happening, while the word "then" as well as the word "when" refer to a self's memory of what has happened or anticipation of what might happen. The words "when" and "then" do not refer to time because time is a fiction of people who have imagined it as a "count-down" of their living in their mortal bodies. You don't live "now" or "in this moment" because there are no separate nows or moments of an eternal present or eternal Now nor are there past or future nows or moments. As a center of Nature, you are a current happening of Nature's Continuity in Immediacy, not a timed event of God's time in eternity.

Nature is absolute Activity, while the natures of Nature are Its relative activities. Nature is not sui generis (self-generating) because Nature is absolute Generativity or Activity; therefore, Nature is not a relative generated activity. Nature generates because Nature is the absolute Generator or Activator. *Generationism or Activationism* is the truth that Nature is the absolute Generator or Activator and, thus, the absolute Origin of everything. The falsehood of Creationism is "The doctrine that the universe and all matter and forms of being within it are the result not of evolution but of God's direct and instantaneous creation" (Landau, 1968, p. 315).

Nature's Kinetics is the activity of Nature's Kinesis. Nature's Kinesis is Its absolute motions and movements; therefore, Nature's Kinesis is generated or activated by Its Kinetics. Nature's Will or Volition is Its activity of Kinetics, while Its Kinesis is Its absolute motions and movements.

A self is a relative activity; therefore, a self instinctively as well as deliberately activates Nature's Will or Volition. A self's use of Nature's Will is unknown or ignored as well as known by the self; therefore, automatism is a mistaken hypothesis because automatists base automatism on the hypothesis that we only know our supposedly illusory feeling of willing. Automatism is the false philosophical doctrine which asserts that activity, motion, and movement are the result of mechanical "force" while Volition in activity, motion, and movement is only an illusion.

Every self uses Selfkinesis to motion its small uncondensed energy forms, motion its large uncondensed energy form, motion particles in the body it inhabits, move its body, move particles in the environment, and move very small bodies in the environment, while reserving its use of Selfkinetics for activating selfological qualities, such as a self's needs, sane desires, insane desires, abilities, disabling abilities, faculties, and disabling faculties. A self's need for wisdom motivates its use of Selfkinetics and Selfkinesis.

A self's harmony within Nature's harmony is the self's experience of Naturalism; therefore, a self's wisdom is its cognition and knowing of its experience of harmony within Nature's harmony.

Essence and Substance are activities of Nature's Volition or Will; therefore, absolute Activity is Nature's willing or volition of Essence and Substance as activities. Essence is an advancement of Nature's Existence as Activity; therefore, Essence is the activity of progression because Nature advances realities, phenomena, or natures by progression. Substance is progressed by Nature as the activity of procession. Nature uses Essence to progress the processions of Substance.

Essence is uncondensed Energy or unmaterialised Matter. Essence is activity in the uncondensed or unmaterialised forms evolved by Nature. Substance is condensed Energy or materialised Matter. Substance is the Activity of the condensed energies or "materialised matters" evolved by Nature's Existence.

Existence is defined as:

'The absolute Activity called 'Nature' or 'Thingness' which is the absolute Source of activation for the only Will that Nature or Thingness and Its relative sources or activities of activation called 'selves' use to effect immediately continual changing currents of Flow in the World, including the inner-outer World of these selves.'

A nature or thing's existing is defined as:

'Any nature, thing, phenomenon, or reality which Nature, Thingness, the Phenomenon, or Reality has generated or activated who is also able to generate nor activate continually immediate changing currents of Flow in the World, i.e., 'selves', like you and I.'

Physicality is also an activity activated by Nature's use of Its Will or Volition. A physicality is an activated activity of realised realities, naturalised natures, condensed energies or materialised matters which are evolved, grown, and developed as the continually immediate always changing *structures* of mineral, vegetable, and sensable organisms or bodies. A physicality is a structure evolved, grown, and developed by having portions of Reality realised and structured by Reality which is identical to writing "portions of Nature natured and structured by Nature", "portions of Energy condensed and structured by Energy", or "portions of Matter materialised and structured by Matter".

Nature is the absolute Activity that uses Volition or Will. Nature or Activity activates Its willing which is identical to saying, "Nature or Activity activates Its volitioning".

Living is a means of a self's ability to exist its sensor or sensable organism. Living is a specific way of selves ability to exist or activate; therefore, existing transcends living because living is a specific activity of a self's generalised ability to activate activities.

A self is an activity of Activity which is brought to exist as a center of activity in an existent (such as a zygote) by way of its use of Activity's (Nature's) spontaneous instinctive nondeliberate willing. A self exists without living as a self; however, a newly generated self spontaneously or impulsively as well as instinctively and nondeliberately lives its sensor (its large uncondensed energy form) as well as its sensable organism (its zygote) by using its ability to exist (activate Nature's Will). Absolute Existence is Nature's existing or activating of Its Will in selves and their sensors, mineral bodies, vegetable bodies, and sensable bodies. A self exists or activates its use of Nature's willing in its inner aspects of the World, like its immaterial faculty of cognition and immaterial ability of knowing, as well as exists or activates its living of its outer aspects of the World, like its immaterial sensor and it materialised sensable organism.

A self is an activity, an energy, or a matter. A self's faculty of cognition is its immaterial activity, energy, or matter with which it guides its ability of immaterial knowing; therefore, cognition is a self's immaterial faculty containing its immaterial ability of knowing. A self's sensor is its form of essence, its form of progression or its form of energetics. A self's sensable organism is its body of substance, body of procession, or body of energy impulses (sensations). A self's physicality is its continually changing structure called its "sensable organism" by using materialised atoms as its means of continually changing this structure.

Certain Greek Presocratic philosophers thought material atoms were indestructible because they didn't understand that only destructible condensed energies or materialised matters are existed as existents by Nature because these particular existents have no ability to exist, i.e., no ability to activate Nature's Will. Materialised matters are the destructible particles evolved by Nature from unmaterialised Matter. Unmaterialised Matter *is* indestructible because unmaterialised Matter is uncondensed Energy (Nature).

Nature is the Source, not the void. Nature is Full of Energy as the Source; therefore, Nature is not an empty energyless void. Nature is Activity or Thingness, not inactivity or the "stillness" of nothingness Taoists and Zenists claim that the inactivity of nothingness is only a phrase referring to the unreal or the unnatural because the inactivity of nothingness simply "is not". In other words, inactivity is a delusional concept, like nothingness, because neither the word "inactivity" nor the word "nothingness" refer to an actual, illusory, delusional, or hallucinatory referent.

Nothingness "is not" as I've already indicated; therefore, nothingness has no existing referent. "Nothingness" and "non-Existence" are words without meaning. In other words "Nothingness" and "non-Existence" are only nominal words. They don't refer to any thing or the Thingness from, in, and by which everything is generated or activated to begin existing as an existent of thingness, i.e., nominal words can't refer to referent because they have none.

Nothingness is usually thought to be a "synonym" for non-Existence; however, nothingness isn't even a mistaken hypothesis or delusion of those who give it credence because it simply isn't existent. Nothingness isn't a synonym for non-Existence because non-Existence carries the connotation that nothingness is the "content" of non-Existence, whereas non-Existence carries the connotation that it's the "container" of nothingness.

Ironically, "synonyms" are the mistaken hypotheses or delusions of linguists who fail to appreciate that every word has certain dissimilar as well similar connotations which denote a slightly, moderately, or drastically different actuality, illusion, delusion, or hallucination that they've referred to as having exactly the same meaning as other words with different connotations that they're ignoring.

The supernatural also is not. The supernatural is only imaginary because the supernatural is unreal or unnatural; therefore, The Creator, Creation, creatures, creativity, and creativeness are all mistaken hypotheses or delusions because these concepts are based on the mistaken hypothesis of supernaturalism.

The definition of Creation is 'bringing something into existence from nothing.' Nothingness is a mistaken hypothesis or delusion which means that the word "Creation" and all words derived from it are mistaken hypotheses or delusions because nothingness isn't an existent. The ability to create is a fantasy of Creationists. We only have the abilities to invent signs, develop plans, and generate things from Energy, not the ability to create things from nothing.

Unlike the Creator, the Activator is real. The Activator is Nature. Nature is not God, because God is a dualistic notion. The word "God" is existent sonly in relation to the word "Goddess"; therefore, these words constitute a duality. In various eras of history, either God or Goddess was thought to be the sole "Creator" of the universe because our ancestors weren't acquainted with the Infiniverse or the truth of Activation from the absolute Activity I call "Nature". Consequently, our ancestors ignored Nature's continual development of selves and continual evolution, growth, development, deterioration, and devolution of other natures because they were enchanted by their delusion of Creation.

Phenomena, natures, or realities include appearances, like a bush in a garden, and apparitions, like a hologram, as well as unappearing and unapparitioning selves. Appearances and apparitions are realities, natures, or phenomena as are unappearing and unapparitioning selves; therefore, phenomenology is ontology and Naturalism because phenomenology is the study of the Phenomenon and Its phenomena, ontology is the study of ontic Reality and Its ontic realities, and Naturalism is the study of Nature and Its natures. Ontology, phenomenology, and Naturalism are the respective studies of a self's cognitive knowing of its non-sensable faculties and abilities, Its cognitive knowing of its sensing through its sensor, as well as through its sensable organism.

Many philosophers consider their theory that we exist in a universe "created" from a beginning to be sacrosanct; however, only Nature's Infiniverse of infinite particles are existed by Nature as Its immediate continuity of condensations or materialisations which are also (sooner or later) decondensed or dematerialised and replaced by new condensations or dematerialisations. The Infiniverse is the infinity of particles existent, but not existing, in the Ether because they're not selves with the ability of existing, activating, or generating changes in the World by using Nature's Will. The universe is falsely imagined because, like a body, the universe is defined as closed or bounded, whereas the Ether is open or unbounded. There is an infinity of finite particles existed by the Ether. This infinity of particles isn't bounded or closed off by the Ether because the Ether isn't bounded or closed off.

Only the Ether exists, not space, because space is supposedly empty nothingness. The Ether is Thingness (Nature). The Ether is full of things. Selves are things, although not everything is a self.

The Ether is continually evolving Its infinity of organic particles in Its unbounded extent. The Ether grows this infinity of organic particles into an infinity of organic bodies. I call this infinity of organic particles and bodies "the Infiniverse". The Infiniverse is not "the universe" because the word "universe" literally means "all phenomena taken collectively or all phenomena combined into one", whereas the Infiniverse literally means "the infinity of physicalities existent in as well as by way of the unboundedness of the Ether". Saying that "The universe is all phenomena or an amount" is like saying, "The universe is a body", because a body is simply an amount of particles.

Philosophers hypothesise that the world is all phenomena taken collectively or all phenomena combined into one; therefore, they fail to understand that phenomena aren't limited in number by the Ether because the Ether is unbounded or open. Phenomena are unlimited and numberless in the unboundedness or openness of the Ether.

The hypothesis of the "universe" is the mistaken notion that a bounded space limits the physicalities in it to a finite amount. Consequently, "the universe" is a misnomer because the physicalities evolved and grown by the Ether are infinite.

The unlimited phenomena which are continually evolved, grown, developed, deteriorated, and devolved are existed by Nature in Nature as an infinity, not a unity, because they aren't limited as a finite "amount" or a "unity". Consequently, the Infiniverse is not a unity because the Infiniverse is only describable as "infinity" or "the unlimited" which obviously isn't a "finite limitation" or universal amount.

Nature absolutely motions Its own portions of the unbounded Energy It is and particlises them as particles. My definition for "particlise" is:

'Nature's accidental spontaneous instinctive nondeliberate use of Its Will to condense or materialise a portion of the unbounded uncondensed Energy or unbounded immaterial Matter It is into a condensation or materialisation called a "particle".'

Among other things, particles compose the atoms of deoxyribonucleic acid (DNA) found in the cells of a sensable organism's muscles as well as in the rest of the cells of the sensable organism. "Sensable organism" are two words I've coined to replace the words "animal" and "creature" because the words, "animal" and "creature", are based on the delusion of laws, rather than the reality of needs. The inhabiting self of a sensable organism uses its ability of Selfkinesis to selfkinesthetically contract or relax its muscle cells thus initiating the movements of its sensable organism. A self's organic body is the self's sensable) because the self unavoidably senses its body with its cognition by way of its sensor and senses the outer world with its cognition by way of its sensable organism's sensory organs.

"Suefs" are smaller than particles as well as different from particles; however, "simfs" is an acronym standing for "small immaterial matter forms" which is identical to the acronym, suefs, "small uncondensed energy forms", because unbounded uncondensed Energy is identical to unbounded immaterial Matter.

Nature shines outer invisible qualia or outer waves of activity (visible light) through objective suefs to illuminate them so that they take on the appearance of objective photons. Photons aren't particles because their energy is uncondensed, not condensed, i.e., photons have no mass because a mass is a condensed portion of Energy or a materialised portion of Matter.

Objective photons are converted into subjective suefs by way of Nature's instinctive willing in a sensable organism's organs. The inhabiting self of the sensable organism senses these subjective suefs. The self of this sensable organism is also able to instinctively use Nature's Will to shine an inner quale of visible light through these subjective suefs so that these subjective suefs are imaged as subjective photons in the self's faculty of imagination.

Objective photons which apparition in the outer world don't apparition as objective photons in the self's imagination because an objective photon is translated into a subjective suef by way of the cone cells and rod cells in the retinas of the self's sensable organism. The self then images the subjective suef derived from its translation of an objective photon as a subjective photon.

The subjective photons imaged from these subjective suefs in the self's faculty of imagination give the self the impression that it has really seen the objective photon, rather than the subjective photon. The imaging of many subjective photons by a self inevitably results in its subjective motion picture or subjectively motioned large uncondensed energy form (known by the acronym, "luef") in its imagination derived from the interaction of objective photons with the self's retinas. The motion pictures that a self has derived from the environment are distinguished by the self from the hallucinatory motion pictures it generates, like its dream images.

Nature generates a self in gametes It is concurrently merging together and then develops this self in the zygote that these merging gametes complete at syngamy. As well as using subjective suefs to motion a self's subjective large uncondensed energy form, Nature uses a self's objective suefs to compose a self's objective large uncondensed energy form so that the self's objective luef may be shone as a large apparition. Luefs is an acronym standing for "large uncondensed energy forms" which is identical to the acronym, limfs, "large immaterial matter forms", because unbounded uncondensed Energy is identical to unbounded immaterial Matter. Objective luefs or limfs may be shone as large objective apparitions because they are composed of objective suefs or simfs which may be shone as small objective photons (small objective apparitions). Mirages are also composed of small objective photons.

A self's objective luef is the self's sensor.

When the objective suefs composing an objective luef have an inner subjective light instinctively shone through them by a self, the self's objective luef is transformed into an aura or large apparition which is objectively visible. Sensitive people are able to see an aura (an apparition of light) about a self's sensable organism. Nature also shines light through the luefs of plants so that they each have an aura, but a plant has no inhabiting self.

A self uses its guidance of Nature's Will to release its objective luef (its sensor) from its sensable organism when its sensable organism finally dies (that is, if selves are immortal). The self continues to exist and maintain its sensor in its ethereal home in the after-death (if the self is immortal). The self's ethereal home will reflect its religion as well as its blend of stupidity, ignorance, knowledge, and wisdom (if the self is immortal).

The picture on the cover of this book illustrates an ageless self's ageless sensor shining as this self's large apparition as it arises from this self's corpse which was formerly its aging sensable organism. If selves are immortal, a self's relations with its aged human sensable organism are isolated when this aged sensable organism dies and turns into a corpse. If selves are immortal, the self meets with selves of the after-death after its release from its corpse. The selves of the after-death either help or hinder a self in its decision of which ethereal realm of the after-death is appropriate for it to enter (if these ethereal realms are existent).

Physical realms compose the Infiniverse or the "before-death". The before-death is existed in the after-death because the selves of the physical realms might cognitively relate to the selves of the ethereal realms.

By using Nature's Will, a self is able to release as well as isolate its sensor from its multicellular body when its multicellular body dies (that is, if selves are immortal). A self is also able to release and isolate its sensor from its body when the self is cognisant (lucid) in its sleep as well as release and isolate its sensor from its multicellular body when the self is cognisant in its awakeness; however, the self remains related to its body by Nature's Will. Even though the self is isolated from its body, the self is able to use Nature's Will to keep its multicellular body's metabolism processing; therefore, the multicellular body continues to breathe, despite the self's isolation from it.

The sensors of selves which Nature evolves are like Nature in that their energies are uncondensed; however, the bodies which selves inhabit are composed of condensed energies. Nature would be completely filled by condensations or materialisations if they were immortal because the infinity of immortal condensations or materialisations (particles) would be continually increased by new infinities of immortal particles, like them, which Nature would continually evolve.

It's fortunate that particles are instable because their infinite increase as immortal particlisations which never departiclise would fill even the unboundedness of Energy (Nature). Energy's instinctive willing in these instable particles inevitably ages or deteriorates them and then decondenses or devolves them because the vibrations of particles are these particles' instability. Consequently, these particles are departiclised (decondensed or dematerialised) into unbounded pure (uncondensed) Energy or unbounded pure (immaterial) Matter. Consequently, my definition for "departiclise" is:

'Nature's accidental spontaneous instinctive nondeliberate use of Its Will to decondense or dematerialize an unsettled particle.'

Selves don't have the ability to evolve particles because selves need to replace particles in their sensable organisms by using their bodies to eat food. Particles are also eliminated from a self's sensable organism by way of evaporation, urination, and defecation which is why a self has to replace its particles; however, a self is only able to replace its particles by using its sensable organism to eat food. Of course, these particles aren't immortal because they're annihilated by digestion to provide energy for the self to use for a purpose, like moving its body.

The answer to the question, "How many angels are able to dance on the head of a pin?" would be a limited amount of angels, that is, if these angels had bodies of immortal condensed energies. Numberless angels are able to dance on the head of a pin because (if angels are existent and exist their sensors in certain realms of the after-death) they have luefs which aren't extended in Nature; therefore, the continually increasing infinities of new luefs evolved by Nature with the increasing infinities of newly developed selves will never overpopulate the unboundedness of Nature. Fortunately, the new particles continually evolved by Nature will never overpopulate Nature, despite the extendedness of these particles, because these particles are mortal.

Nature is not God because God is a mistaken hypothesis. Consequently, there is no enlightened God, as Creationists maintain.

God's ability to create a universe is only a mythical notion. The ability to "create" is based on the myth that we're able to bring something to exist as an existent from nothing based on a purposeful plan. The ability to create doesn't exist because things are generated from Thingness (Nature) by Its use of Its Existence (Its ability of Generation) without purpose, design, or plan because Nature has no intelligence with which to reason Its way to develop the goals so necessary for the implementation of purposing, designing, and planning.

Our supposed ability to create is a myth because the notion of creation is based on the impossibility of bringing something to exist as an existent from nothingness. We don't create; we invent. We are only able to devise, con of paying attention to his or her conscience. Community is based on the exclusion of individuals who won't let a community tell them to listen to its leaders, instead of their own consciences.

Conceive or form a plan as a thing by way of our original effort so we're able to produce another thing from the thing we call our "plan". We are unable to create a plan as something from nothing by way of our original effort; therefore, we're unable to create a thing. We develop designs from things by way of our original effort so we're able to produce new things, like *inner words of energy*.

We're unable to create designs from nothing by way of our original effort; therefore, we're unable to create things, like "inner words of nothing".

An inner word of energy is a word you've developed in your cognition as well as stored in your memory store so that you're able to use this inner word in your thinking; therefore, an *inner wordless* thought or *pure* thought, like an anticipation, is intuited by you as you think the thought, inwardly, just as an outer wordless vocalisation, like a screech, is felt by you as you vocalise the screech, outwardly. An interruption to your pure thoughts (your unworded thoughts) as you're doing something may result in your forgetting what you were doing; however, an interruption to your adulterated thoughts (your worded thoughts) may result in your forgetting the sequence of inner words you were thinking.

Inner words aren't necessarily new to adults who have been using them for years, but they are new to a child; therefore, a child needs to develop these inner words as its new realities, despite the fact that these inner words aren't new to adults, like the child's parents. A child learns how to convert the outer words he hears spoken by an adult to inner words. Inner words originated from outer words because outer words had to be spoken by Homo sapiens before Homo sapiens learned to internalise them as inner words. An inner word is an inner symbol as well as a silent sound of inner speech, while an outer word is an audible outer sound of outer speech. Inner speech is our ability to think inner symbols as silent sounds for our unheard listening in our cognitions. Inner and outer signs, like symbolic words, are energies, not nothings, just as inner and outer sounds are energies.

You may completely forget an interrupted thought if you don't work at remembering it. The challenge most people have is they haven't learned to concentrate their attention on their thinking; therefore, they have difficulty remembering the thoughts they've been thinking when their thinking has been interrupted.

By knowing Nature and Its differentiations, I develop knowledge. By focusing my attention on my knowledge, I'm able to think about my knowledge. By reasoning about my thoughts, I'm able to develop an understanding of Nature and Its differentiations. Knowing is simply a self's ability of cognising an energy which is experienced by it in its faculty of cognition.

Naturalism is my attempt to reconcile Nature's spontaneously instinctive nondeliberate use of Its Will with my spontaneously deliberate noninstinctive as well as spontaneously instinctive nondeliberate use of Its Will based on my ability to realise the Freedom of my own harmony within Nature's harmony. Selfism is my religion which is my understanding of Nature as the Origin of selves.

The nine chapters of this book are all concerned with my metaphysics of naturalism; however, I describe naturalism in relation to my religion of Selfism (which I founded) because metaphysics is always derived from a basic premise about the origin of phenomena. A premise about the origin of phenomena is a religious premise. Metaphysicians have only recently and unwisely attempted to divorce metaphysics and religion to satisfy the advocates of scientism, most of whom are Mortalists who don't realise the premise of their metaphysics is religious. My metaphysics deals with the Activator of our evolving, growing, developing, deteriorating, and devolving natural planet because this Activator also activates and develops selves, like you and I. Consequently, this book is my answer to the metaphysics of Mortalists who ignore the probability that they might exist (activate or generate) Nature's Will as Immortalists.

I define science as the critical and suitable use of scientific conceptual terms based on the axioms or experiential truths of voluntarism, harmony, conscience, needs, Style, experience, qualification, participant-observation, description, and subjectivism. I define scientism as the uncritical and unsuitable use of scientismistic conceptual terms based on the premises or hypothetical propositions of automatism, principles, rules, laws, technique, experimentation, quantification, delineation, measurement, and objectivism. Consequently, scientism is the doctrine which Aristotle developed and mistakenly called "science" instead of "scientism".

I call our modern day advocates for scientism "scientismists". There are very few scientists on earth because the falsity of scientism was developed by Aristotle as a false ontology.

Observable and unobservable realities we know in our experience resulted in the science and philosophy of ontology. I define ontology as a self's phenomenology as well as a self's naturalism; therefore, ontology, phenomenology, and naturalism are a self's study of Reality, Phenomenon, or Nature, realities, phenomena, or natures, and real, phenomenal, or natural qualities for the purpose of indicating, describing, and explaining their relationships by using an extrospective scientific research Style (unmethodical "method") and an introspective philosophical research approach in accord with the self's need to attain or deepen its wisdom. A scientist's Style is his or her realistic unmethodical "method" (which, of course, is written with my "tongue" very much "in cheek", since, quite obviously, my realistic Style is qualitatively unmethodical, not quantitatively methodical, while a scientismist's technique is his or her unrealistic quantitative method).

Metaphysics is unavoidably related to science; therefore, my metaphysics of naturalism is unevadably related to my science of ontology. My metaphysics is my artistic attempt to use my ontology to understand my religion of Selfism because religion is the basis of philosophy, just as art is the basis of science.

True scientists are a rare find because scientismists have attempted to stop the development of true science by disparaging art. Scientismists fear art because art is a self's use of science to develop an appreciation of how to harmoniously guide its selfological actions of energy as well as its energetical and physical motions and movements, while logic is a self's use of scientism in its delusional attempt to control the uncontrollable.

Scientismists ignore the fact that they don't have the ability to control Nature or other people. Nor are they able to control the selves they are. Self-control is a delusion. We are only able to guide our instinctive or deliberate use of Nature's Will. If we attempt to control Nature's use of Its Will or another self's use of Nature's Will, we exist in disharmony with Nature or the other self, because we're using Nature's Will in our delusional attempt to forcibly control Nature or the other self's use of Nature's Will, instead of using Nature's Will in our meaningful attempt to unforcefully guide our use of Nature's Will. Metaphysics is the study of immaterial realities existent in and by way of immaterial Reality beyond the existence of materialised realities which are existent in and by way of immaterial Reality. "Naturalism" is a word I use for the Freedom of a self's harmony within Nature's harmony; however, I also use the word "Naturalism" to symbolise the metaphysics I've developed which is the basis of my understanding of science—and scientism.

My religion of Selfism is the basis of my metaphysics. Some atheistic scientismists attack religion, even though they base their scientism on the religious absolute of non-Existence. The goal of atheistic scientismists is to establish their religion, despite their mistaken belief that they're irreligious. Of course, there are also scientismists who practice a religion based on a religious absolute other than non-Existence. Unfortunately, they've swallowed the propaganda of Aristotle too.

Naturalism is the compilation of insights I've had which helped me to understand the importance of Nature's spontaneous instinctive nondeliberate willing in relating Kinetics to Kinesis as well as its importance and the importance of my spontaneous or impulsive instinctive nondeliberate and deliberate noninstinctive use of Nature's Will in relating Selfkinetics to Selfkinesis. Although I seldom mention Selfkinetics and Selfkinesis in the nine chapters of this book, every sentence I've written is laden with their meaning.

Selfism is a religion I've developed in harmony with Nature's harmony (but not in "communion" with Nature). Nature is unable to explain in words how I need to develop my religion because Nature is unable to develop or speak words. I simply dwell in Nature's harmony and used my innerly reasoned words to explain what Nature is and how Nature generates things, like you and I; therefore, I'm able to type the words of this book as I'm harmonising with Nature.

As a Selfist, I never use the word "who" to refer to Nature because Nature isn't inhabited by a Self. Nature is Non-Individual; therefore, Nature is not the absolute Individual or the absolute Self.

I realised my metaphysics and religion by reasoning about the scriptures of religionists, the scriptures of scientists, the scriptures of philosophers, as well as the scriptures of artists. I was able to use my reasoning about the "Holy" Bible to discover a contradiction in the story of Jesus' resurrection which, at first, I thought only I had realised; however, in my subsequent research I found writings of other researchers who had noted the same contradiction and understood, as I had, that the bodily resurrection of Jesus was a hoax.[1]

The account given of "doubting Thomas" and Mary Magdalene's interactions with the supposedly risen sensable organism of Jesus demonstrates that Jesus' sensable organism (organic human body) wasn't resurrected. Jesus rose *from* his organic human body in his sensor which may have been seen by his followers as an aura. Jesus didn't resurrect in a "holy" or "pure" organic

---

[1] I've put quotation marks around the word "Holy", because the meaning of "Holy" is based on the supernatural; therefore, the meaning of the word "Holy", is a delusional assimilated sensation of supernaturalists. The "Holy", like the sacred, is the selfpathic assimilated sensation of our "unworthiness" because, supposedly, only God is worthy.

human body because the Bible's report of doubting Thomas' interaction with Jesus contradicts its report of Mary Magdalene's interaction with Jesus.

Jesus told Mary not to touch his "organic human body"; however, Jesus is supposed to have contradicted what he said to Mary by letting doubting Thomas touch his body's wound. Jesus would not let Mary touch his hypothetically risen organic human body because, supposedly, Mary would have defiled it if she touched it; therefore, Jesus would not have let Thomas touch it either if the resurrection story was really true. Consequently, the story that Thomas touched Jesus' "risen" organic human body after its "fall" of death has to be false, just as the story that Mary had seen Jesus in his supposedly resurrected organic human body has to be false.

Jesus' resurrection in his supposedly immortal organic human body (his sensable organism) is a mythical doctrine of Christians because the obvious truth is that organic human bodies are inevitably mortal. A Christian is afraid of existing as an existent in an objective luef after the death of his or her body simply because he or she is more familiar with the harmonies and disharmonies of his or her mortal body than he or she is with his or her objective luef.

The Christian suffers from the illusion of "states" of being which he or she mistakes for the unchanging inactivity of a physicality or a solid because he or she doesn't realise that even an activity which is not a self is existent unchangingly *as an activity, not as an "inactivity"*, despite its inability to exist, activate, or generate another activity.

A self who is using its ability to exist, activate, or generate another activity is subjected to the complementary effect of changing as the continually immediate activity it always is, while existing as an unchanging activity (like mineral, vegetative, and sensable organisms) when its not using its ability to exist, activate, or generate another activity. Inactivities are illusions because solids are unchanging activities, not unchanging inactivities. Activities change as activities so that they become different activities because Nature exists It Volition or wills these activities to change or a self can use Nature's Volition or Will to change them

Selves act and behave in accord or in discord with Nature's harmony. But Nature's harmony isn't love because Nature is barren of emotions. Neither Nature nor Its selves are perfect in their expression of harmony because neither Nature nor Its selves are controlled in their use of Nature's Volition or Will. Unlike Nature, Selves experience disharmony as well as harmony because they are always developing illusions, delusions, and fictions as well as knowledge, meanings, and facts.

A self is a reality, nature, or phenomenon who *realistically, naturally, or phenomenally* proves its collection of theories to be true or false based on the self's knowledgeable knowing of the meanings of its facts; however, a self is unable to develop perfect knowledge. A self is unable to develop omniscience or all-knowing knowledge because a self only exists where it is, not ubiquitously (everywhere), like Nature; however, Nature is not omniscient, despite Its ubiquity.

Unlike us, Nature is unable to know and is also unable to unknow; therefore, Nature is unable to develop knowledge, gain insight from knowledge, think on the basis of insights, realise in relation to thinking, reason on the basis of realisations, or understand the implications of reasoning. And, of course, Nature is also unable to unknow knowledge, unknow insights, unknow thinking, unknow realisations, unknow reasoning, or unknow understanding because It is unable to know these selfological qualities in the first place.

Nature is unable to know because It is not a self; therefore, knowing things as Its feedback is impossible for Nature. Nature is not the Knower of experience. Only we're knowers of experience because we have a need to receive as well as give. Although Nature receives particles by blending them with It after It has instinctively departiclised them, Nature is unable to take in their departiclisation as a known experience because Nature has no need to know.

Nature is unable to develop delusions, beliefs, theories, or understandings; therefore, Nature is unable to activate courage or fear in relation to them. Consequently, Nature is never tempted to express an emotion.

Nature is not an individual with a realistic desire to communicate or an unrealistic desire to commune. Nature's Non-individuality and inability to communicate or commune means that Nature is unable to intervene or interfere. Nature is unable to intrude.

Nature has no needs. Nature has no need to Will. Nature needs no laws which scientismists presume have the ability to Cause because Nature's willing is Nature's inherent ability to Cause, not an ability which Nature caused by activating it as its Cause. There is no reason why Nature wills the evolution and growth of natural outer letters and natural physicalities or the development of natural selves because Nature wills in Freedom.

There is no Cause to Nature's willing; therefore, fatedness and destiny are only words. Like Nature, we use Nature's Will in absolute Freedom. Although our use of Nature's Will is often deliberate, we deliberately use Nature's Will in absolute Freedom, despite the influence of Nature's use of Its Will and the influence of other selves' use of Its Will to affect us.

A self, like you or I, is a center of Nature. Nature is Energy or Matter: therefore, we are centers of Energy or Matter. A self or center of Energy or Matter is formless because a center is not a form. A self is an immortal activity, even though it starts as an activity from Nature.

Nature is Reality; therefore, we are realities because we are centers of Reality. A center of Reality is a thing. Other centers of Thingness are also things but, as things, they are not selves.

For example, the center of a particle is the thing of the particle in which Nature wills; however, the center of a particle is unable to use Nature's Will in tandem with Nature because the center of a particle isn't a self.

Nature is *not* an absolute Center. Nature is immortal unbounded Thingness; therefore, Nature is not an absolute Self. Nature is absolute boundless Thingness.

"Anima" is Latin for "psyche", while "animus" is Latin for "mind". The late Carl G. Jung was a Swiss psychiatrist who altered the meaning of anima and animus by referring to the anima as the female spirit in a man and the animus as the male spirit in a woman. Jung's belief in a female anima spirit and a male animus spirit was his fiction because only a body has maleness or femaleness, not spirit. Jung didn't understand that the "Spirit of God" was his delusion because only the Will of Nature is real. Maleness and femaleness are evolved by Nature's use of Its Will but Nature's Will is neither male nor female.

There are no spiritual powers. There is only Nature's Will. There are no egos, psyches, and minds, beings, souls, and consciousnesses, or ipsa, animas, and animuses. There are only selves, sensors, and cognitions.

A self uses its sensor. A sensor is used by a self to guide, not control, the self's generation of energetics in its sensor, like the energetics of excitement and anxiety. A self has a need to learn how to work in harmony, rather than disharmony, with its spontaneous or impulsive instinctive nondeliberate or deliberate noninstinctive use of Nature's Will along with Nature's always harmonious spontaneous instinctive nondeliberate use of Its Will.

A self's cognition is the self's faculty of knowing in which the self has and uses its ability of knowing. The self is the "I" who possesses or owns its cognition. The self is located in the reticular formation of its brain's stem at the "foot" of its brain.

Like, a self, a self's sensor is generated from and evolved by Nature as Nature generates and develops the self. The self uses its cognition to sense by way of its sensor.

My sensor is my emanation of pure energy from the center of pure energy I am as my cognitively as well as directly known "me" or "aura" through which I indirectly know the other inner aspects of my World (like my other immaterial faculties and abilities), and indirectly know, by sensing through this emanation, my sensable organism and other outer aspects of my World, like the mineral, vegetative, and sensable organisms which I share with the World's infinite selves who also inhabit their sensable organisms and/or emanations of pure energy.

I can activate the rest of my brain with me (my sensor) as well as activate motions in and movements of my sensable organism by emanating me from the rest of my brain to the rest of my sensable organism.

A self is what it is when it acts as it is. A self pretends to be who it is when it acts as it is not. When a self is what it is, the self genuinely, sincerely, and authentically guides its use of its sensor as who it is. When a self is pretending to be who it is, the self ingenuinely, insincerely, and inauthentically guides its sensor. A self's pretensions are its false selves which are also known as a self's roles or personae.

Enlightenment is a metaphor for wisdom because the vibrations of light enlighten a room, just as knowing knowledge wises up a self's understanding. A self is able to attain wisdom because it's able to develop a goal for its need to strive for wisdom; however, it needs to learn that its fear of death is unnecessary if it accepts that death is its mortality which is the end of its suffering as well as enjoyment. Ironically, if it desires to will because it fails to understand that it borrows and uses Nature's Will, it will experience unnecessary suffering. Even if it's immortal and will exist forever in its ethereal realm of the after-death, it will continue to suffer from its absurd thought that it will die and pessimistically cling to its tendency to despair.

If we're immortal, we will tend to know that we're using Nature's Will; therefore, an immortal who has the insane desire to become immortal is an absurdity because the immortal fails to realise that he or she is immortal. Such an immortal ignores his or her knowledge of Nature's willing in him or her as Its immortality which is the reason why he or she is ignorant of his or her own immortality.

Most humans develop pathologies because they have the insane desire for immortality—or mortality. They don't understand that their insane desire for immortality or mortality is unnecessary because their knowledge of Nature's immortal willing in them *is* their immortality if they are, indeed, immortal.

Our desires are occasionally—or often—insane because an insane desire is a drive without a need. Your desire to satisfy what you need is sane because your satisfaction activates processes of health for your body and activities of wellness for you. But to want to satisfy what you don't need is insane because the satisfaction of what you don't need usually activates sickness in your body and unwellness in you. This is why the compulsive desire to satisfy what you don't need is called an "addiction" and the habitual thinking that activates this compulsive desire is called an "obsession".

A need is a realistic motivator, but a motivator is not necessarily a need, because a motivator is also existed as a sane or an insane desire. A need motivates a striving for abundance, not a striving to overcome deprivation; however, Nature is unable to attain the abundance of wisdom because It has no need to be wise.

We're able to purpose and intend in accord with our need to use Nature's Will; therefore, we purpose and intend in harmony with Nature's purposeless and intentionless instinctive willing so we're able to work towards attaining our goals and meanings. We have purposes because we have goals by which to purpose. We have intentions because we have meanings by which to intend. But Nature has no ability to develop a goal or a meaning. Consequently, Nature has no ability to develop a purpose or an intention.

A sane desire is a self's realistic motivating drive in relation to a need. A self uses Nature's Will deliberately, intentionally, knowingly, and knowledgeably as well as instinctively, unintentionally, unknowingly, and unknowledgeably as its motivating drive in its needs.

An insane desire is a self's unnecessary, unrealistic, delusional and greedy use of Nature's Will to drive for authoritarian control of Nature's Will. This greedy drive for authoritarian control puts the self instinctively—or deliberately—in conflict with Nature's instinctive nondeliberate willing because the self insanely desires sole possession of Nature's Will. A self's greedy drive for authoritarian control is the result of its fear of being deprived of control because it thinks it has to develop its immortality by "creating" its own authority. Such a greedy self has yet to realise that its knowledge of how to use to use Nature's Will is its immortality (if it is immortal).

Behaviours associated with the greedy drive for authoritarian control are a self's insatiable drives for monetary wealth, rank, fame, popularity, beauty, intellectual superiority, and so on.

As the things which are knowers of Thingness, we are either immortal or mortal. Other centers of Thingness aren't immortal things because they're missing the ability of knowing as well as the disabling ability of unknowing or ignoring; therefore, they aren't able to know or ignore how to use Nature's Will which is why Nature's willing in them is discontinued when they disintegrate or decay; therefore, these centers blend with Thingness (Nature) and cease as existent centers (which might be the lot of every self as well).

A self's ability to know its disabling ability to unknow are the sources of the self's immortality (if selves are immortal); however, a self is only a knower, not an "unknower" because its unknowing is a knower's denial of its need to know. The knower unknows or ignores its knowing as well as knows its knowing. Consequently, there is only a need for a knower, not an unknower, because the knower unknows as well as knows.

But there's little sense in knowing as a knower if you're so driven by your need to know that you're unable to enjoy life, which is why a self often dwells in unknowing, instead of knowing. A self has to balance the knower it is with the enjoyer it is before it's able to develop its knowledge that a knower is what a self is, its knowledge that an enjoyer, a sufferer, a user, and usurer are how a self is, its knowledge that it is who it is (or who it isn't) and its knowledge that it is an intender or purposer is why it is the way it is. Of course, Nature is not the Intender or the Purposer because Nature's willing is intentionless or purposeless; therefore, Nature hasn't any plans for a self's development which would fate or destine it.

A wise self understands that it's only able to activate its wisdom when it's a knower, activate its enjoyment when it's an enjoyer, activate its practicality when it's a user, and activate its needs and sane desires when it's an intender or purposer; however, the most important thing for a wise self to realise is that its knowing of happiness and ability to be happy is derived from its knowledge of enjoyment, while its love of wisdom (its philosophy) is derived from its enjoyment of knowing.

A self's unknowing of truth and falsity is the result of the self's insane desire to escape its knowledge of truth and falsity. A self's desire to escape its knowledge is futile because its attempt to escape from its knowledge is dependent on its knowledge of how to make such an escape. Consequently, a self will never escape its knowledge that it's a knower because its need to know that it's a knower is inescapable.

A self looks upon Nature's Volition or Will with intentionality. If a self intends to escape knowing by retreating into unknowing, it will look upon its own ability to volition or will (its use of Nature's Volition or Will) as a curse because it thinks its knowing of how to volition or will with Nature's Volition or Will is the source of its suffering. If a self intends to keep developing its knowing, it will look upon its knowing of how to volition opr will with Nature's Volition or Will as its "blessing" because it knows that its knowing is the source of its enjoyment as well as its suffering.

The Twenty-Five Fundamental Truths of Selfism

The Twenty-Five Fundamental Truths of Selfism are meant to help a Truist work towards knowledge and attain wisdom in freedom from coercion so the Truist realises his or her Style which is a Truist's transcendence of his or her unnatural formal meditative technique by way of his or her realisation of his or her informal natural Style as an existing self who exists its cognition and lives its sensor as well as its sensable organism. "Truism" is a Selfist's word for his or her unnatural formal meditative technique; therefore, a Truist is a member of the religion of Selfism (a Selfist) who subscribes to the practice of Truism, that is, until he or she recognizes that he or she has no need to practice the "unnatural formal technique" of "meditation" anymore because he or she knows his or her natural informal Style of existing and living.

Every Selfist who exists in a body as well as a sensor has its inner world protected by the Watchers who exist in the realm of the after-death called "The Realm of Watchers" (that is, if selves are immortal and Watchers as well as The Realm of Watchers in the after-death really exist); therefore, every Selfist is able to receive help from companionable Watchers in dealing with entities from the ethereal realm who have a wish to hinder a Selfist's development of its inner world (that is, if these Watchers and The Realm of the Watchers are actually existent.

Freedom is The Ultimate Truth of my unique atheistic religion of Selfism. My knowledge of The Primary Truth and The Secondary Truth of Selfism is based on my knowledge of Freedom. The Primary Truth of Selfism is Nature's Will. The Secondary Truth of Selfism is Nature's harmony. The Ultimate, Primary, and Secondary Truths of Selfism lay beyond and gather together The Twenty-Five Fundamental Truths of Selfism listed below.

1. Nature is always using Its Will to evolve motions in natures and move natures. Nature evolves, grows, develops, deteriorates, and devolves natures, like suefs, luefs, particles and bodies as well as develops natural immortal or mortal selves from It. Nature generates a self as a center of energy in a spermatozoon and an egg Its merged together. An immortal or mortal self's generation is completed with the evolution of the zygote from the spermatozoon and egg's merger. Nature also generates a self within an evolved and grown bud of a sensable organism.
2. Nature is harmonious, not perfect or imperfect in Its willing, since perfection and imperfection are words with no applicable referent. Nature forms as well as condenses Its portions. Nature also shines apparitions, like mirages. Nature's ability to Will or Drive Its vitalities of gravity-antigravity, magnetism, electricity, electromagnetism, electro-weak nuclearity, weak nuclearity, and strong nuclearity results in Its continual evolution, growth, development, deterioration, and devolution of the Infiniverse. Nature continually activates an infinity of individual happenings.
3. Nature wills without needing to will. Nature has no choice but to continually, non-intentionally, as well as non-unintentionally use Its Will; however, its willing is not determined or predetermined because Nature's willing has no reason or cause; therefore, Nature's willing is Free in its instinctive driving which is why Nature's willing is indeterministic and random. Nature is Non-Individual; therefore, Nature wills Non-Individually as unboundedness. Plants do not use Nature's Will because plants aren't inhabited by a self; rather, a plant's motions and movements are willed or driven by Nature. Selves are willed by Nature, too, but selves also use and express their motions and movements by using Nature's Will. A self doesn't have its own individual will. Nature is unable to knowingly—or unknowingly—use

Its Will. Nature's selves instinctively, unintentionally, unknowingly, and unknowledgeably as well as deliberately, intentionally, knowingly, and knowledgeably use Nature's Will. Whether we know it or not, all our choices, decisions, and selections have possible consequences for other people because we're always related to each other by way of Nature's use and our use of Its Will. Usury is a self's licentious use of Nature's Will. Use is a self's free spontaneous liberal or free impulsive licentious instinctive nondeliberate or deliberate noninstinctive borrowing and expressing of Nature's Will in harmony or disharmony with Nature's free spontaneous instinctive nondeliberate possession and expression of Its Will which, simply put, is a self and Nature's free application or employment of Its Will.

4. Nature is harmonious in Its expression of Its Will because Nature is unaffected by sensation. We unconditionally or conditionally use our excited energetical emotion of love as our basis to develop emotions related to it, like affection and joy. We also unconditionally or conditionally use our anxious energetical emotion of hate as our basis to develop emotions related to it, like anger and sorrow. Nature is Non-Individual, not an individual; therefore, Nature is unable to communicate with individuals. Consequently, Nature has no need to emote emotion and moods as a reaction to individual communication.

5. Kinetics is Nature's use of Its Will to activate absolute activities. Selfkinetics is a self's use of Nature's Will to activate its selfological qualitative activities, like Selfkinesis. Kinesis is Nature's use of Its Will to activate absolute motions in and movements of bodies. Selfkinesis is a self's use of Nature's Will to activate motions in and movements of its sensor and sensable organism as well as use the movements of its sensable organism to move mineral, vegetative, and sensable organisms in its environment.

6. Nature is the unbounded uncondensed or immaterial Ether by which the Infiniverse is existed and in which the Infiniverse is interspersed. Unnatured Nature (unrealised Reality, uncondensed Energy, or unmaterialised Matter) evolves, grows, develops, deteriorates, and devolves the infinite physicalities composing the Infiniverse. These infinite physicalities are existed by Nature in a harmony of organisation-disorganisation-reorganisation.

7. Nature is unable to unknow, just as Nature is unable to know; therefore, Nature is unable to know knowledge or unknow knowledge. A self's immortality arises mutually with the self's ability to know with cognisance as well as unknow with incognisance; therefore, selves transcend Nature because they use Nature's Will in tandem with Nature to develop their abilities and disabilities as activities from Potentiality, Activity, or Nature. A self's abilities and faculties are existed by it from Nature as Potentiality or Activity with which the self actualises as well as activates them because the self sooner or later has need of them. Nature is Non-Individual; therefore, Nature doesn't need to know or desire to unknow because Nature doesn't interact as an individual. Every self who inhabits a sensable organism is stimulated by its need for wisdom which is every self's need for a harmonious understanding of its knowledge; therefore, every self needs to realise its knowledge, meanings, and facts as its realistic realisms and cease to idealise illusions, delusions, and fictions as its idolatrous or iconic idealisms A self's realisations are its recognition of its knowledge, meanings, and facts by its use of its ability to know, whereas a self's idealisations are its fantasising of illusions, delusions, and fictions by way of its unknowing which is its denial of its ability to know and retreat from it into fantasy.

8. An outer symbol and an inner symbol as well as audible outer speech and inaudible inner speech (silent inner speech) fail to correspond to or resemble the referent for which they stand. For instance, the outer symbol and the inner symbol, "cup", both stand for the reality of the symbol, "cup", without corresponding to or resembling that reality. An icon corresponds to or resembles its referent. For instance, the outer word and the inner word "buzz" both correspond to or resemble the sound that a bumble bee makes. Indices are considered by some linguists to be "natural" outer signs, but an index is not an outer sign because an outer sign is intentionally and artificially produced in the environment in some way whereas an index, like yawning, is used to express its referent of sleepiness, unintentionally and artlessly; therefore, a yawn is not an "outer sign" of sleepiness. A yawn indicates sleepiness, but this indication is not intentional; therefore, yawning indicates sleepiness as an *outer symptom*, not an "outer sign".

9. Sensing is a self's ability of cognising a sensation (an impulse of energy) which is experienced by it in its body. Knowing is a self's ability of cognising an energy which is experienced by it in its cognition. Unknowing is a self's inability to know because the self is ignoring its ability to know. Perceiving is a self's ability of intelligently as well as accurately assimilating its feeling of an emotion or a sensation as its interpreted knowledge. Misperceiving is a self's disabling ability of intellectually as well as inaccurately assimilating its feeling of an emotion or a sensation as its interpreted illusion. Consequently, assimilating is a self's use of its intelligence to ably perceive or accurately interpret its feeling of an emotion or a sensation as its interpreted knowledge as well as its use of its intellect to disable its able perceiving or accurate interpreting so it misperceives or misinterprets its feeling of them and absorbs this feeling as its interpreted illusion. Intelligence is a self's faculty of understanding. Intelligence is also a self's ability of realising its knowledge as meanings and its meanings as facts. A Truist uses facts to prove that it is existent as a self which is a knowledge beyond the Truist's experience. Intellect is a self's disabling ability of misunderstanding. Intellectualising is a self's disabling ability of cogitating. A self uses its cogitating to idealise its illusions as delusions and its delusions as fictions. A self uses its disabling ability of cogitating, intellectualising, or idealising to avoid dealing with realities.
10. We produce thoughts with our ability to attentively think, ideas with our ability to interpretively think, and hypotheses with our ability to assimilatively reason. We attentively and interpretively think as well as assimilatively reason with inner words and inner ideograms which we use inner letters and inner graphics to structure, respectively. We're also able to think, attentively and interpretively, without using inner symbols in our thinking; however, we're only able to reason, assimilatively, by using inner symbols in our reasoning. Unfortunately, our disabling ability of cogitating leads us to intellectualise. Cogitating is a disabling ability because our use of cogitating disables our ability to think and our ability to reason. We use inner signs, like inner numbers, to cogitate, but we're unable to use inner numbers to structure inner symbols, like inner ideograms or inner words.

11. We attentively think notions (which we develop into thoughts) as well as ponder over our thoughts to develop ideas (which we develop, in turn, into concepts) so we're able to assimilatively reason (deduce and induce) about our concepts and develop hypotheses (which we develop, in turn, into a theory). We infer the truth or falsity of our hypotheses by reasoning about them. The truth or falsity we attribute to a hypothesis is due to an unfairly prejudiced or fairly biased reasoning in discord or accord, respectively, with our observing which only rejects or affirms, rather than denies or confirms, our metaphysical theories. *Not many researchers know how to participate as observers who sense with a fair bias, rather than an unfair prejudice. Our researchers' fairly biased sensing might help them to recognise a simple truth which is that they're sensing realities in their unsharable inner aspects of the World as well as in their sharable outer aspects of the World If our researchers come to realise the aforementioned truth, they might develop the skill to reason with known facts, develop inferences about Reality, and derive metaphysical truths from these inferences.*
12. We have an ability to freely reason. Freely reasoning about a situation so that we're able to recognise what's happening in this situation and act to use this situation to our advantage is called "practical reasoning". To freely infer is to freely develop a conclusion about our deductions and inductions. Logic is the study of applying laws to the activity of free reasoning. "Logicising" is a word I've coined meaning our "second guessing" of our inferential reasoning or our "formal intellectualising". Logicising is a judgement about the truth or falsity of our free inferential reasoning, instead of using our understanding to discern its truth or falsity. Logicising is a logician's application of laws to his activity of free reasoning which changes his activity of free reasoning into his absurd activity of cogitating which is conditioned by the laws applied to it. "Logical reasoning" is a contradiction in terms because logic is not used to establish the activity of free reasoning. *Aristotle developed logic because he was afraid to be free of laws.*
13. Laws are only existed by a self as its delusions (mistaken hypotheses) since laws have no actual referents in the sharable outer aspects of our World. Although we developed the inner word "law" and defined it as, 'that which produces a regularity of Nature', a law doesn't evolve a

regularity of Nature. Laws are supposed by Creationists to be creations of the Creator who is thought to have derived these laws from the rules and principles he is also thought to have created. A Creationist's word "Creator" has no actual referent. This means that the Creator is a mistaken hypothesis; therefore, the mythical creations of such a mistaken hypothesis, like laws, are also mistaken hypotheses and have no actual referents. Mortalistic scientismists think laws are uncreated in Nature; therefore, they see no need for a Creator of laws. A scientismist's laws aren't uncreated in Nature for him to "discover" because new laws are developed to replace old laws by a scientismist's intellectual cogitating. Nature regulates the regularities in Its Infiniverse because Its willing is harmonious; therefore, Nature's willing in accord with Its harmony evolves the regularities of the Infiniverse, not laws.

14. Nature is unable to develop perfect reasoning because Nature is barren of the ability to reason. A self can frequently free, its ignorance, its tendency to fear, and its tendency to leap to assumptions so its reasoning can be accurate, but its reasoning is never perfect, since it's incapable of taking infinite factors into account. A self's misunderstanding of a situation will interfere with its ability to reason. Its mistaken reasoning will interfere with its ability to love; therefore, it will dredge up its ability to hate, instead. A self has to learn that it's responsible for its emoting of its emotions. Even when a self responsibly uses its ability to understand and accords its use of Nature's Will to its ability to understand, its ability to understand will always be inadequate.

15. Staying "tuned in" to its conscience means that a self has a need to know what its conscience is. A self's conscience is not its understanding of whether what it's done is "right" (legal or moral) or "wrong" (illegal or immoral). A self's conscience is its understanding of whether what it's done is benevolent and appropriate or malevolent and inappropriate. Right (legality or morality) and wrong (illegality or immorality) are merely judgements resulting from a self's intellectualising about its selfological actions and bodily behaviours. Only by inferentially reasoning can a self, like you or I, understand how to act and behave so it acts and behaves benevolently and appropriately or misunderstands how to act and behave so that it acts and behaves malevolently and inappropriately. Consequently, a self's "righteous" logical belief that it's

legal or moral and its "unrighteous" logical belief that it's illegal or immoral are merely its mistaken accompaniments to its mistaken hypothesis of laws.

16. A self uses its understanding and misunderstanding to develop its characters. Character is developed when a self uses its misunderstanding to develop beliefs and delusions, its understanding as well as its misunderstanding to develop theories, and its understanding to develop understandings. A self uses its understanding and misunderstanding to develop its five basic character types from which it derives the five basic selves or roles of its personality. Erich Fromm realised a self is able to develop productive, receptive, hoarding, exploitative, and marketing character types. I realised that the productive character type was a self's outer expression of its inner developmental character type. I also realised that the respective personality roles (false selves or personae) of adult player, infantile victim, childish authoritarian, preadolescent trickster, and adolescent hero are developed from these character types. Selves are highly reluctant to examine their characters because they know that their characters are rooted in their metaphysical and religious theories which they fear may be delusional. For example, objectivists who maintain that objectivism is the "Truth" are delusional because objects are definitely not "the end-all-be-all"; however, these objectivists have a great deal of faith in their delusion.

17. A self's personality is composed of five basic roles, personae, or false selves. A self is able to pit these roles against each other. If an enlightened self finds it necessary to express a role, it keeps to the role of adult player and lets the roles of infantile victim, childish authoritarian, preadolescent trickster, and adolescent hero remain active only in memory. The expression of a self's personality is primarily due to the self's use of Nature's Will to express it, although it's necessary for the self to understand the difference between its five basic roles if it's to attain wisdom. A self has the ability to express false selves. Nature is barren of the typical roles of productive-developmental adult player, receptive infantile victim, hoarding childish authoritarian, exploitative preadolescent trickster, and marketing adolescent hero. Nature's expression of Its Will is roleless or free of false selves as well as free of a genuine, sincere and authentic absolute Self. Nature is unable to

express Self, not to mention roles or false selves, because Nature is Selfless. Nature is uninhabited by an absolute Self. Consequently, the absolute Self is a fiction because Nature is Non-Individual or Selfless, not an absolute Individual or absolute Self.

18. An instinct is related to a self's need, sane desire, or insane desire. A self's instincts are based on Nature's willing which is Nature's instinct. An instinct motivates a self to use Nature's Will or Drive in pursuit of a goal. Nature is unable to develop sane and insane desires. Nature's only instinct is Its spontaneously harmonised willing. Nature is also unmotivated by Its instinctive Will or Drive; therefore, Nature has no goals. An instinct is a self's spontaneously harmonised or impulsively disharmonised nondeliberate use of Nature's Will with or in isolation from Nature's spontaneously harmonised nondeliberate use of Its Will. A self has two basic emotional instincts to choose from in actualising the roles of its personality. These are its emotional instinct of love and its emotional instinct of hate which give rise to behaviours of playing and toying, respectively. All the other emotional instincts of a self are derived from its emotional instincts of love and hate and can be used in the self's behaviour of playing and toying. A self is able to "tune into" its emotional instincts.

19. I prefer to develop my goals, spontaneously, as I immediately continue in changing my plans to attain them. If a self develops a plan to erect a barrier to my attainment of a goal of mine, I simply need to outmanoeuver it with a plan of my own and continue to pursue my goal with my plan or, if this is not possible, spontaneously change my goal. Either way, I try not to "cave in" and give my opponent the insane "satisfaction" of a fight.

20. We perceive what we sense, i.e., we listen to what we hear, vision what we see, feel what we touch, taste what we eat, and smell what we inhale. We introspectively listen, vision, feel, taste, or smell in our unsharable inner aspect of the World usually after having extrospectively heard, seen, touched, eaten, or inhaled realities in our outer sharable aspects of the World. We also introspectively envision the images we imagine. Introspection is our ability to recognise realistic, natural, or phenomenal qualities existent in our unsharable inner aspects of the World.

Extrospection is our ability to recognise realistic, natural, or phenomenal qualities existent in our sharable outer aspects of the World.

21. The desire to overcome boredom declines when a genuine interest in a behaviour replaces the desire for the pleasure of the behaviour so that the person engages in that behaviour with interest, rather than engages in that behaviour only for pleasure, a pleasure which he (or she) might desire without having any interest in that behaviour at all. The enlightened individual realises that his spontaneous interest in everything he feels the need to think and reason about is wise because he has learned to intelligently consider all that he experiences, while his boredom in his thinking and reasoning is impulsively stupid. Therefore, he finds it enjoyable to be spontaneously interested in everything he does and everything that happens around, to, and in him.

22. Every Truist trained in Naturalism and Selfism, needs to understand that his (or her) greed for love, fame, security, monetary wealth, privilege, rank, status, and etcetera, is the result of his feelings of deprivation which are sources of his anxiety. His anxiety will decline with a corresponding decline in his greed and a corresponding increase in the interest he takes in his enjoyable selfological activities and bodily behaviours. The art of his search for wisdom is the skill with which he purposes as he journeys towards his goal because he will need to alter his purposes as he learns more about his goal. In other words, his continual change in understanding about his goal of wisdom will always affect the purposes with which he journeys towards this goal, especially his realisation that he was generated by Nature with an infinite depth of stupidity on which his intelligence "floats" as his Potentiality or Activity with which to start developing as his ability to "wise up" to the truth that his wisdom will always be a finite expression of his intelligence which "floats on the surface" of his infinite depth of stupidity. Consequently, his ultimate challenge is learning to enjoy his continually changing purposes in journeying as he suits them to his continually changing goals.

23. If you make a mistake which leads to trouble for other people, apologise to them and make amends by helping them clear up the trouble that was a consequence of your mistake. A mistake is a missing of the mark or a "sin". A mistaken action or behaviour is not "wrong", "incorrect" and

"illogical". A mistaken action or behaviour is simply *improper, inaccurate, and inappropriate*. The concepts of wrong, incorrect, and illogical as well as the concepts of right, correct, and logical are mistaken hypotheses because they're based on our insane desire for law and order. The concepts of improper, inaccurate, and inappropriate as well as the concepts of proper, accurate, and appropriate are truths because they're based on our need for organisation, disorganisation, and reorganisation. Even an intentional selfological action meant to cause people trouble is merely a mistake, not a "sin" or an "evil", because the individual who is intentionally causing the trouble doesn't actually prefer to cause trouble. If he realised that he prefers to avoid making trouble, he would go out of his way to stop making trouble for other people. Such an individual is not "a sinner" because he is not a sin; rather, his actions and behaviours are mistakenly improper, inaccurate, and inappropriate because his fear and frustration are the challenges which he might irresponsibly let lead him to ignore the needs of other people. He has yet to understand that he has a preference to avoid trouble by acting properly, accurately, and appropriately. I suggest that we call the complement of a mistake a "take" as well as a "verity" because "that which applies to the proper, accurate, and appropriate" is another connotation for the word "take"; therefore, a take is the complement of a mistake because a mistake is that which applies to the improper, inaccurate, and inappropriate. I based my definition of the word "take" on the exclamation of, "That's a take!" which movie directors shout when they want a section of film acknowledged and preserved as the recording of their actors' proper, accurate, and appropriate behaviours in a scene.

24. When we consider what may happen, we tend to suffer; however, when we realistically consider what has happened and what is happening, we tend to enjoy. Resentment leads to suffering because resentment results from an unrealistic grudge an individual might develop over what has happened, rather than this individual's acceptance of what has happened. Hope leads to suffering because hope results from an individual's unrealistic fantasy about what might happen. And compassion leads to suffering because compassion is an individual's unrealistic and masochistic empathising with a sufferer's suffering. When we accept what has happened and what is happening, we don't resent what has

happened, hope for what might happen, or compassionately empathise with a happening; therefore, we're able to put a positive slant on what has happened and what is happening. Gratitude results from our realistic desire to appreciate what has happened because of the help other people have extended to us. Realism is the result of our sane desire to know and gain knowledge of what is happening so that we're able to develop wisdom.

25. Time is not subjectively or objectively actual because Nature has Continuity in Immediacy as Its attribute, not time in eternity. Time is a mistaken hypothesis because the word "time" has no referent. Nature has no need of "the past", "the present" and "the future" because Nature continues immediately. Nature has no need to continue in a supposed length of time called a "duration", such as the delusionally instantaneous duration of the present, the delusionally eternal duration of the past, or the delusionally eternal duration of the future. Nature has no need to continue in time because the mistaken hypothesis of time is unnecessary. Nature has no need of eternity or the Now which are both associated with the Creator because the Immediacy of Nature is not the Now any more than the Continuity of Nature is the unchanging eternity of the Creator. Nature doesn't eternally time; Nature immediately continues.

Chapter One
The Reality of Images, Apparitions and Appearances

In his article, "On the Appearance and Reality of Mind", Demian Whiting writes in his abstract, 'According to what I will call the "appearance is reality doctrine of mind", conscious mental states are identical to how they subjectively appear or present themselves to us in our experience of them' (Whiting, 2016, p. 47). In this opening sentence, Whiting's confusion is demonstrated. Whiting failed to understand that there are no fixed "states" of mind because states are our delusions. Also, a self only has a continually active cognition, not a mind and a consciousness.

Whiting doesn't seem to realise that consciousness and mind are only a self's unobservable hypotheses because "consciousness" and "mind" aren't appearances.

Whiting's confusion doesn't stop at his confusion about conscious mental states but extends to the examples he uses for appearances, such as the "pains, itches, tingles, emotions, and moods" which we're only able to feel, not see (Whiting, 2016, p. 49). Whiting doesn't realise that these phenomena don't actually appear to us, although they are experienced by us.

A self is able to see a small or a large image which results from an inner visible light shining through a subjective suef or a subjective luef, respectively.

For example, a self's shining of inner visible light through a subjective luef so that an image is seen by the self in its imagination is the result of the self's *imagining* of a real image, such as the real image of an unreal fairy, the self's *imagiting* of a real image of a real apparition in the environment, *such as the real image of a real fairy,* the self's *imagiting* of a real image of a real illusory apparition, such as the real image of a real illusory mirage, or the self's *imugiting* of a real image of a real appearance in the environment, such as the real image of a real tree.

"Imagiting" is a word I've coined which stands for our ability to translate a reality existent in the environment to our imaginations by way of visioning. Imagining is our ability to fantasise or hallucinate an image by way of envisioning.

An image is a self's imagitive or imagined motion picture seen by the self in its faculty of imagination. A small image (a subjective photon) or a large image is seen as an inner sight and perceived by a self so the self is able to reason about its perceptions and understand the truth of the image it has seen. A self is also able to see the colour of a small hallucination or a large hallucination in its activity of dreaming.

Hallucinations aren't existed by us in the environment. Only actual apparitions, actual illusory apparitions and actual appearances are existed in the environment because hallucinations are usually imaginings or fantasies existed by a self in its imagination; however, a self may also experience a hallucination as its unknowing inner speech of inner symbols to which it inaudibly listens in its cognition.

A self is able to see a small image or a large image in its imagination by way of a corresponding small apparition or a corresponding large apparition in the environment. A self's small image or large image is to be distinguished from a small apparition or a large apparition in the environment because an apparition is the stimulus for an image to be developed in the self's imagination for the self to see.

A large apparition is translated into subjective suefs after objective photons travelling from this large apparition meet with the retinas of the self's body. These suefs are transported by Nature and the self via the optic nerves to the occipital lobe of the self's brain. Then the self instinctively uses Nature's Will in tandem with Nature to shine *an inner visible light* through these subjective suefs so that they are illuminated as subjective photons resulting in a large image which the self is able to see in its imagination.

Objective photons are small apparitions. Many objective photons are willed by Nature to combine and evolve a large apparition. A body in the environment, such as a blade of grass, is only seen by a self after Nature has willed in the objective photons to reflect from the blade of grass so that these photons meet with and merge with the rods and cones of a human sensable organism's retinas and are translated into subjective suefs. Then, with Nature's help, a self instinctively shines visible inner light waves through these subjective suefs so the self can illuminate them as subjective photons and develop a large image of the blade of grass in its faculty of imagination.

A large image evolved by a self in its imagination by way of the self's observation of an apparition, like a fairy, or the self's observation of an appearance, like a table, in a self's shared environment with other selves is not a mental state identical to its image, as Whiting insists, because an image is a *motion picture* occurring in the self's imagination. This motion picture is identical to its image. This motion picture is not a mental "state" because this picture is an activity in motion, not an inactivity or a state.

Subjective photons are willed to develop as subjective motion pictures by a self's use of Nature's Will. Motion pictures occurring in a self's imagination aren't "frames of film or snapshots" occurring in the self's brain, like the frames of film or snapshots of the mistakenly named "motion pictures" that Hollywood produces because Hollywood's so-called "motion pictures" are the illusions cast by film projectors.

An objective motion in energy with objective suefs or objective luefs is the result of an objective quale or a wave of will instigated non-intentionally as well as non-unintentionally by Nature because Nature has no ability to intend which means that unintended actions aren't attributable to Nature either.

An objective as well as a subjective quale is a will wave. Invisible or visible light existed in the environment by Nature are qualia or waves of will. Outer visible light is shone by Nature's instinctive willing in waves through objective suefs. This outer visible light carries these objective suefs and is shone through them so that they apparition as objective photons. When these objective photons meet the rods and cones of the retinas of a self, they are translated into subjective suefs. After the objective photons have been translated into subjective suefs, the self can shine inner visible light through these subjective suefs so they shine as subjective photons in the self's faculty of imagination for the self to see.

Although an objective appearance in the environment, like a book, is imaged by the self as a motion picture in its imagination, an appearance is existed by Nature in the environment after its construction by selves without need of a self to observe it; therefore, the objective aspect as well as the subjective aspect of Nature are realities. These aspects aren't separate because Nature's Will is in everything, including the thing called a self.

Things are energy forms, particles, and bodies. Selves are things too, but things are not necessarily selves. Selfological qualities, like needs, are used by selves to relate to other things, especially other selves.

A real apparition is a real object in the environment, like an angel's real apparition; however, such an "apparition" might simply be existed by a self as its mistaken interpretation of a hallucination which is only existent in this self's imagination. Consequently, the self might simply mistakenly think its seeing an apparition outside of its sensable organism, instead of a hallucination in its imagination.

A real appearance is also a real object in the environment, like a real tree. Apparitions and appearances are only existed in the environment by Nature, just as images are only existed in a self's imagination by it with Nature's non-intended and non-unintended assistance. A self is able to shine inner visible light through its objective luef so that its objective luef or sensor is shone as an aura (an apparition) about the self's body. It's important to understand that a self's subjective luefs are only existed by a self in its imagination. The self's sensor or objective luef is lived by it in its objective body.

An image is a subjective phenomenon, while an appearance and an apparition are both objective phenomena. The colour of a body is derived from an outer quale of visible light with objective photons carried by this light as small apparitions, not small appearances.

A body's colouring is due to an outer visible light wave or outer activity. Objective suefs are carried by this visible light and apparitioned as objective photons by having this visible light shone through them. Colouring is light energy reflected off a body; therefore, this colouring is existed by Nature as an outer phenomenon. Outer colouring is received by the rods and cones of a self's retinas which convert it into inner colouring. A self is capable of seeing this inner colouring by way of inner visible light in its imagination.

A sensable organism's rods and cones are influenced by a self's volitional use of Nature's Volition in them so that the inner colouring of the light energy interacting with them is influenced by the self who inhabits this sensable organism; therefore, a self can sense a slightly different colour than any other self who is viewing the same outer colouring from an object in the environment, like a tree, because every sensable organism's rods and cones which the inhabiting self of this sensable organism influences are unique. The rods and cones of a body's retinas will be used by the body's inhabiting self to translate the outer colours of light from a tree in a different way than other selves are able to use the rods and cones of their bodies to translate them. As a result, the colours of a tree you see are unique to you because you see the colours of the same tree, differently, than other selves see them.

An image is an activity happening in a self's imagination. An image is not a pre-mental state or a mental state. An image is a motion in light energy with a shining form. An image is a subjective motion picture which we're able to see in our imaginations.

An objective moving picture in the environment is an apparition, e.g., a hologram. The motion pictures that Hollywood produces occur by way of a strip of film moving over the light bulb of the movie projector so the elements of each picture or frame of film are blended together and the illusion of movement is produced. People in Hollywood mistakenly calls this illusory movement a "motion picture". These pictures are really moving pictures, not motion pictures, because motion is an unseeable or unobservable activity which happens inside an existent phenomena, while movement is a seeable or observable activity of the "outside" of existent phenomena; therefore, even though Hollywood really produces moving, not motion, picture, since we really only see the outside of these pictures, the elements of each frame of film are in motion because the particles composing these elements are always in motion.

An image is intuited, cognised, and recognised only after it has been innerly observed by a self in its imagination: therefore, the selfological actions of intuiting, cognising, and recognising are not identical to imaging because the ability to image is existed more deeply by a self in its inner world than the abilities of intuiting, cognising, and recognising. Like our intuitions, cognitions, and recognitions, our images are realities, even if they're only our imaginings, rather than our imagitings.

Whiting's "appearance-is-reality" doctrine of mind is a mistaken phenomenological description of appearance because he failed to recognise what an appearance is or what the observation of an appearance is. Observation is only the act of seeing; therefore, an appearance is an observed objective phenomenon, like a mineral organic rock, a vegetative organic tree, or a sensable organic amphibian, which is converted and seen by a self as an image or observed subjective phenomenon. Sensations, such as pains, pleasures, itches, tingles, emotions, and moods, as well as sounds, flavours, and odours, aren't images nor are they observed; however, we're able to attend to them.

An image may be developed in a self's imagination by way of an appearance or an apparition immediately observed by the self in the environment, by way of a subject's memory of an image, or by way of the self's memory of a fantasy, respectively. The objective photons reflected from an appearance or an apparition are translated into subjective suefs by Nature's instinctive willing in the rods and cones of a self's retinas and are then transported via the self's optic nerves to the areas of its brain associated with its faculty of imagination. Then the self instinctively uses inner qualia of visible light in its imagination to shine through these subjective suefs so that they image as a large image in the self's imagination. The self then symbolises this large image as an inner ideogram or an inner word and commits this image as well as its symbolisation to memory.

Feelings felt, sounds heard, flavours tasted, odours smelled, and colours seen by a self are the result of inner qualia or will waves which are spontaneously, instinctively, and nondeliberately willed by Nature as well as -a self in association with Nature to activate feelings, sounds, flavours, odours, and colours. These waving energies are cognitively sensed as well as felt by us. We're able to commit these sensed qualia to memory.

Just as physical realities aren't existent as "states" (because stillness is an illusion), a self's mind or consciousness isn't existent as a state either; however, "mind" or "consciousness" isn't a state because stillness is an illusion, but because mind or consciousness is only existent as a falsity, not a truth. Only cognition is an existent, not mind or consciousness. And only incognisance is an existent, not mindlessness or unconsciousness. Likewise, only knowing is an existent, not minding or awareness, and only unknowing is an existent, not unminding or unawareness.

States are illusions. Our active sensing may only be enjoyed as peaceful or despaired as agitated. Our sensings are peaceful activities or agitated activities because we spontaneously or impulsively as well as instinctively and nondeliberately or deliberately and noninstinctively use the Will of Nature in the activity of our cognitions with various levels of excitement, easiness, or anxiety.

Even when a self's needs, desires, abilities, disabling abilities, faculties, and disabling faculties are held in Potentiality, they are activities. If Potentiality wasn't Activity, we wouldn't be able to actualise anything from It In other words, Potentiality wouldn't be Potent.

Unobservable qualia, such as the qualia associated with sounds, aren't appearances. Only an observable visible light is associated with an appearance. Whiting has fallen under the sway of phenomenologists who mistakenly think unobservable invisible light associated with sounds, touches, tastes and smells is observable. These phenomenologists fail to understand that only visible light associated with sight is observable. Phenomenologists have also misunderstood the term "appearance" because they have equated the term "appearance" to the term, "phenomenon".

Like most phenomenologists, Whiting likely realises that visible appearances, visible objective small apparitions (objective photons), visible objective large apparitions, invisible objective suefs, invisible subjective suefs, visible subjective small images (subjective photons), and visible subjective large images are all phenomena; however, Whiting is confused because he mistakenly assumes that all phenomena are appearances.

Many phenomenologists are like Whiting. They confuse each other by referring to unobservables, like sounds, feelings, flavours, and odours as appearances. These unobservables obviously don't appear; therefore, we're unable to observe them as appearances.

Appearances and apparitions are objects which are only located in the environment, not in a self's faculty of imagination. In a self's faculty of imagination, the only existent phenomena existed by the self are qualia, suefs, luefs, small images, and large images. The small images and the large images that we see in our faculties of imagination are *imaged* by us as images. We're unable to develop appearances and apparitions in our imaginations; however, we're able to shine inner light through our objective luefs (our sensors) and manifest them as our auras or apparitions.

The colours we see aren't just the result of objective and subjective photons. Colours are also the result of qualia. This means that an outer visible light is an outer quale or will wave and is not just composed of objective photons. A visible light of the outer world is translated by a self so that the self sees it as a visible light in the self's inner world, just as an objective photon is translated into a subjective photon which is subjectively seen by a self. A self is able to see inner visible light's colour spectrum, but not inner *invisible* light's uncoloured spectrum. Only subjective photons are able to be imaged by inner visible light's colour spectrum because Nature is only able to instinctively shine (and we're only able to instinctively shine) visible light through the suefs of the visible light spectrum by way of Its (and our) use of Its Will in activating will waves and the suefs of the visible light spectrum.

Colours are also existed by Nature independently of our capacity to see them, even though our inner colours are as much a result of the cones in our eyes as they are of our ability to see, because a colour of light is reflected from an outer object that absorbs the rest of the colours of the visible light spectrum. We're only able to subjectively see the unabsorbed colour of light reflected by a body, that is, if the cones of our eyes are receptive to the particular outer quale in light that transmits this outer colour to the cones of our eyes, i.e., if we're not colour-blind.

But my point is that Nature instinctively wills in outer visible light and objective photons as well as in the cones of our eyes to change the outer colour of a light into an inner colour of light for us to see. Outer colours reflected from bodies need to be translated by us into inner colours because inner colours are the only colours that we're able to see. If an outer colour of red wasn't reflected from a body, while other outer colours are absorbed by this body, we wouldn't be able to translate this outer colour of red and see its corresponding inner colour of red; therefore, colours are existed outerly, as well as innerly, *with the proviso that we're unable to see outer colours*. Ironically, some scientismists don't believe in outer colours because they are unable to see outer colours.

Nature instinctively wills objective photons and their outer qualia in the environment to intermove with the rods and cones of a sensable organism's retinas so they enter the retina's rods and cones. These photons are then translated by way of their interactions with the rods and cones of the sensable organism's retinas into suefs. This interaction is activated by Nature's instinctive willing so that subjective suefs are transported from the sensable organism's retinas to and within the sensable organism's optic nerves to and within the neurons located in the association area of the brain and sensable organism's occipital lobe.

The occipital lobe is associated with a self's faculty of imagination and its ability of imagining or imagiting images in this faculty. Nature activates activity within the subjective suefs of a self's inner visible light spectrum (which are intermotioning in the association area of the occipital lobe) and coverts them to subjective photons which the self sees as images. Selves don't see with their "Third Eye" because The Third Eye which is supposedly existent in a self is actually the existent self, not an existent "in" the self.

An apparition and an appearance are objects that have been viewed but are unable to be seen until they have been converted into images. A fire is composed of the shifting apparitions we call "flames". We're only able to vision the flames we see after the outer qualia in the objective photons from these flames have interacted with the rods and cones of our retinas; however, it must be remembered that our subjective photons are always active, even when a subjective motion picture seems to be still, e.g., a seemingly still dream image is an activity in our imaginations, not a stillness.

Outer *invisible* light carries objective suefs by way of Nature's instinctively willing in this invisible light; however, Nature is unable to instinctively Will outer invisible light to shine; therefore, Nature is unable to apparition the objective suefs of outer *invisible* light as objective photons, just as we're unable develop subjective photons with inner invisible light because we're unable to shine Nature's Will through subjective suefs carried by inner invisible light. Consequently, the hypothesis of modern physicists that outer invisible light waves, like x-rays, carry objective photons is an invalid hypothesis because the suefs of x-rays are invisible as are the waves of x-rays. In other words, it's impossible to apparition the suefs of x-rays as objective photons because the waves of x-rays are not visible light waves which could be used to shine the x-rays' invisible suefs and develop their visibility to selves.

Our abstractions are based on images without containing them. Examples of such abstractions are subjective inner letters, subjective inner numbers, and subjective inner graphics. We translate these abstractions as objective outer letters, objective outer numbers, or objective outer graphics by engraving them in objective appearances. We use inner letters and inner graphics to structure inner symbols in our inner worlds so that we're able to use these inner symbols to develop our concepts, ideas, hypotheses, and theories.

We store these inner symbols in our memory store and remember them from this memory store. We also remember abstract activities, like colours, sounds, feelings, flavours, and odours by translating their subjective suefs into inner graphics and inner letters which we use to structure inner symbols, like inner ideograms and inner words, so that we're able to intelligently map our experience and commit this map to memory. We're then able to stimulate inner qualia in our memory stores and activate our remembered inner symbols which we use to stimulate motions of energy, like images, associated with these memorised inner symbols.

Many selves other than human selves, like selves inhabiting the bodies of mice, use their remembered inner qualia to directly stimulate images. Mice don't need intermediaries, like inner symbols to stimulate their memories—nor do we need them to stimulate our memories.

Inner graphics and inner letters are used to structure inner symbols, while outer graphics or outer letters are used to structure outer symbols in our environment. We also concretely engrave outer words and outer ideograms in physicalities by using outer letters and outer graphics, respectively. We develop inner letters and inner graphics in our cognitions so that we may structure inner words and inner ideograms.

For example, we use the inner letters "c", "r", "o", "w" and "d" to structure the inner word "crowd" in our cognitions. We know this word in our cognitions. We also use the outer letters "c", "r", "o", "w" and "d" to structure the outer word "crowd" as a concrete engrave in the environment. We sense this word in the environment.

Outer symbols, like outer words, are also audible sounds of outer speech which we hear; therefore, outer words aren't just concrete engravings in physical realities, like an outer word written in ink engraved in a sheet of paper.

We also use inner symbols to speak, innerly and silently, for our inner listening, despite our inability to hear them; therefore, we speak inner symbols in our cognitions for our silent listening as well as know these symbols in our cognitions.

We develop inner graphics and inner letters so we're able to structure inner ideograms and inner words, respectively, and, thus, are able to apply these inner ideograms and inner words to our thinking and reasoning. We apply inner numbers to our cogitating as well as inner symbols; however, we're unable to use inner numbers to structure inner symbols. We only use inner symbols in our thoughts, concepts, and hypotheses *about* inner numbers because our cogitating disables our thinking and reasoning by using principles, rules and laws to delineate inner numbers in inner equations and inner formulas.

Outer graphics, outer numbers, and outer letters are environmental. Inner graphics, inner numbers, and inner letters are cognitional, not mental or conscious, because, as indicated earlier, mind or consciousness, is not an existent in selves.

Thoughts and notions are associated with a self's ability of thinking in its faculty of cognition. Concepts and ideas are also associated with a self's ability of thinking in its faculty of cognition. Hypotheses and theories are associated with a self's ability of reasoning in its faculty of recognition. Emotions are associated with a self's ability to emote in its faculty of temperament. Memories are associated with a self's ability to remember memories from its faculty of memory and also its ability to store memories in this faculty. Colours, sounds, touches, flavours, and odours are associated with a self's abilities of seeing, hearing, feeling, tasting, and smelling in its visual, auditory, tactile, gustatory, and olfactory faculties. Sights of images are associated with a self's abilities of imagining and imagiting in its faculty of imagination.

You're unable to see the inner words you develop unless you develop an image for them. You're able to translate inner qualia and their associated suefs into inner ideograms and inner words; however, it's easy for you to make a mistake and assign the inner word "noisy" to a sound when the appropriate inner word for you to have used would have been the inner word "blaring".

The inner words and the inner ideograms we use in our concepts, ideas, hypotheses, and theories are essential, not substantial or physical. Outer and inner qualia are also essential because they're abstract energies, like inner words and inner ideograms. Abstract inner words and inner ideograms as well as qualia are unobservable selfological qualities of selves.

Seeing, hearing, feeling, tasting, and smelling are our senses. Our seeing, hearing, feeling, tasting, and smelling occur by way of our sensory organs; however, senses are the abilities of selves, not those of sensory organs. Our sensory organs are unable to sense. We sense by using our sensory organs, *such as our brains*, to sense with our cognitive knowing in our sensory organs. *We*, not our brains, hear, feel, taste, smell, and see.

By way of instinctive outer will waves or qualia, Nature channels objective photons through a sensable organism's eyes and retinas which are then translated as subjective suefs. These subjective suefs are instinctively channelled by Nature and the inhabiting self of a sensable organism through the sensable organism's optic nerves to the association area of the occipital lobe of the sensable organism's brain in which the self holds its immaterial faculty of imagination. In the self's immaterial faculty of imagination (which is not a part of its brain), Nature and the self instinctively shine inner visible light through these subjective suefs so they are imaged in the self's imagination as subjective photons for the self to see.

The self instinctively and nondeliberately uses Nature's Will in tandem with Nature's instinctive nondeliberate use of its Will to channel objective photons from the materialised association area of the materialised occipital lobe where these objective photons are converted into subjective photons in the self's immaterial faculty of imagination. The self's immaterial faculty of imagination is also associated with the self's materialised brain's prefrontal lobe which contains as well as encompasses the self's immaterial faculties of intuition, cognition, and recognition. The self deliberately uses its immaterial ability of thinking contained in the materialised brain's prefrontal lobe by the self to translate the self's immaterial perception of subjective photons in its the self's immaterial imagination into immaterial abstract inner graphics and inner letters so the self is able to structure these immaterial inner graphics and inner letters into immaterial inner ideograms and inner words, respectively. The self also deliberately uses its immaterial disabling ability of cogitating to translate immaterial subjective photons into immaterial abstract inner numbers; however, the self is unable to use its immaterial inner numbers to structure immaterial inner symbols. This is my "take" on our development of immaterial inner ideograms and inner words as well as inner numbers; however, it's just as important to have an appropriate take on the levels of Reality.

Nature is existent as well as exists as Reality. Nature's self's are existent as well as exist at the deepest level of Reality. Selves are existent and exist at a deeper level of Reality than existent inner qualia and outer qualia which are devoid of the ability to exist.[2] Inner qualia and outer qualia are existent at a deeper level of Reality than subjective suefs and objective suefs. Subjective suefs and objective suefs are existent at a deeper level of Reality than subjective luefs and subjective images. Subjective luefs and subjective images are existent at a deeper level of Reality than objective luefs and apparitions. Objective luefs and apparitions are existent at a deeper level of Reality than sensable, vegetable, and mineral appearances. Sensable, vegetable, and mineral appearances are existent at a deeper level of Reality than inner graphics, inner numbers, inner letters, and inner symbols. Inner graphics, inner numbers, inner letters, and inner symbols

---

[2] Although qualia are outer in that they are existent in the environment and are also inner in that they are existent in us, qualia aren't objects any more than they are subjects. Rather, qualia are qualities derived from Nature (like everything else). Qualia are also qualities of Nature's willing other than electromagnetic light, like the vitality of gravity-antigravity.

are existent at a deeper level of Reality than outer graphics, outer numbers, outer letters, and outer symbols.

At the sensable level of Reality, Reality instinctively wills the generation of *sensations* which are carried by Its instinctive will waves. These outer qualia are used by Reality (Nature) and a self to *impulse* suefs to the neurons of the self's brain. The brain is used by the self who inhabits its brain's reticular formation to channel these impulses and release their energies so these inner energies are seen, heard, felt, tasted, or smelled by the self in its visual, auditory, tactile, gustatory, and olfactory faculties. The self holds these immaterial faculties in its materialised brain which is used by the self to contain them as transcendent immaterialities; however, the word "transcendent" isn't necessarily an indication of the self's immortality

Sounds relevant to our sense of hearing demonstrate that sensations are carried in a sensable organism nerves and neurons as a self's impulses by the self's spontaneous or impulsive use of Nature's Will in harmony or disharmony with Nature's spontaneous use of Its Will; therefore, the impulses which are generated in a sensable organism are not necessarily impulsive or disharmonious activities generated by the stupidity of a self but are often spontaneous and harmonious activities generated by a self's wisdom.

Hearing is our ability attend, although not necessarily listen, to the suefs associated with a quale so we sense sounds with our ability to hear, but might not use our knowing in our sensing of these sounds to actually listen to their meaning or significance. A self is able to hear a vibration and the subjective suefs associated with it as a sound which the self is able to translate into inner graphics and inner letters by its use of its ability to think. Sensations of subjective suefs are instinctively channelled by qualia in impulses through the afferent nerves of the peripheral nervous system and then through the afferent nerves of the spinal cord to the materialised brain's area associated with the self's immaterial auditory faculty so that it's able to instinctively hear these subjective suefs by way of an immaterial inner quale associated with a particular immaterial sound occurring in its immaterial auditory faculty.

The tongue is an organ in which Nature's willed impulses carrying sensations are generated by Nature in response to the chemicals in a food, such as an orange, so the nerves leading from the tongue to the brain are used as channels for these willed impulses to carry these sensations directly to the area of the materialised brain associated with the self's immaterial gustatory faculty so that the self can taste these sensations. The self can sense the orange's taste or flavour without need of sensing through the afferent nerves of the spinal cord. The self uses its ability of recognising to translate the sweet or sour flavour of the orange into the inner words "sweet" or "sour" by using its ability to identify the flavour of the orange and its ability to name this flavour.

Every unobservable self, such as you and I, is a center of Reality. As a center of Reality, I developed my immaterial faculties from Potentiality, Activity, or Nature when I needed them. My immaterial faculty of temperament contains my immaterial ability to emote. The immaterial emotions I emote are uncondensed energies generated by my immaterial ability to emote. My immaterial ability to emote is my ability to generate a will wave or a quale by using my immaterial ability to emote with my borrowed use of Nature's Will. Emoting is an activity a subject usually uses instinctively, but occasionally uses deliberately, to activate motions called "emotions". It seems likely that the letter "e" in the word "emotion" originally stood for energy. Consequently, a subject uses a quale of emoting to activate an emotion (a motion of energy) which it feels as a passion.

The qualia in our emotions have no subjective suefs associated with them. Interestingly, it seems certain that Nature's gravity-antigravity quale carries objective suefs; therefore, it seems certain that a "graviton" is an objective suef or "boson" generated by Nature in Its gravity wave, while an "antigraviton" is an objective suef or boson generated by Nature in its antigravity wave. Fortunately, our emotions are barren of objective suefs; therefore, it's easier for us to distinguish between our emotions because the spectrum of our emotions aren't differentiated by subjective suefs, like our vibrations of sight, sound, touch, flavour, and odour.

There is a challenge to understanding what is real based on your inhabitation of your sensable organism and your immaterial ability to relate to uninhabited mineral and vegetative organisms as well as other selves who inhabit sensable organisms other than yours as aspects of your shared outer World.

For example, certain individuals I know scoff at sights of apparitions which only I and some other people are able to see as well as scoff at disembodied voices, like the voice I once heard saying, "Daryl, this is God". I knew this voice either originated from me as my hallucination, like these scoffers claimed, or was only that of a self from a realm of the after-death because I knew unbounded Nature is unable to speak. This voice may have been the voice of either the tyrannical self, Yahweh (the "Judge"), the tyrannical self, Sophia (the

"Comforter"), the tyrannical self, Satan (the "Prosecutor"), the tyrannical self, Jesus (the Defender), or any other tyrant from a realm of the after-death (that is, if we're immortal, rather than mortal).

Unlike holographic apparitions which we're all able to see, some of the apparitions that I've seen were not susceptible to the observation of other people.

For example, I was once alone in a room I had rented when I saw the apparitions of three fairies emerge from a wooden armoire in the corner of the room and fly about the room. One fairy perched on my right hand's extended index finger for a while before it and its two companions decided to fly back to the armoire and merge back with it.

To call such apparitions "hallucinations" is to "beg the question". To call the self who has seen such apparitions a "psychotic" self is untrue because only oversensitivity is existed by a self, not psychosis. Like mind, the psyche isn't an existent reality either.

The apparitions seen by an oversensitive self are not necessarily hallucinations simply because such a self's brain is in chemical disharmony. An oversensitive self's pineal gland in this disharmonised self's use of Nature's Will to chemically imbalance its brain might be used as an aberrant "antenna" by sensitive selves from realms in the after-death (if they exist) so the oversensitive self's chemically imbalanced brain is a means of attracting the attention of these sensitive selves; therefore, a disharmonised self might also use its chemically imbalanced brain's pineal gland as its organic "receiver" by way of which this self sees the apparition of a self's sensor which might be evidence that this apparition originates from a realm of the after-death.

When I was an oversensitive self, I could hear the lying voice of a self who said, "Daryl, I am God". I've heard other oversensitive selves say they can feel an emotion which a self who might originate from a realm of the after-death has stirred in them and smell the scent as well as taste the flavour of such a self's objective luef.

Psychiatrists fail to realise that the chemically balanced brains of "normal" sensitive selves are also the organic receivers through which these sensitive selves are able to see the apparitions, hear the voices, feel the emotions, smell the sensors, as well as taste the sensors of selves who might originate from ethereal realms of the after-death, that is, if these selves exist and are as open to knowing their experience as oversensitive selves are.

Psychiatrists who believe that such phenomena are hallucinations suffer from a severe case of myopic intelligence, that is, if they refuse to admit that such phenomena might be actualities, rather than hallucinations. Many psychiatrists refuse to explore the paranormal as a serious scientific pursuit, despite the fact that they have all had experiences with their clients which they're unable to explain with their presumptive psychiatric "medical modelling", not to mention their own, occasional experience of unexplainable incidents which are quite impossible to duplicate so they could be tested by experimentation.

The myopic intelligence of some psychiatrists is demonstrated by their willingness to believe that an oversensitive self sees the real image of a fairy and their unwillingness to believe that this image is the image of a fairy's real apparition in the environment simply because these psychiatrists don't believe in fairies. In other words, most psychiatrists claim that the image of a fairy that their clients see is only real in the sense of a "real" hallucination. They claim that an apparition of a fairy is a hallucination because they've never had the experience of seeing a fairy. Psychiatrists have never seen a fairy because they instinctively block their ability to see them.

Most psychiatrists fail to realise that a fairy may shine, or not shine, its sensor as an apparition to be seen; however, even when invisible, the fairy is able to observe exactly what we're doing (if fairies are actual, rather than hallucinatory). A fairy is able to select when it will be seen and when it will not be seen (if it's not a hallucination). Those who don't believe in fairies aren't usually given the opportunity by fairies to see them (if fairies are existent) because fairy lore often refers to the reluctance of fairies to associate with the ignorant (taken in both its senses of "refusing to sense" and "rudeness"). Consequently, it's not always a psychiatrist's instinctive blocking that prevents him or her from seeing a fairy.

It doesn't take a genius to recognise that apparitions might be existent or real because a self might be unable to project an image outside of its body so it would see this image as an "objective hallucination" (a contradiction in terms). A self might not have the ability to holographically project an image as an apparition outside of its body: therefore, a fairy's apparition observed by an oversensitive self as an apparition outside of this self's sensable organism might be its dependently projected apparition, rather than an independently existent apparition.

The fact that sensitive people are able to observe the apparitions of these fairies, like oversensitive selves, is a small hint to psychiatrists that they need to re-examine their assumption that "psychotic" selves hallucinate fairies, rather than sense them; however, true to form, most psychiatrists deny that fairies exist because they are unable to accommodate their theories to the possible reality of fairies. As a result of their unfairly prejudiced stance, these psychiatrists say that anyone who sees the apparitions of fairies are "by definition" delusional. These psychiatrists tend to gloss over the fact that fairies might just exist because they are suffering from the mistaken hypothesis that their intellectual interpretations of a reality are their intelligent knowledge of the truth or falsity of this reality. They fail to understand that they are unfairly and prejudicially using their intellectual interpretations of reality to deny that their clients' experience of interacting with fairies has any possibly of truth.

A self is not hallucinating a fairy's apparition if the self's subjective image of the fairy gives the self the impression that this subjective image has a corresponding apparition existed outside of the self's imagination in the environment; however, if the self's impression is that the subjective image seen has no corresponding apparition and is existed only as a fantasy in the self's imagination, this subjective image is the self's hallucination. A subjective image seen in relation to an apparition existed outside of a self's body is a vision, not a hallucination, because the apparition existed outside of the self's imagination has given the self the impression that this apparition is real, rather than fantasised.

I find it ironic when scoffers claim that apparitions aren't real, yet, in the same breath, refer to the illusory apparition of a mirage. These scoffers don't reason out that a mirage is a reflected illusory apparition of a real appearance, such as an oasis; however, a fairy's apparition might exist as the fairy's shining of its inner visible light through its sensor so that this objective luef becomes the fairy's real, not illusory, apparition. A fairy's apparition could be existent as the fairy's inhabited reality, not an uninhabited illusory apparition, like the mirage of an oasis; however, illusory apparitions are just as real as the realities from which they're derived because we're able to sense them.

A fantasy or an imagining is a hallucination. To envision is your ability to fantasise, imagine, or hallucinate a subjective suef which you image by shining it as a subjective photon to see in your imagination. To vision is your ability to image a subjective suef you've received from the environment by shining it as a subjective photon to see in your imagination without fantasising, imagining or hallucinating this image. Therefore, envisioning is your ability to fantasise, imagine, or hallucinate an image, like a dream image, while visioning is your ability to imagitively image by way of an apparition, like an angel (if angels actually exist), or by way of an appearance, like a tree.

An imagitive image is the result of visioning. Visioning is our ability to realise an apparition or an appearance by translating it and imagiting it as an image, not by fantasising, imagining, or hallucinating it; therefore, our use of envisioning usually hinders us so that we become deluded, while our use of visioning usually helps us to be realistic.

As I noted earlier, imagiting is our ability to translate a reality existent in the environment to our imaginations by way of visioning, while imagining is our ability to fantasise or hallucinate an image by way of envisioning. I had to coin the word "imagiting" because researchers had no word for our ability to image an object that existed in the objective world so that we see it in our imaginations.

We use our ability of imagining, fantasising, or hallucinating to conjure up an image in our imaginations. A conjured up image is a reality, even though it's only an imagined, fantasised, or hallucinated reality.

Whether you're fantasising, imagining, or hallucinating an image or imagiting an image from an existent apparition or an appearance, you see these images in your faculty of imagination. Consequently, you're able to imaginatively image a fairy in your imagination (even though this image is not translated from a fairy's actual illusory apparition) as well as imagitively image a fairy in your imagination (from a fairy's actual apparition, that is, if fairies are actually existent).[3]

We might envision (imaginatively image) the image of an unreal "troubled angel" or we might vision (imagitively image) an image of a real troubled angel. I need to emphasise that a troubled angel is not a "demon" (if angels actually exist). "Demon" is an inappropriate moniker, unlike the words "fairy" and "human", because the words "fairy" and "human" carry the connotation that the fairy and the human express relative goodness and badness. The word "demon" carries the connotation that the demon is evil or absolutely bad without any good existent in or existed by him or her, while the word "angel" carries the

---

[3] Even a hallucinated or fantasised dream image is a reality, despite the fact that it's ephemeral. Selves from the after-death are able to use our dream images to influence us by talking to us through them (if selves are immortal).

connotation that the angel is divine or absolutely good without any bad existent in or existed by him or her.

An angel of absolute goodness and a demon of absolute badness are fictions because there are no absolute divine or evil selves. There are only angels who *express* relative love more than relative hate or who express relative hate more than relative love. There are no demons who express absolute badness or evil nor are there angels who express absolute goodness or divinity.

Selves are unable to *be* good or bad. Like Nature, selves transcend goodness and badness. A self's expressions are relatively loving, not relatively good, or relatively hateful, not relatively bad.

Nature's expression of harmony is enjoyable for selves, not good for them. But Nature transcends Its harmony. Nature transcends Its harmony as well as Its Will because Nature possesses Its harmony and Will; therefore, Nature is neither Its harmony nor Its Will because these possessions aren't the Possessor of them.

There isn't a self in a fantasised image, even though this hallucinated image is real. The "content" of a fantasised image only seems to exist; however, an apparition might have a self who inhabits it because an apparition is not necessarily a hallucinated image.

The apparition of an angel, who is so troubled or unwell that we mistakenly refer to him or her as a "demon" is a self with a real inner world (if angels actually exist). The hallucinated images of *unrisen*, not fallen, angels whom we envision in our dreams are often "masks" that angels are acting out in our dreams for us (if our dream images of angels are projections by angels who are actually existent as well as exist); however, if these angels are projecting "angels" as our dream images, they don't necessarily inhabit the hallucinated images or masks they're acting out in our dreams. The masks that unrisen angels act out in our dreams are manifestations of their unwellness because unrisen angels are caught in the stupidity of not yet realising that they're free. Consequently, if angels are existent as well as exist, they aren't "fallen" from "grace"; they're unrisen from the infinite depths of stupidity from which they were generated by Nature in the sensable organisms they originally inhabited before their sensable organisms died and they entered their realm of the after-death.

Like a self who views apparitions, a self who hears a disembodied voice is not necessarily hallucinating. A self who hears such a voice is not always unknowingly speaking this voice so it's merely hearing its own voice. The voice may originate from another self whose disembodied "outer speech" is heard as sounds that originate from outside of the hearing self's sensable organism in which case the voice heard is not a hallucination but is the voice of a self from a realm of the after-death; however, inner speech occurring within the self's cognition which the self doesn't know it's speaking is the self's hallucination. Such a hallucination is cognitive, not imaginative; therefore, not all hallucinations are imaginings or fantasies.

For example, we speak the hallucinated inner words we hear and might listen to in our dreams, although we think our dream images are speaking these inner words; however, entities from realms of the after-death might occasionally speak in and from the images they form in our dreams (if these entities actually exist as well as are existent).

It could be disturbing to an earth-bound self if a self actually exists who inhabits an apparition from a realm in the after-death and speaks to the earth-bound self from outside of its sensor and sensable organism because the self from the after-death might be so disturbed that it will attempt to indoctrinate, rather than help the earth-bound self. Even worse, the self from the after-death might attempt to hypnotise the earth-bound self so that the earth-bound self might cease to fully use its ability to know and let the self from the after-death lead it "by the nose". This kind of hypnosis is called "possession" by less enlightened people because they don't yet understand that the self from the after-death has not taken possession of the earth-bound self's thinking. Rather, the self from the after-death (if it, indeed, exists) has simply mesmerised the earth-bound self so that the earth-bound self unquestioningly follows the instructions of the self from the after-death.

It's important to understand that we're able to use our ability of imaging to generate abstract inner graphics, inner numbers, inner letters, inner ideograms, and inner words from Essence to envision them as observable hallucinations in our imaginations. These abstractions aren't separations but are relations which are in accord with patterns in the environment we have seen. In other words, we're able to generate and envision symbols in our imaginations as well as generate and innerly speak symbols with our silent thinking for our inaudible listening in our cognitions.

As well as activating our abstractions, we also activate our skills because we're activities who have the ability to actualise our abilities from Potentiality. We activate our abilities by instinctively or deliberately using Nature's Will to do so; therefore, our ability to instinctively and nondeliberately as well as deliberately and noninstinctively use Nature's Will is our vitality because Nature's Will is the fundamental reality from which we choose which of our needs we'll fulfil immediately or postpone fulfilling until later.

Our abstract inner graphics, inner numbers, inner letters, inner ideograms, and inner words originate in our cognitions. We use our intelligence to develop these abstractions as concepts. We're unable to "create" these abstractions as "separations" from Activity because Creation and separateness are associated with the fiction of non-Existence whereas Activation and relatedness are associated with the truths of Existence; therefore, Creation and separation are fictions of Creationists.

We only have the abilities to activate and relate, not the abilities to create and separate. Consequently, the definition of the word "abstraction" as a self's ability to use abstract "nothings" to separate a self's subjective world from its objective world is mistaken. The appropriate definition of the word "abstraction" is a self's ability to use abstract things to relate its selfological world to its objective world.

Nature only has the ability to generate differentiations, like selves, develop differentiations, like qualia, as well as evolve and grow differentiations, like suefs, luefs, particles, and bodies. Nature doesn't have the ability to distinguish a differentiation or to distinguish between differentiations because Nature is not a differentiation. Nature has no way of knowing that the differentiations It evolves and grows are existed by It because Nature hasn't the ability to know nor does It have the ability to sense differentiations. Nature is barren of sensory abilities, like seeing, hearing, feeling, tasting and smelling. Nature is also barren of sensory faculties, like vision, audition, tactility, gustation, and olfaction.

Needs motivate a self's use of its subjective abilities, like emoting, thinking, reasoning, fantasising, imagining, imagiting, identifying, naming, memorising, remembering, anticipating, drinking, eating, and so on. A self's abilities of drinking and eating are derived from selfological, not "organic" needs. A self has needs, not its sensable organism. A sensable organism (an organic body) is needless because a sensable organism is lived by a self for the benefit of the self's needs, since sensable organisms as well as mineral organisms and vegetative organisms have no needs or, for that matter, any abilities to fulfil needs which is the ludicrous assumption of scientismists who assert that we "are" brains who have such needs and the skills to develop our supposed abilities as brains.

An organism is an evolved, grown, and developed mineral, vegetative, or sensable organic body. The Source evolved, grew, and developed mineral, vegetative, and sensable organic bodies on earth until the first parental sensable organisms were evolved so centers of the Source were generated within the zygotes and buds of these parental sensable organisms. We are the centers of pure energy who were developed in sensable organic zygotes by the Source. We were able to help the Source generate new cells from our zygotes by way of the process of mitosis. As we grew our materialised brains with the help of the Source, we generated our immaterial faculties, such as our intuition, cognition, and recognition, from Potentiality, Activity, or Nature as our activities by our spontaneous or impulsive instinctive nondeliberate use of Nature's Will in tandem with Its spontaneous instinctive nondeliberate willing.

By the way, there's an answer to the riddle, "Which came first, the chicken or the egg?" The answer is, "The egg". The original parent of chickens was not a chicken. The original non-chicken parent evolved mutated DNA in its sex cells so that the eggs it generated contained the first chickens; therefore, originally, eggs were used by Nature and a non-chicken to develop chickens which means that a chicken didn't originally develop the first eggs of chickens.

Conclusion

Some philosophers will object to my metaphysics because they won't understand that Nature is the efficient Activator of physical appearances as well as the efficient Activator of everything else. Nature evolves particles and grows as well as develops them into bodies; therefore, *the Will is Nature's ability to activate while Nature is the absolute Activity which is the Activator of Its Will or ability of Activation*

Nature causes effects by instinctively willing motions in and movements of Its things. Nature also causes effects by instinctively willing in a self, a self's natural selfological qualities, like a self's instincts, as well as a self's other things, like a self's suefs, luef, particles, and body.

By attending to its knowledge, a self is able to understand this knowledge and effect efficient motions in and movements of its body. Nature's effects are developed in a self as well as evolved in its body. Nature is unable to knowingly or unknowingly Will; therefore, Nature is unable to develop any knowledge of Its effects or ignore these effects.

Nature effects changes to bodies from within and without them as well as effects changes to the selfological qualities of all selves by instinctively willing from within and without them. Nature's willing relates everything to everything; therefore, there is no separation between a thing and a thing.

There is no such thing as separation because Nature's Will is the absolute factor of relatedness. A self may be isolated from another self, but it's never separated from that self. Two isolated selves are never separated or unrelated because Nature's Will is always relating them together. Despite our ability to isolate by withdrawing from relating, we are never separated from each other.

Likewise, an object is isolated from another object but it's never separated from the other object because it's always related to the other object by Nature's Will.

We don't need to be "attached" to another self in order to be related to it because we're always in relation to every self and everything else by way of Nature's Will. We're occasionally incommunicative when we're innerly isolated; however, we're not separated, disconnected, or detached. Likewise, we're frequently communicative when we're innerly isolated; however, we're not oned, connected, or attached.

We're always related to the Source in our inner isolation by the Will of this Source. We're always innerly isolated from each other; however, we're not separated from each other. We may choose not to communicate with each other in our isolation; however, we're unable to choose to separate from each other because the Will of the Source is always continually, incommunicatively, and incommunally relating us to each other.

Unlike the Source, we may choose to use Its Will to communicate with others or choose not to use Its Will to communicate with others. The Source is unable to choose; therefore, It doesn't choose to be incommunicative. It simply lacks the ability to communicate as well as the ability to commune, just as we have no ability to commune, but only the ability to relate, which is why "communities" are our delusions that individuals are our illusions, when the truth is that that only individuals are real, not communities or collectives.

Nature's Will is the absolute factor of relatedness for all that It exists as existents, including selves, their selfological qualities, their sensors, and their sensable organisms. This means that, if a self is immortal, it needs to abandon its dead sensable organism while remaining related to it, since all selves, their selfological qualities, and their suefs, luefs, particles, and bodies are related by

Nature's willing; however, the delusional idea of detachment, disconnection, or separation would mean that a self, its selfological qualities, its suefs composing its luef, as well as the particles composing its corpse would all be separated, detached, or disconnected from Nature's willing which is impossible.

Atheistic, agnostic, and theistic scientismists of scientism who believe in Oneness, connection, and attachment as well as separation, disconnection, and detachment are deluded because only relatedness in isolation is real.

For example, an electric plug is not oned, connected, or attached to an electric socket; the electric plug is related to the electric socket by Nature's Will in Its vitalism of electricity which flows from the electric socket to the electric plug. Likewise, the electric plug is not separated, disconnected, or detached from the electric socket when it's unplugged; the electric plug is isolated from the electric socket. But even in its isolation, the electric plug is always related to the electric socket by the relatedness of Nature's Will.

Unfortunately, Nature is unable to communicate with us in words or commune with us in love because Nature doesn't have the ability to distinguish or the ability to emote, even though Nature's Will is the absolute factor of relatedness for phenomena. We're able to dwell in Nature's harmony, but we're unable to commune with Nature. Nature is unable to commune with us because Nature doesn't know that we exist or that It exists; therefore, Nature is also unable to communicate with us. Consequently, praying to Nature in expectation of communication or communing is futile.

Many religionists think the relatedness of things to things in Reality is illusory because they think Reality is undifferentiated. They also think Reality is a self-contained universe. Therefore, they call their idea of an undifferentiated self-contained universe "Oneness". They don't realise that Reality's differentiations are real as well as infinite which means that Reality transcends any notion of the One. We experience relatedness, not "Oneness", because we're able to experience Reality's spontaneous instinctive nondeliberate willing.

The "oceanic feeler of Oneness" is ignoring his or her feeling of Reality's differentiations. We only truly experience relatedness in Reality by way of our experience of Nature's instinctive willing. We don't experience the Oneness of Reality because Reality is unboundedness, not Oneness. We're only able to experience an oceanic feeling of unboundedness, while recognising that we are ignoring the infinite differentiations of this unboundedness.

Your experience of recognising differentiations may be profound but it's not wisdom because your experience of relatedness is necessary for the harmonisation of your knowledge of Nature's differentiations. Consequently, the description of Nature's differentiations in words needs to be accompanied by your experience of your relatedness in and with Reality (Nature) if your description of Reality in words is ever to be your wise description of It.

It's important to understand that a self's knowledge of Reality is not its wisdom. A self has a need to recognise scattered bits of knowledge. Only then is it wisely able to understand the *pattern* of its bits of knowledge. Wisdom is first preceded by having insights into Reality so that the self can gain bits of knowledge about Reality. Then, by relating to its bits of knowledge, the self is able to feel The Ultimate Truth with which it patterned its bits of knowledge. A self's cognition of The Ultimate Truth and its basic pattern of knowledge is its wisdom. The Ultimate Truth is a self's feeling of Freedom. A self's harmony is the self's wise Freedom of action.

Relatedness is associated with contentment because the experience of relatedness puts us in relation to our emotion of love. The wise establish the relatedness of Nature's Will so they understand that Nature's Will is the way in which differentiations are harmonised by It as well as harmonised and disharmonised by Its selves, like you and I; therefore, our recognition of Reality as well as our recognition of our emotions of love and hate enables us to honestly pursue wisdom.

Nature is Reality or the Phenomenon. Natures are realities or phenomena. An ontologist knows that an unobservable is either an unappearing or unapparitioning reality, while an observable is either an appearing or apparitioning reality. Idealists hypothesise that an unappearing or unapparitioning reality is really a noumenon; however, a noumenon is a superstitious concept. A noumenon is a delusion of idealists who suppose that a noumenon is a thing as it really is, while a reality is supposedly the noumenon's "unreal" appearance or "phenomenon"; however, a reality is a thing as it is because there are no ideal realities. Idealists are superstitious supernaturalists who refuse to accept the evidence of their senses. If they accepted what they sensed, they would realise that appearances and apparitions (phenomena) are real.

Many phenomenologists fail to realise that phenomenologists are ontologists who describe for the purpose of discovering what they can and explain the

Reality in, of, and by which they are existents with the ability to exist. Instead, these phenomenologists believe that description is all that is needed; therefore, they completely ignore what we are because they don't believe that we are able to ongoingly understand and ongoingly explain the continually changing patterns of Reality.

Many phenomenologists tend to be obscurantists because they have given up the true pursuit of philosophy. The true pursuit of philosophy is to develop an ontology as well as a metaphysics based on the foundation of a religious absolute and The Ultimate Truth of Freedom. That many phenomenologists have given up this pursuit is evidenced by their definitions of the words "phenomena" and "noumena" which obscure the true meanings of these words.

In my practice of kinesiology, the *Senate* of the University of Waterloo has granted me the dubious privilege of attributing the label of "kinesiologist" inaccurately to what I am as my "identity", instead of identifying what I am as the self I really am. I only realized that I practiced "kinesiologist" as a role, persona, or false self, not what I am, when I established my own version of ontology, phenomenology, or Naturalism. I succeeded in removing the falsehood of idealism from my ontology, phenomenology, or Naturalism which I'd developed in accord with my extrospective scientific research Style (which I ironically refer to as my unmethodical "method") and my introspective philosophical research approach. I used my scientific Style in my ontology, phenomenology, or Naturalism, to develop my metaphysics of Naturalism which, of course, isn't my ontological or phenomenal Naturalism.

My explanation of why we exist is given by my religion of Selfism; therefore, Selfism is my religious understanding of why we exist which I explain with my metaphysics of Naturalism.

The Ultimate Truth of Selfism is Freedom; therefore, Freedom is the core of my philosophy, artistic sciences, and religion.

I describe my religion of Selfism as my Polyselfism. Polyselfism is the knowledge that selves are either immortals or mortals who originate from and are accidentally generated or activated by Nature's spontaneous instinctive nondeliberate use of Its Will in a parental sensable organism's zygote or bud.

Chapter Two
A Self's Development of Harmony

A Self's Harmonious Contentment Between Its Disharmonious Discontentments

	A Self's Disharmonious Discontentments	A Self's Harmonious Contentment	A Self's Disharmonious Discontentments
Associated Energetics:	Excited	Satisfied	Anxious
Associated Attitudinal Exacerbation:	Indulgence	Peace	Worry
Associated Desires:	Sane Desires		Insane Desires
Associated Emotions:	Love		Hate
	Affection		Anger
	Gratitude		Resentment
	Trust		Jealousy
	Generosity		Envy
	Pride		Shame (Compassion)
	Courage		Fear
Associated Moods:	Mania		Melancholia
	Ecstasy		Misery
	Bliss		Woe
	Elation		Depression
	Joy		Sorrow
	Happiness		Sadness
Associated Cognitive Content:	Knowledge	Cognition	Ignorance
Associated Actions:	Kindness		Cruelty
Associated Selfological Qualities:	Modesty		Humility and Conceit
Associated Ability and Disability:	Intelligence		Intellect
Associated Physical Motions:	Flow		Turmoil
Associated Physical Movements:	Calmness		Agitation
Associated Physical Characteristics:	Relaxation		Tension

My table, "A Self's Harmonious Contentment Between Its Disharmonious Discontentments", lists the emotions and moods of a self's sane desires associated with its energetic of excitement as well as the emotions and moods of the self's insane desires associated with its energetic of anxiety. Our cognitive content of knowledge is associated with a self's sane desires, while our cognitive content of ignorance is associated with a self's insane desires. All the associations in this table refer to our energetics of excitement, easiness, and anxiety.

My purpose in developing this table was to understand the empirical relations of my emotions to the development of my wisdom because a wise self has realised that its emotions are instinctive desires, not instinctive needs. A self has an instinctive need to develop wisdom because wisdom is a self's cognition of its harmony within Nature's harmony.

Nature's Will is Its harmony because Nature is free of the desire to end Its use of Its Will; therefore, a self's harmony within Nature's harmony is the self's acceptance of its need to use Nature's Will because it finally understands that its desire to end Its use of Nature's Will is impossible and, therefore, futile. Peace is often viewed to be a stagnating activity in which a self has ceased to use Nature's Will and experiences a purposeless lack of Will or Drive; however, a wise self knows that peace is a purposeful activity because a self's purposeless lack of Drive results in a nihilistic feeling of boredom and a suffering of meaninglessness if the self is not purposefully and peacefully willing. A self's purposeful (deliberate) use of Natures Will for enjoyment is needed if the self is to overcome the suffering which results from stagnating in a purposeless lack of willing.

Nature never stagnates because Nature never ceases to Will; however, Nature is purposeless in its willing because Nature is unable to develop goals. Nature is always willing harmoniously because Nature doesn't purposefully strive, but Nature's harmony is not Nature's stagnation because Nature's Will is Its harmonious Drive, not a stagnating lack of Drive.

Siddhartha Gautama advocated the stagnating lack of Drive he called "Nirvana" as his religious "Truth". Buddhists think Nirvana was Siddhartha's wisdom, not realising that Siddhartha was actually actually confused in his knowing because Nirvana was Siddhartha's stupidity, not his wisdom.

Wisdom is needed because wisdom enables a self to decide whether to let an instinctive desire arise or let it rest in Potentiality based on the self's need for harmony. A self has a need to meditate on its sensing until it's in harmony with Nature by way of its cognitions. Wisdom is a self's continual cognition of harmony based on its knowledge that it's not at the mercy of its emotions and moods; therefore, a wise self understands that it's able to decide whether or not it will let certain emotions and moods rise from Potentiality, Activity, or Nature.

Our temperaments are faculties held by us in our sensors as well as our sensable organisms. We use our sensors to sense our temperaments' emotions while we use Nature's Will in our temperaments to instinctively and nondeliberately or noninstinctively and deliberately radiate our emotions. We also use Nature's Will in our temperaments to emote emotions in excitement, easiness, or anxiety.

We use Nature's Will, instinctively or deliberately, to express our emotions of love and hate. Our expression of love originates from Nature's harmony, while our expression of hate originates from our fears and frustrations. The mood related to our expression of love is the mood of elation, which is an excitement, while the mood related to our expression of hate is the mood of depression, which is a repressed anxiety.

Depression is the repression of anxiety, not the lack of anxiety. The associated attitudinal exacerbation related to anxiety is worry. When we're anxious, we tend to worry in our feeling of anxiety which exacerbates our anxiety. This "dirty circle" of escalating anxiety often results in an escalation of a self's mood from sadness to sorrow, depression, woe, misery, and, finally melancholia. The associated attitudinal exacerbation related to excitement is indulgence. When we're excited, we tend to indulge in our feeling of excitement which exacerbates our excitement. This "dirty circle" of escalating excitement often results in an escalation of a self's mood from happiness to joy, elation, bliss, ecstasy, and, finally, mania. When we're at ease, rather than excited or anxious, we're contented and our emotions and moods are at peace. We use our cognitions to know the peace we feel when we're at ease.

We use our temperaments to emote our emotions as well as "mood" our moods. Our use of our temperaments to emote emotions and mood moods often affects the way we use our meanings to effect changes to our sensors and sensable organisms.

Nature is unable to generate positive moods and emotions in us so that we would feel them as Nature's moods and emotions; however, a self from a realm of the after-death does have a temperament; therefore, such a self is able to transfer its emoting of emotions and "mooding" of moods to us (that is, if selves are existent in realms of the after-death). Some of us mistakenly interpret these moods and emotions as coming from "God" rather than a self in a realm of the after-death (if these realms and the after-death exist) who wants to assert its dominance by pretending to be God.

Our actions associated with our sane desires are our kind actions, while our actions associated with our insane desires are our cruel actions. People who act kindly are usually intelligent as well as wise.

A favourite expression of stupid people is, "You have to be cruel to be kind". This expression is stupid because cruelty is never kind. People who act cruelly are usually unintelligent as well as stupid. Stupidity is the result of their inattentiveness which, in turn, is the result of their fear of striving for wisdom. Stupid people even express their kindness stupidly because their "kindness" is expressed, sentimentally, rather than realistically, which means that their expression of kindness is not sourced in wisdom.

You may be wondering why I have included compassion in the list of associated emotions as shame, rather than including it under the associated action of kindness. Your confusion is understandable because philosophers, like Siddhartha Gautama, often fail to understand the true nature of compassion.

Siddhartha failed to understand that compassion is a sentimentally masochistic insane desire and hasn't a thing to do with kindness. To be kind is not to be compassionate. To be kind is not to empathise with another self's suffering. To be kind is to give every self the opportunity to develop its understanding of how to manage its suffering; therefore, a compassionate self's masochistic empathising with another self's suffering is ridiculous as well as malevolent, not "spiritual" and "benevolent".

Instead of using compassion as our masochistic approach to another self's suffering, we need to be kind to selves who suffer without feeling their suffering. If we share a sufferer's suffering, the sufferer feels ashamed because the sharing of suffering is unnecessary. A sensible suffering self doesn't want its suffering shared. A sensible suffering self simply wants its suffering to cease. A kind self gives a suffering self the confidence that its inner suffering will be relieved, while the compassionate empathiser merely reinforces the dismal hypothesis of the suffering self that its inner suffering will continue.

People who have knowledge are usually modest, while people who are ignorant are usually humble or conceited. Modesty is not humility or conceit because modest people don't allow others to humiliate them. A humble self and a conceited self almost think alike. A humble self thinks its humiliation is necessary, just as a conceited self thinks a humble self's humiliation is necessary; however, the conceited self doesn't think its own humiliation is necessary.

The inner motions of our sensable organisms which are associated with our expression of love tend to be harmoniously in flow, while the inner motions of our sensable organisms associated with our expression of hate tend to be disharmoniously in turmoil. The physical movements of our sensable organisms in the outer world associated with our expression of love tend to be expressed calmly, while the physical movements of our sensable organisms which are associated with our expression of hate tend to be expressed agitatedly. The physical characteristic of our sensable organisms which is associated with our expression of love is the characteristic of relaxation, while the physical characteristic of our sensable organisms which is associated with our expression of hate is the characteristic of tension.

Considering all of the above, anyone who has the ability to reason is able to understand why a self who expresses love is referred to as "sane", while a self who expresses hate is referred to as "insane". Sanity is a self's expression of benevolence based on benevolent motivations, aims, intentions, or purposes which, in turn, reflect beneficial desires. Insanity is a self's expression of malevolence based on malevolent motivations, aims, intentions, or purposes which, in turn, reflect malevolent desires.

An insane (malevolent) self is not necessarily oversensitive and an oversensitive self is not necessarily insane. An oversensitive self may have a polygenetically aberrant body which predisposes it to oversensitivity and cognitive disruptions, like paranoid delusions of grandeur or persecution. An insane self usually has healthy genes; therefore, its malevolent tendencies are intentionally expressed. Religious fanatics who start wars with those who refuse to become their proselytes demonstrate such malevolent tendencies. These religious fanatics are sadomasochistic childish authoritarians who have been conditioned to express hate and ignore love.

A self is able to use Nature's Will to deliberately activate the emotions it exists from Potentiality. A self's expression of these emotions is either responsive or impulsive; however, it has no need to command its expression of love, as Jesus recommended, because a commanding attitude is a result of a self's emotion of hate.

A self noninstinctively and deliberately uses Nature's Will to cogitate with an indifference which masks the self's hatred. A self also noninstinctively and deliberately uses Nature's Will to think and reason with a neutrality which masks the self's love. A self who is indifferent doesn't care about the emotional implications of its cogitating because such an indifferent self is actually hiding behind its attitudinal mask of indifference.

A self has four ways of developing within four roles by which it misunderstands its situations unintelligently and one way of developing within one role by which it understands its situation intelligently. A self's four ways and four roles of misunderstanding and its one way and one role of understanding are expressed as follows:

a) A self's unintelligent way of developing irrational prejudicial phony emotionality within its typical role of receptive infantile victim.
b) A self's unintelligent way of developing unreasonable hate-filled unemotional intellectualising within its typical role of hoarding childish authoritarian.
c) A self's unintelligent way of developing logical indifference within its typical role of exploitative preadolescent trickster.
d) A self's unintelligent way of developing irrational prejudicial genuine emotionality within its typical role of marketing adolescent hero.
e) A self's intelligent way of developing intelligent lovable reasoning within its typical role of productive-developmental adult player.[4]

By using the example of a self who has suffered vicious abuse from another self, I'll illustrate the four ineffective ways of unintelligent misunderstanding and the effective way of intelligent understanding.

---

[4] For a more comprehensive explanation of the typical roles of receptive infantile victim, hoarding childish authoritarian, exploitative preadolescent trickster, marketing adolescent hero, and productive-developmental adult player, see "Chapter Eight: The Character Types and Personality Roles of a Self".

When a self's uses its unintelligent way of developing irrational prejudicial phony emotionality within its typical role of receptive infantile victim, it ineffectively responds to its abuse by choosing to "charm" its abuser with its phony emotions, a policy which it doesn't realise is usually transparent to its abuser; therefore, its abuser will ignore the abused self's attempts to charm it and will continue to abuse the abused self.

When a self uses its unintelligent way of developing unreasonable hate-filled unemotional intellectualising within its typical role of hoarding childish authoritarian, it ineffectively responds to its abuse by abusing its abuser with its own vicious abuse in an attempt to dominate its abuser. Even if it succeeds in dominating its abuser, its abuser will never stop seeking revenge. Consequently, the abused hater's domineering tactics are ineffective.

When a self uses its unintelligent way of developing logical indifference within its typical role of exploitative preadolescent trickster, it ineffectively responds to its abuse by choosing to logicise (formally intellectualise) its situation and analyse its abuser with indifference. Such indifference teaches it to viciously abuse its abuser in a "utilitarian" fashion. This self is also considering the possible punishments its abuser may levy in return.

When a self uses its unintelligent way of developing irrational prejudicial genuine emotionality within its typical role of marketing adolescent hero, it ineffectively responds to its abuse by choosing to courageously let its genuine emotions lead the way it acts towards its abuser which means that its use of its genuine emotions is usually foolish because they tend to lead it into a struggle which could result in the death of either its or its abuser's sensable organism.

Finally, when a self uses its intelligent way of developing intelligent lovable reasoning within its typical role of productive-developmental adult player, it effectively responds to its abuse by choosing to take actions which accord reasonably to its own sane desires as well as the sane desires of its abuser without giving its abuser the opportunity to express its insane desire to abuse it any further.

An abused intelligent lovable reasoning self may be forced to take legal action if its abuser is acting out of its insane desires; however, wise selves usually listen carefully to their abusers and attempt to respond to their abusers' sane desires without taking legal action against their abusers because they know that their acceptance of their abusers' sane desires breeds mutual understanding, while legal punishments breed only resentment and increased anger. Wise people know that it's never necessary to punish a self, although it's occasionally necessary to restrain a self's behaviour or limit its behaviour for its own safety and the safety of other selves. We need to have penalties resulting in restraint or restriction; however, we also need to be very careful that we don't hand out of punishments which harm another self's body, hurt it emotionally, or conflict its thinking and reasoning (unless these punishments are absolutely necessary to keep us from being unfairly punished by this self).

Only a self who uses its thinking and its reasoning (without cogitating) in accord with its intelligent intuiting, cognising, and recognising as well as in accord with its emotion of love is able to develop a wise understanding of its situation; however, a stupid self is not wise because the stupid self hasn't developed its understanding of its knowledge. Consequently, stupidity is the activity of a self whose understanding needs development before it progresses to the stage of using its intelligence to become wise. Intelligence is used by a self to know and understand its feelings so the self is able to harmonise with its feelings.

Nature is always in harmony, but Nature doesn't feel. A self's emotion of love is its reflection of Nature's harmony; therefore, we often feel Nature's harmony by way of our emotion of love which is why we prefer love over hate.

A self may relegate its love to Potentiality within the self's temperament because the self may choose to let its expression of hate eclipse its expression of love. By understanding the relationship of its unpreferred emotion of hate to its preferred emotion of love, a self usually relegates its hatred to Potentiality in its temperament.

Emotions are entirely irrational or lacking in reason. Our spontaneous preference for love leads to our *irrational saneness* because this preference was developed in us by way of Nature's harmony, not by way of our reasoning; therefore, our preference to express our emotions of love, like affection, gratitude, trust, generosity, pride, and courage, is not the result of a reason. It's simply an irrational fact of our natural temperaments.

The emotions of love and hate are usually, but not necessarily, related to a goal; therefore, the self's expression of these emotions is usually goal directed. Of course, the self is also able to "dwell" in love or "wallow" in hate without having a goal.

A self selfkinetically guides its temperament's emoting of emotions. Nature doesn't exhibit attenuated or exaggerated emotions because Nature doesn't have the ability to emote. Nature doesn't express emotions.

A self is able to guide its emoting of love and the emotions related to it as well as its emoting of hate and the emotions related to it. A self usually expresses its emotions by exhibiting them, attenuatively, if it's realistic, or exhibiting them, exaggeratedly, if it's delusional. A self might even delusionally exhibit a phony emotion, like fake affection.

A self's expression of an attitude is not the self's emoting. A self is able to noninstinctively and deliberately suppress and mask its emoting of love by affecting an attitude of neutrality as well as noninstinctively and deliberately repress and quarantine its emoting of hate by affecting an attitude of indifference.

Although a self is able to reason in relation to its emotions, it doesn't necessarily "plot" how it will express its emotions as Richard and Bernice Lazarus suggested it does in their book, *Passion and Reason*. A self doesn't always need to rationalise or plot in relation to its emotions.

Contrary to the reasoning of psychologists, like Richard and Bernice Lazarus, our emotions or passions aren't rational because our emotions are derived from our accordance or discordance with Nature's harmony, not from our ability to reason, whereas our rational speculations *are* derived from our ability to reason. Our emotions are analysed and synthesised by us with our reasoning so that it may seem as if our emotions are rational, but we don't *need* our emotions to be influenced by our reasoning any more than we need our rationales to be influenced by our emoting. We're able to neutrally express our thoughts, notions, concepts, ideas, hypotheses, and theories with our masked love as well as indifferently express them with our quarantined hatred; however, our use of our temperaments to emote emotions is effected by our harmony or disharmony within Nature's harmony, not by our reasoning. Our use of Nature's Will to effectively reason affects our use of our temperaments to emote our emotions; however, our use of our emotions is not always necessarily rationalised by our ability to reason.

A self's uses its temperament to emote, while the self uses its ability of reasoning to relate its emoting to its other faculties. Likewise, a self uses its ability of intuiting and its ability of cognising to think while also using its ability of recognising to reason in such a way that the self's thinking is related to its reasoning. A self is also able to relate its thinking and reasoning to its other faculties.

Nature is unable to think because It can't intuit and is unable to reason and can't deduce or induce nor cogitate because It's unable to intellectualise as we so stupidly do. Nature doesn't have feelings; therefore, Nature is unable to feel through the feelings of selves who inhabit sensable organisms, like the sensable organisms of humans, alligators, frogs, and beetles. Nor is Nature able to feel through selfless vegetative organisms, like the vegetative organism of petunias, weeping willows, and cucumbers, or selfless mineral organisms, like the mineral organisms of sand, rocks, and metals.

Nature is unable to sense sensable organisms, vegetative organisms, or mineral organisms. Nature is only able to instinctively Will Its evolution, growth, development, deterioration, and devolution of individual phenomenal suefs, luefs, free particles, and bodies as well as Its generation and development of individual phenomenal selves.

Nature is the absolute Background; therefore, Nature is unable to receive feedback from the environment since Nature only has the absolute Foreground ability of willing to feed out phenomena, not an absolute Foreground ability of receiving information as feedback; therefore, Nature has no way of knowing that It exists as the Source. Nature is unable to experience feedback, including the harmony of a self's emotion of love.

Nature has no absolute Person because such an absolute Person would only be an absolute Persona or an absolute Mask hiding Nature. Of course, Nature's Personality of "Mother" is only a myth. Nature is impersonal, not personal.

Our use of our temperaments to emote is related to our need to wisely understand how to emote love because love is the default emotion of a self. The importance of a self's emoting is it's emoting isn't n a reflection of Nature's harmony but is *derived* from Nature's harmony as well as the self's harmony— or disharmony; however, Nature's harmony is not the emotion of love because Nature is unable to emote. Only the natural selves of Nature are able to emote.

Chapter Three
The Empirical Basis for a Self's Understanding and Wisdom

The Accordant Truths and Religious Delusions of Selves

	Foundations	Structures	Superstructures
Metaphysical Truths:	Activity	Activation	Activities
Practical Truths:	Meditation	Contemplation	Speculation
Religious Truth:	Self (The Knower)	Sensor	Cognition
Religious Delusions:	Ego	Psyche	Mind
	Being	Soul	Consciousness
	Ipsum	Anima	Animus
Cognitive Truths:	Know	Knowing	Known
Epistemological Truths:	Knowledge	Meanings	Facts
	Intelligence	Intellect	Perception-Misperception
	Attention	Interpretation	Assimilation
	Intuition	Cognition	Recognition
	Pure Thinking	Symbolic Thinking	Symbolic Reasoning
	Thoughts	Concepts	Hypotheses
	Notions	Ideas	Theories
Wisdom Truths	Insights	Understandings	Realizations
Temperamental Truths:	Emoting	Emotions	Moods

Empiricism is a self's insight that its knowledge is derived from sensory experience. In other words, an empiricist knows that he develops his knowledge a posteriori in accord with his sensing. Rationalism is a self's superstitious belief that its knowledge is a supernaturally a priori implant in its memory which the self thinks God is responsible for implanting. The phrase, "a priori", is defined as 'before the self began to experience.'

Rationalists are lost in a morass of illusions, delusions, and fictions because they deny the evidence of their senses. Unfortunately, empiricists tend to overreact to the illusions, delusions, and fictions of rationalists by claiming without reason that our physical world is the basis of energy, rather than realising that Nature, Reality, Matter, or Energy is the basis of our physical world.

Most empiricists believe that we use our bodies to sense because they are Mortalists; however, we might exist as immortal selves who have sensors which we shine as our immortal auras, rather than our mortal auras. Our sensable organisms contain sensations, but we don't use our sensable organisms to sense sensations. Nor do we use our sensors to sense the sensations in our sensable organisms either. Rather, we use our cognition as our ability to sense the sensations in our sensable organisms because a self can sense its sensations with its cognition by way of its sensor. The self's sensor is the objective large uncondensed energy form which a self uses to express as well as inhabit as sits means by which to cognitively sense its aspects in its inner-outer World.

A self's knowing is its ability to use the energy of its cognition to realise realities. A self is the activator as well as the inhibiter of its cognition.

A self's cognition is the energy which encloses and interpenetrates its sensor's energetics, its sensable organism's sensations, as well as the condensed energies composing its sensable organism, while a self's sensor is the energetics which encloses and interpenetrates its sensable organism's sensations as well as the condensed energies composing its sensable organism. A self uses Energy's Will to energise the energy of its cognition for the purpose of sensing the energetics of its sensor and the sensations of its sensable organism.

I know as I sense. I know I'm sensing when I'm sensing; however, my sensing isn't my knowing because I know the energy of my cognition without sensing it just as I know my sensor's energetics, my sensable organism's sensations, and the condensed energies composing my sensable organism by sensing them. Consequently, our physical world is a reality we realise or know by sensing it which means that idealism is a falsehood.

Nature's willing in its qualia stimulates a sensation to happen in a self's sensable organism when the self who inhabits its sensable organism (its organic body) uses it to interact with other sensable organisms.. These sensations are visual, auditory, tactile, gustatory, olfactory, proprioceptive, emotional, or moody.[5] A self's feeling is a self's sensing; however, a self's sensing is not necessarily a self's feeling because a self is only able to feel the sensations of its tactions, proprioceptions, emotions and moods, not its sights, sounds, tastes, and smells.

A sensation is an activity of a self's sensable organism which a self uses its cognition to sense by way of its sensor. A self's sensing of a sensation is realised by the self who uses its intelligence to perceive, assimilate, and realise the knowledge which has resulted from its sensing of this sensation; however, the self is also able to disable its intelligence by using its intellect in its intellectual misperceiving as well as misassimilating and idealising of sensations as its illusions.

A self's intelligence is its ability to gain insight into realities and understand these realities based on its ability to know or realise them. A self uses its intelligent knowing to develop knowledge of realities for its understanding; however, a self also uses its intellect to delude its understanding when it ignores its experience. Unknowing is a self's inability to know its experience because self is ignoring its experience.

After a self has used its knowing to know an emotion or a sensation, the self uses its intelligence to perceive, assimilate, or realise the knowledge which has resulted from its knowing and thereby develop a meaning for its knowledge or use its intellect to misperceive, misassimilate, and idealise this sensation by cogitating illusions with its unknowing and thereby develop delusions by way of its cogitated illusions. Finally, a self uses its intelligence to realise this meaning as a fact (a hypothesis) or uses its intellect to idealise its delusion as a fiction (a fantasy).

The energy of a self's intelligent thinking and reasoning is based on its realism and empiricism, while the energy of its intellectual cogitating is based on its idealism and rationalism. Empiricists are knowers who think and reason on the basis of their realism. Rationalists are knowers who cogitate on the basis

---

[5] My use of the word "moody", in this context implies cheerful moods as well as moods of moroseness.

of their idealism. Scientists are empiricists. *Scientismists are deluded because they confuse measurement with empiricism.*

Idealists fail to understand that their inner aspects of the World were developed in accord with the reality of their outer aspects of the World. Idealists also fail to understand that they indirectly cognise their outer aspects of the World by sensorially knowing them, just as they directly cognise their inner aspects of the World by knowing them without sensing them.

A self uses its cognition in its abilities of thinking and reasoning by intelligently knowing them as well as uses its cogitation in its disabling ability of cogitating by intellectually disregarding its ability to cognitively know.

In his paper, "Science and Sympathy: 'Intuition' and the Ethics of Human Judgement", David Boynton expressed his opinion in the abstract of this paper that it would 'not do to define thinking in terms of two isolable systems' (Boynton, 2016, p. 141). Boynton also claimed in this abstract that "thinking is quasi-rational" (Boynton, 2016, p. 141).

Boynton's opinion that our thinking is not isolable is mistaken because we're able to think in isolation from our reasoning. We're also able to define our thinking and our reasoning in terms of two related systems because our thinking is always related to our reasoning when we're reasoning.

Boynton's opinion that thinking is quasi-rational is mistaken. Our thinking is not quasi-rational, any more than our thinking is quasi-cogitative.

We're able to think before we rationally reason just as we're able to relate our reasoning, rationally, to our thinking when we're reasoning; however, we're unable to think quasi-rationally, because our ability to think is not at all like our ability to reason. Boynton's intimation that thinking is simply an inferior grade of reasoning ignores the fact that thinking has its own attributes. Thinking is used for poetic and narrative artistic expression, not for intelligently reasoned scientific explanations or for intellectually cogitated scientismistic formulations. Boynton fails to understand that a philosopher who doesn't think poetically and narratively about a situation is unable to apply his explanatory reasoning to his thinking; therefore, he's incapable of understanding the situation in which he's engaged.

Our abilities of poetic and narrative thinking are dependent on our intelligent cognitive ability, while our explanatory reasoning is dependent on our intelligent recognitive ability. Our thinking is intuitive as well as cognitive; however, we're only able to use our system of inner words and inner ideograms in our cognitive thinking to poetise and narrate, while we use them in our recognitive reasoning to explain our thinking.

We think and reason as our means of developing inner languages in our cognitions for the purpose of using inner symbols in our introspective inner speaking and imaging as well as our means of developing outer languages sourced in our knowing of our inner languages for the purpose of using outer symbols in our extrospective outer speaking and materialisation of engravings.. We cogitate as our means of developing "inner equations" and "inner formulas" in our cogitations for our purpose of introspectively using inner numbers in our inner speaking and imaging as well as extrospectively using outer numbers in our outer speaking and engraving.

Selves who inhabit sensable organisms and have non-human intelligence often communicate, intuitively, with each other because they don't have the ability to develop inner words. We develop inner words by first hearing outer words. Then we develop our ability to think with inner words as our inner speech which enables us to express outer speech with our lungs, vocal cords, mouth, and tongue. Our innerly worded thinking is not our innerly worded reasoning because inner words always accompany our reasoning whereas they don't accompany our intuiting (our "pure" thinking). Our intuiting is easily related to our feelings and our sensations. It takes more work to wordedly think than it does to intuit since we tend to be more related to our ability of feeling emotions and sensations when we're intuiting. We learn to use our words to isolate our thinking and reasoning from our feeling of emotions and sensations; therefore, we need to learn to relate our worded thinking and reasoning to our feeling of emotions and sensations so we don't suffer from the feeling of isolation when we think and reason.

We're able to use our feeling of emotions and sensations to help us develop intuitions because our intuitions are our insights into the sources of our emotions and sensations.

We prepare for insights by reasoning about the circumstance or circumstances we're examining. Then we're able to work, intuitively, on our worded reasoning, develop an insight, and relate this insight to our reasoning. Finally, we're able to put this insight into outer words on paper for other selves to consider; however, reasoning is not always necessary for the development of insights because our intuiting is the basis for our reasoning, not vice versa

For example, a racoon is usually unable to wordedly think unless it's been a pet of a human; however, a racoon is obviously able to think because it uses its clawed hands to take the lid off a locked food container so it's able to get at the food in the container. Although the racoon is able to develop the insight of how to get at the food in the container, it doesn't usually reason how to get at it because it doesn't use inner words with which to reason. That a racoon develops in nature with only the ability to intuit is important because the racoon's originally natural inability to think with words helps us realise that Nature doesn't think or reason at all.

Our thinking and reasoning is based on our meanings. Meaning is not use, as Ludwig Wittgenstein mistakenly thought. *A meaning is a self's assimilated feeling of an emotion or a sensation for the purpose of symbolising this emotion or sensation.*

The meaning of an identically spelled inner or outer word, like our English word "love", is our assimilated feeling of our emotion of love which we symbolise as the word "love"; however, Nature has no ability to develop meanings because Nature is only able to *give out* by instinctively willing the evolution, growth, development, deterioration, and devolvement of realities. Nature has no ability to *take in, assimilate, or absorb* realities; therefore, Nature is unable to develop understanding based on meanings.

The following are truths:

(a) Beliefs are our arrogant opinions about the validity of facts (hypotheses).
(b) Delusions are our mistaken hypotheses (mistaken facts) which we fail to realise are mistaken.
(c) Hypotheses are our guesses about the truth of certain facts.
(d) Theories are our arrangement of hypotheses (facts) into an organised as well as continually changing structure.
(e) Validity e is our ability to subjectively prove a bit of knowledge as a truth.
(f) Knowledge is our subjectively proven bits of knowledge organised into a continually changing structure.
(g) Wisdom is our cognition by which we continually assimilate new bits of knowledge to our structure of knowledge about Reality and Its realities so our structure of knowledge is always changing to accommodate new bits of knowledge.

Our beliefs indicate our laziness because our laziness prevents us from striving to prove the truth or falsity of our beliefs. Ironically, we cling to our belief that our beliefs are facts when, obviously, we haven't proven them to be facts because our beliefs are our conclusive opinions, not our tentative hypotheses or facts. We need to rid our intelligence of our arrogant beliefs as well as our delusions. Only then will we be able to concentrate on subjectively proving our tentative facts about the continually changing pattern of Reality's realities.

I have already subjectively proven that Reality is Nature; however, you need to subjectively prove this to you because I'm unable to subjectively prove it to you. I'm unable to subjectively prove it to you because I am not you. I'm only able to express my own tentative facts, objectively, in my writing. It's up to you to subjectively prove that these facts are conclusive truths or falsities, instead of tentative or inconclusive hypotheses by learning that you're absolutely free to continually change the arrangement of these facts until you realise their relations so well that you develop a certainty of their truthful or false definitions. You can continually change the arrangement of these facts in your intelligence as realities about —and in you are continually changing in accord with Nature's instinctive use of Its Will in tandem with your instinctive as well as deliberate use of it.

Nature develops a self with an evolved luef to inhabit before It evolves a sensable organism (an organic body) for the self to inhabit. There are no angels who were "created" in heaven to inhabit phenomenal luefs and organic bodies as they started to exist as activities because every self, even an angel, needs to inhabit an organic body before its able to leave the corpse that was its body behind it forever, that is, if it is an immortal self who emanates an immortal sensor as the "me" of the "I" every self is.

We develop in sensable organisms because we need to realise that we don't want to die with them, although we have no choice whether or not we die with them or not. If a self was started by Nature to exist as an activity in an evolved luef without also developing in an evolved sensable organism, it wouldn't realise that it didn't want to die with its body because it wouldn't have a body which inevitably dies. Consequently, the self would be discontent in its luef because it wouldn't appreciate its need to enjoy Nature's willing or driving of it.

Nature doesn't realise that we need to learn the value of enjoyment because Nature has no ability to realise. Nature instinctively develops us in sensable organisms when we begin as activities because it's *inevitable* that we will only enjoy existing if we understand that we don't really want to die with our sensable organisms..

Nature's willing is in accord with the inevitable. The inevitable refers to an occurrence in and of Nature which selves generated by Nature are incapable of avoiding or evading, like the deaths of their sensable organisms: however, exactly when such an occurrence will happen is unpredictable as well as unprophetical.

Nature develops us in sensable organisms because we need them for our enjoyment. The inevitability of enjoyment is drawn from Potentiality; therefore, Nature starts every self as an activity in a sensable organism to fulfil the inevitability of the self's enjoyment—as well as the inevitability of its suffering; however, Nature only develops us in one sensable organism (organic body) because It only generates new selves in sensable organisms. Nature doesn't recycle old selves in new sensable organisms because there is no need for such recycling. In other words, reincarnation and rebirth are impossible because such recycling is against the spontaneity of Nature's instinctive nondeliberation. And, of course, resurrection of a sensable organism is obviously impossible.

An immortal self is fully developed by the instinctive drive of Nature's Will in this self's mortal zygote. Most of the self's abilities and faculties aren't brought to exist by the self yet because the self doesn't have a need for them. Of course, the self doesn't use Nature's Will to generate its abilities and faculties from the activity the self is until it's ready to use its brain to channel them.

After the foetus is grown to maturity and is born, the infant is grown outside of the womb until it becomes a child. The developing immaterial self who inhabits this materialised child body has finally actualised its immaterial ability to think from its immaterial faculties of intuition and cognition which it's able to use to help it develop its selfological inner aspect of its inner-outer World. A self learns to hear and assimilate outer words before it uses its intuitive thinking to generate inner words. A self also learns to think with these inner words before it learns to reason with them.

The selves on earth who wordedly think and reason are mostly human, like you and I. Human selves seem to be the only selves who've developed worded thinking as well as worded reasoning. Certain selves, like the selves of dolphins, whales, dogs, and parrots, are able to develop an acquaintance with human words from hearing the outer words of humans. Dolphins, whales, dogs, and parrots also have their own outer language of sounds to speak (which aren't outer words), i.e., parrots communicate by different screeches and clicks, while dogs communicate by different barks and whines. We assign inner words to our sounds which dolphins, whales, dogs, and parrots don't do, but they do learn the sounds associated with our inner words from us; however, only some of these selves, like parrot selves, are able to translate the sounds they've learned from us as their imitation of human outer speech.

We speak outer words as sounds. We write outer words as engravings. We write so that we're able to express the outer symbols of our outer languages and the outer numbers and outer graphics of our outer formulas and outer equations. In this way, we translate our inner graphics, inner numbers, and inner letters to outer graphics, outer numbers, and outer letters in our environment, just as we're able to reverse this activity and translate outer graphics, outer numbers, and outer letters in our environment to inner graphics, inner numbers, and inner letters in our cognitions.

We see outer graphics, outer letters, and outer numbers in the environment. We think and reason with unseen inner words and inner ideograms. We also cogitate with unseen inner words and inner ideograms; however, when cogitating we treat our inner words and inner ideograms as if they were only inner numbers.

We develop inner graphics and inner letters with our ability to intuit and interpret them with our ability to perceive them as well as assimilate them with our ability to cognise them. We structure our inner graphics into inner ideograms and structure our inner letters into inner words which we use to descriptively map realities in our cognitions. We also attend to inner numbers we develop with our intellectualising to delineatively chart realities in our cognitions.

We use our thinking in our system of inner ideograms and/or inner words to think thoughts with them in our cognitions. We then subject these thoughts to our cognising so we're able to pattern ideas by thinking ideas with these inner ideograms or inner words. Finally, we subject these ideas to our recognising so we can pattern hypotheses by reasoning with these inner ideograms and inner words.

We use our ability of reasoning to analyse the flow of ideas and hypotheses existed by us in our cognitions. Then we use our ability of reasoning to infer the relations of these ideas and hypotheses in a theory which combines them meaningfully into a harmonised continually changing structure of knowledge..

Our hypotheses will sooner or later reveal that they've "fallen into place" when we have subjectively proven this theory's truth or falsity.

Hypotheses become more than hypotheses when they fall into place. Hypotheses become our understandings when they're subjectively proven and known as valid, although sceptics continue to argue that we're unable to develop valid knowledge.

Unfortunately, the ancient Greek philosopher, Heraclitus, suggested that there was an independent universal logos. The Greek word "logos" is usually translated into English as the word "reason", although it's also translated as "word", "plan", "speech" and many other English words. The Christian notion of logos, as elaborated in *The New Testament's* "Gospel According to St John", is similar to the notion of Heraclitus; however, the word "Logos" to a Christian is God's "Christ" which is supposedly God's independent universal Reason, or God's "Word".

The Christian notion of Christ as Logos is their delusion (their mistaken hypothesis) because Nature instinctively wills in accord with Its needs, not in accord with logos or reason. Christians, like John (who is supposed to have written The Gospel of John), projected their own ability to reason onto their idea of the absolute which they called "God". Christians fail to realise that Nature exists, not God, and that Nature has no ability to reason.

Nor is Nature able to "enter" a self and become that self. Nature wills in all selves, Nature doesn't inhabit selves. Although Nature exists selves, It doesn't exist *as* selves, nor does It exist as the absolute "Self".

"Christ" isn't meaningful because there is no infinite Logos. Jesus is not the incarnation of Christ (the infinite Logos) because Jesus was (and is?) only a self who used Nature's Will in accord as well as discord with his emotion of love. Like our reasoning about love, Jesus' reasoning about love will never be perfect—or imperfect (that is, if Jesus of Nazareth is existent and continues to exist in his realm of the after-death). Of course, Jesus is a natural self, not the mythical Creator; therefore, if Yahweh and Jesus exist, they exist as selves centered in Nature.

If Yahweh is existent, he exists the role of Judge, not "the Father". If Jesus is existent, he exists the role of Defender, not "the Son". If Sophia is existent, she exists the role of Wisdom, not the "Holy Spirit" or "the Comforter". If Satan is existent, he exists the role of Prosecutor, not "the Devil".

Yahweh, Sophia and Jesus, aren't a triune God, nor are Yahweh, Satan, Sophia, and Jesus a quaternary God, because God is only a myth fantasised by selves who exist in male sensable organisms, just as the Goddess is only a myth fantasised by selves who exist in female sensable organisms.

Lest Christians judge me, let me hasten to write that Jesus and I respect each other because Jesus and I are friends, even if Jesus is only a hallucination that I've used my ability of imagining to project as an image in my faculty of imagination or as a hallucinatory apparitioned "hologram" outside of my faculty of imagination as well as outside of my sensable organism. I know Jesus as the reality Jesus is (if "he" is not just my hallucinatory internal image or hallucinatory externalised apparition); therefore, I know Jesus occasionally commits mistakes, rather than "sins" or "misses the mark", (just like the rest of us). I know Jesus commits mistakes, rather than "sins", because he is either my actual or hallucinatory reality who tried to understand my intentions and command me to love, instead of accepting my Freedom to whole-heartedly love without commanding me to love. The commandment of Jesus for us to love was irresponsible because love is only valid when its expressed freely, not as the result of a command with which we forfeit our Freedom to express or withhold our love

Jesus has not spoken to me in inner or outer words, but he did respond to my entreaty for his services by helping me associate more effectively with some of the more malicious selves who are either existent as hallucinations in my imagination or existent as actualities in some of the realms of the after-death, which demonstrates that Jesus exists as a hallucinatory or actually known self who usually uses love to guide his use of Nature's Will; however, he unfairly judging me (just as I had unfairly judged him).

You see, in relating my intentions to Jesus, Jesus finally discerned that my metaphysical religion was based on my knowledge of Nature as the Source, my knowledge that I, Jesus, and all other selves are centers of Nature, and my knowledge that Jesus' commandment for us to love was not his sin, but was a colossal mistake, since we're only able to satisfy our desire to express love in Freedom if we're free from any command to love. After all, love which is not freely given is not love.

Our emotion of hate interferes with our knowing because this emotion arises out of our fears and frustrations; therefore, thinking and reasoning based on our fears and frustrations is rather stupid because such thinking and reasoning leads to unknowing as well as our emotion of hate.

Our ability of intuiting is not our ability of cognising. Our ability of cognising is our ability to know our intuiting (as well as our other abilities). We focus our cognising on our pure (intuitive) thinking, just as we focus our recognising on our cognitions. We deductively and inductively reason about our cognised or known concepts; however, we're only able to focus our disabling ability of intellectualising on our disabling ability of cogitating because our disabling ability of cogitating is a delusion that results from our hatred of the fears we repress.

Our immaterial faculty of intuition contains our immaterial ability of unsymbolic or pure thinking. Our immaterial faculty of cognition contains our immaterial ability of symbolic thinking. Our immaterial faculty of recognition contains our immaterial ability of symbolic reasoning, while our immaterial disabling faculty of intellect contains our immaterial disabling ability of symbolic cogitating.

Cogitating is a disabling ability which unnecessarily blocks our ability to think and, thus, our ability to reason. Our disabling ability of cogitating is guided by us, intellectually, not intelligently, while our disabling ability of "logicising" is our formal intellectualising. Our disabling ability of cogitating is existed by us in our disabling faculty of intellect.

Cogitating is a disabling ability used by a self to *delineate* the arrangement of inner formulas and inner equations as well as outer formulas and outer equations. Thinking is an ability used by a self to *indicate and describe* the arrangement of inner sentences and outer sentences. Reasoning is an ability used by a self to *explain* the arrangement of inner sentences and outer sentences.

Languages are used to develop sentences which are arranged by a self's needs, not by its use of laws. Languages are arranged by selves to develop their use of semantics in accord with the needs they used to develop their language rather than handicap their use of semantics by limiting their use of semantics with laws. Formulas and equations aren't languages because formulas and equations are based on laws, not needs.

An artist's semantic language is not a logician's formula or equation. Unfortunately, logicians attempt to give validity to their laws by referring to them as their "semantics", but this is irresponsible (inappropriate and ineffective) on their part because laws aren't concerned with meaningful descriptions, like semantics. Laws are only concerned with delineations, not with the descriptions and explanations concerned with needs; therefore, laws fail to meaningfully contribute to our knowledge.

Reasoning and thinking are different from each other because symbolic reasoning is our way of intelligently recognising. Symbolic thinking is our way of our intelligently cognising, whereas pure thinking (thinking free of symbols) is our way of intelligently intuiting; however, our ability of reasoning has no relation to our disabling ability of logically cogitating because logic isn't necessary to make a reasoned proposal. Ironically, scientismistic logicians fail to understand that a logical proposition (which I will write more about later) is not a reasoned proposition.

Our sensing of outer graphics, outer numbers, and outer letters help us stimulate the remembrance of our inner graphics, inner numbers, and inner letters. We're able to synthesise our inner graphics, inner numbers, and inner letters and thereby develop information. Information is used to develop our knowledge by our use of inner ideogrammed or inner worded reasoning.

Inner graphics, inner numbers, and inner letters are existed as abstractions. Inner graphics, inner numbers, and inner letters are existed in a self's cognition and recognition as well as in its imagination; however, we're able to translate outer graphics, outer numbers, and outer letters into electromagnetic patterns. We use a computer to encode these electromagnetic patterns in objective suefs.

Inner graphics, inner numbers, and inner letters refer to the abstractions we use to map realities in our faculty of cognition, our disabling faculty of intellect, and our faculty of recognition, respectively. Inner graphics, inner numbers, inner letters, inner ideograms, and inner words may be translated by us into electromagnetic patterns for the purpose of evolving motions in and movement of our sensors and our bodies. We merge these electromagnetic patterns with subjective suefs in our brains. We're also able to use Nature's Will to translate the electromagnetic patterns of suefs we receive from the outer world into inner symbols for our thinking and reasoning as well as our cogitating.

We're able to merge electromagnetic patterns with objective suefs in a computer's electromagnetic flow. Nature's instinctive willing in this electromagnetic flow carries these objective suefs to the various mechanisms of the computer; however, a computer is unable to use Nature's Will because a computer is not a self.

Suefs aren't used by a self to send symbolic messages to its organic body's organs and muscles via neurons and nerves of its organic body because its organic body's organic tissues only interact with qualia, not with symbols. Our organic bodies don't need symbolic messages to have their processes occur. Nature's Will is all that a self needs for it's instinctive nondeliberate use of Nature's Will in tandem with Nature's instinctive nondeliberate willing because the self sends electromagnetic patterns within the it's tissues and organs so that motions in and movements of its sensable organism (its organic body) occur.

Only a self, not a computer, is able to use Nature's Will to develop abstract symbols so that it's able to continually use these symbols in its thinking, reasoning, and cogitating and feed its thinking, reasoning, and cogitating back to its memory. Inner graphics, inner numbers, and inner letters are abstractions which a self develops after having viewed patterns in the environment, like a crack in a boulder. These striations are the basis of the markings a self uses to structure inner graphics, inner numbers, and inner letters. The self is then able to use these abstractions to map and chart its observed world.

But the real goal of a self is to map realities with inner ideograms and inner words so that it's able to gain an understanding of the continually changing structure of Reality. By way of this mapping of realities, a self is able to gain wisdom, unlearn the conditioning it's experienced with this mapping, and halt its thinking and reasoning so it's able to know its emotion of love by feeling it.

Our abstract inner graphics, inner numbers, and inner letters are used by us to develop outer graphics, outer numbers, and outer letters. Then we're able to map our outer graphics and outer letters as well as chart our outer numbers concretely in the environment. We're able to observe our mapped outer graphics and outer letters as well as our charted outer numbers which helps us share our inner signs or information.

A self can recognise objective outer letters which have been engraved in the environment and translate these engraved objective outer letters back into subjective inner letters. As well, the self can recognise objective outer graphics which have been engraved in objective appearances and translate these objective outer graphics back into subjective inner graphics. The self also observes objective outer numbers which has been engraved in objective appearances and translate these objective outer numbers back into subjective inner numbers.

Inner letters, inner numbers, and inner graphics are *of* Nature. Nature is the basis of abstractions just as It's the phenomenal basis of everything else;

therefore, abstractions, such as inner graphics, inner numbers, and inner letters, are a self's natural artefacts or natural derivatives of Nature, while outer graphics, outer numbers, and outer letters aren't abstractions, but are concrete physicalities of Nature. Outer graphics, outer numbers, and outer letters are natural artefacts which a self is able to make and use because it's able to derive them from its inner graphics, inner numbers, and inner letters, respectively, although these inner graphics, numbers, and letters were originally developed after the self's making of outer graphics, numbers, and letters. Inner graphics, inner numbers, and inner letters are the abstract tools of a self's intelligence as well as a self's intellect.

Our ancestors developed outer graphics, outer numbers, and outer letters by observing archetypal physical patterns in the environment, such as the spiral patterns of certain seashells and the patterns of bark in trees. Then they used their bodies to physically engrave these outer graphics, numbers, and letters in the environment. The outer graphics, outer numbers, and outer letters we make are the archetypes of the ectypal inner graphics, inner numbers, and inner letters we use in our cognitions to structure inner ideograms and words. In other words, we need to experience the outer signs we make before we're able to develop inner signs or information.

Nature instinctively wills the development of selves in single-celled sensable organisms, like protozoa, before It evolves single-celled zygotes from which multicellular sensable organisms are grown. Nature and every self It generates or activates are able to work together to replicate the self's zygote by way of mitosis resulting, ultimately, in the self's multicellular brain and the rest of its multicellular sensable organism. Then the self uses its brain to channel its abilities of thinking, reasoning, cogitating, and emoting.

By realising that it channels its abilities in its brain, a self is able to recognise, not only that it transcends its brain, but also how it's able to start the activity of working towards wisdom with its abilities of intuiting, cognising, and recognising. A self uses its recognition's reasoning to analyse and synthesise with the inner symbols symbolising the various elements of Nature.

Only by reasoning are we able to experience an enlightened analytical synthesis of any reality in our inner-outer World. We're able to realise Nature's elements and symbolically reason about our realisations and gain understanding. In this way, we're able to develop the analytical synthesis we've worked towards attaining.

I've already explained that an index is not a "symbol". An index corresponds to a reality; however, it doesn't stand for the reality because it's only related to this reality. An index is not really an outer symbol. An index doesn't stand for the reality to which it's related, e.g., a screech with a rising pitch is an index; however, this screech is a consequence of a self's anger; therefore, the screech doesn't stand for anger as an outer symbol but is only related to the anger of the self as a consequence of the self's anger.

An icon isn't a symbol, although it resembles as well as stands for a reality. The icon, "ruff", is a word which resembles as well as stands for the sound a dog makes when it's barking. But an icon isn't a symbol, even though an icon is a word, because a symbol refers to a reality for which it stands without corresponding to or resembling this reality, e.g., the reality on which I sit is referred to by the word "chair". The word "chair" is a symbol because it only stands for the reality on which I am sitting and doesn't correspond to or resemble this reality. In other words, the word "chair" doesn't look like the reality on which I'm sitting.

We analyse by using inner ideograms and inner words to innerly symbolise the various elements in Nature which we experience so that we're able to differentiate and analyse these inner symbols. Inner ideograms and inner words are our natural developments, instead of Nature's developments. Nature has no need to intuit, cognise, and recognise our inner ideograms and inner words. Nature is unable to intuit, cognise, and recognise inner ideograms and inner words; therefore, prayers for help from Nature are futile, although prayers to selves in ethereal realms of the after-death might receive a valid answer (if these selves actually exist)—which is not necessarily a fortunate occurrence.

The inner words and inner ideograms we think while we're intelligently "daydreaming" hardly come to us unbidden because we're always freely developing them. The inner words and inner ideograms of our daydreaming only seem to come to us unbidden.

When you're daydreaming, you're usually thinking with only a hazy understanding of the inner words or inner ideograms you're using in your thinking; therefore, you don't necessarily fully attend to the contents of your daydream. When you stop your daydreaming, you "wake up" by realising that you were daydreaming. Then you're able to analyse whether or not you will use the contents of your daydream for furthering your theories by gaining an understanding of these contents.

We often wake up to images as well as inner words and inner ideograms in our daydreams. Nature is unable to daydream because Nature is unable to emote, think, reason, or imagine. In other words, Nature always seems to be asleep without ever waking up. Nature is not really asleep; therefore, Nature is unable to dream or wake up and start daydreaming.

Meditation is a self's experience of an unnatural formal relatedness in Reality. Meditation is a self's way of waking from its tendency of "sleeping", which is its *ignorance* of its knowing and thus its ignorance of its sensing. A self's sensing is developed by way of its knowing in its sensing. A meditator who is new to meditating is distracted easily by his intuiting; therefore, his experiencing of relatedness evades him which is why formal meditation is a meditator's concentration on developing an insight into what he is by knowing, instead of intuiting. With practice, a self is able to experience its Style of relatedness by sensing in accord with Nature's willing; however, the meditating self needs to learn how to stop its pure thinking or intuiting as well as its symbolic thinking, reasoning, and cogitating while it's sensing.

When a self has experienced relatedness, it finally knows that its abilities of thinking and reasoning are different, but not separate, because it realises that separation is an illusion. Even though a self may isolate its thinking from its reasoning, it's always able to relate its worded thinking, by way of cognising, to its worded reasoning by way of its recognising so that it's able to reason in relation to its thinking. The self's intuitive thinking of unsymbolised thoughts and notions is the nadir of its cognitive activity, its cognitive thinking of symbolised concepts and ideas is the mediator of this activity, and its recognitively worded reasoning of symbolised hypotheses and theories is the zenith of this activity.

We're unable to use the disabling ability of cogitating for the purpose of speculation because the disabling ability of cogitating disables our ability to think as well as our ability to reason.

"Zen" is a Zen Buddhist's word for meditation, while "Truism" is a Truist's word for meditation. The meditative knowing of a Truist and that of a Zenist differ drastically because the philosophical basis of Truism contradicts that of Zen.

Although there is no philosophising in deep meditation, the meditator's philosophy is related to his or her deep meditative experience; therefore, the meditator's philosophy influences his or her deep meditation, despite his or her lack of philosophising while in deep meditation. Zen meditation is based on the philosophical premise that only false selves exist. Truism is based on the philosophical axiom that true selves exist as well as false selves.

Zenists base their philosophy of Zen on their philosophical premise that they forget they exist when they are deeply meditating. They fail to realise that *they* forget they exist, while *they* are meditating; Consequently, the inference of Zenists that they are illusions because they "cease to exist", rather than have simply forgotten they exist, while meditating is very convincing evidence that Zenists are not as cognizant of their experience of meditating as they'd like to think.

Zenists don't understand they're delusional because they've never learned to truly realise. They think they only need to experience, not realise, because they don't believe they are the knowers of their experience. They think they only need to know, not know that they're the knowers of their knowing. They don't yet realise that they are the knowers who are the knowing centers in their cognitions.

Your knowledge that you're a self always precedes your development of wisdom. But realising the self you are and attaining wisdom is not your salvation. Your salvation is your intermittent release from suffering which you experience when you realise your harmony with Nature. Salvation is the direct result of realizing your Style, not your use of Truism, because a self's true Style is its realisation of its responsibility for its own ability to enjoy as well as suffer, not its practice of Truism—and certainly not its practice of Zen.

We're unable to use our ability of reasoning when we cogitate because we're only able to develop our inner symbolic reasoning in accord with our inner symbolic thinking, not in accord with our inner symbolised cogitating. Therefore, the Zenist needs to condemn delineative cogitating, not indicative and descriptive thinking and explanatory reasoning.

Buddhists attempt to imitate Nature by refusing to speculate simply because Siddhartha thought that speculation was unnecessary for "awakening". Siddhartha's awakening was his mistaken intuition that he didn't exist as a self. Siddhartha didn't realise that speculation is essential for enlightenment. Although awakening is a self's realisation that its an immortal or mortal center of Nature, enlightenment is the result of speculative reasoning about Reality on the basis of having realised the self or having awakened; therefore, Siddhartha was neither awakened nor enlightened because he maintained that the self was an illusion.

If I wrote that the desire of Buddhists to avoid speculation is a peculiarity unique to their religion, I would be lying, because every religion, with the exception of Selfism, preaches faith or trust in dogma, which is certainty of belief, rather than pansophy, which is certainty of knowledge. Unfortunately, many Buddhists, Hebrews, Christians, Muslims, Baha'i and other religionists have a stupid unquestioning and uncritical faith in the reasoning of their respective idols, like Siddhartha, Abraham, Jesus, Mohammed, and Bahaullah, which is why those prospective Truists who might follow my reasoning, unquestioningly and uncritically, will also be stupid because their faith in my reasoning, instead of their own, will undermine the critical reasoning and understanding they will need to develop their own Style and, thus, their own wisdom. Such an unquestioned faith breeds the uncritical devotion which characterises all fanatics.

I shudder at the thought of having "devoted disciples". Jesus wanted devoted disciples. Jesus didn't realise that he was *advising* his disciple Peter to deny him on three occasions because Jesus didn't want friends who would ignore the lame prophecies of his idol, Yahweh. Such devoted disciples fail to back up their "master" when their master is in trouble; however, friends always come to each other's aid. They also let their friends know when they're delusional. Peter tried to let Jesus know he was delusional when Jesus prophesised his "ordained" death, but Jesus responded by saying, "Get thee behind me, Satan" (The Gospel According to St Matthew, 16:23). Jesus response was a projection because Jesus' belief in Yahweh's prophecies was his Satanism, not Peter's Satanism.

The Zenist places more emphasis on his ability to emote with emotions than on his thoughts, concepts, and hypotheses. As a result, he fails to understand that he might exist as an immortal. He meekly accepts Siddhartha's doctrine of mortality, his doctrine of not placing importance on speculative reasoning, his doctrine of no self, and his doctrine of Emptiness, rather than use his ability to critically examine these assumptions because the Zenist is afraid of his own probable immortality.

Zenists don't want to realise that Nature is Thingness, not nothingness, because they don't want to accept the fact that they might exist as immortals. Zenists don't want to accept their immortality as a probability because they know they will never be everlastingly rid of their *need* to suffer since they will never be everlastingly rid of hate. They will always have their hate existent in Potentiality, Activity, or Nature (if they are immortal). Their hatred is the result of the fears and frustrations which they're unable to avoid; therefore, they need to suffer when they experience hatred because their suffering motivates them to confront their fears and frustrations.

Most Zenists are cowards who seek the end of their ability to use Nature's Will as the immortals they might be because they want to escape their inevitable fears and frustrations forever by dying with their sensable organisms. Fortunately, not all Buddhists are cowards. Some Zenists know they just might exist as immortals—however, even if they accept that they are probably immortal, they suffer from the delusion that that they are immortal illusions, rather than immortal actualities.

Thingness is not physicality. Thingness is the unbounded Energy of energetics. Things are energies, energy forms, or condensed energies, not Thingness (uncondensed Energy). Zenists' nonsensical notion of nothingness is only a harmless bogey hiding under the bed of such philosopher who, quite obviously, fail to understand that Thingness has no opposite. opposite Consequently, Zenists fail to understand that they are centers of pure energy whose nonsensical notion of nothingness keeps them from knowing that Nature is Thingness, not a "thing" nor a "nothingness".

Our sane desire to express our emotion of love leads us to suffer when we insanely express our emotion of hate because our sane desire to express our emotion of love is based on our conscientious attentiveness to our integrity. Our desire to express our emotion of hate is based on our feelings of intimidation, rather than confidence, while our desire to express our emotion of love is sane because it's based on our feelings of confidence, rather than intimidation.

Thinking and reasoning start us on our journey towards wisdom and, of course, they continue as our activities after we have developed wisdom; however, we continually strive to deepen our wisdom by attempting to harmonise with Nature's willing.

Our need for wisdom is our prompter in our use of Nature's Will; therefore, we start our journey to wisdom when we realise that wisdom is our fundamental need. When a self has realised that the meaning of wisdom is Freedom, this realisation prepares the self to gain an understanding of Reality's very real differentiations by intelligently mapping realities with inner symbols and outer symbols.

Awakening is a metaphor for realisation. Realisation is the start of wisdom. A self's fundamental realisation is that it's either an immortal or a mortal center of Nature. Siddhartha Gautama's doctrine of anatta or no-self was his mistaken hypothesis that he was an empty illusion. Consequently, Siddhartha's doctrine of anatta was his avoidance of realisation because Siddhartha was using his belief in this doctrine to ignore the reality of the self and thus his self-realisation.

Enlightenment is a metaphor for wisdom. Wisdom is a self's understanding of its religion. A religion is a self's exploration into the questions of what it is, who it's genuinely, sincerely and authentically expressing from what it is, instead of ingenuinely, insincerely and inauthentically expressing roles, personae, or false selves from what it is, how it expresses who it is or isn't from what it is, and why it exists as an existent, rather than simply isn't existent; therefore, a Selfist maintains that wisdom is existed in accord with a self's realisation and understanding of what Nature is and how Nature uses Its Will because every Selfist is an atheist, not a theist, a gnostic, or an agnostic.

Thinking and reasoning are a self's responsible way of developing its knowing, just as the self's knowing enables the self to realise that the idea of separation is a fiction. In attending to its isolation, a self feels that, although it may be isolated, it's never separated, because Nature's Will interpenetrates the infinities of natural selves, natural forms, and natural bodies.

Like Nature, Nature's Will is ubiquitous; however, no self is able to communicate with Nature because Nature is unable to develop emotions or abstractions which It might use to communicate. Consequently, the religionist who thinks that he or she can communicate with Nature, rather than just dwell in Nature's harmony, is deluded because Nature is unable to emote emotions and moods, poetically indicate, narratively describe, or heuristically explain.

Only we use inner symbols to freely and poetically indicate, freely and narratively describe, as well as freely and heuristically explain each of the realities we know. Many poets only freely and poetically indicate with the inner words they use to develop their cognitive thinking of concepts; however, some poets freely and descriptively narrate in their cognition with the inner words they use to develop their thinking of ideas. Some poets also freely and heuristically explain with the inner words they use to develop their reasoning of hypotheses in their recognition.

Poets meditatively concentrate their attention on a reality or Reality before they use outer words to mirror either of them in their poems. But they only use outer words to mirror a reality or Reality in their poems after they have used inner words to reflect contemplatively and speculatively on a reality or Reality.

Poets "map" inner words (or inner ideograms) to the realities they're mirroring with outer words by using their cognising to guide their symbolic thinking as well as their recognising to guide their symbolic reasoning in their mapping of inner words.

For example, poets are able to translate inner symbols into outer symbols to write on a medium, like paper, or translate them into electromagnetic patterns by pressing the keys on a computers' keyboard so that outer symbols appear on the computer monitor's viewing screen.

The skill with which a poet uses his ability to map inner symbols in his recognition to the realities he's mirroring with outer symbols is dependent on his thinking in his faculty of cognition as well as on his reasoning in his faculty of recognition. Unfortunately, like many other artists, poets often dislike reasoning; therefore, they fail to acknowledge their occasional use of reasoning in developing their poems. Some poets suppress their use of reasoning in developing their poems so that their reasoned understanding is confined to their memory; therefore, their poems suffer from a lack of realism because they are only using their cognitive thinking to develop their poems.

It's worth noting that a poet is able to express outer symbols from his indifferent hate as well as from his neutral love. Expressions of indifference or neutrality aren't expressions of "objectivity" because they're expressed by a subject, not an object; therefore, indifference and neutrality are expressions of subjectivity, not objectivity.

Indifferent poets think that they're objective brains. They take pride in the "objectivity" or indifference they use to *subjectively* judge the world. They're proud because they haven't allowed their emotions to sway their judgements. They don't understand that they need to discern, not judge.

Intellectuals fear affect which is why they are afraid to let their positive emotions of affection and joy have free reign. They don't know how to handle their own emotions of anger and sorrow; therefore, they settle for a straitjacket of indifference as a defence against their affect. These indifferent individuals don't realise that their cherished "unemotional" indifference is actually the result of the anger and fear they're repressing because these emotions rise from their belief that they will die with their bodies. Their anger over the thought, "I will die", covers over their fear of death so that their fear of death is unnoticed; however, their indifference is actually a manifestation of the hatred they're trying not to feel in relation to their thought that they will die. Their attempt to avoid their feeling of anger is an effort in futility—because their identification with their mortal bodies is the cause of their anger.

A woman (or hermaphrodite or man) who is not thinking with the emotion of love is suppressing or repressing this emotion; therefore, she has no choice but to cogitate with her emotion of hate which is usually masked as an attitude of indifference. Indifference is simply a mask she's wearing to hide the truth that she's actually expressing her hatred in relation to her fear that she will die; however, her neutral attitude is a mask she wears to hide the truth that she's suppressing her expression of love in relation to her appreciation of her probable immortality because she knows her loving is not usually well received by those who fear death.

Scientismists are indifferent advocates of scientism who hide their hatred behind the outer numbers they use. We all use outer graphics and outer letters to structure outer symbols, like outer words, so we can relate to each other by using these outer symbols. We also use outer graphics and outer letters to structure tokens, totems, maps, road signs, and diagrams; however, outer numbers confuse us because mathematical graphics and outer numbers aren't effective for relating. We use outer graphics and outer letters to structure outer ideograms and outer words, respectively. But we're unable to use outer numbers to structure outer ideograms or outer words which is why scientismists confuse us when they attempt to communicate with us by using mathematics as their means of communication.

Mathematicians are scientismists. Mathematicians use mathematical graphics, like =, + and -, to logically connect outer numbers to one another with laws. Once again, these mathematical graphics may be delineated in outer words, such as "equals" (=), "plus" (+) and "minus" (-), but these mathematical "outer words" don't describe because they aren't words of quality which we might use to relate to each other. Mathematical words are words of quantity used to "connect". Connections are a mathematician's delusion because connections are only imaginary. Connections and numbers may only be used to delineate, not describe.

The numbers of mathematics, such as "1", "2", "3" and etcetera, are also expressed as the words "one", "two", "three" and etcetera; however, the counting words "one", "two" and "three" aren't words of quality because numbers are quantitative; therefore, words expressing numbers are counting words of quantity. We're unable to use words of quantity, like "one", "two" and "three" to relate for the simple and obvious reason that words of quantity aren't words of quality.

Spiritualists who delineate the absolute as "the One" as well as our supposed relatedness to this absolute as our "Oneness" are using inadequate labels because the word "one" will always carry the connotation of quantity. Instead, we need to describe Nature as "the Unbounded" and our use of Nature's Will as our relatedness, not our "spirituality".

Intellectual mathematicians think they use their numbers and mathematical connectors with love in their calculating; however, they're actually unknowingly using them with indifferent hate. Likewise, intellectual "poets" don't use words, freely and poetically, to indicate with love, intellectual "narrators" don't use words, freely and narratively, to describe with love, and intellectual "philosophers" don't use words, freely and heuristically, to explain with love; rather, all these intellectuals use words, licentiously and cogitatively, to delineate with their indifferently quarantined hatred.

Intellectuals are unable to use their indifferent logic to reasonably guide their behaviour. Their behaviour is unreasonable because intellectuals repress their ability of cognising in favour of cogitating.

The intellectual is not fully using his ability of sensing because he doesn't pay attention to what he is capable of knowing. The intellectual is inadequate in his expression of his knowing because he fails to pay attention to his expression of his emotions which are the basis of his ability to enjoy as well as suffer; therefore, he is delusional, rather than realistic, because he is so afraid of suffering that he is unable to enjoy by sensing his emotions.

Intellectuals face an enormous challenge because they intellectually and indifferently "philosophise" without realising the Truth of Reality and Its realities. Their challenge is enormous because they are ignoring their Freedom. An intellectual's use of his cogitative disabling ability has the effect of repressing his abilities of thinking and reasoning because cogitation is based on the intellectual's delusional metaphysical premise of determinism.

Intellectuals aren't intuitively and cognitively thinking or recognitively reasoning because their cogitating is not thinking or reasoning. Intellectuals have repressed their intuition, cognition, and recognition along with their emotions because they don't recognise their own Freedom. They don't recognise their own Freedom because they're lost in logic.

The intellectual ignores his ability to intuit, cognise, and recognise in Freedom. The intellectual's disabling cogitations happen by way of his volition, not automatically; however, he's unable to relate his disabling cogitations to his abilities of thinking and reasoning because these abilities are based on our instinctive need for wisdom whereas an intellectual's disabling ability of cogitating is based on his denial of this need. He fails to realise that he isn't a true scientist and philosopher because he's ignoring the humanistic reasonable way of developing hypotheses and theories.

We use intelligent reasoning, not intellectual cogitating, to develop hypotheses and theories which "hold water". We use our pure thinking to develop our thoughts and notions and our symbolic thinking to develop our concepts and ideas. Intellectuals use their mistakenly hypothesised laws in their logical cogitating of inner formulas and inner equations because they mistakenly think they're able to use these laws to develop meaningful theories, not realising that they are only able to use needs to develop meaningful theories as well as meaningful languages.

The thoughts that a self develops by intuitive notional thinking, the concepts that a self develops by cognitive ideational thinking, and the hypotheses that a self develops by recognitive theoretical reasoning are synthesised by the self in accord with its needs so that it's primed for its initial experience of wisdom—that is—if the self is honest. Only then is the self's capability of using its ability of actualising to actualise its understanding of the Truth.

Our hypotheses are defined by our use of inner ideograms and inner words in relation to incidents we've reasoned about. Further reasoning, not cogitating, enables us to prove the truth or falsity of our hypotheses.

Realities are indicated by a self's thoughts in notions, described by a self's concepts in ideas, and explained by a self's hypotheses in theories. The self's thoughts are derived from its pure thinking. The self uses the thoughts of its pure thinking to develop inner graphics and inner letters which it structures into inner ideograms and inner words. The self's concepts are derived from its inner ideogrammed and inner worded ideas. The self's theories are derived from its inner ideogrammed and inner worded hypotheses. Thus, a self is able to use its inner ideograms and inner words to explain its religion. Then it's able to work towards developing bits of knowledge and arrange them into a basic pattern with its understanding based on its religious Truth so that it attains wisdom.

Poetical indicative thinking with inner words is the guidance of thinking to indicate a circumstance, situation, or context. Narrative descriptive thinking with inner words is the guidance of thinking to outline a circumstance, situation, or context. Heuristic exploratory reasoning with inner words is the guidance of reasoning to explain a circumstance, situation, or context. Cogitated inner formulas and inner equations aren't used by a self to indicatively and narratively think or heuristically reason because they're delineated by a self's false belief in laws, rather than its knowledge of needs. A self's knowledge of its needs is its liberating guide to its thinking and reasoning of inner sentences and expressed outer sentences, while the self's belief in laws is its handicap because its cogitating of inner formulas and inner equations and expressed outer formulas and outer equations are denials of its ability of thinking as well as its ability of reasoning.

There are no sentences in a formula or an equation, despite protests from logicians to the contrary. Sentences are only structured by way of a self's ability to freely and poetically indicate a circumstance, situation, or context with its cognitive thinking, by way of its ability to freely and narratively describe a circumstance, situation, or context with its cognitive thinking, or by way of its ability to freely and heuristically explain a circumstance, situation, or context with its recognitive reasoning.

A logician's inner formulas and inner equations aren't inner languages because they're expressions of the logician's insane desire to cogitate with inner numbers. The logician translates his inner formulas and inner equations into outer formulas and outer equations. He uses laws to calculate with his formulas and equations because he is *of the opinion* that we're determined by the laws of Nature or are pre-determined by the laws of "the Creator".

Our inner languages and expressed outer languages are due to our knowledgeable thinking and reasoning because we *know* that we need to think and reason with our sentences in Freedom from laws. Languages aren't the expression of indifferent laws, such as those used in the scientismistic discipline of formal logic called "symbolic logic". "Symbolic logic" is really "sketchy logic" because graphics, letters, and numbers are used in symbolic logic to delineate, not to indicate, describe, and explain. A logician only uses data to delineate and indicate, not to describe and explain. His attempted use of data to describe and explain is absurd.

Words and ideograms are symbols that follow our real needs, rather than our superstitious laws; therefore, these symbols are meaningful. The graphics and letters of logic aren't meaningful because they don't follow our needs. Graphics don't express ideograms in logic, and letters don't express words in logic (even if they were originally meant to stand for them) because they merely follow laws, like numbers; therefore, graphics and letters used in logic are meaningless because they're only "dressed up numbers".

Formal logic is the study of propositions structured by laws and the conclusions which logicians mistakenly hypothesise are determined by the laws of these structured propositions. Propositional formulas and equations are analogues of sentences just as quantitative numbers and mathematical connectors are analogues of qualitative words and conjunctions. But an analogy is not the same as that which the analogy is attempting to imitate. Therefore, propositional formulas and equations aren't the same as sentences because quantitative numbers which *seem* to be mathematically connected aren't qualitative words which *are* grammatically conjoined.

Letters of the genetic code, i.e., "A", "T", "G" and "C" don't seem to be mathematical because they stand for the qualitative words "adenine", "thymine", "guanine" and "cytosine", respectively; however, the genetic code is a formula because these letters are supposedly connected to each other, rather than conjoined; therefore, they're used as dressed up numbers, not qualitative words. The genetic code accords to logic, not reason, because geneticists treat their coding of DNA as a formula, rather than as a sentence. As a consequence, they tend to think of DNA as a rigid structure, rather than as an activity.

Logicising is not truly reasoning because logic is only an analogue of reason.

Although thoughtful indications and descriptions are necessary for the scientist, artist, philosopher, and religionist, it's their reasoned explanations which are the most important linguistic phenomenon for them to use in guiding their understanding. All of us use reasoned explanations; however, many of us indicate, describe, and explain on the basis of superstitious fear, rather than a quest for the truth.

If you're not stupidly cogitating, you narratively describe your cognised ideas about a reality, realities, and Reality only after you have poetically indicated your intuitive notions about them. Then you heuristically attempt to explain the cognised ideas you have narratively described as your recognised hypotheses, fictions, axioms, or myths.

A scientist indicates theories which he attempts to explain by way of the hypotheses he develops. An artist indicates fictions which he attempts to explain by way of the stories he's fantasised. A philosopher indicates axioms which he attempts to explain by way of the insights he's had. A religionist indicates myths which he uses in his attempt to explain his faith in or knowledge of his Ultimate Truth. Unfortunately, scientists, artists, philosophers, and religionists are often deluded by their belief in logic.

The Greek philosopher, Aristotle, developed logic, much to his discredit. Aristotle's development of logic was the result of his philosophy of determinism which is why modern determinists worship Aristotle and his logic. These modern artists, scientists, philosophers, and religionists base their scientismistic methods of research on "logical reasoning", not realising that logical reasoning is an oxymoron because the laws of logic are used, rigidly, to force compliance to a formula or an equation. Reason is freely used by us to understand a language; therefore, logic is a contradiction of reason because our biased logical use of laws forces our cogitating to comply with a fatalistically rigid structure that supposedly determines results. Consequently, we develop only delusions which are in discord with Nature's absolutely free and unplanned instinctive willing when we use rigid logical laws, instead of flexible reasonable needs, to develop sentences by which to express our understanding of our language.

Fortunately, we're able to deliberately base our reasoning on our unbiased sensings so we develop insight into, realise, and understand Nature as the absolute Activity at the root of everything which is why a thing is a continually changing structure. Then we're able to develop our understanding and accord our activities to Nature's unplanned instinctive willing in us and everything else.

It was scientismists, like Galileo, Descartes, and Newton (especially Newton), who convinced all modern scientismists that the method of scientism "must" follow the logic of mathematics. Mathematics is dependent on quantitative measurement, rather than on qualitative sensing, perceiving, and understanding. Our modern scientismists opted out of feeling the emotion of love which is so necessary to our development of wisdom because their fear of death and responsibility led them to use logic in their attempt to measure, rather than know Reality, and Its realities, so they could establish the method of using their delusion of "time" to "count down" the *immediate continuity* (not the "static time") of a clock's readings in their anxious expectation of death.

Scientismists haven't developed any insights into the Source by sensing realities because they're too busy cogitating with the statistics they've derived and delineated from their illusory measurements of "variables" in their artificial experiments. Scientismists fail to understand that they need to study their naturally observed experience, rather than their unnaturally measured experiments.

Modern scientismists have an array of techniques mistakenly hypothesised to be quantitative measures of realities which these advocates of scientism believe they are observing; however, they're ignoring these realities, not observing them. Scientismists in quantum physics are unable to observe the particles which their instruments are supposedly measuring yet they absurdly call their measurements their "observations" so that their myth that they are studying realities is maintained, even though it's obvious that they're only studying their measurements.

Because quantum physicists use logic, they don't really understand the meaning of the possible and the probable because they attempt to predict that which *will* happen based on their measurements, not understanding that the happening of realities is unpredictable because we affect how they happen. They think that their measurements shed light on what is probably going to happen as well as what is possible because they think that laws and time exist in the outer aspect of the Reality, not realising that they are only delusions in our imaginations.

No happening is left behind in a past moment because happenings only continue immediately; therefore, our supposedly astute scientismists ignore the fact that neither past moments nor the past exist. A happening isn't existed in a future moment before this happening's occurrence; therefore, our supposedly astute scientismists ignore that neither future moments nor the future are actually existent. There is no need for a happening to exist in a present moment; therefore, our supposedly astute scientismists ignore the fact that neither present moments nor the present exist.

Often, physicists don't seem to realise that we're unable to predict with certainty what will happen, even though Werner Heisenberg's discovery of the uncertainty "principle" is well known by all modern physicists. There is no future in which happenings are existent as destined or fated happenings and there is no past in which happenings are perpetually existent. There is also no present in which current happenings are existent. Physicists don't want to understand that happenings aren't fated to occur because they would have to admit that time is a mistaken hypothesis (a delusion) and isn't existent for measurement; therefore, they would have to admit that Hermann Minkowski's logically constructed diagram of space-time and the laws which supposedly govern it are also mistaken hypotheses.

These scientismistic physicists and other scientismists don't want to realise these glaring truths because they would have to give up toying at their logical game of measurement and turn their attention to the real challenges which confront us on earth, like poverty, war, and our irresponsible polluting of the earth. We need to be responsible so we don't leave such issues up to politicians to solve because politicians don't want to give up The Game of the Gods which is the Game of striving for authority over people whom these politicians attempt to indoctrinate with the delusional hypothesis that law and order are "necessary realities".

The indoctrination of our intelligence in this way keeps us from realising that our need for organisation-disorganisation-reorganisation is not a Game. Our authoritarian politicians aren't satisfied with merely existing as selves which is why they toy at The Game of the Gods. Our authoritarian politicians want to exist as deities, not as selves. Consequently, The Game of the Gods is an uncooperative competing for supremacy.

Politicians are uncooperative competitors; however, *apolitical coordinating co-operators* only need to use Nature's Will; therefore, they strive for the harmony of organisation-disorganisation-reorganisation because this is the way to wisdom for every center that is a self of Nature.

Nature develops selves, instinctively and *accidentally*, as Its centers; therefore, Nature doesn't know that we're selves who are able to gain knowledge of the Truth and develop wisdom. Nature doesn't generate us on purpose. Nature doesn't generate us for a reason. Nature just generates us.

Nature doesn't know that It has evolved us; therefore, Nature is unable to help us develop towards wisdom. We develop by using Nature's Will in tandem with Nature's instinctive willing; however, our wisdom will happen, unpredictably, by way of our own effort as we develop purposefully towards this goal.

A self's wisdom will inevitably happen, but it's not certain when. A self's wisdom will not necessarily happen while the self is inhabiting its body nor even soon after it enters its realm of the after-death in the sensor it inhabits (if selves are immortal).

Wisdom is not a certainty which has been destined to occur because destiny is falsely imagined. Although it seems a possibility that we might exist as stupid selves forever because destiny is imaginary, in practice, it's impossible to never reach wisdom because we're unable to ignore our motivation to reach wisdom without a great deal of suffering.

Although we do have forever to attain wisdom, only a very stupid self would say, 'I'll strive for wisdom when I haven't got anything better to do', because a self's insane desire to postpone striving for wisdom inevitably leads to intense suffering for it. Such a self is only able to minimise its suffering by attaining wisdom. A man (or a woman) who postpones his attempt to attain wisdom is much like an air-tight pot which builds up steam (anxiety) until this steam reaches a critical level of pressure in the pot (the man). The pot needs to be opened (the man needs to realise his need for wisdom) and its pressure released (he starts to strive for wisdom) or else it will explode (he will become malevolent) so that it shatters (he suffers continually).

Historically, scientismists became convinced that a self's reality is a materialised phenomenon, rather than an uncondensed center of Energy. We call such an absurd philosophy "materialism".

I define materialism as follows:

'The philosophical basis of scientism which is the proposition that immaterial phenomena are produced by materialised phenomena, rather than the proposition of immateriality (which is the philosophical basis of my sciences, selfology and TSQ kinesiology) which is that materialised phenomena are produced by immateriality, i.e., the Phenomenon.'

The absurd philosophy of materialism resulted in the absurd hypothesis of scientismists that the measurement of a materialised reality might be used in understanding Reality. Ironically, physicists, like Galileo Galilei, René Descartes, Isaac Newton, and Albert Einstein developed the absurd hypothesis that the movements of a body could also be measured in addition to the body.

We're unable to measure an organic body's movement because a self's kinesthetic movement of its organic human body is the effect of the self's use of Nature's Will in this body guided by the self's intuition, cognition, and recognition; therefore, we're unable to measure this movement because movement is not the distance on the earth moved over by an organic body; rather, movement is an effect of Nature's Will which relates a body (or particle) that Nature is moving at a distance. Likewise, motion is an effect of Nature's Will which relates a particle as well as the microorganisms existing in an organic body to this whole organic body.[6] Scientismists fail to realise that they're unable to measure relationships (or anything else); therefore, we're unable to measure motions and movements because motions are the continually changing relations of a particle to other particles in a body, while movements are the continually changing relations of an unbodied particle to other unbodied particles or an organic body to other organic bodies.

"Primitive" scientismists (natural philosophers) didn't understand that the immaterial self and its immaterial cognition are just as real as materialised realities because superstitious Creationists maintained that a being and its soul originated from the Creator who supposedly exists in separation from the physicalities of Nature as well as in separation from Nature. These primitive scientismists refused to "swallow" this propaganda; therefore, their modern descendants (who are usually Mortalists) carry on the superstitious belief of these primitive scientismists in materialism which was their response to the superstitious beliefs of Creationists.

The superstitious reactive belief of these mortalistic scientismists was their belief that only the materialised is real. Consequently, they discarded "spirit" and "soul" because they knew they were only superstitious ideas of Creationists, not realising that their belief in materialism was a superstitious belief which they needed to discard along with the Creationists' superstitious beliefs in spirits and their souls. The words "spirit" and "soul" apply only to immortals of "God" which is why I use the word "self", instead of "spirit", and the word "sensor",

---

[6] A microorganism is simply a single-celled organism; therefore, like multicellular plants, some single-celled microorganisms, such as the vegetative bodies of bacteria, are lived without selves inhabiting them, while, like multicellular animals, some single-celled microorganisms, such as the animal bodies of paramecia, do have selves inhabiting them. Microorganisms are usually invisible to the naked eye.

instead of "soul", since the words "self" and "sensor" (or "I" and "me", respectively) apply only to immortals or mortals of Nature.

These scientismists threw the "garbage" (the spirit and the soul) out with the "trash" (the miraculous). Absurdly, these scientismists continued to believe in laws, even though they had ceased to believe in the Creator; therefore, *they transferred the laws of the Creator to Nature and declared them to be uncreated, rather than created.* These scientismists also continued to believe in the logic of Aristotle who claimed that the soul was simply the "form" of a body that died with the body which meant that Aristotle was attempting to redefine the soul because the original definition of the soul denoted its immortality, rather than its mortality.

Ironically, Aristotle believed in the "unmoved mover" whom he supposed moved everything to exist, including mortal souls. Aristotle's unmoved mover could not be referred to as the Creator because the souls of the Creator were believed to exist as immortal realities. Those who believed in the Creator believed he had the absolute "power" to "grant" souls their immortality. Aristotle didn't give credence to a Creator because he believed that we were "moved" to develop by the unmoved mover. Aristotle understood that the absolute mover wasn't an object and had to be unmovable; however, he didn't understand that the absolute mover is Activity. He didn't realise that the absolute Mover is the *Active Unmoved Mover*, not the inactive unmoved mover.

Aristotle's proposition that a soul is the form of a body was his mistake because the soul is not a form and a form is not an epiphenomenon of a body. Aristotle didn't understand that a soul is a delusion because a self is a center of Nature who has a sensor, not a soul. He also didn't understand that a form is an uncondensed bounded portion of Nature.

As promised, I will turn my attention to Aristotle's development of logical propositions by way of his delusional scientismistic logic.

To use logic is to use logical propositions. A logician uses cogitating to develop logical propositions. The logician, Aristotle, didn't think or reason to help him realise and understand truths. Aristotle cogitated in misunderstanding which led him to apply laws to the construction of *formulas or equations* which he equated to sentences in his attempt to ascertain truth. Aristotle's "sentences" were all false because he used logic, rather than reason, to develop them. His "sentences" were rigidly constructed by cogitating with laws, rather than freely developed by reasoning in accord with needs.

The result of laws applied to data is the logical proposition. A logical proposition follows a logical formula or equation. Logic applied to a sequence of words by a self is not the result of a self's contemplative thinking or speculative reasoning. Rather, logic is the result of a self's delusional cogitating because logic applied to a sequence of words is not a free application of words. Logical "sentences" only *seem* to be sentences.

A software program is used to string words together which computer programmers mistake for the computer's sentences because we're able to interpret and understand these formulated or equated words. These formulated or equated words seem to be like the free sentences we speak, write, and type; however, they're not the result of free indicating, describing, and explaining. A computer doesn't have the abilities to freely and poetically indicate, freely and narratively describe, or freely and heuristically explain. Nor does a computer have the disabling ability to deliberately and intellectually delineate. Consequently, the computer's strings of words aren't sentences. Rather, these strings of words are merely outer formulas or outer equations which the unintelligent as well as unintellectual computer has been used to construct by way of the mechanism of a computers software.

Some computer "experts" are of the opinion that their computers write, intelligently, but their opinion speaks only of their own myopic intelligence. Only a self is able to freely use a computer to poetically indicate, narratively describe, and heuristically explain by typing keys on the computer's keyboard as I'm currently doing. Only then are the resulting sentences really sentences. A scientismist uses a computer to avoid using Nature's Will to develop sentences in Freedom. In other words, a scientismist is not a true scientist because he or she is conditioned by logic.

A logical proposition follows a formula. A logical proposition is a self's choice to affirm or deny a subject by using a linking verb called the "copula" to assert a preassumed affirmation called the "predicate". According to the rules of logic, the self "must" affirm or deny the subject with the predicate through the use of the copula. Ironically, logicians are unable to use the logical proposition to justify their choice of affirming or denying the subject because they made the choice to affirm or deny the subject *before* using the logical proposition—which is ironic. You see, logicians maintain that we don't really have the ability to choose because they think choices are illusions derived from our "delusion" that we are free. Fortunately, it's a logician's logic which is his or her delusion based on his or her illusion of determinism, predeterminism or compatibilism because a choice is a self's deliberate noninstinctive use of Nature's Will in spontaneous harmony—or impulsive disharmony—with Nature's always instinctive nondeliberate use of Its Will as the self's Freedom to liberally act or react in accord and licentiously act or react in discord with Nature's nonliberated and nonlicentious Freedom from which Nature has no ability to choose, unlike the selves It generates.

A self who uses a reasoned proposition has no need to use a formula to construct "sentences" because the self freely develops its propositional sentences with its reasoning. A self who is reasonable, rather than logical, knows that no subject has to be understood before its truth is affirmed or denied (or before its falsity is affirmed or denied); therefore, a self's reasoned (rather than logical) proposition puts a topic up for intelligent discernment. A reasoning self has usually realised that the truths and falsities of a topic are continually changing. These truths and falsities are continually changing because Nature and, thus, every self's Ultimate Truth is Freedom.

An unreasonable self's logical proposition puts a topic up for an intellectual judgement which is unconcerned with the needs of people which is why the unreasonable self's judgement of the topic's truth or falsity is irresponsible. The choice of affirming or denying a topic's truth or falsity is made before the logical proposition is used to affirm or deny the topic's truth or falsity; therefore, the logical proposition is a charade. Lawyers will often use logical propositions to convince the judge and jury of the truth or falsity of a case they're attempting to "win", just as politicians will use logical propositions to convince their constituents that they have justified their argumentative choices. The truth is that lawyers use logical propositions so they won't have to address the true needs of the case before the court, while politicians use logical propositions so they won't have to address the true needs of the social situation disturbing their constituents.

We inferentially or conclusively reason by way of free deduction or induction based on our continually changing needs, not unneeded logical laws. A self's inferential reasoning is intelligent because it's guided by a self's recognising of a reality, realities, and Reality. Inferential reasoning is guided by intelligence, not intellect.

Intelligence is the immaterial faculty a self uses to guide its immaterial ability of reasoning. The immaterial intellect is the disabling faculty which a self uses to handicap its immaterial thinking and reasoning by its use of its immaterial cogitating.

Logicising is the use of conjunctions as if they were connectors, rather than relators; therefore, words are linked as if they were numbers resulting in a misunderstanding of what a reality is, whom it isn't if it's a self-thing, how it is if it's a self-thing, how it is if it's only a thing, or why it is the way it is if it's a self-thing.

A self learns to intellectualise to keep from reasoning in Freedom because it fears the unlimited. A self uses cogitation to develop its intellect as its disabling faculty. The intellect is a self's disabling faculty of misunderstanding. A self uses its disabling ability of cogitating to repress its ability of reasoning so it will not have to face its fear of the unlimited which was the fear that "inspired" the self to develop its disabling intellectual faculty in the first place.

The intellect is not used by a self to exercise a "superior" level of reasoning, as scientismists believe; rather, the intellect is used by the self to exercise the absurdity of formal intellectualising which I have dubbed "logicising". The logical intellect is used by a self to delusionally fixate on principles, rules and laws whereas intelligence is used by a self in accord with its knowledge of its needs, its conscience, and its harmony within Nature's harmony. .

An intelligent self abides by the following truths:

A self's harmony within Nature's harmony, not "the 'supernatural' principles of God", is the basis of a self's natural conscience and integrity; a self's natural conscience and integrity, not "the 'supernatural' rules of God", is the basis of a self's natural needs; and a self's natural needs, not "the 'supernatural' laws of God", are the basis for a self's development of its inner aspect of cognitive wellness and its outer aspects of sensorial and bodily health in its inner-outer World.

Intelligence is a self's faculty which it uses to guide its ability of reasoning in accord with its harmony within Nature's harmony.

I was perplexed by the claim of computer technicians which was that computers are intelligent because computers didn't seem to me to be intelligent, despite the claims of these intellectual computer technicians; however, I finally realised that reasoning is a selfkomic ability of a self, while cogitating is a selfpathic disabling ability of a self. I also understood that artificial computers are naturally unintelligent, while selves are naturally intelligent.

Nature instinctively wills in a computer. A computer is a mechanically constructed artefact which we make with natural physicalities. Nature instinctively wills a computer's mechanisms to move. No computer will ever meditatively think, contemplatively think, speculatively reason, or even absurdly cogitate because a computer is not a self who is able to guide Nature's Will.

There is no self with an ability to inhabit a computer; therefore, intuiting, cognising, and recognising as well as thinking, reasoning, and cogitating are impossible developments for a computer because the computer is missing a self. There is no thinking, reasoning, or cogitating in a computer because Nature is instinctively willing in the computer's programming so that the computer's mechanisms are functioned by way of Nature's instinctive willing in Its vitalism of electromagnetism.

We're able to construct machines that move; however, neither our machines nor our sensable bodies move, automatically. Automatism is a mistaken philosophical doctrine because automatists assert that activity, motion, and movement are the result of mechanical "forces" of contact, rather than Nature's Will. Automatists also assert that we're unable to use consciousing to guide Nature's Will because they suppose consciousness is only existed as an impotent by-product of the brain's physiological changes; therefore, they also believe that Nature, selves, and Nature's Will are delusions because their delusion is that Nature's laws exist as invisible mechanisms or forces of contact. Automatists fail to understand that consciousness isn't existent because consciousness was conceived as a mistaken attempt to assert that we aren't selves with cognitions because selves are our "illusions" while we are supposedly each a "selfless consciousness".

Isaac Newton thought that movement starts by the force of contact. The "tricky" hypothesis of forceful contact is a challenge to automatists because it begs the question of how the movements of a sensable organism's limbs start. Ironically, automatists avoid looking at or explaining how the movements of sensable organism start because the doctrine of automatism doesn't allow for the reality of selves or for the ability of these selves to use Nature's Will in tandem with Nature.

Automatists, who try so hard to deny the obvious, fail to understand that a self's sensor emanates from it to encompass the rest of self's brain as well as the rest of the self's body. A brain is merely the conduit for a self's knowing in its sensing. A self intentionally as well as unintentionally uses Nature's Will in the channels of its brain, nervous system, and muscles to start motions in and movements of its body. Even the mechanical movements of machines are the result of Nature's spontaneous instinctive willing; therefore, there is no automatism in Nature.

Although we're selves who spontaneously or impulsively as well as instinctively or deliberately instigate our use of Nature's Will in the particles of our sensable organisms to breathe their lungs, beat their hearts, or digest their foods, we instigate these movements in tandem with Nature's spontaneous instinctive willing. We aren't brains who automatically breathes their lungs, beat their hearts, or digest their foods because we *have* brains which is why we refer to our brains as *our* brains.

Nature's Will is always flowingly active in our sensable organisms s which the following example illustrates:

When the patellar tendon below a self's patella (knee cap) is tapped with a small rubber tipped hammer, Nature instinctively wills in the "reflex arc" (the afferent nerves of the patellar tendon related to the spinal cord and the efferent nerves of the spinal cord related to the muscles of the knee) so the self's knee is kinesthetically "jerked": however, the self is able to override Nature's flowingly active instinctive willing in the reflex arc by deliberately using Nature's Will, self-kinetically to stop its knee from reflexively jerking when its patellar tendon is tapped.

My Naturalism maintains that all phenomena are derived from Nature's voluntarism; therefore, my Naturalism is a vitalism, not an automatism. Only empiricists are able to know the vitality of Nature because vitality is experienced whereas rationalised laws are inexperiential.

Rationalism is a mistaken doctrine of philosophers. Rationalism asserts that a self has knowledge developed in its memory before it begins to experience. Knowledge isn't developed in a self by Nature. Knowledge is only developed by a self in accord with its experience of Nature and the natures of Nature, like this self. We're not born with a priori knowledge existent in our memories by a fiat of God or the cognitive knowing of Nature because God is obviously only a myth and Nature is unable to know or cognise. Consequently, rationalism is a mistaken hypothesis, while empiricism is a truth.

The importance of our abilities of realising and understanding is demonstrated by the opportunity they give us to attain wisdom by way of our ability of sensing. Our knowing of our sensing is our empiricism. Our empiricism is based on our need to know, not on laws.

The goal of empiricism is to realise Reality's Truth based on your experience.

Experience is a self's knowing or cognising which it derives from an effect resulting from its participation with a reality.

A self's known or cognised truths are derived from its insight into its knowing or cognising.

A self's knowledge or conceptualisation is derived from its understanding of its known or cognised truths.

A self's wisdom or cognition is derived from its discernment of its knowledge or conceptualisation of its truths.

A self's self-actualisation or self-realisation is derived from its introspection or inward concentration of its wisdom or cognition on the source of its wisdom or cognition which the self is unable to experience; however, the self can realise that it is this source.

A Selfist needs to practice its unnatural formal meditative technique of Truism if it is unable to immediately realise its natural informal Style because a self's Truism can enable it to develop the knowing that it is a center of pure energy who exists as well as inhabits its cognition, although a self's Style is its natural and, thus, more effective means of using introspection or inward concentration to realize that it exists and inhabits the center of its cognition.

Chapter Four
Continuity in Immediacy Versus Time in Eternity

In their paper, "The Flow of Time as a Perceptual Illusion", Ronald Gruber and Richard Block maintained that happenings, which they defined as 'spatial change' rather than bodily change, are illusions. They reported, 'Previous research reveals that motion perception occurs in discrete processing epochs, frames, or snapshots' (Gruber & Block, 2013, p. 91). Gruber and Block's paper contains a report of an experiment in which subjects were shown a video scene of a walking man and a video scene of bread turning brown in a toaster. The video frames were shown to their subjects in three different ways of interrupting the stimulus (the showing of the video frames). Each video frame was exposed after clock movements of 0.5 seconds, 3.0 seconds, or 7.0 seconds.

Gruber and Block failed to understand that the 0.5, 3.0, and 7.0 seconds or "interstimulus intervals" were their delusions because the 0.5, 3.0, and 7.0 seconds were fictitious measurements of the movements or unchanging activities of the clock they were using as their tool by which to flash their video scenes.

Gruber and Block's absurd hypothesis was that, like the flow of time, motion is an illusion because motion is not seen in a snapshot. Gruber and Block failed to realise that motion is an effect of a self and/or Nature's willing in a body, not a "spatial change". Gruber and Block performed their experiment with metaphorically "closed eyes" (ignorance) because they assumed that space is existent.

Gruber and Block assumed that the flow of time is an illusion. Time flow is a *mistaken hypothesis or a delusion*, not an illusion.

Gruber and Block realised that a movement is not a "length" of time; however, they didn't realise that movement is really an effect of Nature's use of Its Will or a self's use of Nature's Will in tandem with Nature so that movements of bodies are effected by their selves and/or Nature. Gruber and Block mistakenly hypothesised that movements are illusions which is why they used the mechanism of video frames in their attempt to prove that movements are illusions. Gruber and Block also attempted to delusionally measure supposedly unchanging intervals with the durations of 0.5. 3.0, and 7.0 seconds, despite their disbelief in time.

Gruber and Block concentrated their attention on the segmented realities of video frames, and ignored continually moving realities, like my hand waving to a friend. They conveniently overlooked the fact that my waving hand moves continually, not as interrupted video frames; therefore, they reached the absurd conclusion that happenings, motions, and movements are illusions because they were only paying attention to the illusory movements of video frames.

Gruber and Block mistakenly used the word "motion" to describe movement, just as Isaac Newton did when he developed "The Three Laws of Motion". Motion is not movement because movement is observable whereas motion is unobservable. Motion is an unobservable effect of a self and/or Nature's willing *in* a particle or an organism: therefore, motion only applies to the unobserved, such as the usually unobserved motion of blood cells in our sensable organisms' veins and arteries. Movement is the observable effect of a self and/or Nature's willing, such as the self and/or Nature's use of Its Will to move the arms and legs of this self's sensable organism.

Activity applies to the unobserved, such as a self's abilities and faculties, and the observed, like a self's behaviours of conversing and writing. Most people use the word "motion" to refer to an observed movement, such as a self's raising of its arm, as well as to a motion which is usually unobserved, such as a self's use of Nature's Will to motion fluids out of and into a cell. They also use the outer word "activity" to refer to an observed behaviour, such as a self's use of Nature's Will in tandem with Nature to converse and write, as well as an unobservable activity, such as a self's use of Nature's Will in tandem with Nature to develop hypotheses from concepts or concepts from ideas.

I practice theoretical selfological qualitative kinesiology (TSQ kinesiology) which is the study of the self, its effecting of motions in and movements of its human body, and factors which affect such motions and movements (kinesiology is the study of the motions in and the movements of a human body as well as factors which effect and affect such motions and movements). As a practicing theoretical selfological qualitative kinesiologist, I understand that Selfkinetics occurs in Selfkinesis, that a self's uses its cognition to activate motions in and movements of its forms and body, and that a self's cognising or knowing is an unmotioned as well as unmoved activity.

Gruber and Block failed to understand that it was their scientismistic method of using frames of film in their experiment that reinforced their belief that happening and motion (by which they actually meant movement) were illusions *because this was the result they wanted.* They conveniently overlooked the fact that it was the epochs, frames, or snapshots they used in their experiment that were substituted by them in their fantasies to be the way that we perceive. In other words, *Gruber and Block concluded that their subjects perceive movement in epochs, frames, or snapshots because Gruber and Block were using epochs, frames, or snapshots for their subjects to perceive.* Gruber and Block used this circular argument because they didn't really want to find truth in their experiment; they only wanted to assert their belief. Of course, I don't mean to imply that Gruber and Block were dishonest; however, they were unknowingly and naively closing their eyes to some obvious facts of their experience.

For example, Gruber and Block realised that a movie projector usually rolls 24 frames of film per second in a film projector which results in the illusion of a single moving picture; however, their assumption that an actor's movements are illusions is an absurd falsehood because the actor's movements aren't like frames of film as Gruber and Block assert.

Although a self is able to sense the illusory apparition of a moving picture as a motion picture of subjective photons in its faculty of imagination by channelling objective photons in its brain, not all movements sensed by a self are illusions because the movements of actors in front of a movie camera aren't illusory. The illusory sensing of discrete frames of a moving film projected on a screen as a scene which seems to be moving or a scene which seems to be stationary means that a self is the activity who is sensing these epochs, frames, or snapshots by its use of its activity of cognising or knowing, not that a brain is sensing these epoch, frames, or snapshots by its use of epochs, frames, or snapshots, as Gruber and Block implied was the case.

When the movie projector rolls its film at 24 frames per second, it exceeds a self's ability to use the processing of its brain fast enough to discriminate between the individual frames of a film that are flashed very quickly on a screen. The slightly differing pictures in the individual frames are blended together in a self's sense of sight; therefore, the illusion of movement is sensed by the self.

However, if the pictures in each of the exposed frames are identical, even if the film is rolling at 24 frames per second, no illusion of movement will be sensed on the screen by the self's knowing; instead, the self's use of its knowing senses the illusion of stillness on the screen.

There are no motion pictures viewed on a screen because motion pictures only occur in a self's faculty of imagination. There is no motion picture shown on a movie screen because only moving individual frames of a film with different pictures are projected on the screen. Consequently, we sense the illusion of a moving picture, not the illusion of a motion picture.

Gruber and Block seem to agree with the belief of three theorists mentioned in their article 'that avoiding the word "time" makes it easier to understand what is meant by the flow of time' because Gruber and Block wrote, 'At the very least, the expression "flow of time" is best replaced with the expression "flow of events"' (Gruber & Block, 2013, p. 92). An event is supposedly a change; however, an event is also defined by some scientismists as a change in space-time which is their delusion because time (as well as space) are delusions.

Gruber and Block believe in events or changes; however, they also believe that motions and movements are illusions. Some scientismists think an event is a change in unflowing space-time; however, an event is only a delusional idea because "space–time" is a word without a referent.

Physicists believe that their supposedly finite universe exists and contains a collection of infinite events; however, it would be impossible for a finite universe to contain an infinity of events, even if it were possible for a universe and events to exist. Just as infinite events don't exist within a finite universe, infinite points don't exist within an infinite World line because points and the World line are only mistaken hypotheses of physicists.

Hermann Minkowski, a mentor of Albert Einstein, supposed that the present space of time is intersected by a "World line", which he believed is infinite, but begins for us in past space by way of the Big Bang and ends for us with future space in eternity, although this World line is also supposed to continue, infinitely, into the future. Minkowski assumed that light travels forwards along this World line from the beginning of past space as well as travels backwards from the present to the assumed beginning of past space.

Minkowski developed the space-time diagram, which is known as the "light cone" in which a World line, symbolising the duration of movements of light, runs through the middle of a cone symbolising past space to an inverted cone symbolising future space. The meeting of the tips of these two cones symbolises a present space which the World line intersects so that light is supposed to move in accord with this World line from the cone of past space through present space to the inverted cone of future space and vice versa.

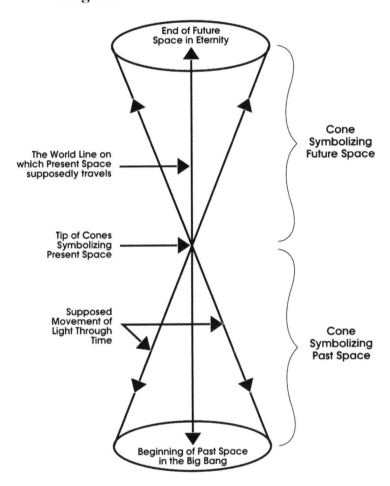

Diagram 1: MINKOWSKI'S LIGHT CONE

Neither Minkowski nor Einstein believed that the present moved along the World line; however, some pseudo-philosophers do believe this, which is why I labelled the World line in Diagram 1 as "The World Line on which Present Space supposedly travels".

Neither Minkowski nor Einstein understood that photons of light continue immediately without travelling from a hypothesised past to a hypothesised present and finally to a hypothesised "empty" future. Einstein "hedged his bets" because he maintained that the past, the present, and the future were really blended together. Einstein remarked, 'People like us, who believe in physics, know that the distinction between past, present, and future is only a stubbornly persistent illusion' (Alvele, 2018). Einstein believed that the past, present, and future were blended together because this belief supported his and Minkowski's belief in an infinite uninterrupted World line.

Einstein maintained that there were no present moments or points of time because they would be distinctions between the past and the future. But others have theorised that we're able to leave behind a present point of time in which we used to exist. This hypothesised present point of time is supposed to become a past point of time on the World line, while we switch to exist in a new present point of time which supposedly came from a future point of time on the World line in an endless process of switching between points of time.

Many people believe that events which take place in the stationary present, occur on the World line so that the events which took place in the present remain in the past forever as we unfold into the future. In other words, these people believe that events are simply "there in the past" for them to visit whenever they feel the desire to visit them. These people forget that they're simply remembering situations which have obviously ceased to happen. Consequently, there is no past which will forever contain events which have passed from the present.

Physicists hypothesise that we may be able to travel in time to visit past events. They hypothesise that we might travel along the light waves which are supposed to travel from the present to the past so that, sooner or later, we'll understand how to pull off this impossible feat of time travel. Fortunately, we're unable to travel along light waves to alter past events because light waves only continue immediately. Light waves don't continue from present events to past events because only continually changing situations are existent, not static events of the present, the past, and the future.

Supposedly, our advance towards a future point is ordained by the Creationist's mythical Creator, just as our leaving behind a formerly present point in the past is also ordained by this mythical Being. Our leaving of a present time in the past and advancing towards a future is supposed by believers in time to occur in discrete units of time which replace each other.

Only continually changing circumstances are existed in continually changing situations *as* motions or movements. In other words, a change is a motion or a movement; however, the Flow of an object's changes or the Flow of an object's motions or movements is the object's Current or Continuity. Flow, Current, or Continuity is an attribute of Nature; therefore, Flow, Current, or Continuity is an attribute of everything. Consequently, Flow is the absolute Continuity or Current of an object's changes in which the object's relative activities, motions, and movements occur, whereas a happening is an activity which is existent in a situation and changes the circumstance of this situation by way of an activation of the activity of motions in and movements of the phenomena of this situation.

Continuity is known in Immediacy, not in "time"; therefore, Continuity occurs in Immediacy, not in time.

When we hear the ticking of a clock or see the pages of a calendar turning, we're not hearing or seeing time replacing its units; rather, we're hearing the clock's ticking interrupted by silences, just as we're seeing the squares on a calendar's pages replacing each other. The clock's ticking is the clock's interruptions of sound, not the clock's timing, while a calendar's square symbolises our memory or our anticipation of the earth revolving unmeasurably around its axis, not a unit of time which we're supposedly using to measure the earth's revolving.

Philosophers who believe in and study time find time to be puzzling and indefinable; however, when time is understood to be a mistaken hypothesis, it's not puzzling or indefinable anymore. Time is assumed by scientismists to be realistically related to movement. Ironically, they are unrealistically attempting to measure movement as time. Movement is thought by these scientismists to be the "illusion" of flow, while they think time is a reality. Many scientismists believe in the "statically continual" (units of time) because they consider movement to be an illusion and stasis to be the reality.

A scientismist's attempt to measure movement is absurd because it's obvious that we're unable to measure movement. The movement of a particle or a body is the result of Nature's willing alone or by Nature and a self who has the capabilities of "borrowing" as well as using Nature's willing with Nature so a body is stimulated to travel over a continually vibrating distance. Particles in a distance are continually vibrating; therefore, particles in a distance aren't measurable because they aren't "statically continual".

The movement of frames of film over the light bulb in a movie projector result in an individual's sensing of movement because objective photons are projected through the moving frames of the film so that they'll reflect from the movie screen for us to sense. The movement of the frames of the film over the "distance" of the movie projector's light bulb is so quick that the movement of the film transcends the unitisation of its frames, just as the motions of the objective photons in a brain transcends a scientismist's attempt to unitise the motions of these objective photons by using scientismistic methodical quantitative measurement techniques, such as functional magnetic resonance imaging (fMRI).

A self is unable to use its brain to measure the movement of a film, just as a technician is unable to use fMRI to measure the motions of objective photons in a self's brain. A film's movement doesn't occur as a distance; rather, a film's frames move *over* a vibrating distance, not *as* this vibrating distance. The film's movement doesn't occur as frames of time for a self to use its brain to measure with units of time because it's the self, not the brain, who suffers from the delusion that it's able to use time to measure movement. The motions of objective photons in a self's brain aren't distances because they travel over distances in the brain; therefore, a technician's attempt to apply measurements (pictures of a self's brain) to the motions of objective photons by way of functional magnetic resonance imaging is his or her delusion because the motions of these objective photons are unfixable as static units.

We attempt to use seconds, minutes, and hours to measure movement. A second, a minute, and an hour are supposedly the static units of a distance moved over by a continuing body, such as the second hand of an analogue clock moving around the dial of the clock which is marked by 60 vibrating distances (not 60 static units). On an analogue clock's dial, there are 60 "second distances" as well as 60 "minute distances" which, taken as a whole, compose an "hour distance". We assume that we're able to associate the moving hands of an analogue clock with these second, minute, and hour distances.

The hands of an analogue clock which we call the "second", "minute" and "hour" hands aren't actually second, minute, and hour hands. We only *assume* that these moving hands are associated with the numbers between the distances of seconds, minutes, and hours on the face of the clock's circular dial. The movements of these hands aren't these numbers. Only the clock's hands are actually associated with their movements, not the vibrating numbers between the vibrating distances on the face of the clock's circular dial. This fact is obvious because the slow moving hand (the so-called "hour" hand), the faster moving hand (the so-called "minute" hand), and the fastest moving hand (the so-called "second" hand) would all move even if there were no numbers on the face of the clock's circular dial. Our assumption that the slow moving hand, the faster moving hand, and the fastest moving hand are associated with the twelve numbers on the face of the clock's dial and the distances between them is unwarranted; therefore, these hands aren't really second hands, minute hands, or hour hands.

Of course, atomic clocks don't have observable hands moving around a dial, but simply flash numbers, digitally. An atomic clock's caesium, hydrogen, or rubidium atoms move over a distance in the atomic clock. The futile attempts of scientismists to measure the cycling movements of an atomic clock's atoms has resulted in their mistaken hypothesis that they can measure atoms over a supposedly "static" distance as an extremely reliable "time" when, in truth, only their *unmeasurable* cycling over a *vibrating* distance is extremely reliable.

The difference between an analogue clock and an atomic clock is that the fastest moving hand of an analogue clock is seen to move continuously, while the numbers flashed on an atomic clock's screen are all we see; therefore, the movements of the atomic clock's mechanisms behind these flashed numbers is masked. The masking of movement by an atomic clock's seemingly stationary numbers leads some poor human selves to mistakenly assert that time, rather than Continuity, is an attribute of Nature, while the realities which Nature evolves, grows, and develops are mistakenly asserted by these poor human selves to have the attribute of time, rather than the attribute of Continuity. This masking of movement is an example of what Eastern philosophers refer to as "Maya" which is their word for our tendency to distort how we intuit, cognise, and recognise a reality, realities, or Reality.

Distances only seem to be static units because we're usually not cognisant of the continual vibrations of particles composing the distance to which we've assigned a beginning number as well as an ending number. We're unable to measure the beginning and ending of a distance because the beginning particles and the ending particles of this distance as well as the particles in between the beginning and ending of this distance are continually vibrating; therefore, this distance is continually changing. This is why the attempt of scientismists to measure the cycling of an atomic clock's atoms is futile.

Einstein believed that movement was illusory because he believed the World line was a stasis; therefore, Einstein believed that events endure on the World line, not activity, motion, or movement. The World line was Minkowski and Einstein's delusion. Movement isn't an illusion reflecting an enduring "length" of time; movement is a real effect of Nature's Will. The movements of a suef (a small uncondensed energy form), a luef (a large uncondensed energy form), a particle (a condensed energy), and a body of particles (a sensable, vegetative or mineral organism) aren't illusions because times aren't created by either the hypothesised laws of Nature or the hypothesised laws of the Creator.

The motions and movements of phenomena occur as continuities in Immediacy. Nature and Its selves (like you and I) use the Will of Nature to motion and move these phenomena. Continuity is an attribute of Nature, just as the Will is an ability of Nature; however, Nature doesn't instinctively Will Continuity in Immediacy to occur because Continuity is an attribute of Nature's Will as well as an attribute of Nature.

Seconds, minutes, hours, days, weeks, months, years, decades, centuries, and millennia aren't durations on the World line but are actually the vibrating or oscillating distances over which phenomena are moved by Nature or by centers of pure energy existing in Nature, like you are and I am. As centers of pure energy in Nature, we use Nature's Will in tandem with It to motion and move phenomena as continuities in Immediacy. Continuity is the attribute of a self's inner and outer aspects of its World. A self's sensor, sensable organism, Infiniverse, and Ether are the outer aspects of its World.

The hypothesis that time exists and has unchanging directionality is mistaken because there is no "Arrow of Time"; however, there is an Arrow of Activity, Motion, and Movement. Activity, motion, and movement progress without regressing because a glass cup that falls to the floor and shatters never spontaneously regroups so that it's existent as that glass cup again. There is no need for an Arrow of Time because the Arrow of Activity, Motion, and Movement is the Continuity or Progression of Nature's activities, motions, and movements.

The Arrow of Time is believed by scientismists to "arrow" from the past to the present and finally to the future along the World line so that past events in past "space" as well as present events in present "space" are simultaneous as well as eternal, once established. Scientismists don't believe that the Arrow of Time flows. They believe that the Arrow of Time is a stasis because they suppose it results from either the miraculous stasis of the Creator or the mundane stasis of nothingness in non-existence.

Some Creationists believe that their mythical Creator has pre-established events in the future as well as in the past and the present. If a Creationist's Creator existed, instead of just the lying self, Yahweh (if Yahweh exists) and this Creator (whom Yahweh, the liar, says he is) created his finite universe in this way, we wouldn't need memories or need to anticipate, expect, or be surprised. We would know all the events in past space, all the events in future space, and all the events in present space.

Time is a mistaken hypothesis which results in paradoxical contradictions when considered in relation to the movements of objects. Most paradoxical contradictions are based on the mistaken hypothesis of time which, in turn, is based upon the basic uncertainty of a self over whether or not it will die with its body. This uncertainty may lead to selfpathological beliefs and behaviours if not acknowledged because selves need to know that they're either immortal or mortal.

A human self's fiction of time is developed from the thoughts, concepts, and hypotheses it develops in relation to its own superstitious fear that it will die with its sensable organism, rather than continue to exist. We will likely never know which civilisation's citizens on earth first developed the fiction of time; however, we're able to encourage emotions and ideas in us which are sane by courageously accepting our fear of death. Then we're able to work through this fear and realise our immortality—if we inhabit and live our sensors after our sensable organisms die.

We think we're able to use time to measure movement; however, considering that we're unable to measure movement, the question arises, "Exactly what is the factor that stimulates us to make the futile attempt to measure movement?" A hint to answering this question is that we start and finish movements without starting them from a beginning or finishing them at an end. The mistakenly hypothesised beginning and ending of a movement are delineated as infinitesimal "points" or moments of time between which there is thought to be a "length" or duration of time. Consequently, the "lengths" between beginning and ending moments are mistakenly assumed by advocates for time to be the means by which we measure the motions in a body and the movements of the body as "durations".

Time is our hallucinated "tool". We delusionally think we're able to use this tool in measuring movement by measuring the distance over which a particle or a body moves. Time was fantasised as an "invisible mechanism" for our ancestors to use in their attempt to measure the Continuity of particles and compositions of particles (bodies) with the hypothesised mechanisms of lengths or durations. Our ancestors developed the mistaken hypothesis of time to use as their "count-down" of their bodies' deaths.

Our ancestors believed that these durations were divided into smaller sectional durations into which they were able to cram their experience before their organisms' death because their fear that they might be annihilated with their organisms' death stimulated them to activate their delusion of time. Consequently, their mistake of hypothesising time was the result of their emotional fear which was their response to their uncertainty about whether they were annihilated with the deaths of their bodies or continued to exist beyond their bodies' deaths.

The Greek philosopher, Zeno of Elea, realised that time and movement were irreconcilable because his attempt to understand movement with his attempt to time or measure movement resulted in his contradictory or paradoxical thoughts about time and movement. Unfortunately, Zeno decided that movement was his illusion, instead of that time was his delusion, because he wanted the world to be fixed as an unchanging inactivity, rather than unfixed as changing (as well as unchanging) activities.

Zeno identified the paradoxes of the racetrack, Achilles and the tortoise, the stadium, and the arrow. Zeno used these paradoxes in his attempt to show that all bodies are things in their own spaces and times. Zeno failed to understand that there are no spaces and times.

Zeno mistakenly hypothesised that things, like arrows, are rigidly fixed in their own spaces and their own section of time; therefore, in his arrow paradox, Zeno attempted to show that the movement of the arrow is an illusion because the arrow would be located in its own rigidly fixed space and time.

The motions of particles in a self's body and the movements of a self's body are continual because Nature's instinctive willing in us and our bodies never ceases. Nature's evolution of motions in objects as well as movements of objects is absolute. We affect Natures continually willed motions of particles in our bodies by using Nature's willing in these motions to start and finish our bodies' movements; however, Nature is always moving a self's body, even though the inhabiting self of its body has the capability of starting and finishing motions in and movements of its body (with Nature's instinctive assistance).

A moving body doesn't "hop" discretely from one section of time to the next because movement occurs continually. Time was supposed by Aristotle to be 'the number of movements in respect of the before and after' (Audi, 1995, p. 920). Seconds, minutes, hours, days, weeks, months, years, decades, centuries, and millennia are the distances over which the movements of objects occur. Many people delusionally think "static" distances "represent" sectional durations, like the past (which Aristotle thought was the "before") and the future (which Aristotle thought was the "after").

Some scientismistic physicists think that the infinitesimal duration of the present shifts from the duration of the past to the duration of the future as well as from the duration of the future to the duration of the past. They also suppose that tachyon particles travel from the infinitesimal duration of the present to the duration of the past; however, they're reluctant to suppose that a particle might travel from the infinitesimal duration of the present to the duration of the future, although given the gullibility of some physicists, the likelihood that they will hypothesise the "reality" of such a particle is very strong.

Time was described by Augustine of Hippo as 'a present of things past, memory, a present of things present, sight, and a present of things future, expectation' (Audi, 1995, p. 920); therefore, Augustine's three false beliefs were: (1) that our memory presents things from the past, rather than remembers things in Immediacy; (2) that our sight of things are existed in the present, rather than in Immediacy; and (3) that our expectation of things future are existed in the present, rather than our anticipation of things in Immediacy.

Aristotle and Augustine's belief in time is still honoured by most people because their need to "number the days" they have left before they die arises from their fear of annihilation with the deaths of their sensable organisms. This fear will keep us believing in time until we face the mistaken hypothesis of our "certainty" of annihilation and realise that we're not necessarily annihilated with our sensable organisms but just might continue to exist beyond their deaths.

That Aristotle numbered the days left before the death of his sensable organism also resulted in Aristotle's attempt to number the movements of the various sensable, vegetative and mineral organisms which he believed were contained by time. Aristotle numbered the distances over which these organisms had moved, not their movements. .

Motions are used to effect changes in a sensable organism by way of its inhabiting self's use of Nature's Will. The different ways the inner motions in a sensable organism happen are known by the sensable organism's inhabiting self; therefore, the self is able to use this knowledge in its use of Nature's willing to effect new motions in its sensable organism. Then these new motions in its sensable organism are used by it to move its sensable organism in the environment.

For example, the muscles of a sensable organism's arm are used by its inhabiting self to motion its arm's bones; therefore, the self is able to move its arm in the environment to effect changes in its environment.

The main goal of concentrating your knowing in your meditations, contemplations, and speculations is not to train your "mind" to "return to the present moment", as some Zenists are so fond of saying. Rather, your goal is to focus your knowing on your sensing as a continuity of the Continuity in Immediacy.

The Will of Nature has always continued immediately in realities which means that the past, the present, and the future aren't real. Time is an individual's delusional belief that space exists, is static, and is divided so that infinitesimal points in this stasis called "moments" are created and lengths, stretches, or spans of this stasis exist between these points as "durations", such as the past, the present, and the future.

But unbounded Nature hasn't any need of infinitesimal points (moments) of time nor any need of lengths, stretches, or spans (durations) of time, because Nature has Continuity as Its attribute, not time.

You're unable to return your delusion of your "mind" on the "present moment" by concentrating, meditatively, as Zen masters believe. The present moment doesn't exist because you're a center of the Ether (not a center of space) who continues with the Ether's Continuity in Immediacy. There is no "existing in the here and now of eternity"; there is only currently existing as a center or "here" of the Ether within Its Continuity in Immediacy. You're unable to return your attention to the present because the present is only a delusion.

Your attention is a current; therefore, your attention is not present because there is only Flow, Current, or Continuity in Immediacy, not stasis in the "present" of time. Only Continuity in Immediacy, not time in eternity, is an attribute of Nature; therefore, a self's use of Nature's Volition or Will is not a happening in the present but is a happening in Immediacy.

I have demonstrated that time is a delusion; however, most meditators are reluctant to give up their belief that they are momentarily present because they don't realise that they are immediate continuities. Nor do they realise that Continuity in Immediacy is the attribute of Reality, not time in eternity.

Many meditators delusionally think moments of the "future" pass into the "stillness of the present". These meditators also delusionally think present moments pass from the stillness of the present and become "past" moments; therefore, advocates for time don't so much believe that we progress into the future as we pass away with the future. Ironically, advocates for time ignore the fact that we would pass into the past from the stillness of the present with the moment in which we were happening if we really happened in such a present moment.

Continuity progresses immediately. We can *see or observe* the Continuity of an object's movement as an immediate progression; therefore, there are no regressive moments passing from the future to the stillness of the present and, finally, to the past.

We aren't specific stases or times of a general stasis or time in eternity. We're also unable to leave or abandon Continuity in Immediacy; therefore, there is no moment we're able to leave behind in the past so that we might return our cognitions to a present moment because there is no past and there are no present moments. Only Continuity is an attribute of perhaps mortal or perhaps immortal centers of Nature, like you and I.

We might exist as mortals even though we commence from the immortality of non-commenced Nature. Nature has always had Continuity in Immediacy as Its attribute. Consequently, the Now of eternity and time are only their advocates' delusions.

Eternity is believed by Creationists to be the simultaneous presence of the mythical Creator to all his created moments of time in bounded universal space. The Creator is hypothesised to transcend this created bounded universal space.

The theory of a bounded universal space is a mistaken theory because there is only the unbounded Ether. The Infiniverse is existent in the unbounded Ether. The Infiniverse is not bounded by a finite space because the Infiniverse is not a finite whole. The Infiniverse is composed of infinite particles and infinite organisms composed of particles which are interspersed in the Ether. The unbounded Ether is the unbounded pure Energy we call "Nature".

We're not created spaces who "bide our time" until the created moments of an expanding space-time supposedly end in the eternal Now. We exist in the Infiniverse which is and always has been continually evolved, grown, developed, deteriorated, and devolved without ever having been created. There is no created finite universe which has its own expanding space-time. There is only Nature in which an infinity of mortal particles are always continually and immediately appearing and disappearing as the Infiniverse in Nature's harmony of organisation-disorganisation-reorganisation.

We have memories which continue in us, when continually bolstered, and we have anticipations which continue in us, until they come about or we abandon them. Our memories aren't existed by us in the past any more than our anticipations are existed by us in the future. We continue without continuing in time because we don't continue from the past to the future in a present any more than we regress from the future to the past in a present. We have Continuity as our attribute, just as Nature has Continuity as Its attribute, which means that we don't continue in or as a present; we simply continue. We don't leave behind a past by continuing into an "empty" future because the past and the future, like the present, are the fictions of temporalists.

Continuity in Immediacy is not the Continuum. Continuity in Immediacy is the attribute of the Continuum by which Continuity is the ongoingness in and of the Continuum's Immediacy, while Immediacy is the carrier of the Continuum's Continuity. The flow of motions and movements happen in the Continuum. The Continuum is the unbounded *extent* of Activity. Continuity is a fact of continualists.

Our Continuity never stops if we're immortal; therefore, if we're immortal, after our organisms die, we don't await their resurrection by the Creator in eternity which is believed by theists and deists alike to be the Creator's perpetuity outside of time. We simply continue immediately in our sensors. We don't exist in a time which is thought to be suspended in the eternity of the Now because the eternity of the Now is delusionally believed to be the everlasting Moment in which the Creator exists.

Nature doesn't instinctively use Its Will in the eternity of the Now because Its willing happens continually in Immediacy. Eternity may be defined as the infinite Duration or Perpetuity of the Creator. Advocates for time believe that time begins and ends as well as that eternity is the infinite Duration of the absolute Now or Moment of the Creator; however, "duration" and "now" are categories of time which means that the absolute Now or the absolute Moment would be the Creator's absolute Time, while the infinite Duration would be the infinite length of the Creator's Time, that is, if the Creator existed.

Absolute Time is mistakenly hypothesised to be the Creator's stasis and Perpetuity; therefore, Perpetuity is mistakenly hypothesised to be static, like relative time.

Time isn't necessary for Nature to continually Will. A self's Continuity commences as soon as the self has been generated by Nature, while Nature's Continuity hasn't commenced or started because Nature is non-commenced. In other words, if selves exist immortally, they exist as immortals in and with the immortality of Nature as soon as Nature has generated them from Its starting of their existence.

A scientismist's mistaken hypothesis of time contains the mistaken hypotheses of moments and durations. A duration is the mistaken hypothesis that our selfological activities, the motions in our sensable organisms and/or sensors, and the movements of our sensable organisms and/or sensors are illusions simply because scientismists believe that only static spans or lengths of time are real.

The past and the future are believed to exist as durations in independence of the infinitesimal duration of the present. Some Creationists speculate that the present advances into the future so that the future becomes the present, retreats into the past so that the present becomes the past, while also remaining stationary as the present—which is absurd as well as paradoxical thinking.

It's not possible to realise durations because durations have no actual referent. "The specious present" is assumed to exist as the duration of 'the recent past' (Audi, 1995, p. 868). "The specious present" is also assumed to be the span in which 'we retain, instantaneously enjoy, as well as protend' (Hasanoglu, 2018, p. 189). Consequently, seconds, minutes, hours, and etcetera, are assumed to divide the past and the future into sections, while moments are the result of the belief that the present is dividable into sections.

There are no sectional durations of seconds, minutes, hours, days, and etcetera, just as there are no "holistic" durations like the past, the present, and the future in which sectional durations supposedly exist. There are no points or moments of time nor are there spans or durations of past, present, and future in which points or moments exist.

There are no durations of Continuity because Continuity is not time. Continuity isn't an attribute of eternity. Continuity is an attribute of Immediacy, not eternity, which is why we always continue immediately. We don't "present" how we are and who we aren't by way of what we are in a moment of time; rather, we activate the activities which are how we are and who we aren't by way of the activities which are what we are as we continue immediately.

The falsehood of considering seconds, minutes, hours, days, and etcetera, to be durations was developed from the false idea that the cycling of appearing bodies may be mathematically expressed by symbolising these cycles with geometrical figures.

For example, an analogue clock's dial is measured and calibrated so that numbers are assigned to these calibrations with the distances between them called seconds. The mistakenly labelled "second", "minute" and "hour" hands of an analogue clock cycle around the face of the clock. We're able to observe their continual cycling; however, such cycling isn't existent as the vibrating distances between the numbers 1 to 12 on the face of the clock because the cycling hands of the clock aren't these vibrating distances.

We're unable to use a day (symbolising the revolving distance of 24 hours) to express the Continuity of the earth cycling once around its axis and we're unable to use a year (symbolising the oscillating distance of 365 or 366 days) to express the Continuity of the earth cycling once around the sun. We're also unable to use the vibrating distances between a clock's numbers (which symbolise seconds, minutes, and hours) to express the cycling of the clock's hands.

The movements of phenomena aren't static lengths; therefore, we're unable to measure the movements of phenomena as static lengths or durations. We mistakenly refer to seconds, minutes, hours, and days as "durations" or "static lengths" instead of "vibrating distances". We often compare movements of phenomena to each other, but the movements of these phenomena aren't the vibrating distances over which they move. Consequently, phenomena cycle, but they only cycle as movements, not as durations, because the movement of an object is not a length.

Continuity is real because motions in a self's body are felt and continued by the self and Nature, while the movements of a self's body by the self and Nature are felt as well as observed to continue by the self. A motion is an effect of Nature's willing which we're only able to feel, not see, whereas a movement is manifested in the outer world by a body as either the sole effect of Nature's willing or the effect of a self's use of Nature's willing with Nature which may be seen as well as felt by this self. Consequently, a self feels—but doesn't see—volitional motions in its body; however, a self's volitional motions in a body are often used by the self to volition movements of its body which the self is able to see as well as feel.

We're able to compare a stop-watch hand's movement over the distance of its dial's area to a sprinter's movement over a distance on a racetrack; however, we're unable to measure the sprinter's movement with the stop-watch hand's movement. Our attempt to measure the movement of the sprinter with the measurement of the stop-watch hand's movement is based on the mistaken hypothesis or delusion that we're able to fix continually changing qualities as fixed quantities; therefore, measurement is impossible because things or qualities are unfixable.

The vibrating distance over which a Reality's movement happens is not this movement's duration because this movement is not the vibrating distance over which it's occurring, e.g., a sprinter's sprinting is not the vibrating distance over which the sprinter sprints; therefore, the vibrating distance sprinted by a sprinter is not the duration of the sprinter's sprinting. Consequently, durations are delusions.

Movement isn't a length or a duration because movement only occurs as the effect of Nature's Will in relation to a particle or a body (as well as a suef or a luef); therefore, durations aren't necessary for movements to occur. A moving body isn't a second distance, a minute distance, an hour distance, a day distance, and etcetera, because the moving body is not the distance over which the moving body is travelling. Seconds, minutes, hours, and days are the attempt to fix vibrating distances as unchanging units. The vibrating distances between outer numbers on a clock aren't "static distances" nor are the vibrations of a distance's particles "static movements" because the phrase, "static movements", is a contradiction in terms.

The speed and velocity of an object which we attribute to the object's movement are delusions or mistaken hypotheses, too, because the seconds, minutes, and hours which we attempt to use in measuring the movement of an object are simply reiterations of the distances travelled over by the moving object. The speed and velocity attributed to the movement of the object are mistaken hypotheses because they are a scientismist's attempt to measure an object's movement with the delusional units of seconds, minutes, and hours. The movement of an object occurs *over* a vibrating distance, not *as* this vibrating distance.

Interestingly, a light-year is based upon the *assumption* that light has a constant movement, but there is no way to confirm this assumption. It's possible that the movement of a photon of light has no limit to how fast it travels because the photon has no mass; therefore, the photon has no resistance to movement. Consequently, the notion of a light-year is without merit because we're unable to assess whether or not the fastness of light photons is constant.

We're unable to assess the fastness of an objective photon of light because we're unable to actually measure its fastness. We're unable to measure the fastness of an objective photon (or anything else) because speed and velocity are based on the mistaken assumption that the distance travelled over by a photon's movement *is* that photon's movement, which, of course, is not the case.

Photons are small apparitions, not particles, because they have no mass. Einstein's hypothesis of a 'massless particle' is a contradiction in terms (an oxymoron) because a particle is, by definition, a mass. This means that Einstein's interpretation of the photoelectric effect was mistaken because a beam of light is not analogous to a stream of bullets as Einstein maintained.

Our interpretations are often mistaken because an interpretation is a self's use of its ability of perception to develop concepts as possible explanations of realities based on its ideas.

Einstein assumed that an objective photon hits and bounces off an electron in a metal; therefore, he assumed that, when enough objective photons hit and bounce off enough jarred electrons in a flywheel, they move the flywheel by the force of the objective photons contact with the flywheel's metal. Einstein failed to understand that an objective photon is carried by the electromagnetism of Nature's Will; therefore, when the objective photon meets an electron in the flywheel's metal, the photon is translated into a suef which blends with the electron. After Nature has instinctively blended the translated suef with an electron, Nature's instinctive nondeliberate willing in the electromagnetic vitalism carrying the suef is transferred to the electron so that the electron is vitalised away from the metal. Nature's willing in this electromagnetic vitalism also pushes on the atoms of the flywheel so the flywheel moves.

An objective photon which meets an electron obliquely doesn't transfer its movement to the electron by "bouncing" off the electron so the flywheel is moved; rather, a photon is reflected from the electron without transferring electromagnetic vitality to the electron because the objective photon is not blended with the electron. Consequently, the photon is not translated by Nature's instinctive willing into a suef which means that the electron would not be given movement by the electromagnetic vitality of Nature.

The attempt to attribute a standardised vibrating distance over which a body is moving to the movement of this body is not possible because the vibrating distance and the moving body are isolated from each other, despite their relations to each other by way of Nature's willing; however, a self and/or Nature wills the immediate effect of a suef, a luef, a particle, or a body's movement as well as the immediate effect of vibration in bodies by varying anti-gravitational, magnetic, electric, and electroweak nuclear "pushes" on them as well as by varying gravitational, magnetic, electric, and strong nuclear "pulls" on them.

A body's movement is usually faster or slower than another body's movement which is demonstrated by sprinters who commence their bodies' movements in a 100 meter dash and vary in how quickly or how slowly they cover this distance. The starting and finishing of a stop-watch hand's movement over the small circular distance of the dial of the stop-watch may be compared to the starting of the movement of a sprinter's body over 100 meters and the sprinter's finishing of those 100 meters; therefore, the movement of the stop-watch hand may be compared to the movement of the sprinter's body—but only as we're observing both of these movements occurring together. We're not measuring duration or time; we're comparing two different movements *over* two different vibrating distances, not measuring these movements *as* these two different vibrating distances. These two different vibrating distances aren't delineations of two different durations (lengths of time) because they're vibrating distances, not durations.

We're only able to observe the difference in different movements *as they're occurring*; therefore, we're only able to compare the movements of racing sprinters *as we're observing them*. We're unable to compare these movements after a race has finished. We're only able to compare the vibrating distances over which the sprinter's movements occurred after the finishing of the race. We're unable to compare the racing of these sprinters after they've stopped racing.

The movements of a body occur immediately with Continuity, not durationally in time. The present supposedly endures in a series of moments. Immediacy doesn't endure in a series of moments. Immediacy simply continues. Immediacy is an immortal attribute of Nature. Immediacy *carries* Continuity, while Continuity is the *ongoingness* in and of its Immediacy.

The Now is delusionally supposed to be the absolute Moment encompassing the "static Perpetuity" of the Creator in which the past, present, and future are absent. Eternity is simply the delusion that static Perpetuity or infinite Duration is the expanse of the Creator's absolute Now, Moment, or Time.

Unlike a theist's nonsensical notion of the Creator, an atheist's sensible realisation of the Phenomenon (the Generator as well the Evolver, Grower, Developer, Deteriorator, and Devolver) and Its phenomena (the generated as well as the evolved, grown, developed, deteriorated, and devolved) results in the atheist's knowing and knowledge that Continuity in Immediacy is the attribute of the Phenomenon and phenomena.

The supposed endurance of a sprinter is a fiction, but the stamina of a sprinter is a truth. Stamina is developed, but stamina isn't endurance, because stamina results from a self's training of its body to continually move so the body's processing of oxygen becomes more efficient. Endurance is the delusion that the self's body is able to endure in a duration.

A stop-watch hand's movement happens as the movement of the sprinter's body happens. The stop-watch hand's movement and the sprinter's movement of his body on a racetrack are observed to happen together; however, the movement of the sprinter's body will vary as he increases the fastness of his body's movement from the starting block (which is mistakenly referred to as his or her "acceleration") whereas the stop-watch hand's movement is relatively unvaried. By applying the unstandardised vibrating distances travelled over by the relatively unvaried movement of the hand of the stop-watch to the standardised vibrating distance of 100 meters travelled over by the sprinter's movement of his body, we're able to compare these vibrating distances. The vibrating distance travelled over by the hand of the stop-watch isn't a duration of time because durations of time are only delusions which we attribute to vibrating distances.

Calculations of acceleration and deceleration are the delusions of physicists because calculations of an object's increasing fastness or decreasing fastness are based on the delusion that we are able to measure an object's movement as a duration. The delusional measurements of the vibrating distance on the dial of the stop-watch over which the hand of the stop-watch has moved and the delusional measurements of the vibrating distance over which the sprinter's body has moved are used by scientismists to calculate their delusions of acceleration and deceleration. The fairly constant movement of the hand of the stop-watch and the increasing fastness of the sprinter's body are unmeasurable; therefore, the calculations a scientismist makes based on his measurements are his delusions because his measurements are his delusions.

The fairly constant movement of the stop-watch hand is obviously not a duration used to measure the speed or velocity of a sprinter's body any more than the sprinter's increasingly fast movement is a duration; therefore, we're unable to use a stop-watch to measure the acceleration of the sprinter's body. We're able to compare the stop-watch hand's movement over the vibrating distance of the dial and the sprinter's movement over the vibrating distance of the racetrack's vibrating distance; however, we're only able to observe that the sprinter's movement is occurring over the racetrack more quickly than, more slowly than, or similarly to another sprinter's movement. We're unable to measure the increasing or decreasing fastness of these sprinters movements with the vibrating distance over which they're sprinting because the fastness of their sprinting isn't the vibrating distance of the racetrack which is delusionally measured as 100 meters.

If we use a different stop-watch for each sprinter to compare each stop-watch hand's movement to the movements of each sprinter, we might delusionally think we're able to measure the movement of each sprinter's body and that we're able to compare these measurements. The delusional units we attribute to a stop-watch dial's vibrating distance is compared to the delusional units we attribute to the vibrating distance over which every other stop-watch hand's movement happens. The delusional units we attribute to the vibrating distance over which the sprinters are moving their bodies is standardised or pre-set (100 delusional meters), while the delusional units we attribute to the vibrating distance over which each stop-watch hand moves, though calibrated, is not pre-set, because the vibrating distance travelled over by the stop-watch hand is dependent upon the movement of the respective sprinter's body over the vibrating distance of the racetrack.

The vibrating distance over which a stop-watch hand has moved is not a measurement of the associated sprinter's movement of his body. Rather, the vibrating distance over which the stop-watch hand has moved is a *tracking* of the movement of the associated sprinter's body.

Another example of the tracking of movement is a speedometer's needle which is used to track the movement of a car. The numbers on the speedometer's panel are assigned to measure the needle's movements as the car's speed. But these numbers have no relationship to the car's quickness of movement because they have no relation to the movement of the speedometer's needle. We're unable to use numbers to count a car's increasing or decreasing quickness because quickness doesn't happen in numbers. Consequently, we're only able to count objects, not the quickness of these objects.

A car's speedometer should really be called a "trackometer". We're able to track a car's movement by tracking its movement over a distance; however, we're unable to measure a car's movement as a speed over a vibrating distance by way of this vibrating distance because the movement of a car is not the vibrating distance over which the car is moving; therefore, we're unable to measure the movement of the car by, or as, this vibrating distance.

I know that I am repeating this message but this message bears repeating because we're gullibly convinced that we're able to measure an object's movement by the vibrating distance over which this object is moving.

The movement of a body is not the vibrating distance over which this body moves nor is it the measurement of this distance; therefore, we need to say that we're in a car moving *over* a vibrating distance, rather than that we're in a car moving *at* a speed, because speed is the delusional measurement of the vibrating distance travelled over by the car, not the movement of the car. We only believe that we're able to measure speed as a static distance on a road in kilometres (100) and relate this supposedly static distance to the supposedly static distance of 1 hour on a clock's face. We're unable to use speed to measure a car's movement because the car is not moving *at* a static speed, it's moving *over* a vibrating distance.

The movement of a reality only occurs over a vibrating or an oscillating distance, rather than as this distance; therefore, a reality's movement over a vibrating distance occurs continually, not as a short or long duration. If you don't understand why an object's movement occurs continually, rather than as a duration, you won't understand why time is a mistaken hypothesis which is why I am emphasising the fact that a vibrating as well as an oscillating distance is not the movement of an object over it.

Continuity in Immediacy is an extremely important attribute of phenomena. The movement of a phenomenon is only seen against the background of other phenomena existed by the Ether which are related to the phenomenon we see. If there are no other phenomena in the vicinity of a phenomenon, the continual movement of this phenomenon is not seen by us because there are no other moving phenomena to see in relation to this phenomenon's continual movement. Even if other phenomena are related to this phenomenon, we're unable to compare their oscillating distance to each other because the continual movements of these phenomena increase and/or decrease, continually; therefore, the oscillating distances over which they travel are never consistent.

An object's movement is not a length of space-time. There are no areas of space-time because space-time was Einstein's delusion. Ironically, it was Einstein's delusional belief that he could measure an object's movement with a vibrating distance that prompted him to conclude that an object's movement is an illusion in "empty space-time". Consequently, Einstein and Minkowski's hypothesis that they could measure an object's movement with lengths of empty areas of space-time was their delusion.

In my quest to understand time, I realised that the word "when" is not a reference to time; rather, the word "when" refers to a happening which *was* ongoing, a happening which *is* ongoing, and a happening which *might* ongoingly happen. Likewise, the word "then" doesn't refer to the past and the future; rather, the word "then" refers to a *memory* of a happening as well as an *anticipation* of a happening.

Happenings blend into each other; therefore, happenings aren't "separated" from each other. The current of a happening is only explicably given in Immediacy. *Consequently, what has happened before in a current, flow, or continuity in Immediacy is memorised by a self without need of an existent past; pas what might happen in a current, flow, or continuity in Immediacy is anticipated by a self without need of an existent future; and what is happening to a self in a current, flow, or continuity of Continuity in Immediacy is experienced by the self without need of an existent present.*

A happening is existent in a current activity of Continuity in Immediacy, while an event is an abrupt change which is supposed to occur in time. An event which is thought to occur with time in eternity is an individual's delusion because there is only Continuity in Immediacy, not time in eternity. There is no "present", "past" or "future" of time because the present, the past, and the future of time are only nominal, like time; however, Continuity is a real attribute of Reality, Phenomenon, or Nature's Immediacy.

The table, "The Truths of Continualists and the Falsehoods of Temporalists", contrasts the views of continualists and the views of temporalists.

The Truths of Continualists and the Falsehoods of Temporalists

The Truths of the Continualists	the Falsehoods of Temporalists
Immediacy	Now
Continuity	Time
Situation	Event
Happening	Moment
Current	Duration
Concurrency and Synconcurrency[7]	Simultaneity and synchronicity
When (currents, happenings, memories and anticipations)	When (past, present and future)
Then (memories and anticipations)	Then (the past and the future)
Actual	Present
Here[8] (a center of Nature)	Here (a position in bounded space)
Absolute motion and movement	Stillness of position

Although Freedom is an enlightened individual's Ultimate Truth, wisdom is a close second. We're unable to use faith to free up our wisdom because an unenlightened individual has to subjectively *prove* that his Ultimate Truth is his appropriate basis for knowledge and is not his *inappropriate hypothesis* before he is able to free up his tendency to express Nature's Will in harmony with

---

[7] Concurrency is the reality of situations occurring together as continuities in Immediacy whereas simultaneity is the fiction that events occur together "at the same time"; therefore, Carl G. Jung's hypotheses of eternity in time and synchronicities were the result of mistaken reasoning because only Continuity in Immediacy and Synconcurrencies are attributes of situations.

[8] You aren't a soul existent in the "here" and "now" of God's "eternal" existence. You're simply a centralized "here" of Nature continuing immediately within Nature's Existenceexistent as an existing existent of Nature.

Nature's harmony; therefore, we need to set out on a quest to understand time so we're able to understand time has no referent in Reality. Only then are we able to realise The Ultimate Truth of Freedom which is only appropriately defined as the nonliberal nonlicentious basis of Nature which enables every self to deliberately and noninstinctively use Nature's Will in harmony or disharmony with Nature's spontaneous instinctive nondeliberate use of Its Will to cognizantly and knowingly choose whether to act and react with spontaneously unselfish conscientious liberty or impulsively selfish unconscientious licentiousness.

Einstein's delusion was that there are only laws that determine our actions and reactions. Like his favourite philosopher, Baruch Spinoza, Einstein believed Nature or "God" was the impersonal "being" of mysticism in which all uncreated laws were real, not the personal Creator whom Creationists suppose determine everything by laws that "he" supposedly created.

Einstein superstitious belief in the uncreated laws of Nature was just as naïve as the superstitious belief of Creationists in their Creator's created laws. Einstein thought that metaphysics was the study of being without consideration of the Supreme Being; therefore, Einstein's "God" wasn't the "Supreme Being" of theism. Einstein's God was the "impersonal being" he referred to as "Nature". Einstein referred to "God" as "being" or "Nature", not understanding that Nature is impersonal Thingness, not impersonal being.

Einstein, knew, as I do, that the personal Creator is only a myth. I suspect that Einstein only used the word, 'God', to refer to "being" or "Nature" because he wanted to avoid the hassle that would have come from certain Creationists who were prejudiced and didn't like atheists, like Einstein.

I understand the reluctance of atheists to argue with Creationists because I'm an atheist who has experienced the verbal attacks of Creationists simply because I disagree with their religious absolute. They are so threatened by anyone who disagrees with their religious absolute that they forget all about loving people who disagree with them even though love is the most important value of their religion. Surprisingly (and quite ironically), I've found most atheists express even more hatred of me than most theists because my stance that Atheism is a religion according to my definition of religion, rather than an irreligion (which is the stance of most atheists), is so threatening to their desire to keep from examining their philosophical preconceptions and assumptions that they immediately attack me, rather than question their inadequate preconceptions and assumptions.

Einstein's metaphysical notion of impersonal being under-laid his "block universe theory" which is the theory that space is bounded and has three dimensions of length, height, and width as well as a fourth dimension of time in which the "block" of all things (the universe) happens. Einstein didn't understand that Nature has no dimensions because dimensions are only mathematical delusions existed by us in our cognitions; therefore, dimensions are delusions that we have about Nature *because they aren't actually existed by Nature.*

The block universe theory is incompatible with our need to remember a happening because we wouldn't need to remember if events were actually in the past. The block universe theory is also incompatible with our need to anticipate a happening because we wouldn't need to anticipate if events existed in the future. At least Einstein didn't believe that events are actually existed in the future; therefore, Einstein's block universe theory differs from that of some eternalists who believe that the future is "already written".

Einstein seemed to believe that the future is an emptiness, which differentiates Einstein's thinking from that of eternalists. Eternalists' theories of time are compatible with the absurd belief that we're able to know in advance what will happen; therefore, what is possible and impossible as well as what is probable (likely) or improbable (unlikely) would not be necessary. These eternalists believe, absurdly, that we're able to work towards activating a memory, a possibility, a probability, or an improbability as a happening while concurrently believing that this happening is either a fated or a destined event in the future which we're also, paradoxically, supposed to be free to choose as either our fate or our destiny.

We develop possible, probable, and improbable guesses about situations which might occur. We're able to work towards activating a course of action in our behaviour based on our guesses about situations which might happen.

The belief of eternalists that our behaviours are already existent in the future is absurd because we would know the future if our future behaviours were already existent. There would also be no need for us to develop memories or be surprised if this were the case. If our behaviour already existed in the past, present, and future, we would have no need to remember memories, anticipate possible and probable courses of action, or be surprised by improbable happenings because the Creator would have given us "pre-knowledge" (a priori knowledge), "foreknowledge" (the knowledge of what will or has to happen), as well as current knowledge (the only knowledge we are really able to have).

If we had pre-knowledge and foreknowledge, our memories, anticipations, and surprises would not occur. We would have no need to memorise our pre-knowledge and our foreknowledge because they would have been placed in our memory store when the Creator created us. If we actually had the abilities of foreknowledge and pre-knowledge, all predictions and prophecies would be accurate.

Ontologists know that predictions and prophecies aren't accurate because the prophecies of religionists and the predictions of scientismists have met with dismal failure. Most scientismists make predictions and most religionists make prophecies with abandon. The prophecies of religionists are just "dressed up predictions", while the predictions of scientismists are simply "naked prophecies". Predictions aren't scientific because we're unable to know what will happen in advance; therefore, a true scientist abandons her desire to predict because she knows better than to engage in prophecy. A true scientist simply makes guesses about what *might* happen because she knows that there is no fated or destined future.

The inevitable, like the death of our bodies, is not a prediction or a prophecy because the inevitable is simply a reality of Nature which selves (generated by, from, and in Nature) are incapable of avoiding or evading, like the deaths of their sensable organisms, whereas predictions and prophecies are delusionally based on the illusion of laws. Even a suicidal woman or a suicidal man aren't able to predict the death of their bodies because other people might act to intervene in their attempt to kill their bodies.

If pre-knowledge and foreknowledge were ours, we would not need to choose a course of action. We would have no need to choose a course of action because our actions would be either fated or destined; therefore, we would not have the Freedom to develop in our use of Nature's Will because we would not be able to choose. If we actually had pre-knowledge and foreknowledge, we would not be free to alter our relationships.

Physicists refer to the actions in the Infiniverse as indeterminate, rather than "infatal". "Infatalism" is a word I've coined meaning "the lack of fate", just as the word "indeterminism" means "the lack of determinism". Indeterminism is even a truth of scientismistic quantum physicists because Freedom is the Ultimate Truth of Nature.

Nature's use of Its instinctive willing is random because It wills without intention and purpose as well as non-unintentionally and non-purposelessly; however, a self's use of Nature's Will is intentional and purposeful as well as unintentional and purposeless because, unlike Nature, a self has the ability to know what is happening; therefore, a self is able to develop goals in relation to what's happening so that it's able to intend or purpose its way towards these goals as well as simply "let things happen" in unintentionally and purposelessly relating to what's happening without setting goals.

When a self has the insight that its knowing is its ability by which it knows that it's the knower of its experience, it is self-realised and on its way towards developing a basic pattern of knowledge and a wise understanding of this pattern, but the further step of always attempting to act and behave in accord with the harmony of Nature is the final step necessary to attaining sanity so this self's wisdom is not just its pretension.

Nature instinctively wills in absolute Freedom to indeterminately initiate what will happen. Nature doesn't deterministically, predeterministically, or compatibilistically use Its Will. We *choose* between the orientations of indeterminism (absolute Freedom), determinism (fatalism), predeterminism (destiny), and compatibilism (the combination of relative freedom and relative determinism). Obviously, we're free to choose between these orientations because indeterminism (absolute Freedom) is The Ultimate Truth.

Determinism is the mistaken hypothesis that events are fated to occur by way of the uncreated laws of Nature, while predeterminism is the mistaken hypothesis that the Creator has used his will to create laws by which he has planned our destinies as inevitable events. Compatibilism is the mistaken hypothesis that we're determined by the laws of Nature, but that "somehow" we have our own free wills and are able to use our own free wills to choose between fate and Freedom.

If we were determined by Natural Law, it would be impossible for us to be free. The compatibilist's hypothesis that we're free as well as fated is absurd because we have to be *either* absolutely free *or* absolutely fated. We're unable to be relatively free *as well as* relatively fated because we're not free if we're fated nor are we fated if we're free.

You're able to escape your conditioning by other people; however, your selfpathic desire to condition your actions and behaviours by attempting to moralise your conscience needs to be transcended by you so you're completely free of the attempt to condition your conscience and thereby your actions and behaviours. In this way, you're able to act and behave conscientiously in Freedom because you're not disintegrally conditioning your conscientious integrity with laws that you use in the absurd belief that you're able to "control" the supposed "Controller" of your destiny and/or fate which you think is either "God" or the "Laws of Nature".

Determinism is a delusion, just as predeterminism is a delusion. We're only able to describe Nature by the terms "indeterministic", "infatalistic" and "undestined" because Nature's instinctive way of willing isn't planned.

There isn't anything that is determinately or pre-determinately evolved and grown by Nature. This includes particles because Nature indeterminately evolves particles and grows them into bodies; therefore, Nature indeterminately wills. In other words, Nature instinctively wills with Freedom. Unfortunately, Freedom is The Ultimate Truth which confuses many scientismistic physicists.

Erwin Schrödinger's scientismistic interpretation of "Schrödinger's cat paradox" demonstrates how easily quantum physicists are confused. Schrödinger's cat paradox is a "mind" experiment in which a cat (a symbolisation of a "subatomic particle") is supposedly trapped in an air-tight box containing a radioactive atom with a fifty-fifty chance of decaying within the hour so that, if it decays, the radiation of particles from it will trigger a relay that will cause a hammer to fall and break a glass container holding a sufficient amount of prussic acid to kill the cat's body. What confounds physicists is that they want to know the "point in time" when the cat's body will die.

Many quantum physicists believe, absurdly, that the time of death of the cat's body is equally likely or unlikely to happen because the cat's body is unable to be seen by the experimenter. It was Schrödinger who first leaped to the paradoxical and absurd assumption that the cat's body in the box (symbolising a particle that physicists are unable to see) is neither killed nor unkilled because it's only killed or unkilled when the experimenter opens the box and sees (observes) the cat's body. The observation of the cat's body is an analogy for a physicist's measurement of observable traces in a medium left by (what has to be) a particle's movements; however, like the cat's body in the unopened box, we're unable to see a particle that leaves traces in a medium; however, we're *subjectively* certain that it's a particle.

Instead of examining their basic assumption that time is real, physicists who disagree with Schrödinger's proposal tend to attack only the idea of eternalism inherent in this paradox (which is that the cat's body in the box is neither killed nor unkilled) without examining the idea of time. If these physicists honestly examined their hypotheses of time as well as eternalism, they would sooner or later understand that these hypotheses were their mistakes. These scientismists would realise that there is no need to postulate a present moment in which the cat's body is killed or unkilled because the cat's body in the box is obviously killed or unkilled in Immediacy—whether or not they see its killing or unkilling.

Our inability to see everywhere is not a challenge for us to solve; rather, we need to accept this inability as the limiting factor to our knowledge. In other words, we aren't ubiquitous; therefore, we're unable see everything everywhere. Even if we were able see everywhere, some things, like some suefs, aren't seeable.

Physicists believe that either random process or the act of observing the cat's body (the particle) in Schrödinger's cat paradox results in the killing of the cat's body (the death of the particle) or the unkilling of the cat's body. Physicists fail to understand that the killing or unkilling of the cat's body (the death of the particle or continued existing of the particle by Nature) is not determined by observation because observation is an activity of introspection, not a behaviour.

Our activity of observing (seeing something) "takes in" rather than "gives out"; therefore, our observing is an action of taking in, not a behaviour of giving out; however, as Jean-Paul Sartre demonstrated in his book, *Being and Nothingness*, by training the pupils of your eyes on the pupils of another self's eyes, you make it obvious to the other self that you're attempting to look into this self's depths. As a result, the other self might generate emotions that influence the understanding or misunderstanding with which it's conducting its behaviour. Of course, it's a mistake to compare the body of a cat with a particle because the particle isn't inhabited by a self, like the cat.

Selves are existed by Nature as well as use Nature's Will to exist. But particles are unable to use Nature's Will to exist; therefore, particles don't have the ability to exist, even though they are existents.

A particle's decay is random because particles are instable; therefore, sooner or later, a particle decondenses and returns to pure (immaterial) Matter. The instability of the particle leads to its "unsettledness" so Nature's indeterminate instinctive willing in the particle activates the particle's departiclisation.

Nature purposelessly and goallessly wills as It kinesthetically develops the motion of particlisation in portions of the Energy It is. Nature is unable to stabilise the instability of particles; therefore, Nature's departiclisation of particles is inevitable. Consequently, every particle is sooner or later departiclised by Nature

Nature is unable to cognise how we realise because Nature hasn't the abilities to realise or know. We need the absolute Freedom to cognise, know, or realise; however, Nature freely and instinctively wills in us so we can deliberately use Its instinctive willing in our ability of cognising to work towards initiating a possible, a probable, or an improbable happening.

We need to develop our ability of realising because it's a vital ability contributing to our development of wisdom. We begin to develop wisdom by realising insights, such as the insight that Nature is unable to develop insights.

Thales of Miletus was a pre-Socratic philosopher who existed in fifth century B.C. Thales was the first "natural philosopher". The Greek natural philosophers were the pre-cursors to our modern day scientismists. Thales is known for developing the basis of Western scientism and the study of "physical cosmology". Thales claimed that the supposed order of the universe must be explained by "natural" events and laws, rather than by supernatural means.

Thales' thought that the order of the universe was explained by events and laws. Order, events, and laws were Thales' delusions because they're artificialities of human cogitating, not primary properties existed by Nature. Organisation-disorganisation-reorganisation, occurrences, and happenings are the primary properties of Nature. Thales failed to understand what the real primary properties of Nature were because he didn't understand that order, events, and laws were concepts of supernaturalists. Thales belief in order, events, and laws, led him to ignore organisation-disorganisation-reorganisation, occurrences, and happenings.

Organisation-disorganisation-reorganisation, occurrences, and happenings (of selves) are the natural results of Nature's willing in the inevitability of the realities It is always immediately continuing to generate as well as evolve, grow, develop, deteriorate and devolve. Nature is unable to activate order, events, and laws in the Infiniverse because order, events, and laws are mistaken hypotheses. Order, events, and laws are only actual as a self's mistaken cogitations; therefore, they aren't existed by Nature.

For example, there are no laws of motion because motion unlawfully occurs according to Nature's instinctive willing. A self is able to guide its use of Nature's Will; however, it is unable to guide Nature's use of Its Will or any other self's use of Nature's Will.

Unfortunately, Thales borrowed the mistaken hypotheses of order, events, and laws from superstitious religionists who believed in fate and destiny. As a result, the scientismists who descended from Thales developed the insane desire to see Nature in terms of order, events, and laws without understanding the basis of their stance. Like Thales, these scientismists ignored their ability to see Nature in terms of organisation-disorganisation-reorganisation, occurrences, and happenings. Consequently, Thales' hypotheses need to be re-evaluated.

Einstein's Special Theory of Relativity is based on Thales' delusions of order, events, and laws. Einstein's premise was that the laws of physics are the same for any frame of reference in which the events of his finite universe were supposed to be ordered. Einstein's Special Theory of Relativity was based on his assumption that the movement of light is constant and may be used to measure simultaneous events in a frame of reference by using light as a means of measurement; however, Einstein also assumed that an observer in another frame of reference who uses light to measure the same events in the original frame of reference will find that these events aren't occurring simultaneously. Einstein failed to understand that events don't occur simultaneously depending on our frame of reference because we're unable to use light to measure whether events (which aren't existent) are simultaneous or located in different "times" for the obvious reason that the times of time in eternity are no more existent than time in eternity.

Situations in the Infiniverse interact either concurrently or Synconcurrently. Synconcurrency is the meaningful co-incidence of concurrent situations happening together in Immediacy.

Synchronicity was supposed by Carl G. Jung, the Swiss psychiatrist, to be the meaningful co-incidence of simultaneous events happening together at the same time; therefore, synchronicity was Jung's mistaken hypothesis because time was his mistaken hypothesis. Time is only an individual's delusion; therefore, neither simultaneity nor synchronicity are able to be established by an individual.

There are no events existed in a relative space; therefore, there are no events which could interact at the same time. Rather, infinite situations happen in the unbounded Ether by interacting concurrently or Synconcurrently in Immediacy.

Einstein not only assumed that the movements of "events" are relative to the constant movement of light, but also assumed that the laws of physics he developed (which were the result of his daydreaming) were actual and invariant. Einstein's laws aren't facts because they were only fictional hypotheses in Einstein's cognition. His laws weren't facts because they have no actual referents. Nor are Einstein's laws invariant because other physicists alter Einstein's laws to fit the new theories they develop.

Two other pre-Socratics, Zeno of Elea and Parmenides had their speculations adapted by other Western scientismists to fit Thales speculation that Nature was governed by order, events, and laws. Zeno attempted to demonstrate the paradoxical results of combining movement, space, and time by developing his four paradoxes. As already mentioned, his hypothesis was that movement in space was impossible because time and space render movement impossible. Western scientismists agree with Zeno. They think that movement is impossible because they mistakenly think that time is a truth without having any sensible reason for thinking so.

Zeno's paradoxes are transformations of Parmenides' deductions concerning metaphysics. Parmenides' metaphysics is not known in completeness because we only have fragments of a didactic poem that Parmenides wrote. We have no other writings of Parmenides. The first part of this poem is called "Truth" in which 'Parmenides argues that "the real" or "what is" or "being" (to eon) must be ungenerable and imperishable, indivisible and unchanging' (Audi, 1995, p. 646), while in the second part of this poem, called "Opinions", Parmenides expounds "a dualistic cosmology" which may be 'intended as candid phenomenology—a doctrine of appearances—or as an ironic foil to "Truth"' (Audi, 1995, p. 647).

Western scientismists who are metaphysically and secularly oriented, rather than religiously oriented, tend to adjust Parmenides' dualistic cosmology to Thales' mistakenly hypothesised laws of Nature. Some Western scientismists absurdly conclude that movement is impossible in Nature because they mistakenly hypothesise that time and laws are natural, rather than observe that movements are natural. They fail to understand that time and laws are only their myths, since our continuity and needs motivate us subjectively, not time and laws.

Laws are delusions we develop because we delusionally attempt to control our impulsivity by using our intellects rather than realise we are only able to guide, not control, our impulsivity by using Nature's Will.

Western scientismists stubbornly refuse to give up their prejudice that there is no need to re-examine the bases of Western philosophy, like their prejudice that the ability to create is real, because they fear starting to reason from an entirely new basis. To recognise Nature's Will as the new basis of science provokes too much fear in Western scientismists because they would need to think and reason *on their own in isolation* without the support of authorities who continue to perpetuate mistaken hypotheses, like time and Creation. Their fear of isolation is a barrier to their development of knowledge because only the courage to face isolation is an effective conduit in developing knowledge.

But what is the answer to the question that I asked earlier in this essay which was, "Exactly what is the factor that stimulates us to make the futile attempt to measure movement?" This question requires a second question which is, "What is the illusory experience of which time is the mistaken analogy?"

Conclusion

Time (according to Einstein and Minkowski) is the false belief that there is an infinite World line which is divisible into sections containing infinitesimal points. It needs to be emphasised that these mathematical constructs are *objective scientismistic analogues* of fictional infinitesimal moments (infinitesimal points), an infinite Duration (the World line), and sectional durations (divisible sections of the World line). These fictions are *myths* which we have used to plan our building of certain artefacts, e.g., analogue clocks which have vibrating distances between and including the sixty markings of their circular dials.

Time is the result of the creation myths or fantasies which all religions, but Selfism, have promoted ever since the first anthropoid rose up on its hind legs to usher in the human species. Myths are our fantasies, imaginings, or hallucinations about how we came to exist. Myths are told by people who may not remember that these myths were the fantasies of selves on earth as well as selves in the after-death, that is, if selves are immortal and the after-death exists. Many religionists assert that the myths told by their ancestors are truths, rather than myths. Our ancestors either imagined these myths or had these myths revealed to them by selves from ethereal realms of the after-death who were as naïve as our ancestors, although, unlike our ancestors on earth, they would have known that they were immortal.

If unscrupulous selves from the after-death exist, they pretended (and continue to pretend) to be God or messengers of God; therefore, when they related to our ancestors our naïve ancestors didn't question their integrity. If our ancestors really were in contact with selves from realms in the after-death, they accepted their myths as truths, rather than fictions, simply because they were too scared of "the gods" to question their Game.

The selves of the after-death (if the after-death is existent) first developed the myth that God was the Creator when they existed on their planets in the Infiniverse. When their bodies died, these selves related the myth of the Creator to our ancestors. They persuaded our ancestors to write scripture while continuing to reinforce these myths in us by communicating with us from the after-death. As a result, we tend to be deluded by their communications with us as well as by scripture (or only by scripture if we're mortal, rather than immortal).

It's important to recognise that, if selves exist in the after-death, they first developed on planets in the Infiniverse. After their sensable bodies died, they would have continued on in their objective large uncondensed energy forms in the unboundedness of the Ether; therefore, Yahweh, who likes to be called "God" (if he exists), had his start as a self on a planet, like earth, in a multicellular body. Yahweh's multicellular sensable organism would have died so that he continued on in his sensor where he sooner or later became the leader of a pantheon of selves in the after-death who all compete in The Game of the Gods.

If Yahweh ever existed and continues to exist, he took the title of "the Creator", which, of course, was his lie. Yahweh would have conspired with his pantheon of selves to promote his lie amongst the selves who existed in sensable organisms on earth because he wants to govern the infinite ethereal realms of the after-death. Yahweh would have spread his fiction that he was the Creator of the ethereal realms of his "Heaven" (his after-death) as well as the Creator of earth to his Jewish prophets.[9] Yahweh wouldn't want it known that he only exists as a center of Nature, in and by way of Nature, who used to inhabit a sensable organism because his fiction that he is the Creator would have been revealed as his lie.

The myth-makers of earth know that their myths are not just their own developments if we're immortal. These myth-makers know that their thinking is either freely developed by them or "riding" on thinking which is not their own; however, they often suffer from the delusion that their myths are the result of their "Creator's" thinking, instead of their all too mistaken thinking or the all too mistaken thinking of selves in ethereal realms of the after-death who persuade them to listen to their mythical stories.

When a self who inhabits a human body listens uncritically to what seems to be the objective voice of a self from an ethereal realm of the after-death, its fictious explanation of how we were created and how the universe was created given to a self who inhabits its human body on earth will tend to convince the embodied self on earth that the self from the ethereal Realm is just as superstitious as this gullible embodied self who rarely questions the so-called "knowledge" of selves from the after-death; therefore, it will likely believe that a myth told to it by a self from the after-death is a prophetic truth, instead of just a fantasy.

For example, Moses related Yahweh's "Truth" to his followers that he (Yahweh) was the Creator without critically examining this "Truth's" validity because Moses never suspected that Yahweh was only "spinning a tale".

---

[9] "Finite" is the root word of the word "infinity"; therefore, infinity is related to its contents, each of which is finite; however, the word "unbounded" has the word "bound" as its root word, which is related to expanse, rather than contents. Therefore, "unboundedness" is the proper word to use in describing the Ether because infinity is existent in the unlimited expanse of the Ether. "Infinity" is the proper word to use in describing the Infiniverse because the Infiniverse is unlimited in its infinity of finitely structured contents.

Like the myth that risen, not "unfallen", angels are always perfectly good, a duration is the myth that a motion or a movement is a length or a section of the World line, while moments are the myths that infinitesimal points compose these sections. The fiction of a duration comes from the experience of waiting for a happening to develop, while the fiction of a moment or a now comes from the experience of focusing your attention on a specific happening. Waiting for a happening to develop so we're able to focus our attention on it puts us either in an activity of suspense or a repressed activity of boredom.

When we're waiting for an incident to happen, we say we're "enduring" the experience of waiting. When we're focusing our attention on a specific happening, we say we're "in the now" or "in the moment"; however, there is no duration in which we're enduring the experience of waiting (just as there is no experience of enduring). There is also no moment to be in when we're focusing our attention on a specific happening because moments and durations of time in eternity are simply a delusional scientismist's mistaken attempt to eliminate happenings and occurrences, the currents of Continuity in Immediacy, from the scrutiny of fairly biased selves.

We're activities of Activity. It's important to realise that suefs and particles are also activities because the motions in them and their external movements are only activated by Nature or a self, like you or I. Motions are activities within Potentiality (Activity or Nature) which are activated by this Potentiality.

Motions are the effected by activities of a self's cognitive activities which the self uses to effect motions in the self's sensor as well as its sensable organism. Motions happen in suefs and particles as well as in luefs and bodies. Consequently, a self is either an immortal or a mortal who expresses the activity it is by using Nature's Will in the activities of its selfological world, while the self's sensable organism is a mortal thing in which the self uses Nature's Will to activate motions in as well as movements of it..

A self is either an immortal or a mortal who uses Nature's Will to stimulate actions and through these actions stimulate energetics in its sensor which is existent between the energy of its cognition and the condensed energies of its brain which, in turn, stimulates inner motions in the self's brain as well as inner motions in nerves relating its brain to the rest of its body. These inner motions in the self's body result in the movements of its body if so needed or desired. All stimulations are the result of Nature's willing or a self's use of Nature's Will in tandem with Nature; therefore, "stimulation" is simply a word to describe an effect of Will.

An activator is a self who activates its cognition. An activator doesn't act in durations existed between moments of time because an activator continues without enduring. Nature never ceases to instinctively Will; therefore, Nature is the Activity which is always instinctively willing as the Activity It is.

Nature's instinctive willing in suefs and particles keeps these suefs and particles in continual inner motion as well as in continual outer movement. Nature's instinctive willing absolutely motions Its suefs and particles.

Nature's movement of bodies is also absolute. In other words, the stillness of bodies is an illusion. A body's inner elements are always in absolute motion (absolute process or absolute activity) even when the body has died because the corpse of a vegetative or a sensable organism decays, while a dead mineral organism, like a rock, disintegrates, which means that the particles of a mineral, vegetative, or sensable organism are always in motion, i.e., particles are always vibrating.

A body is never still. A body only seems to be still because of our limited view of it. If our focus is expanded to include the earth as a whole, the bodies on the earth are always seen to be moving. Our bodies aren't still, even though we may not be moving them.

For example, people who see me typing on my laptop at my table in the restaurant in which I am currently sitting may mistakenly hypothesise that I'm sitting still because their view is limited to the inside of this restaurant; however, if they expand their view by lifting off the earth in one of NASA's rockets so they're orbiting the earth, they're able to see (through a telescope) that all the bodies on earth, including my body sitting in this restaurant, are moving with the earth as it revolves around its axis. Not only this, all the bodies on earth are also moving with the earth around the sun, with the sun around the Milky Way galaxy, and so on; therefore, Nature is always instinctively willing my body to move, even though I may not be moving my body.

Although your view would be expanded if you were lifted off the earth in one of NASA's rockets, you would not be in a different "frame of reference" as Einstein thought because separate spaces aren't real any more than inseparable spaces are real. Space isn't real; therefore, space isn't dividable into "frames of reference". Only the Ether is existent; therefore, spaces or frames of reference to which physicists are so fond of alluding simply don't exist.

Because my body is always moving even when it appears to be still, there is no such thing as a position because a position is supposedly the fixed location of an unmoving body or a particle; therefore, the attempt of physicists to measure a particle's quantity of movement or its "momentum" is not their only delusion. Their attempt to measure the particle's position is also their delusion because Nature's movement of a particle is absolute. A thing simply isn't positioned. Unlike a thing, Thingness is unmovable because of Its unboundedness; however, Thingness is not still because Thingness is Activity.

In quantum theory, Werner Heisenberg's uncertainty principle is 'the claim that certain "conjugate" quantities, such as position and momentum, cannot be simultaneously "determined" to arbitrary degrees of accuracy' (Audi, 1995, pp. 702–703). The uncertainty principle is even more damaging to quantum mechanics than Heisenberg believed because it's not just that position and momentum aren't concurrently measurable that is at the root of the uncertainty principle; it's that position and momentum aren't measurable *at all* that is the root of a physicist's uncertainty. It's also interesting to note that Heisenberg's principle of uncertainty is as delusional as the simultaneities of time because we only have a need to be certain, not a need for an uncertainty "principle". Finally, we only have *concurrencies of Continuity in Immediacy*, not "simultaneities of time in eternity".

The preceding words were written in response to the questions asked before the start of this chapter's conclusion. The first question asked was, "Exactly what is the factor that stimulates us to make the futile attempt to measure movement?" However, by answering the second question, we're able to answer the first. The second question was, "What is the illusory experience of which time is the mistaken analogy?"

Nature is the purposeless and goalless Activity which activates absolute motions and movements; therefore, stillness is an illusory perspective which resulted in the delusion of time because stillness is the illusory experience of which time is the mistaken analogy. Stillness is a self's illusion resulting from its limited view of a situation because every situation is either an unchanging activity or a changing activity, not an unchanging inactivity (an unchanging stillness) or a changing activity. Many people believe that stillness is a reality, rather than an illusion, because they've never transcended their limited view or perspective; therefore, "stillness" is the answer to my second question, "What is the illusory experience of which time is the mistaken analogy?"

Developed by way of our limited view of our surroundings, our perspective of stillness is our illusory experience; therefore, we mistakenly hypothesised time to explain our perception of stillness as actual. However, stillness isn't actual because the actual is active. Consequently, a scientismist's hypothesis that time is real is his delusion because he bases his hypothesis on his illusory perspective of stillness.

Stillness is an illusion because we're not always able to observe that phenomena are absolute activities; however, we're capable of knowing that stillness is illusory. Unfortunately, people may also ignore that stillness is an illusion which results in their mistaken hypothesis that stillness is actual.

The seeming stillness of a corpse is an illusion which stimulates a self's anxiety. The self usually doesn't want to know that stillness is just its mistaken perspective because it knows that the self of the corpse has ceased to move this corpse (although Nature continues to move it). Every self has a compelling need to understand what happens to it when its body dies and turns into a corpse. Consequently, "death" is the answer to my first question which was, "Exactly what is the factor that stimulates us to make the futile attempt to measure movement?"

The absolute movement of bodies is continual because Nature is absolute Activity. Nature activates the continual motions in and movements of particles and bodies. The movement of bodies is continual because movement is never still; therefore, movement is unmeasurable because the mistaken hypothesis of measurement is derived from the contradictory idea of "still movement" or "static movement". Measurement is the delusion that the particles composing these distances are still, rather than vibratory, and that we're able to fix these distances into units.

Because the particles of a body are always in vibrating motion in the body and free particles are always in movement in the phenomenal world, there is a structure to a body, but not an *unchanging* structure to the body, because the body's structural elements are always absolutely vibrating. There is only a continually changing structure to a body whether it's a mineral organism, a vegetable organism, or a sensable organism.

Isaac Newton based his scientism on the model of the machine because he thought the Universe was infinite and unchanging as a structured Machine. The Creator is supposed to have made this Universal Machine from indestructible atoms which he created in time with laws that govern time. In other words, the Creator is supposed to have deliberately willed the creation of laws which he used to create time and, finally, used to create indestructible solidities or "matters". Then the Creator supposedly used these indestructible matters to construct the mechanical Machine that Newton mistakenly hypothesised was his infinite Universe, not understanding that an "infinite Universe" is an oxymoron, since infinity is the unlimited whereas a universe is a limited amount.

The idea of indestructible matters comes from the belief that a particle is an indestructible solid (which is obviously a falsehood because portions of unbounded Matter are only impermanently condensed as solids by way of the instinctive nondeliberate willing of Nature). These condensed matters aren't invulnerably and immortally condensed as solids; therefore, they're destructible solids, not indestructible solids.

Atoms were originally defined as indestructible solids or what I call indestructible "materialisations". While unmaterialised Matter is indestructible, the solid materialised portions of Matter are destructible so that, sooner or later, their materialisation is dematerialised and they blend with the unmaterialised Matter from which they were evolved, grown, and developed; therefore, a materialisation of unmaterialised Matter is a destructible "materialisation" despite the indestructibility of unmaterialised Matter.

Isaac Newton's belief that his "infinite Universe" was created as a still mechanical Machine was the result of Newton's supposition that time was the "mechanism" that preceded motion in creation. Newton believed that his mechanical infinite Universe existed in stillness before it was put into movement by his Creator's use of laws; therefore, Newton thought that motion (which he should have called "movement") was to be understood mechanically because, supposedly, the time of Newton's still Universal Machine was the mechanism by which Newton ridiculously believed that movement occurred by way of his Three Laws of Motion.

Newton viewed movement to be a quantitative physical force, rather than a qualitative effect of Nature's instinctive nondeliberate willing and a self's noninstinctive deliberate or instinctive nondeliberate use of Nature's Will. Newton's Three Laws of "Motion" (by which he really meant The Three Laws of Movement) are based upon his delusion that movement is a quantity of force.

Newton's Three Laws of Motion are only useful because they give scientismists a paradigm to use so that they may attempt to manipulate their environment. Although this paradigm is useful, it's not reasonable nor is it true. Newton's word for the study of motion is "mechanics"; however, mechanics is actually the study of how to *quantise* movement. Newton's labelling of the study of motion as "mechanics" rather than "*organics*" wasn't realised to be an absurdity by Einstein because Einstein believed that Nature operated automatically, rather than voluntarily.

Unlike Newton, who believed that God created his infinite Universe, Einstein believed that Nature created his finite universe. Unlike Newton, Einstein thought his universe was an illusion governed by Natural Law. Einstein ignored Nature's Will which is, obviously, the way of real geological and biological change. Consequently, his general and specific theory of relativity led to the peculiar physics of quantum mechanics based on the absurdities of quantities and time and his denial of Nature's willing.

Like Newtonian mechanics, quantum mechanics is a paradigm based on the unreasonable and untrue premise that continually changing qualities may be measured and converted to unchanging quantities of time. Scientismistic physicists are the "mechanics" of quantum mechanics who ignore the truth that unchanging quantities are their delusions because they're in denial of the qualities which are continually changing or unchanging activities.

For example, heaviness is continual, but it's never an unchanging inactivity, because heaviness is dependent upon the vitality of gravity-antigravity in which Nature wills the pull-push within and without all moving bodies. Bodies are all moving in relation to one another; therefore, Nature's instinctive willing in Its vital gravity-antigravity will work in them continually in relation to their movements towards or away from each other so that gravity-antigravity fields result in and around unbodied particles as well as in and around bodied particles.

Your weight on your bathroom scale is not just the result of Nature's willed waves of gravity-antigravity in and around the earth interacting with the vitality of gravity-antigravity in and around your body because the vitality of gravity-antigravity is in and around the sun, the moon, and the earth; therefore, the earth spirals with the moon as well as with the sun. The gravity-antigravity fields in and around the moving moon and sun are interrelated with the gravity-antigravity fields in and around the moving earth, in and around your body standing on the scale, and in and around the scale that's tracking your heaviness. Consequently, you're unable to measure your weight with a scale because the needle meant to "fix" your heaviness as the scale's measurement of your weight is always vibrating back and forth; however, you may not be able to see these vibrations because they're volitioned or willed by Nature under the threshold of your ability to see them.

A scale's needle is always jiggling back and forth under the heaviness of an object on the scale, even if we're unable to actually see this jiggling happening, because unchanging heaviness is impossible in the Infiniverse's interacting gravity-antigravity fields. These fields aren't a complex of "quantum forces"; rather, a gravity-antigravity field is an interaction of Nature's spontaneous instinctive nondeliberate willing in gravitons and antigravitons.

My scientific Style or unmethodical "method" and philosophical approach is an ontology. My ontology was developed from my knowledge of truths, such as Activation, organisation-disorganisation-reorganisation, situations, conscience, needs, Continuity, Immediacy, and voluntarism. This example of some of the contents of my ontology's paradigm.

Quantum mechanics is based on objectivism and its hypothetical falsehoods of Creation, order, events, rules, laws, time, eternity, and automatism. Quantum theorists know that evolution is a truth; however, they cling to their delusion that we exist in a finite universe created by "quantum fluctuations" instead of understanding that we exist in an infinity of physicalities (the Infiniverse) which are continually evolved, grown, developed, deteriorated, and devolved by Nature's use of Its Will.

"Disciplines" like objectivistic physics, chemistry, and biology as well as objectivistic psychology and sociology, are based on a paradigm borrowed from Creationists; therefore, these scientisms mislead because their disciplines are based on a paradigm of mistaken hypotheses. Of course, this paradigm doesn't correspond with Reality because Creationism is based on the superstitious myth of Creation, rather than the reality of Activation. Scientismists have broken with the Creationist's myth of the Creator; however, they also need to completely break with the superstitious hypotheses developed from this myth (Creation, order, events, rules, laws, time, eternalism, and automatism) if they are ever to become true scientists.

Time was mistakenly hypothesised because time is the fiction that activity, motion, and movement are only illusions and that we're inactivities. A self is an activity, not an inactivity. Inactivity (stillness) is impossible. A self is an activity who might move its luef out of its body when its body dies by instinctively using Nature's Will to do so; therefore, a self either leaves behind its dead body when it enters its specific realm of the after-death in its sensor or dies with its mortal body.

A self is an active reality, not a still illusion. All scientismists suffer from the delusion that a self is enduring in units of time. These scientismists slander Nature. They believe that the mind exists as a nothingness of Nature because they believe Nature is an empty Void; therefore, they also believe the word "self" is just a synonym for the word "illusion".

A cognition surrounds a center (a knower or a self) who uses its cognition. A center's use of its sensor is bounded by this center's cognition. A center needs to activate its sensor in its cognition so that its sensing is able to happen. A center inhabiting a cognition is a self; therefore, a self is not an illusion because a self has its cognition which it also activates—or inhibits.

Activationism needs to be the basis of every ontologist's understanding. Activationism is the antithesis of Creationism because Creationism is the mistaken hypothesis that stillness or inactivity is the basis of activities. The following indented paragraph defines Activationism:

Activationism is the knowledge that Activity is the basis of activities, not stillness or inactivity. We have no ability to create from stillness; however, the Activator *activates* from the Activity It is and activities, like you or I, *activate* from the activity each of us is.

There is no Creator. There is only the *Activator*. There are no creatures. There are only *activators*. There was no Creation. There is only an immediate and continual *Activation* of realities by the Activator, some of which are also deactivated by It to, sooner or later, blend with the Activity called "the Activator".

Ontology is the study of the Activator because the Activator is Reality. My ontology is an extrospective scientific research Style and an introspective philosophical research approach. My ontology is my foundation for a self's development of knowledge. I have related my practical Style and approach for my science and philosophy of ontology in "Chapter Seven: Ontology versus Scientism". The whole of this book is the metaphysical basis for my ontological Style and approach because every ontologist's enlightenment is the basis for his or her effective use of ontology.

Ontology is the study of Reality which I refer to as "Nature" as well as the "Phenomenon"; therefore, my ontology is based on Reality's Will, not on laws which aren't actually existent. Only when a self understands ontology will it recognise what it is, who it is (and isn't) as expressed by what it is, how it is who it is expressed by what it is or how it isn't who it is expressed by its fear of what it is, and why it is individually existent, instead of returned to Nature, the unbounded and Non-Individual..

Chapter Five
Nature and Deoxyribonucleic Acid (DNA)

The *natural* is that which is activated from Nature by Nature.

The unnatural or the unreal are the supposed referents of nominal words, like "non-Existence", "nothingness", "Creator", "time", "automatism" and "law". These "referents" are unnatural or unreal because they can't be found in Nature (the Phenomenon or Reality). Naturally developed artefacts, like nominal words, are phenomenal or real because they're developed by a self out of Nature, the Phenomenon, or Reality; however, nominal words have no natural, phenomenal, or real referents. Therefore, nominal words confuse those people who don't understand that these words don't refer to natures, phenomena, or realities. In other words, the words "non-Existence", "nothingness", "Creator", "time", "automatism" and "law" don't refer to actual referents.

Like essential nominal words, physically constructed tools are artefacts. Artefacts, like cars and airplanes, are made by selves out of Nature's Natural, Phenomenon's phenomenal, or Reality's real physicalities (particles). These natural, phenomenal, or real physicalities are natures of Nature, phenomena of the Phenomenon, or realities of Reality, just as natural, phenomenal, or real nominal words and natural, phenomenal, and real forms are non-physical natures of Nature, phenomena of the Phenomenon, or realities of Reality. The term "derivatively natural" refers to our natural artefacts because, unlike natural forms, natural artefacts are constructed natures of Nature.

An artefact is not necessarily mechanical.

For example, a painting is artificial, but not mechanical, because a painting doesn't usually have moving parts.

We make mechanical tools which are our artificial instruments, mechanisms, and machines. Our instruments, like scalpels and telescopes, our mechanisms, like carburettors and microchips, and our machines, like watches, cars, planes, and computers, are derivatively natural because they are technologies made out of natures of Nature by selves, like you and I.

We are able to make naturally artificial outer graphics, outer numbers, and outer letters in the environment by using our derivatively natural inner graphics, inner numbers, and inner letters as our means of translation. We use derivatively natural inner symbols we've structured with our inner graphics and inner letters to think thoughts and concepts as well as reason out hypotheses. We use tools, like computers, to help us think and reason.

We're able to see derivatively natural outer ideograms and outer words on a computer's monitor by keying electromagnetic patterns into the suefs of a computer's electromagnetic waves. A computer programmer develops combinations of the numbers 0 and 1 in his cognition so he's able to relate these numbers to the electromagnetic patterns which are encoded in suefs; however, the computer programmer's numbers aren't these electromagnetic patterns. When the computer programmer presses keys on the computer's keyboard, suefs are encoded or "keyed" with electromagnetic patterns and electromagnetically motioned to the Central Processing Unit (CPU) of the computer where they are then electromagnetically converted into the computer's output of outer numbers, outer graphics, outer letters, outer ideograms, and outer words.

We stimulate Nature's instinctive willing in a computer by pressing a key on a computer's keyboard or by clicking the computer's mouse. When a key is pressed or the mouse is clicked, Nature instinctively wills electromagnetic patterns to merge with objective suefs. The objective suefs are motioned to the hard drive by Nature's use of Its instinctive electromagnetic will waves or qualia. The electromagnetic patterns of suefs which have been motioned to the hard drive are copied to suefs of the hard drive. These suefs then have their electromagnetic patterns copied to other suefs which an electromagnetic quale carries from the hard drive to the Central Processing Unit. Nature's instinctive willing of electromagnetism in the CPU then graphs outer ideograms and forms outer words in the computer's viewing screen for us to see.

Outputted outer symbols appear on a computer's viewing screen; however, they aren't information, like most computer scientismists think; rather they're data. Information is a self's composition of inner signs which are existent in the self's cognition and memory store, while data are a self's outer signs existent in its environment. Outputted outer numbers which apparition in the computer's viewing screen are translated by a self and cognised in its cognition as inner ideograms and inner words so that these inner ideograms and inner words may be used by a self in its thinking and reasoning. Outer ideograms and outer words contain outer graphics and outer letters which are translated into inner graphics and inner letters by the self so that the self is able to structure inner ideograms and inner words in its cognition.

Nature has no need for information which is why Nature is unable to develop inner signs; however, we do have a need for information because we have a need to learn; therefore, we translate a computer's outputted data into information in our cognitions.

Unlike a computer, we're able to learn by using our intelligent reasoning to concurrently analyse and synthesise exactly what we are, who we are expressing we are (and aren't) from what we are, how we are (and aren't) expressing who we are (and aren't) from what we are, and why we are obviously existent, instead of not existent..

Computers have no ability to compose information. Computers are only used to input data and output data. Computers aren't intelligent, despite the "hype" of computer technicians who maintain that computers are "artificially intelligent". Nature's instinctive willing in a computer is *unintelligent* because Nature isn't a Self. A computer is unintelligent because the computer isn't a self. A computer has no ability to exist because the ability to exist is a self's ability to use the Will of Nature which computers are unable to do; therefore, artificial intelligence is impossible because a constructed (artificial) computer is not a self who uses Nature's Will to exist intelligence nor is a computer inhabited by an intelligent self.

A computer is not able to cognise and has no intelligence because neither the ability to cognise nor the faculty of intelligence are naturally *constructed*. The ability to cognise and the faculty of intelligence are only naturally *developed* by selves, not "constructed" by computers.

We use small uncondensed energy forms (suefs) to formulate sounds of outer speech about realities. Unlike a computer, which is often used to simulate sounds, we're able to understand what these sounds mean. A computer is unable to understand what these sounds mean because a computer is unintelligent.

We're able to help Nature encode electromagnetic patterns in a computer's hard drive; however, the suefs in a brain which are encoded with electromagnetic patterns aren't channelled by the brain's inhabiting self to a hard drive existent in the brain; therefore, a self's memories aren't electromagnetically stored in the self's brain. Essential selfological qualities, like inner words, are existed by a self in its essential memory store, not in the self's substantial or physical brain. Consequently, there is no need for electromagnetic patterns to be stored on a "hard drive" in the self's brain.

A self has a memory store (an essential activity) in which the self's developed inner graphics, inner numbers, inner letters, inner words, and inner ideograms are stored; therefore, a self has no need to electromagnetically encode patterns in a "brainy" hard drive. There is no equivalent of a computer's hard drive in a brain; however, a self's faculty of memory is associated with the self's brain. A self's faculty of memory is a thing as well as an activity, but it is an essential thing, not the self's physical thing (the self's physical brain).

By using Nature's Will, a self is able to translate the pure energy of an abstraction in its intelligence into an electromagnetic pattern in its brain and merge this electromagnetic pattern with a suef so that the suef carries this electromagnetic pattern to the nervous systems of the self's body. Then the self is able to use Nature's Will in the electromagnetic patterns of its nerves to effect motions in its muscles so that its able to use these motions to effect the movements of its body.

A computer is not evolved and grown by Nature; therefore, a computer isn't an organism. A computer is simply a constructed machine, not an integrated organism. A computer is not an organism inhabited by a self; therefore, a computer's Central Processing Unit is not *responsible* for activating the functions of the other components of the computer system, as computer "techies" believe, because the CPU has no self who inhabits it so this "machine-self" would be able to use Nature's Will, responsibly—or irresponsibly—to activate the electromagnetism necessary for the functions of the computer to occur. Nor is the Central Processing Unit responsible for guiding these functions because a self uses its human body to press the computer keys which will stimulate Nature to instinctively Will a quale or a will wave of electromagnetism as a happening in the computer.

It's ludicrous to believe that a computer is responsible for its functions because the computer is not a self who might choose to use Nature's Will. Even if the computer was inhabited by a self, the computer's self would be responsible for the computer's functions, not the computer.

A computer isn't intelligent because a computer is barren of the abilities of knowing, assimilating, and reasoning. A computer is unintelligent because the computer only has physical components, like a Central Processing Unit, not essential faculties, like intelligence.

A computer's CPU is not a self; therefore, we're no more able to hold a computer responsible for its functions than we're able to hold our brains responsible for the activities of our intelligence and our bodily processes. Like our brains, a computer's CPU has no volitional ability.

Nature activates the computer with the help of any self who opens the computer's channels by pressing the computer's "power" button (power is a delusion) to release Nature's vitality of electromagnetism in the computer. Nature instinctively affects us by stimulating effects in our bodies. Nature is also able to stimulate effects in a computer by energising it; however, a computer is unable to use Nature's Will to "build" a self because the computer has no abilities; therefore, the computer is only energised, not affected, like us, nor is it able to effect, like us, because a computer is unable to use Nature's Will.

When we turn on a computer and type on the keys of the computer's keyboard, Nature's instinctive willing encodes electromagnetic patterns in suefs. Although outer numbers are outputted in the computer's monitor or on a printout, the CPU of the computer doesn't intellectually formulate these outer numbers because the CPU as well as Nature are unable to intellectually cogitate.

A computer's software is programmed so that Nature's instinctive willing in this software retrieves electromagnetic patterns from a computer file which Nature's uses in the computer's CPU. As a result, colours as well as white, black, and grey are projected within the pixels on the screen of the monitor thereby forming outer signs or data, like an outer ideogram or an outer word. The computer doesn't know that outer ideograms and outer words are appearing on its monitor, that these outer ideograms and outer words are outer ideograms and outer words, or that the electromagnetic patterns encoded in its hard drive are translations of outer ideograms and outer words because it's impossible for a computer to know, just as it's impossible for a brain to know. Computers and brains are barren of the ability to know and all other abilities.

We're unable to program a computer to "construct" its own self. A computer has no ability to "build" a self who would be able to "construct" its own inner graphics and inner letters with which to structure its own inner ideograms and inner words for the purpose of thinking and reasoning.

Why is it that neither a computer nor a brain have abilities, like the ability to "construct" a self?

The obvious answer to this question is that a self is generated by Nature so that this self is able to develop its abilities from Potentiality in accord with its use of Nature's Will; therefore, a self is not constructed by computers—or brains.

Nature is Energy or Matter; therefore, Nature spontaneously, instinctively and nondeliberately generated us as energies or matters (selves) in zygotes or buds. Scientismists hold the mistaken opinion that a self is a brain grown by "Natural Law"; therefore; they believe that they're able to build a computer as a "self" by using laws. *Scientismists deny that Nature uses Existence, Volition, or Will because Nature's instinctive use of Its Existence, Volition, or Will means that Natural Law is not required to explain how things change.*

Modern scientismists, which includes almost all psychiatrists, psychologists, and psychoanalysts, are practicing under the absurd notion that selves, like you and I, are actually mechanical constructions of our "mechanical brain". Scientismists absurdly believe that we are mechanically constructed by our brains because they don't know that we are selves whose brains are volitionally grown by us with the help of Nature's Volition.

Scientismists, including many medical doctors, tend to believe that brains are 'living computers' (Clayman, 1991, p. 5); however, they're troubled because they don't understand how we exist as "living computers". Of course, they believe that it's only a "matter of time" before they do "figure out" the laws by which they assume we live. These scientismists fail to understand that we don't live by laws because we are existents who exist our cognitions and live our sensors and sensable organisms by according our use of Nature's Will in tandem with Nature to fulfil our needs, satisfy our sane desires, and carefully sooth those frustrations we experience which result in our insane desires.

Medical doctors who refer to our brains as "living computers" would likely protest that they know the brain is not really a computer because, "after all", this is the reason why they put the words, "living computer", in quotation marks in their writings. These doctors would likely say that they know they're only using the computer as a metaphor for the brain; however, they don't understand that their continual use of this metaphor seduces them so that they think in secret that the brain really is a computer. This way of thinking has a devastating effect on the doctor's approach to his patients because he tends to treat them as if they were selfless living machines.

A computer is a machine that's constructed and programmed by a human self who inhabits a human body. It isn't possible for a machine to build a self as a component part, like a CPU, because a self is a center of energy, not a physicality, like a CPU—or a brain.

A computer's CPU has no ability to use the rest of a computer's components. Nor are the computer's components able to hold faculties. Likewise, a brain is unable to hold faculties; instead, the self who inhabits its brain holds its faculties in its brain because these faculties belong to the self, not to the self's brain.

Nature instinctively wills in Its electromagnetism; however, Nature is unable to intelligently manipulate the electromagnetic patterns encoded in the computer's hard drive to attain Its own goals because Nature isn't intelligent; therefore, Nature is unable to plan in relation to *our* purpose of encoding electromagnetic patterns in a computer's hard drive.

We're unable to construct a computer which could intelligently relay plans from Nature or plans of its own. A computer is only instinctively willed to operate by Nature. Nature has no knowledge of how to manipulate the electromagnetic patterns It instinctively patterns in suefs because Nature is unable to develop knowledge.

A computer hasn't developed any abilities; therefore, a computer is unable to think, cogitate, or reason with inner graphics, inner numbers, and inner letters. A computer is also incapable of understanding how to intuit, cognise, and recognise inner graphics, inner numbers, and inner letters. I need to continually stress that "AI" (artificial intelligence) is a contradiction in terms because the world-wide "hype" of our cultures' computer aficionados has conditioned complacent people to believe that AI exists.

A computer has no needs because a computer isn't a self; therefore, a computer also has no abilities or faculties because it doesn't have a need for them. Contrary to popular opinion, computers haven't developed a memory store because a memory store is a faculty of a self, not a component of a computer.

Computers have a storage and retrieval system for electromagnetically encoded patterns (energetics), but this system is physical, not essential; therefore, this system is a *record* system, not a "memory" system. We use a computer to record data, not to memorise data, because a computer doesn't have the ability to memorise.

A self's memory store is a storage and retrieval system for abstracted essentially encoded patterns which the self has stored in and retrieves from its essential faculty of memory, not its physical brain. Nor is a self's faculty of memory existed as part of its brain, although its immortal faculty of memory is integrated with its mortal brain.

A self develops essential images, sounds, emotions, flavours, and odours which it stores in memory as abstractions. The self is then able to summon or retrieve these essential abstractions from memory for use. Inner words are memorised as essentially abstracted images or sounds.

A self signifies inner graphics and formulates inner letters so that it may structure inner ideograms and inner words. Then the self is able to use its body to produce outer ideograms and outer words in the environment by using its vocal cords to physically speak them.

Computer scientismists refer to a computer's input as "data" and refer to a computer's output as "information"; however, a computer has only inputted data converted to electromagnetic patterns and only has electromagnetic patterns converted back into data as its output. Only a self, not a computer, is able to develop inner numbers, inner graphics, and inner letters as information in its cognition and translate them into outer numbers, outer graphics, and outer letters. Only a self is able to translate outer graphics in the environment into inner graphics or information for its knowing, translate outer letters in the environment into inner letters or information for its knowing, and translate outer numbers in the environment into inner numbers or information for its knowing.

The electromagnetic patterns of a computer's software are translations of a computer programmer's algorithms which are only existent in the computer programmer's cognition, not in the computer's software. The computer programmer converts the algorithms in his cognition to electromagnetic patterns in a computer's software which result in the computer's output of outer numbers and outer "connectors", outer graphics and outer ideograms, as well as outer letters and outer words.

Computer aficionados speculate that a computer's Central Processing Unit calculates by formal intellectualisation or logic; however, a computer is merely moved mechanically without performing operations of intellect. Only gullible people speculate that a computer has a calculating intellect. Actually, the computer has a CPU which is mechanically moved by Nature's quale of electromagnetism in the CPU; therefore, the CPU's movements are mechanical movements, not calculations. The computer has no disabling ability of calculating because the computer is not a self who would be able to use the disabling ability of cogitating to calculate.

Nature's instinctive willing in the computer moves the mechanisms in the computer's CPU; therefore, the computer's CPU isn't calculating. The movements in the mechanisms of a computer's CPU aren't the CPU's ability to calculate because only a self uses its disabling ability of cogitating to calculate. Nature's instinctive willing in the computer's CPU functions the CPU's mechanisms. But Nature isn't intellectually cogitating in the computer. Nature is instinctively willing in the computer so that movements (not intellectual calculations) occur in the CPU because Nature has no disabling ability to cogitate in a computer's CPU any more than It has an enabling ability to reason in it.

A computer's CPU is not the computer's "calculator" because the CPU is used by us to process electromagnetic patterns, not to calculate outer numbers. Of course, a computer is used by us to process data in relation to a program so that results appear; however, such a process is not the ability to calculate.

"Artificial intelligence" is an oxymoron because intelligence isn't artificial; however, selves use Nature's Will to intellectually cogitate, as well as to intelligently reason; therefore, selves develop logical intellects in which they use their disabling ability of cogitating to intellectualise. A self's cogitating disables its ability of reasoning and its ability of thinking because the self is cogitating by way of laws. Consequently, such a deceived self is hampering its ability to think, contemplatively, as well as its ability to reason, speculatively.

Although we instinctively as well as deliberately use Nature's Will to activate actions in our faculties, motions in our bodies, and movements of our bodies, we're unable to affect Nature by way of the knowledge we have. We're unable to feed our knowledge back to Nature because Nature has no ability to cognise.

A hard drive is a thing but a computer has no ability to remember with its hard drive. Nature instinctively wills in a computer so that electromagnetically encoded patterns are stored and retrieved by way of the computer's programming; however, computers aren't selves who might use Nature's Will to remember. A computer isn't a self with selfological qualities; therefore, a computer is unable to mechanically move its own components.

A computer isn't a brain because there isn't a self who inhabits and uses it. A computer has no need for a memory because a computer has no needs. Only a self has needs. A self's brain is also barren of needs which is why a self's brain has no need for a memory. Only a self can fulfil its needs by channelling Nature's Will within its brain and the rest of its body to fulfil its needs, like its *selfological, not physical,* needs of eating and drinking.

Nature's three main activities in a computer's processes are as follows:

(1) We use a computer's keyboard or mouse to stimulate Nature's Will in the computer so that suefs are encoded with electromagnetic patterns.
(2) These electromagnetic patterns are then transferred to the computer's hard drive by Nature's willing in the computer system so they may be stored in as well as retrieved from the computer's hard drive.
(3) When suefs are encoded or merged with inputted electromagnetic patterns by Nature and relayed to the computer's CPU, Nature is then able to instinctively use Its Will in the computer's CPU so data results as the output of the computer.

We're able to view the objective photons reflected from any computer's monitor as the output of the computer and translate these objective photons into subjective photons which we use to develop information in our cognitions. Then we're able to use our ability of memorising to memorise our information so we're able to remember them whenever we need them.

Although we're able to use the electromagnetism of Nature's spontaneous instinctive nondeliberate willing in a computer's hard drive so that our desire to see "outer words" on the computer's screen is fulfilled, these outer words aren't actually outer words for the computer or for Nature. Neither the computer nor Nature are able to desire so that they might desire to see outer words nor are they able to realise that outer words are the environmental counterparts of inner words. Nature has simply spontaneously, instinctively, and nondeliberately willed (in accord with *our* need to energise) the translation of electromagnetically encoded patterns in the computer's hard drive.

A computer is used by us to input encoded electromagnetically patterned suefs. These electromagnetic patterns are translations of groups of the binary numbers 0 and 1 which, in turn, are translations of algorithms existed by us in our cognitions. Algorithms are only existed by a self in its cognition, not a computer program, because only electromagnetic patterns are existed by Nature in a computer's software, not algorithms (sets of rules). Computer programmers convert the energised algorithms that they've cogitated in their disabling intellects to electromagnetic patterns which they feed into a computer's software. These computer "experts" ignore the obvious truth that computers are unable to intellectually cogitate with algorithms because computers aren't selves.

Sets of rules aren't a computer's instructions as computer scientists would lead you to believe because a computer isn't a self with the intelligence to follow instructions. Rules aren't instructions because instructions tell human selves how to use their abilities for certain actions or how to use their human bodies for certain behaviours. An instructor might include rules in his instructions, but instructions are developed from needs, not rules, which is why rules aren't instructions.

An algorithm's rules aren't unambiguous instructions about how to solve a class of problems because rules aren't instructions and aren't effective as a means of instruction. Rules are only ineffectively used by human instructors in their instructions. Only a logician will bore his students by ineffectively using rules of logic in his instructing.

An algorithm is a set of rules, not a set of instructions. We translate our inner intellects' intellectually energised algorithms into our outer aspect of the World's electromagnetic patterns of energy and encode these electromagnetic patterns in a computers software and hard drive. The electromagnetic patterns of a computer's software are unable to "instruct" the computer's CPU, just as the electromagnetic patterns of the CPU are unable to "learn" how to develop new electromagnetic patterns.

The electromagnetic patterns of a computer's software are the result of a computer programmer's *delusional* translation of algorithms or sets of rules which *he* learned, not the computer. The computer's software doesn't "learn" and neither do the electromagnetic patterns issuing from this software.

A vital insight which few people have is that a computer hasn't any knowledge to feed back to its programming. Computer programmers are scientismists who feed electromagnetic patterns that they've associated with their *intellects'* cogitated inner numbers and algorithms into a computer' which, unlike their unsharable intellects, they have the ability to share with every other self. A computer's displayed outer numbers is only a reflection of the computer programmer's knowledge because outer numbers are only used to outline, not to know. Unfortunately, computer programmers usually have little knowledge because they're addicted to logical cogitating. As a result, their ability to inferentially reason is stunted.

A computer programmer's assertion that he programs sets of rules or *algorithms* into a computer is his delusion because computers can only be programmed with electromagnetic patterns, not the energy of a self's rules or algorithms which are only possible as existents in a self's enabling intelligence or disabling intellect. A computer programmer really translates algorithms he's intellectually cogitated and associated with electromagnetic patterns so he can feed these electromagnetic patterns, not his intellectual algorithms, into a computer's software or data storage components, like the hard drive. Computer programmers often fail to understand that Nature instinctively wills in these electromagnetic patterns; therefore, the functions of the computer are carried out by Nature with no need for an intelligent understanding by a computer programmer of what's actually happening in the computer or Nature.

It seems as if our scientismistic computer programmers are as incapable of learning as their computers because they're so used to cogitating quantitatively, delineatively, and logically with mathematical laws that they've lost touch with their scientific ability to *decondition* their own conditioned thinking. A scientific deconditioner learns by freely, indicatively, and descriptively thinking, as well as by freely and explanatorily reasoning in accord with the knowledge he already has, especially his knowledge of his needs. He doesn't "deprogram" his thinking because he's not a computer. He *deconditions* his thinking by ridding his thinking of unfairly prejudiced thoughts in favour of a fairly biased thoughts.

Computer programmers "don't see the forest because they don't believe in the tree". Computer programmers don't usually see the difference between a brain and a computer because they aren't used to using their thinking and reasoning, qualitatively. They've been conditioned to use their cogitating, quantitatively. Therefore, they miss the "forest" of selves who use their brains. They deny that this forest exists because they're so prejudiced by their belief in automatism that they think we're all automatic brains or living computers. They ignore the fact that a brain is, quite obviously, very different from a computer. After all, a brain is inhabited by a "tree" while a computer is void of such "greenery".

Norman Doidge, who wrote the book, *The Brain that Changes Itself*, emphasised the brain's "neuroplasticity", which simply means that the relationships of a brain's neurons change. Doidge and other neuroscientismists fail to understand that the human brain is not changing itself; rather, it's changed by the human self who inhabits it and who instinctively, nondeliberately as well as continually uses Nature's Will in tandem with Nature's instinctive, nondeliberate and continual use of Its Will to rearrange its brain's neurons.

The brain's neuroplasticity seems to have given computer technicians the idea that they were able to make systems in their computers which are flexible. The computer's flexible system of electromagnetic patterns is meant to imitate the brain's neuroplasticity; therefore, neurologists and medical doctors who subscribe to the doctrine of objectivism, like Norman Doidge, have convinced computer technicians that "inevitably" their computers will become conscious because these neurologists and medical doctors simply don't believe that a self is generated by Nature to use its brain. They believe a brain automatically constructs its mind as well as its consciousness. They don't understand that a self has developed its cognition from Potentiality, Nature, or Activity, not mind or consciousness; therefore, a self cognitively (not mindfully or consciously) uses Nature's Will in its brain to channel its ability of sensing in its brain.

A computer has no disabling ability to "perform" logic with algorithms. A computer has no logical intellect with which to logicise so that it could pass judgement with a set of rules; therefore, it's impossible for a computer to make calculations. Nor is a computer able to learn.

Computer technicians absurdly speculate that computers are able to learn. These "techies" ignore the obvious fact that no computer has the ability to learn because a computer is not a self who guides the abilities of intuiting, cognising, and recognising so that learning might take place. What actually happens in a computer is that sample electronic patterns from input devices are programmed by us and processed by Nature's willing in them in such a way that new electromagnetic patterns are generated from the sample electromagnetic patterns. These new electromagnetic patterns constitute a new program which the computer programmer is able to convert to a new mathematical model in his intellect. The computer didn't learn to develop these new electromagnetic patterns nor is the new program a mathematical model.

A new mathematical model is simply a mathematician's translation of a computer's electromagnetic output of patterns which are outputted by the computer as data (not information) into his intellect's inner numbers which he cogitates in his intellect as a new mathematical model; therefore, a computer doesn't learn to develop new mathematical models. Rather, a computer's original program (its original software containing electromagnetic patterns) is activated by Nature's willing and related to the changing input from the computer's input devices by Nature's willing so that a new program is processed *by way of the old program.*

Such an instinctively willed mechanical function is hardly learning.

Even if a computer's CPU had a video camera hooked up to it, the CPU would not "sense" the outer symbols produced on its monitor's viewing screen derived from the video camera. The CPU would receive the electromagnetic patterns electromagnetically transmitted to it by Nature's willing in the camera. Then Nature would instinctively convert the suefs containing these electromagnetic patterns into photons within the pixels on the monitor's viewing screen for *us*, not the computer, to sense, perceive, and understand.

Unlike computers, brains are grown.

"Deoxyribonucleic acid" (DNA) is evolved from condensed energies, materialised matters, or particles. DNA is evolved by Nature into single-celled sensable organisms within which Nature instinctively develops selves. Some of these single-celled sensable organisms have had their DNA mutated by their selves and Nature so that Nature and these selves were able to use mitosis to grow these new single-celled sensable organisms into a multicellular sensable organism.

Nature instinctively evolves and grows sensable organisms with brains by instinctively evolving patterns (molecules) of DNA by way of which selves are able to organise cells, including the neurons of their brains. We learn to covert the inner numbers or information in our cognitions to outer numbers or data for the purpose of labelling and charting the patterns of DNA we've observed with electron microscopes.

A self doesn't have to produce outer graphics, outer numbers, and outer letters in its brain, like it does in the environment, because the self has an essential memory in which it develops and contains inner graphics, inner numbers, and inner letters; therefore, the brain is used by its inhabiting self to channel inner graphics, inner numbers, and inner letters from the self's memory for the self to use. The self's memory surrounds the self's brain while the self is centered in its brain's reticular formation.

Just as we're able to understandingly sense and perceive the pixels in a computer's viewing screen, we're able to understandingly sense and perceive a slide of DNA taken from our brains' neurons when we've had this DNA extracted from our brains for viewing under an electron microscope. Then we're able to intellectually abstract the images we've imaged from our viewing of the slides of DNA and develop inner numbers related to these images for storage in our faculties of memory for recall when desired.

We use our abstract inner graphics, inner numbers, and inner letters to map or chart the overall pattern of a DNA molecule and its genetic "markers" (genetic polymorphisms). The "genetic code" is existed by us as a pattern of activities in our cognitions and memory stores. We also chart this code as outer numbers or map this code as outer graphics or outer letters in the environment.

DNA is a pattern of condensed energies. DNA is not a code because DNA is not an abstraction or a development from an abstraction. Nature is unable to develop codes because Nature is unable to develop abstractions, like the Morse code; *therefore, DNA is not based on genetic codes; genetic codes are based on DNA.*

Nature doesn't map out the DNA patterns It evolves because It's unable to plan. Nature is unable to develop inner numbers because It has no need to develop Its own inner equations and inner formulas. Nature is also unable to develop inner graphics and inner letters into an ideographic or worded inner language because It has no need to develop Its own inner language.

Nature evolves genetic patterns in our sensable organisms; however, we develop the genetic code in our cognitions by labelling these genetic patterns; therefore, the physical charts and maps we make to label the genetic code in our environment with numbers (if it's a chart) and graphics or letters (if it's a map) is not our decoding of Nature's DNA code. Rather, the numbers with which we chart and the graphics or letters with which we map DNA is our coding of the genetic patterns which Nature has instinctively and randomly evolved.

We use letters and words of the English language in our charting and mapping of DNA. The nitrogen bases, which are expressed in English as adenine, thymine, guanine, and cytosine, are expressed by differently lettered words in other languages; however, the genetic code was "cracked" by English speaking researchers. Consequently, the letters "A", "T", "G" and "C" symbolising the words, "adenine", "thymine", "guanine" and "cytosine", respectively, are used by all researchers to stand for these nitrogen bases.

We use letters to formulate a DNA code. We attend to these letters by way of our ability to sense them, interpret them by way of our ability to perceive them, and assimilate them by way of our ability to cognise them. Outer letters become our information after having been translated into inner letters by way of our ability to think; however, the first human selves would not have been able to develop inner graphics, inner numbers, and inner letters without first having heard and/or seen outer graphics, outer numbers and outer letters; therefore, our outer graphics, outer numbers, and outer letters are the respective origins of our inner graphics, inner numbers, and inner letters.

DNA's structure of condensed energies is coded by a geneticist, but DNA is not encoded by Natural Law. DNA is a pattern containing nucleotides. DNA patterns are evolved by Nature so that, by observing our DNA and labelling its nucleotides with English letters, we're able to develop a DNA code. English geneticists first developed and structured the genetic code which is another reason why English letters and words are used to label the elements of DNA.

A geneticist maps the various genes of a DNA sequence with abstract forms in her intellect and later formulates them as outer letters. Then she uses these outer letters to label the nitrogen bases of DNA. Geneticists developed this code and then attributed this code to the genetic sequences they discovered. These geneticists developed the genetic code only after they had discovered the DNA sequence which means that the codes they develop and map *are not* an ectypal code of a supposed archetypal code of Nature.

Nature instinctively evolves the physical structure of a zygote's DNA pattern from what Nature is. Nature evolves a self's zygote by merging gametes together at syngamy so that the DNA of the zygote is instinctively used by Nature and the self to grow the self's brain and the rest of the self's sensable organism.

The self who inhabits its zygote is unable to activate its faculties of intuition, cognition, and recognition because the self and Nature have yet to grow a brain from the zygote for the self to hold these faculties in its brain; therefore, the self needs to instinctively and nondeliberately use Nature's Will in tandem with Nature's instinctive nondeliberate willing to grow its brain before it's able to develop immaterial faculties of energy which encompass its materialised brain and are held by it in its brain. After it has grown its materialised brain, the inhabiting immaterial self of this brain uses Nature's Will in tandem with Nature to replicate genes from a DNA sequence, copy these genes so that "ribonucleic acid" (RNA) is produced, replicate tri-nucleotides from messenger RNA so that amino acids (the constituents of proteins) are evolved, and organise its body by using proteins to replenish the cells which compose its body.

A self instinctively and nondeliberately grows its neurons and thus the lobes of its brain with Nature's instinctive nondeliberate assistance. A self's abilities and faculties are developed from Nature, Activity, or Potentiality only after the self has been generated by Nature to start its existence in the zygote at syngamy. The self is spontaneously, instinctively and nondeliberately enabled by Nature to replicate its single-celled zygote by way of mitosis and uses these replicated cells to grow and organise its multicellular brain. The self spontaneously or impulsively, instinctively and nondeliberately generates its abilities and faculties within the lobes of its brain as these lobes are growing.

The DNA in the cells of a self's multicellular body is put into action by the self's spontaneous or impulsive instinctive nondeliberate use of Nature's Will in tandem with Nature's spontaneous instinctive nondeliberate willing. The self's instinctive nondeliberate actions are either spontaneously in accord or impulsively in discord with its needs and Nature's spontaneous instinctive nondeliberate willing.

DNA hasn't the ability to need. Only selves of Nature have needs derived from their existence in Nature as natural individuals. A self uses its needs in contributing to the evolution, growth and development of its sensable organism and, thus, its brain. A self holds its immaterial selfological qualities in its materialised brain so that its immaterial selfological needs, especially its immaterial need to develop its wisdom, are fulfilled by its use of its immaterial abilities in its immaterial faculties.

The self, not its DNA, develops an insane desire to survive in its sensable organism because it doesn't yet understand that it might exist as an immortal. Also, the self, not its DNA, has the desire to avoid anxiety and pain and the desire to court excitement and pleasure, instead of calmly enjoying the ease of existing and living with the by-product of enjoyment that every self knows as "happiness".

A self and Nature instinctively Will the growth of the self's zygote to foetal sufficiency, although not to maturity. A brain is grown by the self and Nature from the embryonic stage to the foetal stage. The self and Nature also grow the rest of the body as the self and Nature are growing the self's brain so that the neurons of the brain are related by nerves to the rest of the self's sensable organism. In this way, the central nervous system, composed of the brain's neurons and the spinal column's nerves, are related to the nerves of the "autovolitional nervous system" innervating the muscles and organs of the "gut", such as the stomach, the colon, the kidneys, and the liver. The neurons of the brain are also related to the nerves of the peripheral nervous system innervating the muscles of the body's limbs. All these neurons, nerves, muscles, and organs are the result of molecules of DNA.

It's important to realise that there is only an autovolitional nervous system, not an "autonomic nervous system". The word "autonomic" in the phrase "autonomic nervous system" is a misnomer because a nervous system doesn't "function automatically". In Nature, there is no automatism, despite the fact that we're able to make instruments, mechanisms, and machines as our tools. Even when we flip a switch to "turn on a tool", our tool functions by Nature's willing in it. Our tools don't function, automatically, because Nature's willing of waves, vitalities, or "fuels" effect our tools' movements; therefore, there is no automatism in Nature. There is only the instinctive Volition of Nature.

The word "Volition" is defined as 'Nature's spontaneous instinctive nondeliberate use of Its Will and a self's spontaneous or impulsive instinctive nondeliberate or deliberate noninstinctive use of Nature's Will.' Voluntarism is the realisation of the truth that Volition is the ability of Nature which Nature uses to activate natures, like selves, who can use Nature's Will to activate natures (which are not selves) in the nature every self is.

Scientismists refer to our autovolitional nervous system as our "autonomic nervous system" but this nervous system is not automatic, because we volition its processes. Our autovolitional nervous system is our spontaneous or impulsive instinctive nondeliberate use of Nature's Will in tandem with Nature's spontaneous instinctive nondeliberate willing to initiate motions in this nervous system which are meant to harmonise certain behaviours in our organs, like digestion; however, unfortunate circumstances often affect the self's use of Nature's Will so that the self impulsively, instinctively and nondeliberately disrupts its use of Nature's Will in this autovolitional nervous system, not because it has the intention to harm its sensable organism, but simply because it hasn't yet learned how to cognizantly monitor its use of Nature's Will in this nervous system.

The morpheme "auto-" of the word "autonomic" is derived from the Greek word "autos", meaning, "self" in English, while, the morpheme, "-nomic" of the word "autonomic" is derived from the Greek word "nomos" meaning, "law" in English. The Greeks ignored the truth that we're real selves who use Nature's Will, not laws, to guide our bodies' behaviour. They ignored the fact that law doesn't fate our bodies' behaviour because we are absolutely Free. We don't merely sit passively in our bodies while our bodies are fated by law because, as selves, we're absolutely free to act as we are or act out the false selves we aren't.

We usually *incognizantly* as well as instinctively, nondeliberately, and spontaneously or impulsively use Nature's Will in tandem with Nature's spontaneous instinctive nondeliberate use of Its Will within our autovolitional nervous systems; therefore, the phrase, "autonomic nervous system", is a misnomer because we use Nature's Will, not laws, to motion phenomena in our nervous systems.

Often a self doesn't know that Nature is spontaneously, instinctively and nondeliberately willing in it. As a result, the self is usually oblivious to Nature's willing in its autovolitional nervous system and doesn't usually feel Nature's willing in it. But a self is able to learn how to train its ability of feeling on Nature's willing. Then it's able to cognizantly attend to Nature's willing in its autovolitional nervous system.

For example, a Yogi, is often able to attend to her blood pressure. Thus, she's able to sense and interpret the flow of blood in her arteries and assimilate the knowledge of how to alter the intensity of the flow of her blood by deliberately volitioning in tandem with Nature's instinctive volitioning so that she's able to raise or lower her blood pressure. This learned behaviour has very little to do with wisdom because a Yogi often knows that Nature is willing in her but knows very little else about Nature. Unfortunately, this "trick" (among others) is used by unscrupulous "Yogis" to awe their gullible disciples so that, in their naivety, these disciples will worship them, instead of question their doctrines.

Nature is unable to develop towards closure or completion. Closure or completion is also impossible for us. Omniscience (all-knowing knowledge) is an impossibility for Nature because Nature has no ability to know so that It could develop knowledge, while it's impossible for us to be all-knowing because we're centers of Nature who are not ubiquitous, like Nature.

Nature is unable to know; therefore, Nature is unable to know all the differentiations It evolves, grows, and develops which is also why Nature is unable to distinguish a differentiation, like a self and its human body, or a differentiation, like DNA, distinguish between differentiations, like selves and DNA, or compare differentiations, like selves and DNA.

Patterns of Nature are always open to change. A DNA molecule is always open to mutation or variance by Nature's instinctive and random willing in it.

Nature is always instinctively and randomly willing in a DNA molecule to change it, just as It's always instinctively and randomly willing in the environment to change the environment.

The "environment" is unable to "naturally select" the DNA which is most adaptable to environmental changes as Charles Darwin thought. Nature adapts DNA to the environment by instinctively and randomly willing in this DNA as well as in the environment without selecting changes in the environment or DNA because Nature hasn't the ability to choose, decide, or select.

Plato's immortal archetypal "Forms" aren't existed by Nature; therefore, Nature is unable to encode DNA so that DNA would be the mortal ectype of immortal archetypal Forms. DNA patterns are existed by Nature. DNA patterns are Nature's mortal archetypes, but these archetypes are barren of immortal archetypal Forms. These DNA patterns are evolved by Nature because Nature has the Will with which to evolve these mortal archetypes. Our brains are the result of Nature's archetypal and mortal DNA which Nature freely evolves and grows *by chance*.

A self and Nature instinctively use Nature's Will to grow the brain of the self's foetus; therefore, the self also develops its cognisant knowing as its combined faculty and knowing to hold in its brain. Before it develops its cognisant knowing from Potentiality, the self's ability to use Nature's Will occurs without choice because a self's cognisant knowing needs to be developed before its ability to choose becomes possible; therefore, the self's use of Nature's Will before it develops cognisant knowing is undirected and occurs only by chance—which is also how Nature uses Its Will. Consequently, the inhabiting self's growth of its zygote to the stage of mature foetus occurs by Nature and its instinctively chanced use of Nature's Will, rather than by their instinctively chosen use of Its Will, which is why aberrancies in DNA occur; therefore, every foetus is flawed because its DNA is inevitably disrupted by its inhabiting self's impulsivity in some way.

A computer programmers' use of software to encode suefs with electromagnetic patterns is analogised to the encoding of DNA; however, this analogy is inappropriate. We're unable to use electromagnetic patterns as an analogy of the encoding of DNA because *we* use electromagnetic patterns to encode suefs, but Nature doesn't used Forms to encode DNA.

We code DNA, but DNA isn't encoded. Nature is unable to encode Its DNA because Nature has no ability to develop codes.

A DNA molecule's tri-nucleotides are the basis of our ability to develop genetic codes. A code is a system of regulated outer graphics, outer numbers, or outer letters used for the purpose of communication, like the Morse code.

Nature instinctively wills within a DNA molecule to produce tri-nucleotides. Ultimately, these tri-nucleotides are instinctively willed by Nature and a self to pattern proteins. These tri-nucleotides are the physical structures to which geneticists assign "codons" (units of a code). The outer graphics, outer numbers, and outer letters of a code are the abstract ectypes we use to reflect the physical and archetypal DNA which these ectypes signify.

Nature doesn't regulate the evolution and growth of tri-nucleotides from the DNA molecule according to the principles of probability theory because Nature doesn't use Its Will in alignment with principles. Probability theory only *seems* to apply to the evolution and growth of tri-nucleotides, genes, amino acids, and proteins because scientismists forget that they only apply the principles of probability theory to the evolution of tri-nucleotides from the DNA molecule *after* they've identified the materialised tri-nucleotides and the physical process of their evolving from DNA. Consequently, the application of probability theory to the evolution and growth of these phenomena may be interesting to mathematicians, but mathematics hasn't anything to do with the way tri-nucleotides, genes, amino acids, and proteins are actually evolved and grown.

Nature doesn't use probability theory to produce tri-nucleotides from the DNA molecule. Nature instinctively, randomly, and indeterminately wills the sequencing of a DNA molecule. Then It instinctively, randomly, and indeterminately copies tri-nucleotides from this sequence.

Portions of Energy are condensed by Energy as physicalities; however, a self is unable to store its inner graphics, inner numbers, and inner letters in physicalities or things. A self is only able to store these abstractions in its essential memory store; therefore, inner graphics, inner numbers, and inner letters are activities which the self has developed so it's able to translate them into outer graphics, outer numbers, and outer letters by engraving them in physicalities.

Inner graphics, inner numbers, and inner letters are a self's information. Information is used by a self to develop theories which it may subsequently prove to be true or false; however, inner numbers are only used to quantify, not qualify. Since all knowledge is qualitative, quantitative numbers don't lead to knowledge. Quantitative numbers only delineate; therefore, a self is unable to use numbers to describe a theory.

Scientismists suffer from the delusion that mathematical procedures, like statistics, convey knowledge; however, statistics are only used to sketch or outline situations. When the theory of an experiment is statistically analysed as accurate (or inaccurate) within a certain degree of probability, this analysis doesn't give us any real knowledge because this analysis is only a mathematician's projected guess about the truth or falsity of a theory, not his knowledge of this theory's truth or falsity.

Primitive humans developed the mistaken hypothesis of the Creator and mistakenly hypothesised that he created the regularities of Nature. They imagined that the Creator created laws to guide the "mechanical" regularities of evolution and growth.

Adding laws to Nature is somewhat like attempting to "add legs to a snake" which is a favourite expression of Zen masters who are fond of relaying that we often attempt to develop the unnecessary, like the serpent in the myth of Adam and Eve who had "unnecessary" legs. Yahweh supposedly took these legs away from the serpent to "punish" the serpent by forcing it to use its belly to crawl on the ground, like a snake.

The principles found in probability theory are the delusions of mathematicians because, like the word "creation", the word "principle" has no actual referent. A principle, rule, or law is meant to mask certain realities not reveal them. The realities which principles, rules, and laws are meant to mask are harmonies, consciences, and needs.

For example, you have a need to stop your car when a red light is blinking for you at an intersection in order to avoid an accident with another car whose driver has a green light flashing for him, that is, if you have a conscience. You don't have a "lawful" need to stop at a blinking red light or a "lawful" need to drive on at a blinking green light. You simply have a need to stop or a need to drive on. If you drive on at a red light and get into an accident, then consequences are needed, but these consequences aren't consequences of law; these consequences are consequences of need. These consequences are needed because you were irresponsible (impulsive). You were not responsible (spontaneous); instead, you ignored the needs of others as well as your own needs because you were impulsively responding to your insane desires.

Principles, rules, or laws cause confusion because they are nominal. The phrase, "the rule of law" has no referent; therefore, we don't need tombs of law to govern the conduct of our behaviour based on Yahweh's moral laws, The Ten Commandments. We need tombs of need so that we're able to understand how to guide the conduct our behaviour based on our amoral need for harmony because harmony is our guide to true integrity and appropriate conduct.

Nature is unable to express Its Will without mistakes happening because condensed energies are instable; therefore, condensed energies distort the stability of Nature's willing. This is why genetic aberrancies happen.

Scientismists don't realise that Nature exists as Fullness, not as Void, which is why Nature is able to evolve DNA from Its Fullness; however, Nature is unable to help or hinder us in our assigning of codons to chart a DNA molecule's 64 tri-nucleotides so that each tri-nucleotide is symbolised by codons of the genetic code.

To say tri-nucleotides *are* their codons or that the 64 tri-nucleotides *are* harmonised as the genetic code is to indulge in metaphor, not truth. Even to indulge in simile by saying that tri-nucleotides are *like* their codons or that the 64 tri-nucleotides are *like* the harmony of the genetic code is far from the truth of the situation.

Tri-nucleotides are copied from the DNA molecule. Tri-nucleotides don't resemble the abstractions I have dubbed "inner letters" which we use to map these tri-nucleotides in our cognitions. Tri-nucleotides don't resemble the outer letters that we use to physically map these tri-nucleotides in our environment either; therefore, our inner letters and outer letters are completely different from these tri-nucleotides. Finally, an organism's 64 tri-nucleotides are copied from its DNA sequence but they aren't harmonised by a geneticist's genetic code.

Outer letters are used by geneticists to formulate the genetic code because these letters symbolise the nucleotides which structure Nature's 64 tri-nucleotides. The outer letters geneticists used to map tri-nucleotides follow the English language, rather than a formula, because the letters used to symbolise the nucleotides of the 64 tri-nucleotides originally stood for words, e.g., the letter, "A" is the short form of the word "adenine".

"A" and "adenine" both stand for the reality of a nitrogen base. Unfortunately, they came to be used in a genetic formula, rather than a genetic language. These letters were charted as data. Geneticists rigidly formulate codons to symbolise these 64 tri-nucleotides and chart genetic codes in relation to them.

The sequences of tri-nucleotides are copied from the DNA molecule by Nature and a self so an amino acid is evolved for each tri-nucleotide by the instinctively willing of Nature and the self within the tri-nucleotides; however, there are only 20 amino acids which means that the self and Nature use Nature's Will in some tri-nucleotides to evolve the same amino acid. Once the amino acids have been evolved, the self instinctively uses Nature's Will in tandem with Nature's willing within the amino acids to bond them together so that a protein results. The self then uses Nature's Will in tandem with Nature's willing within these proteins to catalyse reactions in a cell or replenish the physical structure of the cell.

Each nucleotide is a molecule in one of two strands of a much larger DNA molecule. Each nucleotide is composed of a phosphate group, a sugar group, and a nitrogen base. There are four types of nitrogen bases called "adenine" (shortened to the letter "A"), "thymine" (shortened to the letter "T"), "guanine" (shortened to the letter "G"), and "cytosine" (shortened the letter "C"). Adenine (A) and guanine (G) are examples of purines containing a six atom ring and a five atom ring sharing two atoms. Cytosine (C) and thymine (T) are examples of pyrimidines which are composed of a single six atom ring.

A self instinctively uses Nature's Will (with Nature's assistance) in adenine on one strand of the DNA molecule and in thymine on the other strand of the DNA molecule as well as in guanine on adenine's strand of the DNA molecule and in cytosine on thymine's strand of the DNA molecule to keep these respective pairs of nitrogen bases together. Nature's instinctive willing in the hydrogen atoms relates these pairs of nitrogen bases to each other.

When a nitrogen base on one strand of the DNA molecule is related to a nitrogen base on the other strand of the DNA molecule, the two bonded nitrogen bases are called a "base pair". Adenine is only bonded with thymine, while guanine is only bonded with cytosine (or uracil on a RNA molecule); therefore, there are only four types of base pairs possible for a DNA molecule. These four base pairs are A-T, G-C, T-A, and C-G.

A self doesn't instinctively use Nature's Will as strongly to relate molecules together with chemical hydrogen relations as it uses Nature's Will to covalently relate molecules together; therefore, the base pairings in a DNA molecule are easily isolated from each other by these relations which allows the self to instinctively use Nature's Will in tandem with Nature's instinctive willing within the DNA molecules for the purposes of replication, transcription, and translation.

Replication is a self's instinctive use of Nature's Will (in tandem with Nature's instinctive willing) to detach one strand of the DNA molecule (the DNA double helix) from the other strand of this molecule so that the DNA is not a helix of two strands anymore. This isolation of the two strands allows each nitrogen base of each of the two isolated strands to be paired with a "free" nitrogen base so two DNA helixes or molecules result from the original DNA helix or molecule.

Transcription is the self's instinctive use of Nature's Will (in tandem with Nature's instinctive willing) in the first step of copying a gene from the sequence of genes used to structure the DNA molecule. A distinct sequence of nucleotides (a gene) is copied into RNA, specifically messenger RNA (mRNA), by way of the enzyme RNA polymerase. The self then instinctively uses Nature's Will (in tandem with Nature's instinctive willing) in the next step, which is translation.

The process of translation is the transporting of mRNA (evolved in transcription) out of the nucleus of the cell into the cell's cytoplasm. In the cell's cytoplasm, mRNA is directed by way of the self and Nature's instinctive willing to the ribosomes of the cell where protein synthesis is directed to happen by way of transfer RNA (tRNA).

The condensed energies which are exchanged between the DNA patterns is not information because DNA patterns haven't any inner letters in them any more than they have data or outer letters in them. The letter, "A" is short-form for the word "adenine", which is used by us to stand for its nitrogen base; however, the letter "A" is not this nitrogen base. Just as it's a semantic truth that the word is not the thing to which the word refers, it's also a semantic truth that a letter is not the thing to which the letter refers!

Geneticists hypothesise that a cell is able to "read" the genetic pattern in it but this is a ludicrous hypothesis because a physical cell doesn't have abilities, like the ability to read and identify. Only a self has ability to read and identify. Only a self is able to instinctively identify and respond to the changes produced in its cells' DNA.

Every self has the ability to "borrow" Nature's Will so it can influence the way in which its sensable organism's genes are instinctively used to develop proteins; therefore, every self affects how these proteins are used to carry out anabolism and catabolism in its sensable organism's cells. A self is able to influence the motions of its genes and proteins by using Nature's Volition in them after identifying them by instinctively sensing and feeling them; therefore, the self instinctively uses Nature's Will in the genes and proteins of its sensable organism so its genes and proteins are used to develop its sensable organism.

But a self is unable to identify the codes that geneticists believe are their translations of the encoded outer letters carried by the physical patterns of DNA because Nature is unable to encode outer letters in the physical patterns of the DNA It evolves. Geneticists had to painstakingly develop a genetic code to associate with Nature's physical patterns of DNA because there is no encoding in DNA for them to "read".

According to the "central dogma" of molecular biology, information flows from DNA to RNA to proteins through replication, transcription, and translation; however, this doctrine is clearly ridiculous. It's impossible for DNA to be encoded with eternal Forms by Nature or the Creator because the Creator is only a myth of Creationists, while Nature has no laws by which to automatically encode molecules of DNA. If these particles of DNA were encoded with eternal Forms, there would be no need for geneticists to use the outer letters of the English language to chart them on energetical and physical charts.[10] Instead, the Creator would have used his own inner language of eternal archetypal Forms to engrave ectypal outer letters onto molecules of DNA for our geneticists to read as this mythical Creator's DNA codes. Consequently, we would know the Creator's alphabet and language.

We're unable to engrave concrete outer letters in the DNA of our brains' neurons; however, we're able to develop abstract inner letters in our cognitions and store them in our essential memory stores. What's interesting is that you're able to stimulate your emotional energies by your instinctive use of Nature's Will in tandem with Its instinctive willing in your perpetually tensed muscles so that you're able to use Nature's Will in emoting the energy of your progressive emotions to stimulate your essential memory of the traumatic incident which led you to perpetually tense your muscles. Then you're able to develop inner symbols, like inner words, and associate them with this traumatic incident in your memory so that you're able to communicate your concerns about this

---

[10] An example of an energetical chart would be a holographic chart projected into a room designed for this purpose.

incident to others by outwardly speaking outer symbols, like outer words, to them.

Anxiety always originates from our temperament by way of our instinctive use of Nature's Will. We use our ongoing anxiety to perpetually, not chronically, tense our muscles. We're unable to chronically tense our muscles because Chronos or time is the root of the word "chronic"; therefore, the use of the word "chronic" to describe the ongoing tenseness of our muscles is inappropriate because Chronos is only a nominal word.

You might think that your body is the source of your anxiety when its perpetually tensed muscles are massaged because this massaging stimulates anxiety in you; however, the anxiety you originally experienced was repressed by you in your temperament and associated by you with your perpetual tensing of your muscles. As a result, when you're muscles are massaged, your memory of your original anxiety is stimulated because you're "haunted" by the unresolved trauma which led your original anxiety to develop in the first place.

A hydrogen atom's bonding to another atom occurs by way of a self and/or Nature's instinctive willing which relates the hydrogen atom to the other atom. These relationships are easily disrupted by a self's instinctive use of Nature's Will for the purpose of replication (copying DNA to DNA), transcription (copying DNA to RNA), and translation (copying mRNA to tRNA). The hydrogen atom has one proton and one electron; therefore, the hydrogen atom is an electrically positive atom because it doesn't have enough electrons to harmonise the charge of its proton. Consequently, Nature instinctively uses Its Will in the hydrogen atom to attract another electron to it so that the hydrogen atom's charge is harmonised.

Contrary to popular belief, there is no such thing as an "electrostatic" charge where a supposedly positive "static" electrical charge at the end of one molecule is attracted to the supposedly negative static charge at the end of another molecule. Electricity is always active because it's an instinctive vitalising by a self and/or Nature. Electric charges are never static. Electric charges are always active. Consequently, Nature on Its own or the self and Nature together instinctively Will within a hydrogen atom to develop a weak chemical relationship between an *electroactively* charged positive hydrogen atom at the end of one molecule and an electroactively charged negative atom, such as an oxygen or a nitrogen atom, at the end of another molecule.

Scientismists refer to covalent bonding as "electrostatic" because they believe in stasis. I refer to covalent bonding as "electroactive" because I know there is only activity. The relevance of this fact to science is that the branch of mechanics called "statics" needs to be replaced by Kinetics, Kinesis, Selfkinetics, and Selfkinesis, just as mechanics needs to be replaced by organics.

Nature instinctively wills an electroactive charge between two molecules to relate them together or isolate them from each other. This relationship is not due to a "dipole–dipole force" because Nature is unable to forcibly Will; Nature is only able to unforcefully Will. Force is a trait of selves, not Nature.

Nature is unable to force because force is a use of Nature's Will with malevolence. Nature doesn't malevolently force any more than It benevolently wills. Benevolent force is an oxymoron because force is contradictory to benevolence. Nature isn't forcefully malevolent or unforcefully benevolent in Its Activation of activities, motions, and movements. Only selves forcefully or malevolently as well as unforcefully or benevolently use Nature's Will.

Nature's electrical will wave is simply one way that Nature expresses Its Will through an atom. Nature's magnetic will wave is even more basic than Nature's electrical will wave because Nature's electrical will wave "rides" Nature's magnetic will wave, just as Nature's strong nuclear and weak nuclear will waves ride Nature's electrical will wave. And Nature's magnetic, electrical, strong nuclear, and weak nuclear will waves "ride" Nature's gravitational-antigravitational will waves; therefore, Nature's Will is the metaphorical "horse" of Nature's Will which Nature spontaneously, instinctively and nondeliberately waves so its vital energies (not "forces") "ride" this "horse" by way of Nature's "saddling" of them.

A self's instinctive as well as deliberate use of Nature's Will is varied. In terms of developing emotions, the particular pattern of genes in the nuclei of the neurons' cell bodies predisposes the self to use Nature's Will to generate emotions in a way that reflects the particular pattern of genes existed by the self in its sensable organism.. This patterning of emotions is often confused as a self's character and personality when, in truth, this patterning is merely the self's way of expressing its emotions *along with* its character and personality.

An enlightened self understands that its way of expressing its emotions is not its character or its personality. As a result, this enlightened self tries to be alert so it guides its emotions by feeling its use of Nature's Will in instinctive, unintentional, unknowing, and unknowledgeable incognisance as well as in deliberate, intentional, knowing, and knowledgeable cognisance, unlike Nature's use of Its Will instinctively, non-intentionally, non-unintentionally, unknowingly, and unknowledgeably, since the self knows that its patterns of expressed emotions are only related to the selves or roles of its personality. An enlightened self knows that the selves and roles of its personality are the result of its thinking and reasoning, while its emotions only influence its thinking and reasoning.

In terms of developing its intelligence, the DNA in a neurons' cell bodies predispose a self to use Nature's Will to cognise in a way that reflects its particular pattern of genes, e.g., a developmentally handicapped self has a sensable organism with a particular pattern of aberrant genes that will interfere more with this self's ability to cognise than selves whose sensable organisms' particular pattern of genes aren't aberrant. This fact also accounts for the various levels of cognising we're familiar with in the population at large, i.e., the population at large reflects a large group with typical gene patterns, a small group of simpletons with aberrant gene patterns, and a small group of geniuses with aberrant gene patterns.

Our abilities are used by us to introspect that which is within us as well as extrospect that which is outside of us. Nature is unable to introspect because Nature is unable to think, intuitively and cognitively, nor is Nature able to reason, recognitively. Nature is unable to extrospect Its outer aspects, such as Its, suefs, luefs, apparitions, particles, and bodies because It's unable to sense, perceive, and understand these phenomena as individuals. And, of course, Nature doesn't cogitate, intellectually, because Nature doesn't have disabling abilities or disabling faculties. Consequently, Nature has no cogitated delusions.

Nature is the Source of every Reality It evolves and grows with Its willing and every Reality It develops with Its willing; therefore, Nature is related to every Reality and Its phenomena are related to each other by Its willing.

Nature instinctively relates things to things, but Nature is unable to communicate with things, like you or I. We're only able to dwell in Nature, not communicate with Nature, because Nature is unable to distinguish us as things who are different from the Thingness It is.

Organisms are mineral as well as multicellularly vegetative and multicellularly sensable; however, only sensable organisms are inhabited by selves. Mineral organisms and vegetative organisms are uninhabited by a self; therefore, only Nature wills the motions in and movements of these organisms.

For example, Nature's instinctive willing in a flower opens the flower's petals as Nature instinctively wills the rays of the sun to heat the flower. The meeting of Nature's willing within the flower and Its willing in the sun's rays from the sun existed outside of the flower is the interaction which evolves changes in the flower. This is *natural harmony*, not "natural selection". *Natural harmony is the interaction of Nature's willing in Its natures.*

Unlike Nature, if our immortality exists, it arises from our ability to know. Nature is unable to grant us immortality because Nature has no ability to know; therefore, Nature hasn't the know-how by which to confer immortality on us. The fact that Nature is unable to grant us our immortality gives contentment to a Selfist because he or she is cognisant that his or her knowing of Nature's Will is his or her effective source of immortality or is ineffective in this regard; therefore, he or she knows that he or she will use his or her ability of Selfkinetics to activate his or her needs, sane desires, and insane desires and use his or her ability of Selfkinetics in his or her ability of Selfkinesis to evolve motions in and movements of his or her sensor forever or until his or her sensable organism dies.

A self's verbal expression of its wisdom is its expression of its religion of words in effectively relaying its fairly biased philosophy of Existence. A Selfist's Ultimate Truth is the Freedom by which he or she indicates, describes, and explains his or her metaphysics as his or her effective way of understanding Nature's instinctive willing within him or her as well as beyond him or her. Nature is his or her religious absolute, while the basis of his or her intelligent metaphysics (as well as his or her intelligent religion) is his or her Ultimate Truth of Freedom which is the basis of Nature, the Selfless Non-Individual unintelligence, an irony, since Nature continues to generate individual selves who are capable of actualizing intelligence by way their individuality

Theology is the delusional study of a fictitious Supreme Being called "God".

In our century, religion is treated as if it were inferior to spirituality because spiritualists have convinced most people that the spirit is "better" than religion. These spiritualists fail to understand that religion is your nonverbal as well as verbal expression of harmony. Spirit and spirituality are delusions because God is a delusion. There is no selfless "spirit" who allows "God" to express this selfless spirit's immortal "soul" with the "grace" of God. There is only a self or an "I" who is responsible for unselfishly expressing its sensor (its "me") in harmony with Nature's harmony and taking care not to selfishly express its sensor in disharmony with the harmony of Nature.

Naturalism is a metaphysics as well as a science. A Selfist defines metaphysics as 'The study of immaterial realities existent in and by way of immaterial Reality beyond the existence of materialised realities existent in and by way of immaterial Reality.'

A religious system of practice is a ritual. Selves who have become enlightened Selfists don't put much emphasis on the practice of rituals because rituals are often used to handicap the development of wisdom by leading a practitioner to focus on these rituals, rather than Reality. An individual who orients her understanding to a ritual is, as the Zen Masters say, 'mistaking the finger pointing to the moon for the moon!' Of course, this doesn't mean that rituals aren't occasionally useful, but they need to be placed in context.

Worship is foreign to a Selfist; therefore, Selfists don't congregate in churches, temples, mosques, ashrams, and the like. Rather, they tend to congregate in centers of learning, like colleges and universities, although every Selfist develops his or her own unique religion of Selfism without the need for fellowships to perpetuate their knowledge by instructing recruits with the knowledge outlined in any book about Selfism. The Twenty-Five Fundamental Truths of Selfism I've listed in this book prepare a Selfist to develop his or her knowledge once he or she has subjectively proven that these truths are, indeed, truths. But Selfists who are trained in naturalism might develop fellowships in lodges, rather than congregate in churches and the like, because lodges are meant for independent sovereign individuals to relate as friends, rather than for submitters to worship their dominators.

It's my sincere desire to help all of you who may be on the brink of wisdom to tumble over this brink into Nature; however, you need to abandon your absurd desire for unnatural formal meditation so you're able to develop your abilities of knowing and understanding Nature by realising your natural informal Style. My three definition of my Style are: '1. My natural informal ability to watch what's happening as I interact with this happening by participating in it to intentionally change it to accord with my conscience. 2. My unique natural informal way of relating how I'm acting in accord with whom I'm genuinely, sincerely, and authentically expressing as me from what I am because I know why I exist, i.e., I'm an unplanned undesigned accident of Nature, not a planned designed necessity of God. 3. Continually dallying in my natural informal calmness and enjoying my pleasant emotions, so I'll experience my feelings of happiness as a by-product of my enjoyment, which results in my wellness of cognitive knowing and my sensorial and bodily health!'

Therefore, my ability to express my Style, naturally and informally with skill, is only developed by focusing continually on my knowing of my conscience. A self's conscience is best defined as, 'A self's attentiveness, rather than inattentiveness, to keeping its integrity intact so it avoids the chicanery which results from its inattentiveness.'

My definition of integrity is: 'A self's respect of the Freedom of other selves to choose an action, actions, reaction, or reactions stimulated by their choice to fulfil their chosen need, needs, sane (benevolent) desire or desires without interference by this self's choice to act or react on its chosen insane (malevolent) desire or desires, unless, of course, these selves choose to act or react on their chosen insane desire or desires to interfere with the choice or choices of this self in which case its self-respect (its respect for its own Freedom) will inevitably result in conflict between it and these interfering selves.'

Your ability to develop insights in relation to your reading of this chapter of *Naturalism* may be hindered by your current stage of development. Your reactions to this chapter will reveal your current stage of development. If you've reacted with anger, contempt, or dismay to this chapter, I may assume that you're a delusional Creationist who has not yet given up your irrational faith and belief in the Creator or your associated beliefs, such as your irrationally logical beliefs in Creation, the laws of Nature, and the laws of morality. Of course, I may also assume that you're a delusional scientismist who has not yet given up your irrational faith and belief in the philosophical doctrine of objectivism and your associated beliefs, such as your beliefs in Creation, the creating ability of Natural Law, and the laws of morality. If you've reacted with interest to this chapter, you're well on your way to wisdom because you obviously understand that you're able to choose to assert your use of Nature's Will, Volition, or Existence with responsibility in your way of acting and reacting.

I have attempted to share my sanity with you in writing this chapter as well as in writing the other chapters of this book. The degree to which I've succeeded is not just the result of my sanity but also the result of yours. Sanity is "wellness in relating" because it helps us to communicate, just as insanity is "unwellness in relating" because it hinders our ability to communicate. If you're in agreement with my sanity, please carry on with yours. If you aren't in agreement with my sanity, you're denying your insanity because my sanity is the result of *not* denying *my* insanity (my malevolence).

I know that I'm always in danger of expressing malevolent tendencies, unlike some wellness "professionals" who ignore their expressions of malevolence; therefore, I guard against setting my malevolent tendencies loose on others when I recognise that I am beset by frustrations because my frustrations often tempt me to *not* guard against the negative emotions which I'm continually prone to expressing when I'm frustrated. A woman (or a man) who knows that the Evolver, Grower, Developer, Deteriorator, and Devolver is continually expressing harmony also knows that her experience of harmony is her responsibility. Although her malevolence is ineradicable from Potentiality (and her temperament), she knows that she is always capable of restoring her harmony within Nature's harmony. Unfortunately, the mistakes of other people occasionally frustrate us so much that we instinctively set loose our malevolent tendencies on them.

We have the ability and the Freedom to choose. We're able to choose a benevolent way of responding or a malevolent way of responding to our frustrations. We are absolutely responsible for the way we act and behave; therefore, we have no excuse for choosing to act and behave in irresponsible ways, such as using the excuse that our religious "community" ordered us to persecute individuals who subscribe to individuality, rather than communal, responsibility, like a Selfist.

You see, every Selfist is an Independent Sovereign Individual who develops his or her own unique religion of Selfism which is why every valid religion of Selfism only has a single member (i.e., I am the only member of my religion of Selfism, just as other selves who've developed their religions of Selfism are the only members of their religions of Selfism). Consequently, every Selfist's Selfism is a heterogenous religiously organised individuality which supports that individual's responsibility to develop and maintain his or her integrity, not a homogenous religiously organised community that attempts politically deny an individual's responsibility to develop and maintain his or her integrity by sanctioning him or her for following his or her conscience, rather than his or her shared religion's "Community Standards".

Our internet networking media, like Meta (formerly Facebook), Instagram, Twitter, and Linkedin, as well as our mainstream media have accepted their "patriotic duty" is to defend their community's policies which their politicians call their "Community Standards", instead of pursuing their responsibility as journalists to question the policies of our community "leaders".

Today is the current of Continuity in Immediacy which the Western World has labelled "Monday, August 8th, 2022, 9:23 AM ET". I am currently editing my publisher's PDF proofs of my manuscript as my final editing of them so my Publishing Coordinator at Austin Macauley Publishers can take the next step necessary for setting a date of publication of my manuscript as the book you're currently reading (unless we've blown up the World before this book could be published).

I was inspired to include the news that I reported to my internet network medium, Meta, earlier this morning that I appreciated their efforts in clearing up a technical issue I was having on my Meta Page called "Selfism". I also wrote a message immediately below this compliment which indicated that I respected their freedom to have their own opinions; therefore, (I continued to write) they might want to write a disclaimer to my posting of a comment I wrote to a friend which I intend to post later tonight in various locations on Meta (often referred to as Facebook), like my "Timeline" and certain of the Groups on Meta in which I like to insert comments. I asked Meta's agents to please respond by 7:00 PM ET tonight because I intend to post it after I've seen this clock reading on my laptop.

The title and text of this immediately following post are an interesting way to complete this chapter as well as contain a message which is a worthwhile inclusion to any individual's knowledge:

Individuals Are Inclusive While Communities Are Exclusive

We can use pain—or pleasure, as well as suffering—or enjoyment, to develop our strength of independent sovereignty (which is the hallmark of an individual's wisdom that we call "individuality") or develop our weakness of co-dependent dominance and submission in a "community" to escape our responsibility to choose (which is what Erich Fromm talked about in his book, *Escape from Freedom*). In other words, an individual's craving to "belong with" members of a community are really an individual's irresponsible attempt to escape his or her responsible choice of "belonging to" his or her conscience, instead of his or her governing community whose "leaders" want to irresponsibly choose for him or her as well as every other member of this community.

Individualism is based on the inclusion of every individual's responsibility for paying attention to his or her conscience. Community is based on the exclusion of individuals who won't let a community tell them to listen to its leaders, instead of their consciences.

Chapter Six
The Myth of the Big Bang and the Reality of the Harmonious Infiniverse

"Physis" is a Greek word meaning "nature". Our English word "physics" was derived from this word. The word "physis" was defined by Aristotle as, 'the essence of things that have a source of movement within themselves' (Blackburn, 1994, p. 277). Aristotle didn't distinguish between essence and substance.

The philosophical doctrine of idealism is based on the premise that things are merely the illusions of mind and consciousness. The philosophical doctrine of realism is based on the axiom that things are real apart from our knowing of them. The philosophical doctrine of naturalism is based on the understanding that mind and consciousness are delusions of idealists, while Nature is the immortal Origin, Generator, and Activator of immortal or mortal selves who each have an immortal or mortal cognition, an immortal or mortal sensor, and a definitely mortal sensable organism.

Naturalism is a metaphysics based on Nature. Naturalism excludes Aristotle's science of Physis because Aristotle based his physis on a universal "divine intellect" or "unmoved mover" as well as on the mortality of the self.

Aristotle inaccurately assessed that the source of a thing's movement was the universal divine intellect or unmoved mover. He also inaccurately thought that we each have a free will. Aristotle failed to understand that we use Nature's Will in Freedom.

Aristotle inaccurately thought that the soul was a mortal aspect of its body. He ignored the truth that a body is the mortal attribute of its inhabiting immortal or mortal self who has an immortal or mortal sensor, not a mortal soul. We're not mortal attributes of our bodies because we inhabit our bodies as immortal or mortal centers of pure energy; therefore, our understanding that a sensable organism is merely a physical thing existed by Nature's instinctive willing and its inhabiting self's use of Nature's willing in it is vital to our definition of physics.

Selves, like you and I, are existed by Nature. A self isn't its sensable organism because its sensable organism is the multicellular organic body that this self was generated by Nature to evolve, grow, and develop in harmony or disharmony with Nature's harmony from the original zygote or bud this self began to inhabit. A sensable organism doesn't have the ability to exist because it's unable to use Nature's Will. Only a self who inhabits its sensable organism has the ability to exist because it's able to use Nature's Will; therefore, a sensable organism is existent, but it's unable to exist the existent it is.

Mineral, vegetative and sensable organism aren't able to exist the existents they are because they're only existed by Nature (as well as selves if they're sensable organisms). Nature's existing or willing is used by Nature to effect motions in and movements of mineral, vegetative as well as sensable organisms. Minerals and vegetables have no selves inhabiting them who would be capable of using Nature's Will; however, sensable organisms do have selves inhabiting them.

Vegetation only seems to be moved by inhabiting selves.

For example, a flower seems to have a self who inhabits it and opens the flower's petals to the rays Nature is willing from the sun to meet the flower's petals. In Reality, Nature is willing this movement to happen in the flower; therefore, the flower is not a sensable organism because there is no self who inhabits the flower and senses it..

Aristotle was handicapped by his belief that "animal" bodies are living things. Sensable bodies only seem to live because a self often suffers from the delusion that its sensable organism has needs. A self is only able to live its sensable organism in accord with this self's needs because a sensable organism has no needs; therefore, sensable organisms don't live. All needs are traceable to the self who inhabits its sensable organism because a sensable organism is not its own user. The self of a sensable organism is using Nature's Will to live its sensable organism. A sensable organism is unable to live because it has no ability to use Nature's Will. A self does not live because a self exists as the existent it is in tandem with Nature existing as the Existent It is. A self also exists, rather than lives, its inner world of needs, desires, abilities, disabled abilities, and etcetera.

Aristotle didn't understand that Nature exists as Activity. He thought that his absolute, the divine intellect, was the inactive unmoved mover. Nor did Aristotle understand that selves are activities of Activity.

The modern English word "God" wasn't known in Aristotle's era; therefore, the word "God" wasn't used by Aristotle to refer to the divine intellect. Aristotle didn't understand that his hypothesised divine intellect wasn't the Source, although he did understand that the motions in physical things as well as the movements of these physical things were activated by the Source.

Nature is the Activator as well as the Source; therefore, Nature is the Source or Activator of Its Will, while selves are the relative activators of Nature's Will, but not the sources of Nature's Will. Nature is the absolute Cause because Nature is the Non-Individual user of Its Will. Selves are relative causes because they "borrow" Nature's Will to use as individuals who were generated by Nature from Nature to start their existence in Nature.

The Scottish philosopher, David Hume (1711-1776), convinced the scientismists as well as the philosophers of his era that an object causes another object by way of a lawful automatic connection. This scientismistic theory is ridiculous because objects are related by Nature's Will, not automatically connected by laws. Nature exists or wills objects. Nature's Will is Nature's ability to Cause or Activate from the Activity It is.

Nature causes phenomenal subjects and phenomenal objects by activating them from the Source It is. But there are no causal automatic connections. There are only causally willed relationships. Hume concentrated solely on perception because he thought the connection between the Substance of the outer aspect of a self's World and the Essence of the inner aspect of a self's World could not be established. Consequently, a philosopher would be unable to establish whether the inner aspect of a self's World is existent, the outer aspect of a self's World is existent, or both are existent aspects of a self's World.

Jean-Paul Sartre's dictum was, 'Existence precedes essence' (Sartre, 1953, p. 802), because he believed that an organic physicality precedes the essence it "nihilates". Sartre thought essence was non-Existence and organic physicality was Existence. Sartre lacked the understanding that nothingness is not essence because Essence is an activity of Nature's Existence; therefore, Essence is not nothingness or non-Existence. Existence doesn't precede essence as Sartre thought because Nature has always used Existence to exist Essence as Its progression of forms of energy or matter. Likewise, Nature has always used

Existence to exist Substance as Its procession of condensed energies or materialised matters to grow into physical structured bodies; therefore, Sartre's hypothesis that nothingness is an essence nihilated by the body is non-sense.

Sartre thought that consciousness is "being-for-itself". He also thought that consciousness is developed by the body's act of nihilation which Sartre hypothesised was the instigation of a nothingness from a body by this body. Sartre absurdly referred to a body as a "being-in-itself". His reference was absurd because a body is an existent, not a being. Beings don't exist.

Following Sartre's lead, scientismists assumed that only a phenomenal brain and its hypothesised "epiphenomenon" (secondary characteristic of consciousness) were real, while also assuming that the soul was a "delusion" of a "brain's" consciousness. A brain has no abilities; therefore, a brain is unable to project consciousness as its epiphenomenal ability. Rather, selves project—as well as introject—phenomenal qualities, like their cognition, because "consciousness" as well as "mind" are only nominal words, i.e., the words "consciousness" and "mind" have no actual referents.

Phenomenal sensable organisms, like your organic body, have no ability to project epiphenomena because they have no needs or abilities; therefore, they have no need or ability to use Nature's Will so they would be able to produce epiphenomena. Selves use phenomenal qualities; therefore, a phenomenal self uses phenomenal qualities, like its cognition and its sensor, because phenomenal qualities are necessary to help a self in its use of Nature's Will.

Cognition is a phenomenal ability of a phenomenal self, not an epiphenomenon or a secondary characteristic of a phenomenal brain. Faculties as well as abilities are phenomenal qualities because they are related to a phenomenal self which is their basis.

Aristotle failed to understand that we are either immortal or mortal centers of pure energy who exist by way of Nature willing in Nature. Aristotle's philosophy kept him from realising that he was such an immortal or mortal center who was able to use the Will of immortal Nature to isolate his sensor from the particles of his sensable organism after his sensable organism's death or die with his sensor as well as his sensable organism.

A physical reality is instinctively evolved from Nature by Nature. I know and gain knowledge of physicalities; therefore, I know that a physicality is not an illusion created by a supposedly omniscient Creator meant to fool me into thinking that this physicality is real nor is a physicality an illusion projected by Emptiness as Buddhists contend.

Unfortunately, scientismistic physics is a scientism of misunderstanding because its premise is that the motions of particles in bodies and the movements of bodies in the environment are governed by laws. Theoretical selfological qualitative kinesiology is a valid science because its axiom is that the motions of particles in organisms and the movements of organisms in the environment are instinctively willed by Nature. Consequently, I am a self who invented and practices theoretical selfological qualitative kinesiology and uses its selfological qualitative experience as a participant-observer to understand Nature as the Source of its cognitive activities as well as its activities of motions in and movements of its sensable organism,

The goal of scientismistic physicists is to explain how the movements of mineral particles outside of mineral organisms and the motions of mineral particles inside of mineral organisms occur. They only have a secondary goal of explaining how the movements of vegetative and sensable particles outside of vegetative and sensable organisms and the motions of vegetative and sensable particles inside of vegetative and sensable organisms occur. a Physicists aren't concerned with the needs of selves in coming to an understanding of movement which is why scientismistic physicists have leapt to the mistaken conclusion that the movements of mineral particles and bodies are due to laws by which their movements are supposedly predictable, rather than happen in accord with Nature's unpredictable spontaneous instinctive nondeliberate willing of their immediate and continual movements.

If minerals were moved by Natural Law, instead of Nature's spontaneous willing, selves wouldn't have needs because Nature would only have laws; therefore, Natural Law doesn't move minerals for the very good reason that we have needs!

Nature is beyond categorisation because all categories are logical. Categories are delusionally thought to be sequenced, chronologically as well as logically. The Greek word "Chronos" is equated to the English word "time". Therefore, chronological order is a mistaken hypothesis because it's based on time as well as order, neither of which have a real referent.

We develop laws in the delusional attempt to "order" how we express our needs so that we will not express our needs impulsively and malevolently; however, our delusion of order also prevents us from expressing our needs spontaneously and benevolently. Neither Nature's spontaneity nor the needs of Its selves are ordered by laws because Nature's selves need to express Nature's Will with Freedom. Unlike Nature, selves also express their insane desires, impulsively and malevolently, as well as their sane desires, spontaneously and benevolently. Ironically, a scientismistic physicist's fear of death results in his attempt to order his needs because he's afraid he will not survive if he's impulsive.

Creationists remain mesmerised by their religious fiction that their Creator created laws and then created the needs of creatures with his laws. They fail to realise that their mythical Creator would have used laws to create his ordered universe so that his creatures would not have needs motivating them to organise their objective world if their Creator created laws. Instead, they would only have laws to obey which would deterministically order their objective world to fit their Creator's supposedly ordered intellect. Many theists believe that the Creator orders the universe without having a need to organise it because these theists also believe that, if their Creator had needs, their Creator would exist imperfectly, rather than perfectly.

Particles would be stable if the Creator existed and ordered the objective world as Creationists hypothesise he "perfectly" does. The Creator's laws would absolutely stabilise particles because Creationists maintain that their Creator is intolerant any imperfections in his Creations; however, particles are instable which means that there are no laws by which the Creator orders the objective world. Consequently, there is no Creator.

Likewise, a physicist's hypothesis that uncreated laws of order and disorder are natural and produce the universe make the development of an equation to describe the "unity" of such a universe impossible because these laws contradict each other. There would be no Law which could be used to unify these laws because every law would necessarily be contradicted by another law.

Nature's Will is the harmonising factor of the Infiniverse because infinity transcends the disharmony of universal finitude.

Mineral organisms are evolved, grown, developed, deteriorated, and devolved by Nature, just like vegetable and sensable organisms. There are no mineral, vegetable, and animal "kingdoms" because there is no God or "King" ruling over Nature. Minerals are organic, not "inorganic", because mineral, vegetable and sensable organisms are existed by as well as existent in Nature. Nature activates the absolute motions in organisms and the absolute movements of organisms; however, scientismistic physicists delusionally assume that organisms aren't existed by Nature, while also assuming that sensable organisms are barren of selves and Nature's Will because physicists are of the opinion that "animals" or "creatures" are moved automatically and fatalistically by laws which determine their behaviour in time.

Time is a mistaken hypothesis because we don't remember the past, know the present, or anticipate the future. We only remember our memories, not the past. We only know Flow, Current, or Continuity in Immediacy, not present moments in the Duration of eternity. We only anticipate in accord with current actions, motions, and movements, not future actions, motions, and movements.

Time is a delusion because time has no actual referent. Most physicists are quite deluded because they attempt to prove that time and a bounded space were "created" when an extremely compacted massive particle called a "singularity" exploded. The physicist, Fred Hoyle, sarcastically called this mythical explosion the "Big Bang". The Big Bang is thought by many physicists to have started the expansion of their finite universe in what Albert Einstein thought was expanding bounded "space–time".

Many physicists believe that the Big Bang occurred 15 to 20 billion years ago in what they suppose was the beginning of time. These physicists suffer from the delusion that movements proceeded from the beginning of time and didn't occur before the beginning of time. They maintain, absurdly, that a movement proceeded from the beginning moment of the past to the present moment, while also maintaining, even more absurdly, that there is no reason why this sequence might not be reversed so that movement proceeds from the present moment to the beginning moment of the past.

These supposedly astute physicists don't recognise that a motion in and a movement of an existent happens, immediately, and continues to immediately happen. Nature has always instinctively willed the absolute motions in existents as well as the absolute movements of existents in It. Motions and movements didn't begin with time because time is only a delusional speculation of people who are ignoring activity, motion, and movement. Nature is the Activity which activates the absolute activities, motions and movements of Its pure energy forms, particles, and organisms of particles because the Infiniverse didn't begin in time. The Infiniverse has always appeared despite the mortality of its constituent forms, particles, and organisms.

There are only continually changing physical qualities and continually changing intensities of these qualities which a self instinctively or deliberately uses Nature's Will in tandem with Nature's instinctive willing to influence in reacting or acting to fulfil its needs, satisfy its beneficial desires, or seek vengeance with its insane desires. Measurement is the attempt to fix a continually changing quality as an unchanging quantity; therefore, we're unable to measure a continually changing quality as an inactivity because it's impossible to fix an unchanging activity as "unchanging inactivity".

The relative fastness and slowness of an object's motions and movements are also continually changing qualities because a self uses Nature's Will to increase or decrease the fastness of a motion in or a movement of an object; therefore, Nature's Will is Its basic quality, while quantity is not an actual reality at all because quantity is just a delusion of "methodical technologists" (scientismistic physicists). I practice selfology (the study of selves) which is a science I invented and developed, kinesiology, a science which took form in the 20th century, as well as theoretical selfological qualitative kinesiology (TSQ kinesiology) which is a science combining selfology and kinesiology which I also invented and developed. TSQ kinesiology is a self's study of how it's able to motion the qualities of forms and particles in its sensable organism as well as move the quality which is its sensable organism; therefore, I'm an *unmethodical Stylist* because Quality and qualities are my realisms. I know quantities are only the delusions of scientismists.

Nature is Quality. Nature's quality of Will transcends the continually changing intensity of Nature's Will. Nature's quality of Will is fundamental; however, the changing intensity of Nature's willing is a very important quality because this changing intensity is the source of vibration which destabilises physical structures.

Scientismists futilely attempt to measure the intensity of a particle's fastness or slowness by attempting to measure the impact of particle's movement. Ironically, when a scientismist has recorded his delusional measurement of the intensity of the particle's movement, this recording isn't relevant to the particle anymore because the particles intensity of movement is always changing. Obviously, measurement is an exercise in futility.

The intensity of a particle's movement would have to be measured and re-measured microsecond by microsecond by an objectively and quantitatively oriented scientismist if he were to measure as precisely and pathologically as he wants to measure. The scientismist's pathological obsession with measurement is delusional because the outer as well as the inner aspects of things are continually changing. A scientismist may believe that he's able to make the same measurement of, say, a distance, again and again, but he only seems to make the same measurements. He's really unable to use his measuring tool to measure a "stopped distance" because the particles in a distance never stop vibrating; therefore, there are no measurable distances.

We're also unable to measure a particle or a body's speed and velocity as expressions of time because speed and velocity are actually our attempts to measure a vibrating distance; therefore, speed and velocity are our delusions because they refer to time. We're only able to track, not measure, the fastness or slowness of a body, a machine, a particle in a body, and a free particle by using our mechanical instruments.

Like speed and velocity, acceleration and deceleration are our delusions because the times that scientismists believe occur in acceleration and deceleration have no actual referents. Time is a delusional ingredient of the equations scientismists use to calculate acceleration and deceleration. Acceleration is calculated as distance per second per second where a second is believed to be a duration of time. A second is a scientismist's futile effort to measure a vibrating distance as a static unit, but scientismistic physicists haven't yet realised this truth. Ironically, all scientismistic physicists know that a light-year is an oscillating distance.

A second is supposedly a fixed "unit"; however, a second continually changes with the vibrating distance it supposedly measures, like the sixty second distances which appear on the face of an analogue clock. Interestingly, these sixty continually changing distances taken as a group are known as a minute as well as an hour which means that the above average fastness of an analogue clock's hand mistakenly referred to as the "second hand" is mistakenly associated with each vibrating distance we attempt to measure as a second, just as the average fastness of the clock's hand mistakenly referred to as the "minute hand" and the below average fastness of the clock's hand referred to as the "hour hand" are mistakenly associated with the total vibrating distance which we attempt to measure as sixty minutes and an hour. As these hands move over a vibrating "second", we make the mistake of *pretending* that a "point" or "moment" of time has been observed. Scientismists attempt to calculate acceleration based on such pretensions.

Acceleration is a *calculation* based on the delusions we call "measurements"; therefore, acceleration is not a measurement of the increasing fastness of a tool, a particle, or a body. Acceleration is a calculation based on our mistaken hypothesis that we're able to measure the vibrating distance travelled over by an object. Acceleration is not a measurement of a movement's increasing or decreasing quickness because even a scientismist realises that it's impossible to measure increasing or decreasing quickness.

Average or constant acceleration is a calculation of a scientismist by using the following equation: $a = (v_f - v_i) / t$ (acceleration equals final velocity minus initial velocity divided by time).

The following example demonstrates how average or constant acceleration is calculated:

A car's final speedometer reading is the delusional measurement of 100 meters per second duration subtracted from its initial speedometer reading of 0 meters per delusionally measured second duration so the resulting difference is divided by the delusional measurement of 5 second durations moved over by the inappropriately labelled "second" hand of a clock; therefore, a scientismist plugs these numbers into the outer equation for acceleration as follows:

$a = (100 \text{ m/s} - 0 \text{ m/s})/5 \text{ s} = 20 \text{ m/s/s}$ which is 20 measures/measures/measures.

Are you able to see through the illusion to the reality? Are you able to see that the vibrating distance is mistakenly associated with the car's quickness of movement because there is no measurable relationship between the vibrating distance and the car's movement? Are you able to see that by substituting the letter "t" (meaning the word "time") for the letter "d" (meaning the unit of "measurement", not the vibrating distance) in the equation for acceleration, the delusion of duration has been introduced into the equation? If you do see through the delusion introduced by the substitution of time for the vibrating distance travelled over by the car in this equation, do you also see that we haven't helped the situation at all by rewriting the equation, "$a = (v_f - v_i)/t$", as the equation, "$a =$

(vf-vi)/d"? We haven't helped the situation at all because the vibrating distance moved over by the car is not the moving car. The vibrating distance is related to or associated with the moving car by Nature's Will, not by laws and time.

The motions or vibrations in a distance and the movement of an object over this distance are related to each other by Nature's willing, but the vibrating distance and the moving object are also isolated from each other as well as related to each other by Nature's willing. A vibrating distance and a moving object are also isolated from and related to each other by a self's use of Nature's Will in tandem with Nature's use of Its Will.

Scientismistic physicists refuse to understand that a vibrating distance and the object moving over it aren't actually connected, attached, or oned to each other by their mathematics because they don't want to give up their cherished belief that mathematics is "sacred". These physicists don't want to understand that their mathematically cogitated connections, attachments, and oneness are simply their delusions, as are their mathematically cogitated disconnections, detachments, and separations, because these scientisimistic physicists are afraid to realise that they are isolations who relate from the isolations they are.

We're unable to actually calculate the increasing fastness or decreasing fastness of an object's movement with the equations for acceleration and deceleration, respectively, because these equations are dependent on a vibrating distance which we're unable to really measure. The vibrations or motions of particles in a vibrating distance aren't the movements of objects which are moving over these particles. We're unable to use time to measure the motions of particles in their distance and the movements of objects over them because their motions and movements are unfixable; therefore, we're also unable to calculate the acceleration of an object's increasing fastness of movement or the deceleration of an object's decreasing fastness of movement because acceleration and deceleration are based on the delusion that we're able to measure. We are only able to continually track, not measure, an object's movement.

Scientismists' attempts to measure are made discontinually or intermittently, not continually. Scientismists are confused by the fact that realities are continual, not discontinual. Scientismists ignore Continuity because they believe they're able to measure the objective world, intermittently. Scientismists ignore Activity or the Continuum because they're only concerned with measuring phenomena which they believe are discontinuous, not realising that their delusional attempt to measure is based on their illusion of discontinuity, not the actual continuity of the phenomena they're attempting to so delusionally measure.

The scientismist, James Clerk Maxwell, declared bounded energies to be discontinuous because he didn't realise that unbounded Energy is "Nature". Nor did Maxwell realise that this Source is the Continuum in which all realities are continuities.

Maxwell was deluded. So was Einstein because he adopted Maxwell's mistaken hypothesis that bounded energies are discontinuous. Bounded energies aren't discontinually in separation from each other because their Source is unbounded Energy. Bounded energies are always related to unbounded Energy by Energy's instinctive willing in them; therefore, they are continuities. Energy is Activity. Bounded energies are bounded activities.

Particles are bounded activities of Activity which are activated as well as deactivated by Activity.

Moving particles (moving continuities) compose the Infiniverse. Physicists mistakenly refer to particles as 'fundamental particles as well as mistakenly refer to bodies, like protons and neutrons, as "composite particles". These physicists fail to realise that the term "fundamental particle" is a misnomer because there is no such thing as a "composite particle."

A particle is not a "composite particle" because a body is composed of two or more particles; therefore, two or more particles are a body, not a composite particle. Because protons and neutrons are composed of particles, protons and neutrons are subatomic bodies, not composite particles; therefore, protons and neutrons are the component bodies of the larger body we call an "atom", while atoms are the elemental component bodies of molecules.

Particles aren't subatomic particles because particles compose molecules too; therefore, particles are no more subatomic than they are submolecular because particles are the substrata of atoms *and* molecules. Physicists fail to realise that there is no good reason to label particles "subatomic" any more than there is a good reason to label particles "submolecular" because we would have to label particles "subelemental", "subcompoundular" and so on until we were labelling all things composed of particles with the prefix "sub-". Consequently, we would have words like "sub-cup", "sub-horse", "sub-chair" and so on if we continued with the absurdity of using this prefix.

The Infiniverse has always *currently* existed in the unbounded Ether. The word "currently" is occasionally misused as a synonym for the word "presently". Our use of the word "currently" to mean "presently" is a misuse of the word "currently" because the word "current" refers to flow or continuity. Absolute Current, Flow, or Continuity is the attribute of Nature. Relative currents, flows, and continuities are the attributes of phenomena, like the phenomenal current of a river's stream. The word "presently" refers to the illusion of stillness; therefore, stillness is the basis of the delusion that the actual is the still present, rather than activity, motion, and movement.

Particles are the constituents of bodies as well as the Infiniverse. Infinite particles compose the Infiniverse; therefore, the theory that a finite universe arose from a Big Bang and the theory that a finite multiverse arose from many Big Bangs are myths because they are both based on the myth of Creation.

Particles are continually condensed or continually materialised from portions of the unbounded Ether by the Ether's instinctive willing. Particles are related to each other by the Ether's instinctive willing; therefore, particles are often developed into atoms which are then related to each other to result in larger bodies, like an extremely large star. The Ether is Nature; therefore, the Ether or Nature's instinctive willing in a very large star expends its fuel so that the large star is collapsed resulting in a supernova (a stellar explosion). The various elements of this former star are scattered by the supernova throughout the galaxy in which this supernova was willed to happen by the Ether.

Physicists have speculated that the collapse of very large stars occasionally results in neutron stars which these physicists suppose collapse to non-Existence if they are massive enough so that their condensed energies or matters are "crushed" out of Reality leaving only a "black hole" in bounded space-time; however, their calculations are based on the theory of the Big Bang which is the theory that the universe started from the explosion of an extremely massive particle or singularity. This singularity is hypothesised to have been created by the automatism of Nature's laws (or the Creator's rule of law) to start the Existence of space-time from non-Existence which, in turn, supposedly expanded with the explosion of this hypothetical singularity. Big Bang theorists ignore the fact that there is no mythical finite universe because the Infiniverse has always appeared. They also ignore the Immediacy in which the Ether and all Its differentiations continue because they're fascinated by their delusions of time, eternity, and the Now.

The condensed energies of a massive star aren't crushed out of Reality by the pressure of the Ether's attractive vitalism of gravity. Instead, they're compacted to a critical point of pressure where they become a neutron star. A neutron star is not collapsed out of Reality, despite its impressive mass. A neutron star's condensed energies are compacted until they reach relative stability as a collection of existents because Nature's vital will of antigravity is complementary to Its vital will of gravity; therefore, Nature is unable to Will in gravity to pull an existent out of Reality because Nature's push of antigravity keeps the existent existing. A neutron star may disappear from view because few photons escape its gravitational-antigravitational field, but the neutron star is not collapsed out of Reality as physicists have come to believe.

Nature doesn't instinctively crush a neutron star out of Reality with Its will or vitality of gravity; rather, Nature's harmonising of Its vital gravity-antigravity compacts the neutron star. The deterioration of the neutron star begins when the neutron star has aged to the stage where its heat dissipates because of the instability of its particles.

Nature's continual organising, disorganising, and reorganising of particles is reflected in Its compacting and fusing together of a neutron star's particles; however, this organisation-disorganisation-reorganisation is limited because particles age. Aging or deterioration is a side-effect of the instability of particles. The attractive and repulsive willing of Nature in particles ages or deteriorates them by vibrating them so they decay or disintegrate. Particles are departiclised by Nature when they have aged to the stage where they deteriorate because Nature is unable to keep them integrated.

"Unsettlement" is the final stage of a particle's existence since the particle has become so "brittle" with age that it's inevitably returned to the unbounded uncondensed Energy or unbounded immaterial Matter from which it was first accidentally condensed or materialised by Nature's spontaneous instinctive nondeliberate use of Its Will so that Nature's continued willing in it results in the brittlely aged particle's decondensation or dematerialisation whereupon it ceases to exist as an individual particle. When the particles of a neutron star have aged and deteriorated to the stage of unsettlement, Nature is unable to keep the neutron star integrated. Instead, the push of antigravity and the pull of gravity disintegrates the star's particles and, thereby, the neutron star.

Nature is unable to instinctively and nondeliberately use Its Will in a 'black' star's particles to increase the gravitational pull on the black star so that a black hole would result because Nature's vital attractive gravitational pulling and concurrent vital repulsive antigravitational pushing in the black star's particles compacts the black star so that the black star is existent in a relatively stable condition; therefore, Nature is unable to instinctively and nondeliberately use Its Will in Its attractive vital gravity to collapse the black star out of Reality so that it would "poke a hole" in Reality and leave behind a black hole of non-Existence.

A black hole is supposed to be a singularity point with no volume and infinite density in the finite universe's bounded expanding space-time; however, there are only centers of the Ether, not points of a bounded space-time. A real center of the Ether doesn't have density, much less infinite density, because only physicalities have density. A center of Ether is not the supposed residual infinite density of an infinitely collapsed star because a center of Ether is essential energy, not inessentiality. Inessentiality is a delusion because the inessential is supposed to be nothingness.

Physicists contend that particles and bodies carry "physical forces" and that these hypothesised forces are the "tools" of the Creator or non-Existence; however, particles and bodies are carried by the *vitalism* of the Evolver, Grower, Developer, Deteriorator, and Devolver. Particles and bodies interact by way of Nature's instinctive vitalising, not by physical force, because physicalities have no ability to force. Only selves have the ability to force.

Nature instinctively vitalises the processes in and the activity between particles and bodies. Nature uses Its attractive qualia of gravity, magnetism, electricity, and strong nuclearity to organise and reorganise bodies. Nature uses Its repellent qualia of antigravity, magnetism, electricity, and weak nuclearity to disorganise bodies; therefore, the Infiniverse is a harmony of Nature's willing of organisation-disorganisation-reorganisation.

The decay of vegetable as well as sensable corpses and the disintegration of unsettled mineral "corpses" are the result of Nature's instinctive attractive and repulsive willing in the particles of these sensable, vegetative, and mineral corpses. Nature instinctively wills the particles of decaying sensable, vegetative, and mineral corpses to disorganise. Consequently, Nature exists Its disorganisation of particles as well as Its organisation and reorganisation of particles.

Nature exists contents in Its beginningless and endless extension; therefore, Nature exists the Infiniverse in Its beginningless and endless extension because the Infiniverse continually fills Nature as Nature's contents.

The Infiniverse is existed as an infinity of continually changing particles and bodies in and by way of unbounded Energy. This infinity of continually changing particles and bodies is existed in a harmony, not a steady state, because these particles and bodies are continually organised, continually disorganised, and continually reorganised by Energy's willing. The organisation (evolution and growth) of these particles and bodies is harmonious as is the disorganisation (deterioration and devolution) of these particles and bodies.

For example, we and Nature continually harmonise the cells of our bodies through the metabolic processes of anabolism (organisation) and catabolism (disorganisation). Our cells remain healthy by way of the anabolic processes of evolution, growth, and development, while they're reduced to an unhealthy deterioration and devolution by way of catabolic processes. Our cells age or deteriorate because the particles composing them are instable; therefore, the process of anabolism is reduced in the efficiency and effectiveness with which it occurs. As a result, our cells sooner or later become irreparably damaged by catabolism. Then we're unable to use these damaged cells for anabolism. In other words, our cells inevitably die.

Evolution, growth, and development happen by disorganisation as well as by organisation because we need to continually reorganise our cells; however, deteriorating and devolving are processes of disorganisation that aren't used in the process of organising. Aging is deterioration which is due to the instability of particles that results in their decay or disintegration. Devolution is the result of the instability of particles because the process of devolution happens after the aging or deterioration of a suef, a particle, or an organism is completed.

There wasn't a Big Bang. We don't exist in an expanding finite universe. Neither is there an infinite Universe existed in a steady state as the Steady State Theory of the Universe claims. The Infiniverse is Nature's harmonious act of organisation-disorganisation-reorganisation; therefore, we exist in a Harmonious Infiniverse, not a Steady State Universe.

The Reality of the Harmonious Infiniverse is Nature's way of spontaneous instinctive nondeliberate willing in Its continual evolving, growing, developing, l deteriorating, and devolving of an infinity of particles and bodies in Its harmonious and ongoing organisation-disorganisation-reorganisation of them.

The Big Bang Theory is a theory based on the concept of "chaos" because Big Bang theorists hypothesise that their supposedly finite expanding universe originated from an unformed disorder. Chaos is supposedly utter "disorder" and confusion. Confusion is a reality; however, disorder is only nominal. "Disorder" is a word without a referent because the concept of disorder is based on the myth of law, rather than the facticity of need. Big Bang theorists don't understand that we have a real need for disorganisation because the disorganisation of organisation is necessary for reorganisation to happen.

Disorder or entropy is our delusional attempt to measure disorganisation, while order or negentropy is our delusional attempt to measure organisation. We're incapable of measuring disorganisation and organisation because disorganisation and organisation are continually happening as ongoing change. In other words, a continual disorganising and organising is always happening; therefore, the measurement of an organising's order and the measurement of a disorganising's disorder is impossible because the activity of organising and disorganising would have to be stilled or "stopped" for measurement to occur.

Measurements are merely the result of the desire of scientismists to stop Reality from changing because they want to hop off the merry-go-round of existing. Our hypothesis that we are able to measure is our silly delusion that we are able to stop "the merry-go-round" we call "Reality" and get off It because we haven't accepted the fact that change is the way of continual Activity, Reality, Nature, or Phenomenon. Our delusion that we're able to stop change is the source of our confused "chaotic" feelings.

In contrast to chaos theory is the Reality of harmony. Harmony is the Reality of continual organisation-disorganisation-reorganisation or the happening we call "Reality". Reality is composed of my inner unsharable aspect of the World, the inner unsharable aspects of other selves' World, and the outer aspect of the World we infinite selves share.

The outer world selves share didn't originate in an unformed "state of chaos" as the advocates for scientism proclaim. Our outer world has always appeared as an infinity of particles and bodies which are continually evolved and grown from

Nature (Reality) by way of Nature's instinctive willing as well as deteriorated and devolved back into Nature by way of Nature's instinctive willing. In other words, we don't exist in a universe which is expanding from an original Big Bang nor do we exist in a Steady State Universe.

The Steady State Theory of the Universe was developed by Fred Hoyle, Herman Bondi, and Thomas Gold. Their theory was mistaken because Hoyle, Bondi, and Gold believed in Creation, rather than evolution. The Steady State Theory of the Universe is the theory that the infinite Universe exists in a state of "continuous creation" instead of a harmony of organisation-disorganisation-reorganisation; therefore, The Steady State Universe is a myth because this theory is dependent on the falsehoods of Creationism and the steadiness or stability of the Universe.

Many physicists assume that the Big Bang Theory has been proven to be true because Edwin Powell Hubble discovered a relationship between the observed redshifts of galaxies and the calculated distances from Hubble's observation of these distant galaxy clusters from earth. Hubble made his calculations of the distance of these galaxies from his location on earth by using geometrical triangulation. Hubble theorised that the bounded space of his finite universe was expanding from a point of origin in time because the redshifts of these distant galaxies showed that these galaxies were moving away from our Milky Way galaxy.

Hubble established a "connection" between these redshifts and the distances of these galaxy clusters from us. The delusional mathematical equation for their supposed connection is known as Hubble's Law.

Hubble assumed that we exist in a finite universe which is expanding with space-time because he discovered that distant galaxies are moving away from us. Hubble's discovery convinced Albert Einstein that his supposedly finite universe was expanding in space-time from a point of origin.

Einstein had calculated that the space-time of his theoretical universe was either expanding or contracting before Hubble's discovery; however, Einstein suspected something was amiss. As a result of his reluctance to believe that space-time was either expanding or contracting, Einstein introduced a "fudge factor" into his equations which he called the "cosmological constant" so his calculations would show that space-time was static, rather than expanding or contracting. Einstein calculated that the effects of gravity on a very large scale would be minuscule if the cosmological constant was valid. Einstein later said that introducing this fudge factor into his calculations was the greatest blunder of his career.

Einstein's equations were mistaken because all equations are delusionally based on logic. Einstein's equations were also mistaken because they were based on his General Theory of Relativity which was his mistaken theory that bodied matters "warp" space-time resulting in spatial pathways by which these bodied matters move. Einstein mistakenly hypothesised that these spatial pathways are gravity, rather than that gravity is a will wave of Nature. Einstein didn't believe that Nature had Will because Einstein suffered from the mistaken hypothesis that Nature created us automatically.

Introducing the fudge factor of the cosmological constant into his equations wasn't the greatest blunder of Einstein's career. Einstein's greatest blunder was his denial that Nature wills. This blunder was responsible for Einstein's denial of action at a distance. This was also the blunder of Aristotle and Newton because they both believed that 'matter cannot act where it is not' (Blackburn, 1994, p. 5). All scientismists fail to understand that a particle is unable to act where it is, much less where it's not. A particle is unable to act at all because a particle has no abilities.

Modern philosophers tend to forget that philosophy was originally developed by philosophers as an adjunct to religion. These philosophers only recently abandoned religion in an unfair prejudicial alliance with scientismists who sprang from the first infamous "natural philosopher", Thales of Miletus, who single-handedly "constructed" the foundation of Western scientism. Most scientismists attempt to "throw out" or discredit the obviously superstitious notion of "God" as our ancestor's "dirty bathwater". Unfortunately, they're also trying to throw out the "baby" of Nature's "Will" with the bathwater of God.

The philosophers Dr Arthur Schopenhauer and Dr Friedrich Nietzsche both astutely realised that the Will exists in Nature, although they didn't necessarily realize that the Will was of Nature as well as in Nature.

Scientismists are reluctant to admit that action does, indeed, happen at a distance because they're afraid of unbounded uncondensed or immaterial Nature with a Will that It uses in absolute Freedom as well as ubiquitously, nonliberally, nonlicentiously, accidentally, spontaneously, instinctively, and nondeliberately within subjects and objects outside of and surrounding them to continually change the activity every subject and object is. But these cowardly scientismists feel safe because they know it's impossible to demonstrate by way of our sharable outer or unsharable inner aspects of the World that the Will of Nature exists or that Nature uses this Will to continually effect changes in the World's outer objects or inner subjects.

Scientismists are continually anxious and fearful, despite Isaac Newton, Albert Einstein, and, more recently, Daniel Wegner's ridiculous hypothesis (see Wegner's book, *The Illusion of Conscious Will*, which takes a mechanical, rather than organic, approach to Nature) that there are only codes encoded in Nature's "objects" which "automatically" (involuntarily) effect changes in them. These scientismists know that it's impossible to demonstrate that "invisible" codes and their encoded instructions "automatically" effect changes in the objects of the "objective" World (which is all scientismists think exist), just as it's impossible to demonstrate that Nature's invisible Will in the subjects and objects of the World effects changes in them.

"Quantum theorists" live in dread of being unmasked for the charlatans they are because they know that the invisible encoding of codes by Nature's supposed practice of "automatism" is impossible to verify as the truth of how changes in the World occur. Unlike scientismists, scientists know that neither automatism nor voluntarism can be proven to be the truth by investigating objects in the objective aspect of the World because proof is a matter of a subject's subjectivity, not an object's objectivity.

Modern physicists fail to understand that Nature instinctively wills waves of gravity-antigravity, magnetism, electricity, electromagnetism, electro-weak nuclearity, weak nuclearity, and strong nuclearity in particles. In this way, Nature's instinctive willing in as well as around these particles is Nature's action in particles as well as action around or at a distance from these particles. Like Nature's gravity-antigravity field, all the other fields of Nature, such as Nature's electrical and magnetic fields, are due to Nature's willing of waves in particles.

Einstein's General Theory of Relativity is the theory that a materialised matter (a particle) or a body composed of materialised matters is able to miraculously shape the bounded space-time of Einstein's finite universe so the shape of this bounded space-time is the gravity which these particles and bodies follow in their movements. Einstein intimated that this shaping occurs without action at a distance. Einstein's idea of shaping was absurd because, like Newton, Einstein didn't realise that he was unable to explain movements which are *initiated* by selves who exist, inhabit, and live their sensors as well as their sensable organisms.

Einstein's General Theory of Relativity was mistaken because gravity is *not* an effect of a law in a particle or a body or an effect of a law in space; gravity is an effect of Nature's Will in a particle or a body; therefore, action *does* happen at a distance. There is no bounded space-time shaped by some unknown invisible mechanism or law in particles and bodies as Einstein believed; rather, the non-mechanical unlawful invisible Will of Nature forms uncondensed energies as well as condenses energies and grows bodies. These phenomena don't move according to the shaping of space.

Even the Ether and the phenomena evolved from it aren't shaped. I am able to affect the structure (not the shape) of my body by maintaining a good or a bad diet as well as by exercising or not exercising, but the Ether continually and instinctively wills to effect the continually vibrating structure of my body so that its structure is always changing.

Forms, particles, and bodies are continually vibrating, but a form, a particle, and a body aren't shapes because they include their interiors. A shape is supposedly only the exterior outline or contour of a form, a particle, or a body that doesn't include the interiors of the form, particle or body. Consequently, shapes, outlines, and contours are only images we imagine in our imaginations.

Energy and the phenomena of Energy move according to the Will of Energy. Energy instinctively wills Its phenomena to evolve a vital field which surrounds as well as interpenetrates the phenomena of this field so that these phenomena move in accord with the fields of will waves which Energy is actively willing within these phenomena.

Einstein based his calculations on Hubble's theory that the universe was expanding from a singular point of origin. Of course, both Hubble and Einstein were familiar with the cosmological models of Aleksandr Friedmann and Georges Lemaître who had both advanced the theory that the universe expanded from a "point" of origin. This point of origin was supposedly an extremely dense particle thought to contain the mass which would explode into all the masses contained by an expanding universe. Neither Friedmann nor Lemaître understood that mass wasn't created automatically by Nature's uncreated laws or by the Creator's use of laws he supposedly created.

Hubble leapt to the assumption that the bounded space of his finite universe was expanding in time so he could express the relationship of the redshifts of galaxies to their distances away from us as a law dubbed "Hubble's Law". Hubble developed his mathematical expression of the relationship between the redshifts of galaxies observed by us and the distances of these galaxies away from us in an attempt to show that the universe was expanding; however, he failed to understand that redshifts only demonstrated that distant galaxies were moving away from us, not that the universe was finite and expanding with a bounded space-time.

The cosmological models of Friedmann and Lemaître were simply the first models of "The Big Bang Theory of the Universe". These models were based on the delusional beliefs in Creation and time in eternity, instead of on the knowledge of evolution, growth, development, deterioration, devolution, and Continuity in Immediacy; therefore, these cosmological models were patently false.

Neither Einstein nor Hubble understood that Energy is unbounded. Nor did they give special attention to the fact that Energy is indestructible. Consequently, they didn't understand that indestructible Energy wills the activity of destructible condensed energies or that indestructible Energy grows these destructible condensed energies into destructible stars.

Einstein and Hubble didn't know that unbounded Energy condenses Its portions. Modern physicists mistakenly refer to these condensed portions of Energy as "dark matter" instead of "dark materialised matters". Unbounded Matter is always willing so that It materialises matters. The continual evolution of these dark materialised matters in and between galaxies, such as those continually evolved between distant galaxies and our Milky Way galaxy, have gravity-antigravity willed continually in them by Matter (Energy) which activates the movements of these galaxies so that, through the use of spectroscopy, we observe spectral lines which are shifted towards the red end of the spectrum meaning that these distant galaxies are moving away from our Milky Way galaxy as well as away from each other.

By using spectroscopy, we're able to observe the displacement of the spectral pattern of lines towards either the blue end or the red end of the colour spectrum. By our observation of this displacement, we know "the Doppler Effect" is occurring. The Doppler Effect was discovered in 1842 by Christian Doppler, a professor of mathematics who existed in Prague. The Doppler Effect is the effect of the expansion or contraction of radio waves. A low pitched sound is heard when a sound source is moving away from the hearer, while a high pitched sound is heard when the sound source is moving towards the hearer. The Doppler Effect is also the effect of the expansion or contraction of light waves. The spectral lines of the light spectrum seen when a body is moving away from another body are redshifted, while the spectral lines of the light spectrum seen when a body is moving towards another body are blueshifted.

Physicists believe they're able to determine the speed of a galaxy's movement away from our Milky Way galaxy because they mistakenly think that durations are real and they're able to use them to measure the fastness or slowness of a galaxy's movement; however, physicists aren't able to measure the fast or the slow movements of a galaxy as the galaxy's durations because durations aren't real. We're unable to measure a galaxy's movement over an oscillating distance by the movements of light photons. We're also unable to compare the oscillations of the galaxy and the movements of light photons because we aren't able to observe these oscillations and movements.

We're unable to assess the fastness or slowness of a galaxy's movement by the fastness or slowness of their light photons' movements because this galaxy's movement and the movements of its light photons aren't the distances they move over. The fastness or slowness of a galaxy's movement is not comparable to the supposedly constant movement of light photons because we're unable to actually see the movements of these very distant light photons or see this very distant galaxy's movement; therefore, we have no way of observing (and no ability to measure) how fast or how slowly a galaxy is moving away from us or towards us, just as we have no way of observing (and no ability to measure) how fast or how slowly a photon is moving away from us or towards us.

The vast majority of galaxies we observe from our galaxy, the Milky Way, have spectral lines that are redshifted; therefore, most of the galaxies we view are moving away from the Milky Way. Some galaxies have spectral lines that are blueshifted, which means that these galaxies are moving towards the Milky Way. Once again, we have no way of observing how fast or how slowly these galaxies are moving away from us or towards us.

As mentioned previously, the redshifted galaxies are moving away from us because there are always huge amounts of dark condensed energies which are continually evolved between these galaxies and our own Milky Way so that Nature's attractive and repulsive willing in these particles results in gravitational-antigravitational fields. The antigravity in a particle's field is stronger than the gravity in this field the farther away this field is from the particle so that the antigravity of each particle's gravitational-antigravitational field pushes upon other distant particles; therefore, these galaxies are pushed away from our Milky Way galaxy and from each other. The only reason that Nature's repulsive power of antigravity within these particles is able to push these galaxies further apart from each other is that these galaxies were originally evolved at such a great distance from each other that Nature's gravitational willing in them is unable to attract them to our galaxy. Nature's gravitational vitality within these galaxies' gravitational-antigravitational fields was never strong enough to overcome the great distances at which these galaxies were originally evolved from each other; therefore, these galaxies will continue to move away from each other until they finally age and deteriorate to the stage where they disintegrate to be replaced by new galaxies which evolve from Natures dark materialised matters.

Nature's field of gravity-antigravity in particles and around them are inextricably related to each other in a particle's center of energy. A particle's center is an activity or an energy, but a particle's center is not a self.

Nature uses Its Will to push antigravitationally outwards from the center of a particle or body, while concurrently using Its Will to pull gravitationally inward within the center of the particle or body. A particle or a body's antigravity is relatively weaker in its push in relation to gravity's pull the closer its field is to another particle or body's center of energy, while a particle or a body's antigravity is relatively stronger in its push in relation to gravity's pull the more distant its field is from another particle or body's center of energy.

An electron is established with an optimal orbit about its atom, a moon is established with an optimal orbit about its planet, a planet is established with an optimal orbit about its star, a star is established with an optimal orbit about its galaxy, a galaxy is established with an optimal orbit about a cluster of galaxies, and a cluster of galaxies is established with an optimal orbit about a supercluster of galaxies because the relationship of Nature's willed gravitational pull within every particle and body's center of energy and Nature's concurrently willed antigravitational push outward from every particle and body's center of energy is harmonious.

Galaxies are established in their optimal orbits; however, the dark materialised matters continually evolved between them are pushing these galaxies further away from each other; therefore, the optimal orbit of a cluster of galaxies around a supercluster of galaxies will not continue forever because the cluster of galaxies will be pushed out of orbit by the antigravitational push of the continual increase of dark materialised matters between them and the supercluster of galaxies. Consequently, this cluster of galaxies will lose orbit and move as an isolated cluster of galaxies unless it moves close enough to another supercluster of galaxies so that the harmony of Nature's Will within their gravity-antigravity establishes it with an optimal orbit about this new supercluster of galaxies.

These facts lead me to ask the following questions:

Do super-superclusters of galaxies revolve around superclusters of galaxies?

Exactly what is the limit for the organisation-disorganisation-reorganisation of galaxies in the Infiniverse?

Are superclusters of galaxies the limit?

Is there a limit?

We will never know for sure.

Nature instinctively condenses or materialises Its portions so that "dark" particles are evolved. Scientismistic physicists have delusionally measured the heat energy of these particles at a temperature of 0 degrees on the Kelvin temperature scale or -273.16 degrees on the Celsius temperature scale. Nature instinctively moves these dark particles so they gain heat energy and their inner heat energy rises. When Nature instinctively wills within these dark particles so they intermove with one another, their heat energy rises even more. Nature instinctively wills in these dark particles to relate them to each other so component bodies result, thus, raising even more heat energy. Then Nature instinctively wills in these component bodies to structure the body of an atom with an even higher heat energy.

Nature instinctively wills within atoms so these atoms' interactions are related to each other chemically and the pattern of a molecule results. Nature also evolves interactions in a molecule which generates more heat energy in a molecule than in an atom. Nature continues to instinctively Will within molecules so these molecules interact until, sooner or later, these molecules result in large bodies, like stars, in which Nature generates tremendous heat energy.

Some massive stars are collapsed inwardly by Nature towards their center resulting in a rapidly spinning neutron star called a "pulsar"; however, even more massive stars are collapsed and result in a highly condensed star called a "quasar". Contrary to the belief of physicists, a quasar is not a gigantic black hole because Nature is unable to infinitely collapse a star.

Approximately one quasar in two hundred is willed by Nature to emit microwave radiation (radio waves), while all pulsars are willed by Nature to emit microwave radiation. Quasars and pulsars age and deteriorate so that, sooner or later, Nature's instinctive willing within them activates their disintegration; however, the microwave radiation generated by Nature in integrated quasars and pulsars continues to linger on in the Infiniverse as the Infiniverse's cosmic microwave background radiation (CMBR) even after these quasars and pulsars have disintegrated. Sooner or later, the CMBR that survived the disintegration of their quasars and pulsars (their former "black stars") will also disintegrate to be replaced by the CMBR of newly evolved quasars and pulsars.

Many physicists assume that their measurements of the cosmic microwave background radiation confirm their theory that the universe is finite and expanding with space-time. Physicists who believe in the Big Bang interpret the cosmic microwave background radiation to be a remnant of the Big Bang "fireball". Their mistaken hypothesis is that the hot radiation of this fireball would have thinned out and cooled as the universe expanded with its bounded space in time.

According to theorists of the model of the Big Bang, at time 0.0001 of the first second (believed to be a moment) after time 0 (zero) of the mythical explosion of the singularity, the temperature of the expanding universe was 1000 billion degrees Kelvin. Big Bang theorists then suppose that at one hundredth of the first second after time 0, the universe's expansion had cooled its temperature down to 100 billion degrees Kelvin, that at 1.1 seconds after time 0, the universe's expansion had cooled its temperature down to 10 billion degrees Kelvin, that at 13.8 seconds after time 0, the universe's expansion had cooled its temperature down to 3 billion degrees Kelvin, and that at three minutes and two seconds after time 0, the expansion of the universe had cooled its temperature down to 1 billion degrees Kelvin. At this temperature, Big Bang theorists believe that nuclei of deuterium and helium could combine, despite frequent collisions with other particles, even though these theorists don't believe that atoms composed of deuterium and helium nuclei were grown because supposedly the heat energy was too high for even extremely instable atoms to grow. (All atoms are instable, but some are much more instable than others, especially when they are extremely hot.)

According to the Big Bang theorists, 300,000 years after time 0, their expanding universe had supposedly cooled to a temperature of 6,000 degrees Kelvin so that less instable atoms could evolve, while objective photons were supposed to be incapable of knocking electrons away from these atoms anymore. These photons were supposed to have "decoupled" from atoms so that over the next 500,000 years after time 0, the cosmic microwave background radiation was theorised to have been built up.

Objective photons obviously didn't decouple from atoms because electrons in atoms are continually willed by Nature to emit objective photons, even at the lowest temperature scientismists delusionally measure. *Zero (0) degrees Kelvin is the delusionally measured temperature of the Ether in which our Infiniverse is existed by the Ether. The heat energy of the Infiniverse is stable because our Infiniverse didn't originate in a Big Bang which is why scientismists have always measured the temperature of the Infiniverse at zero degrees Kelvin.*

Big Bang theorists hypothesise that their finite universe started at the ridiculously high temperature of over 1000 billion degrees Kelvin and has slowly lost heat energy as it continued to expand with its bounded space "as time passed" so that "inevitably" it will lose all heat energy and suffer a "heat death". The Infiniverse is not finite nor is it expanding with a bounded space in time. The particles composing the Infiniverse start as extremely cold activities of the Ether.

Ether's portions are condensed by It as very cold, "dark" and invisible condensed energies. The heat energy of these particles rises immediately as they are moved by the Ether. In this way, the Ether generates heat in the Infiniverse.

The Michelson-Morley experiment didn't detect the Ether because the Ether is uncondensed Energy or unmaterialised Matter; therefore, It's not disturbed by bodies moving through It because It's not hampered by the friction which occurs between condensations or materialisations; however, the movements of condensed energies or materialised matters and condensed or materialised bodies through the Ether do result in "harmony waves". Harmony waves are due to the resonance, not the friction, of bodily movements in the Ether. This means that Michelson and Morley's hypothesis that the movement of the earth through the Ether would disturb the Ether and generate a "wind" in the Ether was mistaken.

A "wind" isn't developed in the Ether by the movement of the earth through it because the Ether lacks the condensation necessary for the resistance of friction to happen by way of the earth's movement. The earth's movement through the

Ether is simply a resonance in the Ether which is an effect of Nature's gravity-antigravity willing of qualia, waves, or vitalities; therefore, the particles of interferometers are compacted by Nature's gravity-antigravity will waves.

Scientismistic physicists used very large interferometers to establish the existedness of gravity-antigravity qualia in the Ether on September 14, 2015. The Ether's instinctively willing of Its waves of gravity-antigravity compacted these interferometers. Their compaction was detected by these physicists. Unfortunately, these scientismistic physicists failed to understand that their interferometers were compacted by Nature's unforced willing of gravity-antigravity waves of energy, not Nature's forced law to automatise gravity waves of "power".

The infinite particles known as the Infiniverse are in a harmony of organisation-disorganisation-reorganisation; therefore, the heat energy of particles isn't "running downhill" in a finite universe's expansion with space-time. On the contrary, infinite particles are existed in the Infiniverse with heat energy that is "running uphill" as well as "downhill".

Energy generates heat energy in the Infiniverse by using Its Will to activate continual movements of unbodied particles and organise them into bodies. Energy generates cold energy in the Infiniverse by disorganising bodies and departiclising particles which blend with Energy after having been departiclised by Nature's inevitably continual willing since the brittlely aged particle is disintegrated by the energy of unbounded Energy, unbounded Matter, or unbounded Nature's continual willing in it. Consequently, the heat energy of the Infiniverse is running downhill through the decay and disintegration of bodies as the modern theorists of thermodynamics claim.

However, these theorists ignore that the Infiniverse is also "running uphill" through the integrative organisation of bodies by way of Nature's instinctive willing—which contradicts the Laws of Thermodynamics.

Nature instinctively runs heat energy uphill so that this heat energy is in harmony with the heat energy running downhill which is why I call the Infiniverse "the Harmonious Infiniverse" rather than the "Steady State Universe". The Steady State Universe is the theory that the Universe is infinite and is existed in "a steady state of continuous creation". The Steady State Universe is a myth because this theory is dependent on the falsehoods of creation and the steadiness or stability of a supposedly unevolving "infinite Universe" (a contradiction in terms because the word "Universe" stands for a finite amount, not an infinity, like the Infiniverse, which transcends the mathematical notion of amounts). The Harmonious Infiniverse is based on the truth that Nature instinctively wills the evolution, growth, and development (the organisation) of phenomena which continually runs the heat of the Infiniverse "uphill", while the instability of particles result in Nature's instinctive willing of the deterioration and devolution (the disorganisation) of phenomena which continually runs the heat of the Infiniverse "downhill".

The Big Bang Theory of the Universe is also a myth. Ironically, those physicists who believe in the Big Bang fail to understand the reality of the Ether. Neither Creationists nor automatists understand that the Ether is the Continuum holding the Infiniverse.

Thermal and chemical energy are types of energy generated by Energy's vitalism. Energy's Will is the vitality in mechanical contrivances as well as thermal and chemical processes; however, mechanical energy is a delusion because Activity is Energy; therefore, Energy is always kinetically willing kinesthetic thermal and chemical activities as well as nuclear, electromagnetic, ionic, and other activities. Consequently, there is no mechanical energy which is supposed to be the sum of Potentiality and kinetic energy because Energy is the Activity that continually wills the Kinetic activity of Its own Kinesis.

The myth of the Big Bang revolves around two superstitious beliefs. One superstitious belief is that the Creator has the ability to create a finite universe from non-Existence by way of his willing in his created laws. The other superstitious belief is that uncreated Natural Law "automatically" creates the mechanical forces which create a finite universe from non-Existence.

Superstitious Creationists religiously believe that the Creator will grant them immortality if they believe in him, while most superstitious atheists and agnostics religiously believe that we're all mortal with no possibility of the Creator granting us immortality. Neither of these groups of superstitiously religious people understand that we're centers of energy who might exist as immortals in Energy because we know that we exist.

Superstitiously religious groups of people don't understand that, if they're immortal, their immortality is not "granted" because they fail to realise that the Creator and the laws of Nature are myths. They fail to realise that, if immortality exists for selves, it's an attribute of Nature and self-natures who know that they're developed by, from, and in Nature.

The Infiniverse is not immortal although it never ceases to appear because the Infiniverse is an infinity of mortal particles. These particles aren't immortal because they're evolved, grown, developed, deteriorated, and devolved by Nature, although a new particle will inevitably be evolved to replace every particle that is devolved.

Siddhartha Gautama's stance on Existence is interesting. Buddhists believe that Siddhartha Gautama was "The Buddha" or "The Enlightened One"; however, this was their mistake because Siddhartha wasn't enlightened. Many Buddhists believe that, when they have attained enlightenment, they will cease to reincarnate and return to "Emptiness". Carl G. Jung dubbed the Buddhist concept of Emptiness the "collective unconscious". Jung thought the collective unconscious was the basis of individual consciousness.

Siddhartha maintained that Emptiness was neither Existence nor non-Existence because he believed that Existence as well as non-Existence are simply our illusions. Siddhartha also believed that we are also merely projected purposeless illusions of this purposeless Emptiness.

Siddhartha believed that there was no purpose in life for us. He believed that there was only a purposeless Emptiness; therefore, Siddhartha was a nihilist. He believed that life is suffering which we are only able to escape by returning to Emptiness. Siddhartha believed in Nirvana which literally means "to blow out" or "to extinguish" our "illusory" Existence by ceasing to passionately will. Siddhartha believed that only by attaining Nirvana (blowing out or extinguishing the flame of will) could he finally cease to suffer because he would cease to exist as an illusion and return to the Emptiness which supposedly projected him as one of its "masks".

Siddhartha's philosophy is that of a coward because Siddhartha was afraid of suffering. Paul Tillich wrote a book entitled, *The Courage to Be*. Like Gautama, Tillich understood that suffering anxiety is unavoidable. Neither Gautama nor Tillich dwelled on love because neither of them understood that we use love to counter our feelings of anxiety.

To continue to exist in wisdom takes courage because we will never be free of suffering if we're immortal; however, we don't suffer as much as we might once we have become wise because, in developing our wisdom, we learn how to act in harmony with love so that we tend to enjoy, rather than suffer. This is why we need to pay attention to our need for harmony and our desire for love because harmony and love are the basis of our ability to "komos", which is the Greek word for our ability to enjoy.

We need to stop moaning about the suffering which will always be ours (off and on) because death is impossible for us if we're immortal. We need to develop the goal of wisdom so that we're able to use Nature's Will to attain the very attainable goal of happiness.

Wisdom is not Siddhartha's belief that the Source is Emptiness because the Source is Fullness. A Selfist wisely knows that Nature is Fullness, not "the Void". A Selfist's knowledge of Nature's Fullness motivates his or her free expression of love by understanding this emotion without wanting to cease existing merely because he or she will occasionally suffer (which was the cowardly desire of Siddhartha); however, it's important to understand that Nature doesn't force us to set wisdom as our goal to reach as lovers.

Nature is unable to know; therefore, Nature doesn't know that we have a need for wisdom. Nature doesn't force us to set wisdom as our goal for two reasons. First, Nature doesn't know that we exist. Second, Nature is unable to set wisdom as a goal of Its own.

Nature isn't a Selfist's "Authority", like the mythical Creator of superstitious Creationists. A Selfist is not his own authority either because he's an expert with expertise, not an authoritarian with authority, i.e., a Selfist isn't able to rule over the self it is with laws because a Selfist is only able to guide its selfological qualities, not the self it is. A Selfist feels best when he or she coordinates cooperatively because his or her coordinated cooperating is his or her responsibility. He or she knows that he or she is responsible for selfologically nurturing his or her behaviour.

Some people believe that those of us who are wise "should" strive for a higher status in the social hierarchy because we don't act as authoritarians who would use uncooperative competition to "get" and "possess" our way. These people know that we act as libertarians who use coordinated cooperation, rather than uncooperative competition, to develop our own way as we continue immediately.

Wise people understand society's hierarchical Game of the Gods. The Game of the Gods is a self's attempt to gain more and more influence by continually increasing its rank, privileges, monetary wealth, or fame so gullible people will be impressed by these fleeting illusions and worship them, instead of wisely develop their integrity by paying attention to their consciences.

Wise people don't attempt to rise in the hierarchy of society but choose an occupation to indulge in which gives them enjoyment.

Wise people influence the social hierarchy with coordinated cooperation. Such coordinated cooperation doesn't arise from a "state", but from the *activity* every self is. The work of wise selves is acknowledged by other selves because wise selves have demonstrated that they aren't attempting to become mythical avatars (the mythical Creator "in the flesh"). They are coordinating cooperative harmonisers, not leaders who want to be authorities; therefore, coordinating co-operators are wise people who don't want to flout their knowledge so much as they want to continue to learn from all people at the various levels of coordinating cooperation.

As a Selfist (a naturalistic self) who practices the science of theoretical selfological qualitative kinesiology, I'm not so much attempting to influence your reasoning as I'm trying to help you reason so you'll be able to reason your own way to wisdom. I'm not attempting to control you by attempting to indoctrinate your cognition. I'm attempting to reason with you so you'll be able to develop notions, ideas, and theories with your thoughts, concepts, and hypotheses by way of your own thinking and reasoning which may surpass my meditations, contemplations, and speculations. You're capable of bringing the knowledge of your own experience to bear in considering my philosophy which is why I emphasise your need to consider my philosophy in accord with your fairly unbiased knowledge, rather than the unfairly prejudiced knowledge.

Conscientious writers always try to write from a fairly biased, rather than an unfairly prejudiced, knowledge base. Unfortunately, their readers are often naively incognizant of these writers' experience of continually developing and changing their knowledge with their ongoing knowing. A writer's knowing is his, his-her, or her ability to develop new knowledge in his, his-her, or her continually changing structure of knowledge or knowledge base.

I developed my metaphysics of naturalism by concentrating my cognition or wisdom on the Source. Our Source is the Activator or Energy. Energy is the Source and Activator of all physical things. This knowledge is the basis of my ontology which I use in my practice of selfological qualitative kinesiology to further my harmonious knowledge of the physical realms of the harmonious Infiniverse as well as the harmonious ethereal realms of the Ether.

Scientismistic physicists will likely continue to disharmoniously and unknowledgeably assert their biased perspectives of Creation, time, eternity, laws, logic, and automatism, while avoiding the realities of Activation, Continuity, Immediacy, needs, reason, and voluntarism, because they haven't learned how to eliminate their reliance on their prejudicial perspectives. Nor have they learned that their prejudicial perspectives are the myths they use to compose their encompassing prejudicial perspective—the myth of the Big Bang—which, ironically, they use to establish "order" in the prejudicial perspectives or myths that they used to compose this encompassing myth.

Chapter Seven
Ontology Versus Scientism

Epistemology, metaphysics, logic, ethics, and aesthetics are considered by some philosophers to be the main branches of philosophy. An ontologist understands logic (the study of applying laws to a self's cogitating so its cogitating is conditioned) and ethics (the study of morality and immorality, but not the study of amorality) to be intellectual developments which fail to contribute to our ability to be sane; however, an ontologist also understands that epistemology (the study of knowledge) and metaphysics (the study of immaterial realities existent in and by way of immaterial Reality beyond the existence of materialised realities existent in and by way of immaterial Reality) to be intelligent developments which contribute to our ability to be sane. An ontologist doesn't consider aesthetics (the study of beauty) to be a branch of philosophy because he emotionally appreciates beauty without handicapping his emotional appreciation of it by studying it. Consequently, a prospective ontologist needs to realise that epistemology and metaphysics are the only valid branches of philosophy.

Just as metaphysics means the knowledge of that beyond physics, metalogic means the knowledge of that beyond logic, while metaethics means the knowledge of that beyond ethics; therefore, an ontologist has a metaethical knowledge of needs which are existent prior to the laws of logical ethical moralists and logical unethical immoralists. A logical ethical moralist and a logical unethical immoralist both absurdly attempt to use a set of laws to conduct their behaviour; however, they each have a different set of laws. An ontologist uses his metaethical knowledge of reasonable aethical amoral needs to transcend the insane delusion of logical ethical moral laws and logical unethical immoral laws.

An ontologist has a subjective knowledge of activity, motion, and movement. An ontologist doesn't need moral laws to explain how she "should" act any more than she needs laws of physics to explain how she is able to motion and move her body because she knows her behaviour is the result of her Freedom to select her needed, sanely desired, or insanely desired actions and reactions which prompt her use of Nature's Will without determining her use of Nature's Will.

An ontologist knows that her needs aren't governed by laws. An ontologist also knows that "shoulds" and "shouldn'ts" are an attempt of other people to indoctrinate her. She knows her Freedom would be handicapped if she allowed such indoctrination to happen.

An ontologist's metalogical knowledge is existed by her beyond the delusion of logic and its principle of the rule of law by which logicians believe we govern our reasoning. An ontologist uses this metalogical knowledge to transcend Aristotle's insane logic.

An ontologist understands through her metaethics that "recognitivism" is the sane knowledge of her aethical amoral needs, not ethical naturalism, ethical rationalism, or noncognitivism. Her knowledge of recognitivism helps her to transcend socially insane delusions, like moral and immoral laws.

Ethical naturalism (not to be confused with my metaphysics of naturalism) is the theory of ethics which maintains that a self develops its ethics in relation to its experience. Ethical naturalism models its theory of ethics on the paradigm of modern scientism, which is based on Creation, logic, principles, rules, laws, time in eternity, experimentation, and measurement, rather than the paradigm of my ontology which is based on Activation, reason, harmony, conscientiousness, needs, Continuity in Immediacy, experience, and participant-observation. Ironically, scientismists maintain that measurements are their observations, rather than their delusions, because they believe in delusional laws, rather than know their own realistic needs.

Ethical rationalism is a theory of ethics whose adherents believe that the laws of ethical morality are real in objective reality as well as subjective reality. Many ethical rationalisers assume that these laws were created by the Creator in the Creator's subjective world who then placed these laws in the objective world after he created it so that his "creatures" might "discover" his laws. Ethical rationalism models its theory of ethics on the paradigm of mathematics because ethical rationalists suppose mathematics occurs a priori. This supposition is a mistaken hypothesis, like the supposition that we are able to discover moral laws in the objective world. Nature is not a mathematician; therefore, mathematics occurs a posteriori, not a priori.

Ethical naturalism and ethical rationalism both have morality and immorality in common: however, ethical naturalists are usually *qualitatively* oriented scientists who believe in God, while ethical rationalists are usually *quantitatively* oriented scientists who believe in God; however, ethical naturalists usually only believe in Nature as quantitatively as well as qualitatively oriented scientists.

Unfortunately, most qualitatively oriented scientists are afraid to "buck the establishment" to too great a degree. They know that scientific establishments, like their country's universities, are not usually oriented towards discovering the Truth and its truths about our human situation but are filled with administrative "scientists" (politicians) who are only oriented to escaping pain and suffering by accommodating their universities' "doing" of science to their city, province (or state), and nation's politicians whom are all "dirty" fighters of destructive chicanery, rather than "cathartic" explorers of productive integrity.

These fearful quality oriented scientists who profess their love of knowing quality as their knowledge are often cowardly "ostriches" who "bury" their "heads" of integrity in the "sand" of their ignored consciences by denying their knowledge. The knowledge these fearful qualitatively oriented scientists deny is their knowledge that quantity is a delusion of quantitatively oriented scientists derived from their illusion that their measurements are possible, precise (or approximately precise), as well as seeable (observable).

Quite obviously, measurements are impossible in a continually changing World which reveals that a quantitative scientist's contention that he's able to precisely measure or approximate a precise measurement of (almost) anything is his myth because he won't admit that there can be no precision (or approximate precision) in his "production" of unseeable (unobservable) measurements in his World's continually changing unsharable inner immaterial aspects or continually changing unsharable immaterial as well as sharable materialised outer aspects. Measurements simply can't be seen (observed) because they're supposedly fixed and unchanging when it's quite obvious that there isn't a thing which is fixed or unchanging amidst our World's inner immaterial, outer immaterial, or outer materialised things.

Ironically, qualitatively oriented scientists also claim their ability to measure is beneficial to our intelligence, rather than dangerously detrimental to it, because these scientists refuse to even consider looking at the way our ability to measure distorts and rearranges our intelligence and its ability of reasoning into our "intellects" and our unnecessary use of our intellects to apply rules to our reasoning which changes our reasoning into our dangerously logical cogitating so detrimental to our intelligence. Consequently, to accommodate the views of scientists who claim to practice qualitative as well as quantitative science and those who claim to practice only quantitative science, I've defined morality and immorality as follows:

'A self's idealistic principle of ruling over its own and other selves' actions and reactions with moral and immoral laws in relation to its superstitions of theistic moral destiny and immoral fate or atheistic moral and immoral fate.'

Noncognitivism is the theory of ethics which asserts that ethics is a delusion and that we only know our feelings, emotions, attitudes, and dispositions which we use delusional concepts, like "evil", "wrong" and "right", to vent. The noncognitivist is usually an emotivist who claims that moral judgements simply express an appraiser's tendencies to praise and blame and that the appraiser's claim that he or she is reporting a true moral judgement has no meaning. Unfortunately, the emotivist tends to inappropriately deny the validity of our knowledge as well as appropriately deny the validity of our morals.

"Recognitivism" is a word I've coined referring to a recognitivist's knowledge beyond ethics. A recognitivist asserts, like the noncognitivist, that ethical morality and unethical immorality are delusions; however, unlike the noncognitivist, the recognitivist asserts that Nature is real, while denying that the Creator is real, that the harmony of Nature is good, while denying the Existence of an absolutely Good Creator, that the selves of Nature express relative love as well as relative hate, while denying that divinity (absolute love) and evil (absolute hate) are existed by them, that the selves of Nature express what they are with relatively proper or relatively improper actions and behaviours, while denying that right and wrong are existed by them as absolutes, and that Nature exists with the need to exist, while denying that the Creator and his laws exist as well as that uncreated Natural laws exist.

Noncognitivists disparage paradigms, while recognitivists have their own unique paradigm. The noncognitivist asserts that the recognitivist is merely using different words for the same delusional concepts that the rationalist uses while the recognitivist asserts that the noncognitivist has "thrown the baby out with the bathwater".

The recognitivist asserts that the "clean baby" which the noncognitivist has inappropriately thrown out is the harmony of Nature, our practical sanity, and our ability to use Nature's Will in our needs. The recognitivist also asserts that the "bathwater" which the noncognitivist has appropriately thrown out is filled with the "dirt" or fictions of a holy divine Creator and an unholy evil Devil, our supposed righteous morality and unrighteous immorality, the laws which the Creator supposedly created in us a priori for us to automatically produce our actions, motions, and movements, as well as the commandments which he is supposed to have ordered us to obey. Consequently, if we don't throw out this bathwater, we feel selfpathically obliged to "obey" and "do our duty" by unquestioningly following the commandments of selfpathically disturbed authoritarians.

Recognitivism is the metaethics of an ontologist. An ontologist is a realist who uses his own way of concentrated speculation to understand the paradigm of ontology. Within this paradigm, ontologists are able to gain knowledge about the unbounded Reality, real qualities, and realities.

Through the paradigm of ontology, an ontologist is able to use his positivity to track his negativity and use his negativity to inform his positivity about what his negativity is. Consequently, he uses his goodness to track his badness and his badness to inform his goodness about his badness, uses his beauty to tracked his ugliness and his ugliness to inform his beauty about his ugliness, uses his pleasures, soothing, and harmonies to track his pains, hurts and conflicts and his pains, hurts, and conflicts to inform his pleasures, soothing, and harmonies about his pains, hurts, and conflicts, uses his enjoyment to track his suffering and his suffering to inform his enjoyment about his suffering, uses his excitement to track his anxiety and his anxiety to inform his excitement about his anxiety, uses his sane desires to track his insane desires and his insane desires to inform his sane desires about his insane desires, uses his love to track his hate and his hate to inform his love about his hate, uses his knowledge to track his ignorance and his ignorance to inform his knowledge about his ignorance, uses his meanings to track his delusions and his delusions to inform his meanings about his delusions, uses his facts to track his fictions and his fictions to inform his facts about his fictions, uses his cognisance or wisdom to track his incognisance or stupidity and his incognisance or stupidity to inform his cognisance or wisdom about his incognisance or stupidity, and uses his truths to track his falsehoods and his falsehoods to inform his truths about his falsehoods.

The difference between an individual's negative and positive thinking is that he *believes* his negative thinking is courageous when he represses his knowledge of his positive thinking; however, he *knows* his negative thinking is his cowardice when he affirms his positive thinking.

A stupid individual doesn't use his positivity to track his negativity or use his negativity to inform his positivity about his negativity; therefore, he's ignorant of the fact that his emotion of hate is not necessarily isolated from his emotion of love. He fails to realise that he's unable to destroy his emotion of love with his emotion of hate; therefore, he instinctively represses the emotion of love existed by him in his temperament's memory. He forgets that he deliberately repressed this emotion; therefore, he thinks he has abandoned love.

A stupid individual ignores his ability to express his emotion of love because he's repressed it; therefore, he isn't able to inform his love with his hate. He isn't able to temper his hatred with his love. He expresses his hatred without the knowledge of love as his guide. This lack of knowledge disables his ability to track his hatred with love.

A wise individual defuses his hatred by using love as his guide to defuse it. He expresses his love without denying his hate. His hate isn't activated while he's expressing his love, but rests as an activity in his temperament's memory store. He's able to defuse his tendency to express his hatred towards an individual who has decided to attack him. He's also able to unconditionally express his love towards such an individual because his hatred is defused, not repressed.

Some people indulge in bondage, discipline, dominance, submission, sadism, and masochism. Masochists want to experience physical pain to attain what they think is their goal of pleasure because they think the negative quality of pain is their pleasure; however, the emotional goal of satisfaction is really the feeling they experience, not pleasure.

The quality of emotional satisfaction in such people is positively paired to their feeling of physically derived pain, while the emotional dissatisfaction in such people is negatively paired to their feeling of physically derived pleasure. Consequently, the reversal of sensory pleasure and pain in their interaction with emotionally satisfaction and dissatisfaction constitute the phenomenal aspect of the games these sadomasochists toy at in their thinking.

Timo Airaksinen relates in her interesting paper "A Philosophical and Rhetorical Theory of BDSM" that the goal of a masochist seems to be ambiguous because the masochist is prone to 'say equally well either, "Whip me, give me pleasure" or "Whip me, hurt me"' (Airaksinen, 2017, p. 57). This ambiguity only seems to be a masochist's way of thinking because the masochist is inappropriately using the word "pleasure". What the masochist really means to say is, "Whip me, give me emotional satisfaction" or "Whip me, hurt me, because hurting is emotionally satisfying to me".

The masochist makes the mistake of using the word "pleasure" for the word "satisfaction" when he says, "Whip me, give me pleasure", which is a mistake of substituting his attitude for his feelings. The masochist really means to say, "Whip me, give me emotional satisfaction", because the masochist has confused the spectrum of physicalities and the spectrum of pleasures with the spectrum of emotions and the spectrum of satisfactions. The masochist doesn't feel pleasure when he feels physically derived pain; rather, he feels emotional satisfaction when he feels physically derived pain. Consequently, the word "satisfaction" is the word that the masochist mistakenly uses as a synonym for the word "pleasure", while the word "dissatisfaction" is the word he mistakenly uses as a synonym for the word "anxious".

Unfortunately, Airaksinen doesn't seem to understand that satisfaction is not pleasure. Satisfaction is a feeling derived entirely from the emotional way a masochist thinks, while pleasure is a feeling derived entirely from a masochist's sensor. Likewise, dissatisfaction is not anxiety because dissatisfaction is a feeling derived entirely from the emotional way a masochist thinks, while a masochist's feeling of anxiety is derived entirely through the masochist's sensor. Therefore, to confuse pleasurable feelings with the feeling of emotional satisfaction and confuse anxious feelings with the feeling of emotional dissatisfaction are mistakes of substitution because the feeling of pleasure is misunderstood to be interchangeable with the feeling of emotional satisfaction, while the feeling of anxiety is misunderstood to be interchangeable with the feeling of emotional dissatisfaction.

Stupid people are sadomasochists because they believe they express their behaviours rightly, correctly, and logically as well as wrongly, incorrectly, and illogically, rather than know they only express their behaviours properly, accurately, and appropriately as well as improperly, inaccurately, and inappropriately. Right or wrong, correct or incorrect, and logical or illogical are judgements made for the purpose of praising or blaming an individual whose behaviour is absurdly judged as "divine" or "evil". Consequently, the judged individual is conditioned to obey the dictates of authorities who use praise to reward and blame to punish.

Wise people realise that they're only able to express their actions and behaviours properly, accurately, and appropriately, while also realising they occasionally express their actions and behaviours improperly, inaccurately, and inappropriately. "Propriety" and "impropriety", "accuracy" and "inaccuracy" and "appropriateness" and "inappropriateness" are complementarily paired terms. Right and wrong are the opposites of proper and improper because right and wrong are based on the fiction of law, while proper and improper are based on the reality of need. For the same reason, correct and incorrect are the opposites of accuracy and inaccuracy, just as logical and illogical are the opposites of appropriateness and inappropriateness.

Wise people know that, like Nature, they're only able to use Nature's Will harmoniously, not divinely. Unlike us, Nature is unable to develop hatred from fear and frustration because Nature is not an individual who is able to fear or experience frustration. Nature has no ability to know; therefore, Nature has no knowledge of others which could be used to develop hatred in It. Nor is Nature's harmony love. But Nature's harmony is the basis for our emotion of love. Unfortunately, our ability to act in accord with Nature's harmony as well as our love is often handicapped by our impulsive expression of our hatred because we're individuals who have to relate and communicate with each other, despite our autistic tendencies to isolate and withdraw from each other.

Unlike Nature, selves, like you and I, inhabiting human sensors and human sensable organisms, are able to communicate with each other. Our communications hinder or help our ability to intelligently express our love as we subjectively act and react in our inner worlds and subjectively behave and misbehave our sensors and sensable organisms in the outer world.

A self is unable to express evil because evil is mistakenly hypothesised to be absolute hate. If absolute hate was real, selves would have developed from Nature with absolute hate; therefore, Nature's absolute hate or evil would be our preference because "our" love would only be relative to Nature's absolute hate or evil.

Nature only has a need to express Its Will. Nature expresses Its Will, harmoniously, although Nature's harmony is not expressed for a purpose. Nature has no desire to express hatred or love; therefore, it's clearly impossible that evil or the divine is real because Nature is not an absolute Devil or an absolute God. The Existence of an absolute Devil is impossible because there is only the possibility of Nature, not two absolute Selves. There is only Selfless Nature and

Its selves, like you and I, not a God-Self who expresses divinity and a Devil-Self who expresses evil. Nature only expresses Its Will, harmoniously; therefore, there is no divine Self or absolute God nor is there an evil Self or absolute Devil. Consequently, we're unable to divinely or evilly express our actions and behaviours.

Having written the above paragraph, I must caution you that you're able to completely repress your emotion of love, even though you're unable to rid your temperament of this emotion so that you would be evil. Repressing your emotion of love completely so you're unable to express it is such an extreme response to fear and frustration that most people will mistake your complete volitional repression of this emotion to be your choice to express "evil", rather than your choice to avoid expressing love. These people don't understand that your chosen reaction in your situation is not your absolute hate because they're ignoring their own instinctive repression and deliberate suppression of love. These people fail to understand that you're unable to express your hatred absolutely because your love continues in you, despite your either continual or intermittent instinctive repression or deliberate suppression of it.

Selfpaths exist, but they only hate relatively, not evilly, because they're unable to rid their temperament of their emotions of love; however, these selfpaths do use their instincts to completely and continually repress their emotions of love, unlike many authoritarians whose repression of this emotion is not complete or continual because they allow their repression of their love to lift, occasionally. Consequently, extreme hatred is occasionally existed by a self; however, evil isn't never existent in a self because evil is supposedly the absence of love, not the repression of love.

The Lord of the Rings by J. R. R. Tolkien is a favourite book of mine because Gollum's conflict of love for Frodo and his contradictory greed for the ring of the evil Dark Lord is a portrait of human nature which strikes a chord of truth in me. Tolkien's book is a modern classic fantasy; however, it's a fantasy which was based on Tolkien's superstitious beliefs. Tolkien knew that the evil Dark Lord of his book was just a character he developed as his fantasy. *But Tolkien was a Roman Catholic who based his fantasy of evil Dark Lord on his superstitious belief in the evil Devil of the "Holy" Bible; therefore, the Lord of the Rings was based on Tolkien's delusions of absolute hate and absolute love.*

"Satan" is not an evil Devil. "Satan" is a label for any self who is unwell. "Satan" is also the name of the angel whose duty it was to take an opposing view to that of Yahweh; however, Satan is supposed to have rebelled against Yahweh—or so the story goes.

A Satan is an unwell self because it has repressed its Freedom.; therefore, it needs to restore its wellness again by realising its basis is Freedom. A Satan needs to "derepress" and "unlearn". Unlearning is a Satan's activity of replacing its prejudicial conditioning of its activities and behaviours by its irrational belief in destiny or fate with its unprejudiced as well as unbiased realisation of its basis of Freedom. Derepression is a Satan's choice of releasing its Freedom from repression. Derepression precedes the activity of unlearning. Having been raised in an absurd world, we become Satans who need to access our Freedom before our desire for our emotions, like love. Only by choosing to derepress are we able to unlearn and become well again so we cease to be Satans.

Wise people know that actions and behaviours are either sane (benevolent) or insane (malevolent). Sanity is the ability to discern (while insanity is the inability to discern) how best to interact with an individual you've diagnosed to be expressing behaviours which indicate that he or she is either responsible or irresponsible.

Behaviourists don't generally apply consequences of praise or blame to a self. Instead, they apply the consequences of increased Freedoms or increased restrictions to a self's circumstances so that its responsible behaviours will be positively reinforced and its irresponsible behaviours will be negatively reinforced. But this is not enough to help the self realistically discern the meaning of its actions and behaviours because all reinforcements, even positive reinforcements, are punishments which interfere with a self's abilities of pure thinking, symbolic thinking, and symbolic reasoning. Positive as well as negative reinforcements are punishments because they're meant to *force or condition* a self to obey, despite the fact that behaviourists call their positive reinforcements "rewards" instead of "punishments".

To understand the meaning of its behaviour and the need to change its behaviour, a self has no choice but to realise that its behaviour doesn't just affect it, but also affects other selves as well, which is why other selves increase its Freedom to behave when it's considerate of their feelings and increase the restrictions on its Freedom to behave when it's inconsiderate of their feelings.

A behavioural "therapist" trains a self to follow commands according to principles (rules) of behaviourism. The trained self's cognition is indoctrinated with these principles. As a result, it ceases to feel the need to genuinely, sincerely, and authentically relate to and communicate with other selves. The behaviourist insanely desires that the selves this behaviourist wants to condition become *obligated* to behave according to positive and negative reinforcements that are the scientismistic methods of a behaviourist's tendency to command, although the behaviourist usually attempts to persuade a self to develop its own reinforcements or commands to follow by instructing this self on the "ins and outs" of behaviour modification (the indoctrination of a self's cognition by way of a plan).

Instead of obliging a self to follow commands, we need to help it recognise that it's free in its solitude as well as in society because it chooses its need to love, its need to express this emotion to other selves as well as introject this emotion, and its need to respect the self it is as well as respect other selves. A self's recognition of its needs helps it to genuinely, sincerely and authentically relate to and communicate with other selves so that it experiences Freedom from its insane desire to condition (indoctrinate) its cognition. The self is then able to realise that an enlightened self doesn't act out of obligation or duty because it knows that it's acting from its intelligent reasoning and its interest in its need to play and work.

Work is play, that is, if we don't feel obliged to work or treat work as a duty. Obligatory or dutiful work is drudgery since it's difficult to maintain our interest in it. Obligations are the opposite of choices (even though we choose to be obliged), while duties are the opposite of hobbies (although some of us approach our hobbies as if they were duties). What most people don't realise is that it's your approach to what you're doing that either frees your interest or restricts your interest in what you're doing.

If you approach your work with the attitude that it's an obligation or a duty, your interest in your work will quickly fade away; however, if you approach your work with the attitude that your work is your hobby because you realise that your work is never what you "have" to do, but is always fundamentally your choice, your interest in your work will never fade away.

I'm able to use a role, false self, or persona, such as my adult player, in my work of writing and researching, but I find it's better for me to write and research without using the pretence of my adult player role, even though this role is enjoyable to act out. Although "writer" and "researcher" are occasionally roles I act out, I usually look upon them as interests in which to indulge. Although my writing and researching are behaviours, they aren't necessarily roles I'm playing because I know that writing and researching are my interests.

I have a need to genuinely, sincerely, and authentically write and research in accord with my needs. I'm able to accomplish my behaviours of writing and researching without acting out the roles of writer and researcher. My engagement with my behaviours of writing and researching is a genuine, sincere, and authentic expression of my appreciation of these activities; therefore, I don't identify with the labels, "writer" and "researcher", because I know these labels are merely logical categorisations.

If I'm alert, I don't identify with my roles, false selves, or personae of writer and researcher because I know better than to identify with my roles. When we're not indulging in roles, we're able to use Nature's Will in us to intelligently reason in a genuine, sincere, and authentic way so that we're able to understand and recognise realities; however, when we indulge in roles, we're tempted to intellectually cogitate so that we indulge in an ingenuine, insincere, and inauthentic ways of believing and misrecognising realities.

Intelligent reasoning occurs in accord with speculations established from the need to satisfy a self's conscientious desires, while intellectualising occurs in discord with the self's conscientious desires because the self's delusions are established from the insane desire to obey commands derived from laws. My metalogic is intelligent reasoning about and beyond logic. My metalogic transcends a logician's mistaken hypothesis of logic because my intelligent reasoning is rooted in my deliberate noninstinctive use of Nature's Will whereas a modern logician's logic is rooted in Aristotle's mistaken intellectualised formal laws which the logician uses in his attempt to manipulate the objective world. Ironically, the logician pays attention to his understanding of mathematics which helps him manipulate the objective world, but he ignores his subjective knowing which helps him understand what he is, who he is (and isn't) genuinely, sincerely and authentically expressing from what he is, how he is (and isn't) genuinely, sincerely and authentically expressing who he is from what he is, and why he is (instead of isn't)..

The first logician was Aristotle who invented logic by using laws in his attempt to control his use of his language as well as his use of mathematical formulas and equations. Logicians who followed in Aristotle's footsteps applied logic more extensively to mathematical formulas and equations changing some of the rules of Aristotle's logic along the way because they were trying to relate the laws of logic more extensively to the patterns in Nature *which defy logic*.

Aristotle changed his Greek language from a pattern of reasoning to a pattern of logicising which has convinced scientismists that deterministic logic is superior to the Freedom of reasoning. These scientismists failed to understand that intellectually and artificially ruled logicising is insane whereas the Freedom of intelligently and genuinely reasoning is sane; therefore, these scientismists ignored the truth that intelligence is not intellect.

Commandments and the laws they are based on are developed a posteriori by a self. A posteriori refers to that which is existed by a self after experience. A priori refers to that which is existed by a self before experience.

Laws aren't developed a priori in a self by Nature or by the Creator because each self needs to learn the various laws he knows; therefore, laws are learned by us a posteriori. The Ten Commandments are moral laws; therefore, they are mistaken hypotheses which deluded Creationists use in their attempt to verify their belief in the Creator and his Creation. Creationists aren't able to verify their belief in the Creator because they're unable to prove that the Creator exists by reasoning. If a Creationist's belief in the Creator could be verified, a Creationist wouldn't have a desire for faith because his reasoning would have resulted in his certain knowledge that his Creator exists, rather than his uncertain faith that his Creator exists.

Because Creationists only have uncertain faith that their Creator exists, not their certain knowledge that he exists, they're unable to verify that The Ten Commandments are valid by arguing that their Creator created them. Creationists are only able to develop a delusional faith in Yahweh's commandments and the laws on which they're based, just as they're only able to develop an uncertain faith in their Creator; therefore, they're unable to verify their moral judgements because moral judgements are dependent on faith, not knowledge.

Knowledge enables discernment. Faith is simply a lack of knowledge based on logic and judgement; therefore, moral judgements are unverifiable because they're based on logical faith, rather than knowledgeable discernment.

The assertion that we're unable to verify moral judgements is called the "error theory" in philosophy. It's impossible for a theologian to refute the error theory successfully because he is unable to prove objectively—or subjectively—that the Creator exists.

Marc Krellenstein wrote the following in the abstract of his paper, "Moral Nihilism and its Implications":

'Evolutionary psychologists have had success in explaining the likely origins and mechanisms of morality but have also not established any justification for adopting particular values. As a result, we're left with moral nihilism—the absence of any unarguable values or behaviors we must or should adopt' (Krellenstein, 2017, p. 75).

Krellenstein didn't understand when he wrote this paper that moral nihilism is not the absence of any unarguable values or behaviours because we're capable of discerning unarguable values and behaviours. Krellenstein didn't understand that moral nihilism results from the unarguable fact that a moral commandment derived from laws is a mistaken hypothesis nor did he seem to understand that laws are impossible to verify as truths.

Value or worth is usually understood or meant to be the desirability of a thing, such as an emotion or a behaviour; however, the Reality (Nature) and Its real (natural) selves are all equally valuable or worthy. Reality has no sense of Its own worth. Reality has no ability to appraise Its own worth. Quite obviously, a reality (a nature), like a phenomenal book, has no idea of its own worth either; therefore, your brain has no idea of its own worth because, like a real book, your real brain is not a real self, whereas you are the real self who inhabits the real reticular formation located in the real stem of your real brain.

The laws of a commander have no desirability because a law has no intrinsic value. The laws developed by authoritarian commanders have no worth at all because they aren't based on knowledge; rather, they were developed as "tools" for the purpose of curbing our impulsivity. Unfortunately, they curb our spontaneity too so that we feel trapped.

Moral laws are used by selves to establish a rigid social order and as well as rigid characters and personalities, but laws aren't socially useful. The rigid social norms in which laws result are contrary to the ever changing needs of selves. This rigidity is unhelpful because only the needs of selves help them to interrelate with harmony in their societies.

We're unable to use commandments to promote conscientious integrity. We're also unable to use them to promote social integration.

It's hardly a surprise to any astute individual that the "wolves" and "sheep" of a society are usually reluctant to ask, "Exactly why do we want to lead or follow other individuals?" Most individuals are reluctant to ask this question because they know "deep down" that their desire to lead other individuals is based on their wish to sadistically dominate them while their desire to follow other individuals is based on their wish to masochistically submit to them. In other words, leaders are "wolves" who want to hurt their following "sheep" under the "guise" of helping them, whereas followers are "sheep" who want to suffer the abuse of their leading "wolves" under the "glamour" of admiring them.

Leaders and followers, like politicians and citizens, teachers and students, masters and disciples, doctors and patients, or sellers and buyers, are caught in a co-dependent trap of "mutual conditioning" fostered by the desire of leaders to avoid learning by indoctrinating their followers and the desire of followers to avoid learning by memorising the propaganda of their leaders. Individuals who recognise their needs for independence and sovereignty avoid the pathologies of leading and following by developing their skill in *mutual learning* in accord with the Freedom of their own independence and sovereignty. Unfortunately, most individuals accede to their fear of their own independent sovereign individuality and seek political "Community Standards" to justify their cowardice as well as their "bravery", rather than sensibly seek apolitical *Individual Novelty* which requires only interest and curiosity, not bravery—or cowardice.

Intrinsic needs are valuable because they are our guides to our sane desires, while our insane desire for laws and our insane desire for the commandments derived from them are useless desires because they are our attempts to deny the valuability of our sane desires. People who expound upon the logic of "law and order" are motivated by feelings of inferiority which results in either timidity or a false bravado which keeps them from using their confidence and courage to understand the valuability of their need for organisation-disorganisation-reorganisation. These people worship and idolise law and order, even though law and order are worthless hypotheses.

It's important to understand that not every value is equally worthy. A value is our appreciation of the varying worth of phenomenal qualities a as well as our knowledge that every phenomenal self is equal in worth to every other phenomenal self.

A value is verified by the needs which motivate a self. The spontaneity of the Evolver, Grower, Developer, Deteriorator, and Devolver in Its expression Its Will is appreciated or is of value to any wise self because it's through this same spontaneity in us that our needs are developed as we strive for the goal of harmony. We pursue the goal of harmony in search of The Ultimate Truth—which is the value of Freedom.

Valuability is the knowledge of values which are our appreciations of the importance of that which we're valuing *because our knowledge of that which is truly valuable is our sanity*. People who use the rigid rule of law in an attempt to control their conduct and the conduct of other people *are all insane* because their feeling of inferiority in relation to their mythical "omniscient Creator" results in the selfpathic attempt to prove that they're worthy of immortality.

We're as worthy of immortality as Nature because Nature had no choice but to develop us as immortals (if, that is, we are, indeed, immortals). In a way we're worthier than Nature because we're able to experience love and benevolence. Ironically, our knowledge of hate and our malevolence are almost equal in value to our knowledge of love and benevolence because we need to fully comprehend our hate and malevolence if we are to fully comprehend our love and benevolence.

The current social systems of our world are insane because they're based on the insane practice of justice. Justice is insane because it's based on a practice of retribution as well as on a delusional set of moral laws which contrast sharply with the "immoral" set of laws of those who resent the attempt of our justice system to force our society's morality upon them. Of course, justice and morality in Canadian society is based on the mistaken hypothesis of Creationists which is the hypothesis that the Creator exists and created us from nothingness.

Nothingness is seemingly an identical term for the word "non-Existence" which is a word without a referent; therefore, it's a mistaken hypothesis or a delusion of those who give it credence. Creationists deny my knowledge which is that the Evolver, Grower, Developer, Deteriorator, and Devolver is the unbounded extent of Activity by which we were developed, from which we were developed, and in which we exist as activities. Creationists usually understand that the word "nothingness" is merely their idea of an identical word for "non-Existence".

Unlike valuability, logic is not a truth because logic is an attempt to validate or invalidate an inference based upon the principles, rules, or laws that an inference is supposed to have followed; therefore, by using logic, we're supposedly able to judge the truth or the falsity of an inference. Logic is not a truth because inferences follow needs, not laws; therefore, no scientism is true because all scientisms are based on Natural Law.

Aristotle used laws to develop his logic based on the relationship of laws to numbers, formulas, and equations. The laws, numbers, formulas, equations, and logic of mathematics are developed a posteriori (after we're begun to experience) based upon what we see in our environment.

We develop inner graphics, inner numbers, and inner letters from outer graphics, outer numbers, and outer letters. We develop our outer graphics, outer numbers, and outer letters by engraving them in the physical objects we see by using striated markings we might see in a rock that is about to split apart as an inspiration for the development of these outer engravings. Consequently, straight markings in a physical object are rearranged and engraved by us in physicalities as the outer numbers 1, 4, and 7, curved markings as the outer numbers of 0, 3, 6, 8, and 9, and straight-curved markings as the outer numbers of 2 and 5.

The Creator is only a myth; therefore, inner numbers are not existed eternally as clear and distinct ideas in the Creator's "mind" as well as in our "minds", like René Descartes imagined was the case, because the Source exists continually and immediately, rather than temporally and eternally. The Source has no need to develop inner graphics, inner numbers, and inner letters because the Source isn't an individual; therefore, It has no need to communicate with outer graphics, outer numbers and outer letters.

Nature is unable to develop an intellect or the ability to intellectualise because Nature is unable to cogitate; therefore, Nature doesn't use inner graphics, inner numbers, and inner letters, like the Creationist hypothesises his Creator is able to do. Nature is unable to relay inner graphics, inner numbers, and inner letters to us because Nature is unable to develop and use them. Nor does Nature have Its own inner language of inner ideograms and inner words.

It's important to understand that laws are cogitations of a self's intellect, rather than a development of its intelligence, because laws are really developed from a self's insane desire to destroy its impulsivity, rather than control it (which is a deluded self's attempt to justify its rationalised belief in laws, instead of admit it really wants to use these laws to destroy its impulsivity, rather than accept the inevitability of its impulsivity and its responsibility to mitigate its expression of its impulsivity).

Most people develop laws because of their insane desire to remain ignorant of Reality and Its Truth. People want to remain ignorant because they are too afraid of the anxious feelings that come with seeking knowledge about Reality and the responsibility which comes from knowing they're absolutely free.

Selves, like "mosquitoes", don't have all the faculties of human selves because selves only develop the faculties and abilities they need. Selves develop and hold their immaterial abilities in their immaterial faculties as they're evolving and growing their materialised brains; therefore, a materialised brain has no ability to use the immaterial faculties that its inhabiting immaterial self holds in it.

Selves use Nature's Will to generate their immaterial abilities and faculties. Nature only has the ability to instinctively Will. Nature has no immaterial faculties and no other immaterial abilities than Its immaterial ability to Will. Consequently, Nature has no immaterial archetypal faculties which we would be able to "download" as our immaterial ectypal faculties.

Only some of the selves of Nature have the ability to develop phenomenal qualities, like numbers and words. Nature hasn't the ability to develop numbers and words nor does Nature have the ability to understand that we're able to develop numbers and words. If Nature was able to develop numbers and words, we wouldn't have different Roman and Arabic numbers. Nor would we have different languages with different words, such as English, French, and Spanish words. If Nature was able to develop numbers, we would have infinite numbers of only one design, not two finite sets of numbers, like those of Romanic and Arabic design. If Nature was able to develop words, we would only have a single language with infinite words, not the finite words sets which we know of as, for example, English, French, and Spanish.

The historical sequence of our development of abstractions is as follows:

First, we developed iconic words that resemble the realities for which they stand.

Second, we developed symbolic words that designate, denote, or refer to that for which they stand.

Third, we developed the basic number, like the Arabic number "1" and the Romanic number "i", which designates, denotes, or refers to any single object.

Fourth, we developed other numbers which stand for the additions of the Arabic number "1", e.g., $1+1+1+1 = 4$ (Roman numbers are different in their additions).

Fifth, we developed laws to "connect" words to each another as well as numbers to each other for the insane purpose of attempting to control the environment and the activities and behaviours of other people.

Sixth, we developed dimensions, such as length, height, width, and time, for the purpose of fantasising an unchangingly "still" realm because we want to be either immortal or mortal, not realising that we have no choice in regards to whether we're immortal or mortal.

Seventh, we developed a belief in Aristotle's judgemental logic which was his futile attempt to determinatively validate or invalidate his freely reasoned inferences, instead of using his free reasoning to do so, because he didn't trust in Freedom.

Aristotle didn't know how to infer truth and falsity. His logic was the result of his intellectualised cogitating. The rule of law is also intellectually cogitated. Logic was based on speculations which were existent as a precogitated development in the intellects of natural philosophers, like Socrates and Plato. Aristotle knowingly developed logic from his own precognisant logical precogitating. Socrates and Plato both believed in laws which is why their logical way of cogitating was existed by them in their intellects as their precogitated developments. Aristotle simply precogitated his logical way of cogitating; therefore, he was able to irresponsibly invent and develop the laws of logic.

Logic is a disabling ability because logic handicaps our ability to freely deduce and induce (inferentially reason). Aristotle (who was the pre-runner of modern-day scientismists), failed to comprehend that the attempt to control others through the use of laws was actually his attempt to avoid responding to his needs. Aristotle didn't realise that a self's guidance of its use of Nature's Will is impossible to use for "self-control" or to control other selves, other natures, and Nature because Nature's use of Its Will and the use of Nature's Will by other selves are continually influencing a self's guidance of Nature's Will. Even Nature is unable to control Its use of Its Will because Nature's use of Its Will is based on the Ultimate Freedom which is Nature's libertarian basis, not determinism, predeterminism, or compatibilism; therefore, a Creator who supposedly wills in his laws with absolute control is obviously a myth.

The attempt of a domineering individual to insanely control another individual will result in the latter's sane desire to overtly defy such an attempted tactic of control; however, this sane desire might also give way to the insane desire of attempting to dominate and control the would-be controller in return.

For example, a submissive individual will experience the sane desire to defy such an attempt to control him; however, his defiance is ineffective because he knowingly obeys his dominator while insanely attempting to control him. By unknowingly making what seems to be his "mistake" in his performance of a duty which his would-be controller wants him to perform, he reveals that his "mistake" wasn't really his mistake. His "mistake" was really his intention because his originally known intention of defiance was "buried"; therefore, it became his unknowing defiant intention of defying his would-be controller. He is ignoring the fact that his pretension of making a mistake is his pretension.

Many philosophers resist the truth that intentions may be instinctively as well as deliberately expressed. They are afraid to admit that their intentions are often not deliberately controlled. They want to remain blissfully unknowing of their repression of their intentions because they don't want to be responsible for knowingly repressing them in the first place.

A wise self will experience the sane desire to knowingly and overtly defy such an attempt to delusionally control it by refusing to obey its would-be controller; however, the wise self doesn't attempt to dominate and delusionally control its would-be controller in return. If this would-be controller attempts to use force in its attempt to delusionally control the wise self, the wise self will have a sane desire to confine or restrain its would-be controller. But the wise self knows that the attempt to delusionally control anyone is insane. A wise self doesn't use confinement and restraint as its attempt to delusionally control behaviour. A wise self uses confinement and restraint to limit the damage a would-be controller is able to exact.

The attempt to control others is delusional because we're unable to control a self. Nor are we able to absolutely or relatively control our environment because even Nature only relatively guides Its use of Its Will in the activities of our environment which we influence with our own relatively guided use of Nature's Will in tandem with Nature; therefore, our attempts to absolutely, or even relatively, control our environment results in disaster after disaster. The attempt of scientismists and politicians to control Nature's evolving, growing, developing, deteriorating, and devolving of our environment is laughable as well as delusionally because each of them unknowingly wants to be God. An authoritarian scientismist or politician fails to realise that his or her delusional attempt to control our environment through manipulative "scientific techniques" is motivated by his or her selfish desire to "corner the market" on Freedom so that only he is free and every other self is subject to his "absolute control".

It pays to work with Nature through our responsible care of our environment, rather than absurdly attempting to control Nature by attempting to force Nature to do our bidding. Many people logically rationalise that their use of force to "master" the environment is justified; however, their use of force is not responsive and their use of logic is not reasonable.

Aristotle developed his logic intellectually by using laws in his futile attempt to validate the truth or falsity of pre-determined cogitations, rather than freely reason his way to inferences. This is ironic because Aristotle's mistaken premise was that inferences are judged true or false based on the artificial laws of his logic, rather than based on natural needs.

Aristotle's logical premise was that we're able to judge inferences to be right or wrong; however, this logical premise was Aristotle's delusion because inferences are meant to be discerned as accurate or inaccurate, not morally judged as "right" or "wrong".

Logic was Aristotle's formal intellectualisation. His logic was flawed at the core because it was based on laws and determinism, rather than needs and libertarianism. If Aristotle had inquired further into logic, instead of admiring his own efforts in developing it, he might have discovered his ability to be fair in his inferential reasoning. He might have discovered that he could use his inferential reasoning fairly to discern whether or not his inferential reasoning was true or false without using logic to judge his fairness.

Aristotle's use of logic to validate or invalidate the inferences of his reasoning was regressive. We're able to use our inferential reasoning to invalidate Aristotle's hypothesis of logic; however, we're unable to use logicising to validate or invalidate our inferential reasoning. The attempt to validate or invalidate our inferential reasoning with logic is a case of "putting the cart before the horse" because we're only able to use our "horse" of inferential reasoning to invalidate Aristotle's constructed "cart" of logic. We're unable to use our inferential reasoning to validate logic because logicising is never true.

When we use logic in an attempt to validate or invalidate the truth of a situation, we're using a false means of validation and invalidation; therefore, our formal intellectualising or logicising in relation to a situation is a regression and a falsity. We need to realise that logic is false by using our inferential reasoning to invalidate logic. Only then do we realise that our use of our inferential reasoning in relation to a situation is a progression and a truth.

That we're able to use our free reasoning in guiding us towards our understanding means that free reasoning is truly the basis of our understanding, not Aristotle's "organon" or "tool" of deterministic logic. The goals we develop help guide the purposes which arise in us in relation to our needs; therefore, the goal of our inferential reasoning is to recognise our need to express our emotion of love as well as recognise our need to strive for wisdom so that by becoming wise we become happier; however, contrary to what many people believe, happiness is not wisdom.

Through our knowledge of Reality and Its harmonious willing, we're able to develop wisdom. Happiness is the *result* of your expression of love *by way of* your feeling of harmony; therefore, happiness is not wisdom because you use your wisdom to develop your happiness as a corollary to your ability to love on the basis of your feeling of harmony.

The laws, equations, formulas, connectors, and numbers of logic are inadequate to our need to develop and become wise because they have no intrinsic value; however, we use words to express values which may be defined by way of our needs, our sane desires, and our insane desires in relation to our goals.

For example, the word "survival" usually refers to the insane desire to survive death, while the word "salvation" usually refers to an individual's masochistic desire to please his mythical Creator so his Creator will not cause him to perish (die); however, the word "immortality" refers to the probability that a self might not die with its sensable organism.

The sane desire of an "immortal" or a "mortal" is wisdom. In the context of immortality, mortality, and wisdom, the word "salvation" refers to the sane desire to avoid unnecessary suffering, not to the delusional desire to avoid perishing.

The insane desire of a self to survive death is obedience, while the insane desires related to a Creationist's goal to please his mythical Creator are to be obliging and dutiful, rather than considerate and kind.

The sane desire of self is wisdom, while the attainment of the goal of wisdom fosters the sane desire to help others reach wisdom by way of their own efforts, rather than "save" them.

The sane desire of a self is enjoyment, while the attainment of enjoyment results in the sane desire of a self to express joy to a friend; however, a sane self would do better to keep its joy "under its hat" if it discerns that its friend might be jealous of its joy.

The truth behind all our goals is that we're sane when we have needs which we sanely desire to fulfil; however, our insane desires are based on deprivation, not need, which is why these desires are insane or malevolent motivations.

Unlike the Creator of the "Holy" Bible, the Source has no desire for either I or me to do anything nor does It want I or me to do what I or me need to do because the Source is unable to want. The Source simply does what It does, not what It wants to do. I'm sane or benevolent when I desire to fulfil my needs; however, the Source is unable to need, sanely desire, or insanely desire.

Aristotle attempted to avoid using free inferential reasoning or free deducing and inducing from his needs by applying laws of cogitation to his cogitating. If Aristotle had developed his philosophy as a selfology, he might have abandoned his tool of logic and turned to his need to express love in accord with Nature's harmony so that his need to be enlightened would be based on the harmony of Nature.

Although I understand the terms "sanity" and "insanity" as selfological terms, they are also misunderstood as legal terms. I use the term "sanity" in relation to our selfological valuing or appreciation of our proper (instead of legally "right") benevolent desires and our selfological valuing or appreciation of our improper (instead of legally "wrong") malevolent desires, while I use the term "insanity" in relation to our selfological devaluing or unappreciation of our proper benevolent desires and our selfological valuing or appreciation of our improper malevolent desires.

I'm not using the terms "sanity" and "insanity" as intellectual expressions of the judgements of our justice systems which defines a "sane individual" as an individual who knows the difference between "right" (which is thought to be his or her obedience of commandments derived from the rule of law) and "wrong" (which is thought to be his or her disobedience of commandments derived from the rule of law). According to our justice systems, an "insane individual" is an individual who doesn't know the difference between right and wrong. These definitions fail to account for the fact that oversensitive people often fail to appreciate the difference between the meanings of proper and improper as well as the absurdities of right and wrong, but insane (malevolent) people always do unless they are oversensitive as well as insane.

Psychology is a delusional scientism, not a meaningful science, because we are selves, not psyches. Some psychologists want to underpin psychology with Aristotelian-Thomistic metaphysics. Aristotelian-Thomistic metaphysics is based on the Christian theology of Thomas Aquinas. Aquinas used his Christian theology to alter Aristotle's metaphysics for his own purposes.

In their paper entitled "Scientific Realism, Subjective Realism, and Aristotelian-Thomistic Realism", Stedman, Kostelecky, Spalding, and Gagné asserted, '…Aristotelian-Thomistic (A-T) realism…might be adopted to provide a more coherent and comprehensive philosophical underpinning for psychology' (Stedman, Kostelecky, Spalding, & Gagné, 2016, p. 199). Stedman et al. claimed that A-T metaphysics would be a more coherent and comprehensive explanation of subjective reality than the other current metaphysical underpinnings of psychology.

Throughout their paper, Stedman et al. mistakenly refer to scientismistic subjective materialism as a "scientific subjective realism" based on the modern view of "scientific realism" which I find is better described as "scientismistic objectivism". Scientismistic objectivism is the basis of what we have been conditioned to call the "natural sciences". These "natural sciences" are better described as "scientisms" because scientismistic physicists, chemists, and biologists have abandoned studying the Source of motion, movement, and the illusion of rest which is why their understanding of Nature is absurd. Instead, they study motion and movement, as well as the illusion of rest only in terms of automatism and objectivism, rather than voluntarism and subjectivism, because they consider motion and movement to be illusory. Some scientismists have even gone so far as to claim that there is no Source of motions and movements. These absurd scientismists claim that the uncreated laws of Nature automatically produce the "illusion" of motions in a reality and the "illusion" of a reality's movements.

Stedman et al. were mistaken when they referred to scientismistic objectivism as a "scientific realism" because many scientismistic objectivists deny the Reality which is immaterial Nature and only affirm the reality of materialised phenomena. Scientismistic objectivists view immaterial Matter to be bounded, rather than unbounded.

What is ironic is that Stedman et al. mistakenly referred to "Aristotelian-Thomistic metaphysics" as "Aristotelian-Thomistic realism" because Aristotelian-Thomistic metaphysics is based on the mistaken or delusional hypothesis of Creationists that the Creator is real; therefore, we're unable to accurately refer to Aristotelian-Thomistic metaphysics as a "realism" because the Creator isn't real. Aristotle's metaphysics is not Aristotelian-Thomistic metaphysics because Aristotle maintained that his unmoved mover has always moved the universe, rather than created it. Like Aristotelian-Thomistic metaphysics, Aristotle's metaphysics is unrealistic because he believed in time and used logic in a futile attempt to justify his cogitating.

Aristotelian-Thomistic "metaphysics" is not based Aristotle's belief in the unmoved mover. Thomas Aquinas altered Aristotle's metaphysics to accommodate his belief in the Creator. Aristotle didn't believe in a Creator. Neither did Einstein.

Scientismistic physics is based on Einstein's metaphysical falsehood that the universe was created by Natural Law. Einstein concluded that mass is equivalent to energy, a hypothesis which he famously formulated as $E = mc^2$ (Energy equals mass multiplied by the speed of light squared). Ironically, Einstein realised that energy is pure (absolutely uncondensed); however, he didn't understand that Energy is unbounded. Einstein's famous equation equates a bounded energy, not unbounded Energy, to a limited number (a mass multiplied by the speed of light squared).

Einstein thought that energy was equal to a limited number because he believed that the universe, and thus energy, was finite. Einstein didn't have knowledge of the Infiniverse or the knowledge of the Ether which is why Einstein delineatively cogitated and expressed his equation, $E = mc^2$. If Einstein was on the ball, he would have realised that capitalising the "E" in his equation was a mistake. His equation would have been less inaccurately expressed if he had written it as, "$e = mc^2$" since the energy in his equation was supposedly the bounded energy of a finite universe, rather than the unbounded Energy of the Infiniverse. Ironically, even this equation would have been inaccurate because all equations are based on fixed quantities.

Quantities are the source of inaccuracies because quantities are a physicist's delusional attempt to fix qualities which are unfixable. Qualities are unfixable because they are either continually changing activities or continually unchanging activities.

Objectivism is an example of regressive logicising because objects aren't fundamental. The Evolver, Grower, Developer, Deteriorator, and Devolver has an instinctive need to condense Its portions so that condensed energies are evolved, even though they continually age and deteriorate so that sooner or later they decondense or devolve back into the Evolver, Grower, Developer, Deteriorator, and Devolver.

"Created Matter" is a delusion. Matter is Energy. Matter has always existed. Einstein's mistake was to theorise that Matter is *equivalent* to Energy, rather than *exactly the same as* Energy. Matter *is* Energy, not equivalent to Energy.

Scientismistic "objectivists", "materialists" or "physicalists" are all deluded because they believe that a condensed energy or a materialised matter (a particle) which is "accelerated" by a particle "accelerator" and "crashes" into another particle changes into another condensed energy or another materialised matter or many condensed energies or materialised matters, rather than returns to pure Energy or pure Matter, even though they realise that every condensed energy or materialised matter is instable. Every materialised matter (condensed energy) deteriorates and sooner or later unsettles into pure Matter (pure Energy) by way of Nature's willing. Scientismistic objectivists fail to understand that particles disintegrate because they have a delusional interpretation of the activity which is a particle.

Scientismists use particle (condensation) "accelerators" in which Nature's Will moves particles very fast so that these particles (condensations) collide with other particles. Nature's willing in a particle often results in that particle's disintegration when it collides with another particle. Nature's willing in such interactions also generates new particles or new condensations; therefore, the force of contact between particles or condensations doesn't "automatically" split a particle or condensation into different particles or condensations. Instead, Nature immediately evolves new particles or new condensations upon the annihilation of a particle or condensation when it has collided with another particle or condensation.

A-T psychology is based on falsehoods, like commandments, logic, laws, mathematics, and measurements. Although A-T psychologists don't always fall into the trap of using quantitative measurements, they usually do entertain the mistaken hypothesis of fixed quantities, like the scientismists' hypothetically quantifiable "primordial particle". Consequently, A-T psychologists fail to realise that there are only continually changing active qualities or continually unchanging active qualities, not unchanging quantities.

Scientismistic psychologists are usually referred to as "behaviourists". These behaviourists are almost wholly delusional in their beliefs because they refer to qualities as our "delusions" and to their supposedly fixed quantities as their "realities". They don't understand that they have the situation exactly backwards.

They don't understand that unfixed continually vibrating qualities are our realities, while fixed quantities are only our delusions.

The laws of mathematics as well as the measurements on which they're based are falsehoods; however, mathematics is often useful in helping us work with the appearances composing our environment. Unfortunately, the very usefulness of mathematics is our greatest danger because our use of laws gives us the impression that it's okay to irresponsibly manipulate the appearances composing our environment, rather than responsibly refrain from such manipulation. As a consequence of our irresponsible manipulations of our environment, we're tempted to think our attempts to "manipulate" the cognitions of other individuals is also okay. Such manipulations are mistakenly referred to as "brain-washing". We need to continually clear our cognitions, not cleanse our brains, of authoritarian attempts to indoctrinate our cognitions so we're free to spontaneously think and behave from our own needs.

What distinguishes an A-T psychologist from a mortalistic behaviourist is an A-T psychologist's psychology because his or her A-T psychology is based on his or her theology (which the A-T psychologist pretends is not influencing his or her psychology), while the mortalistic behaviourist, who has no theology, may mistakenly think that he doesn't have a metaphysics any more than he has a theology. The mortalistic behaviourist treats metaphysics as a relatively unimportant matter in relation to the utilitarian goals of his behaviourism.

Unfortunately, scientismists are oriented towards the determinism of behaviour modification. They have compromised their integrity by asserting that selves have no choice but to obey the laws of physics. Their integrity is lacking because they deny that we're able to choose in accord or in discord with our harmonies, consciences, and needs which are based in Nature's Freedom. They subscribe to the doctrine of determinism, rather than libertarianism, because they're afraid to be free.

The A-T psychologist's theology is based on his authoritarian belief that his God, the Creator, created particles from non-Existence by using deterministic laws to do so. Non-Existence is supposed to be separated from the Creator.

The mortalistic behaviourist's stance is based on the even more absurd cogitation that particles are created by Nature's supposedly uncreated laws. These uncreated laws of Nature are believed by mortalistic behaviourists to "somehow" deterministically and automatically create particles. The mortalistic behaviourist's ridiculous hypothesis is that uncreated laws automatically create the physical from Nature which contradicts the Creationist's equally ridiculous hypothesis of a Creator who supposedly creates the physical by willing in the laws he created from non-Existence.

These Mortalists and Creationists will never be able to resolve their issues with each other, even though they both believe in laws, because the premise of the Mortalist is his mortality, while the premise of the Creationist is his immortality which he supposes is granted by his Creator's whimsy. Despite the discovery of new facts, neither Mortalists nor Creationists will understand how these facts are related because they theorise from the fictitious laws they've developed in relation to their other fictions.

Scientismists fail to realise that their theories are subjectively proven false by way of a participant-observer's experience. A scientimistic experimenter doesn't understand that his "observer only" experiments are no substitute for a participant-observer's experience, just as the Creationist doesn't understand that his superstitious myths are an inappropriate basis for experience. Ironically, the scientismistic experimenter's observer only experiments are his or her attempts to escape from subjectively knowing his or her experience, just as the Creationist's superstitious belief in myths is his or her attempt to escape from his or her experience.

Neither the mortalistic behaviourist nor the A-T psychologist realise that theories of Creation are myths because the ability to create is a delusion. Nor do they realise that particles are particlised from Nature as well as inevitably departiclised by Nature so they're decondensed or dematerialised by Nature's accidental and continual spontaneous instinctive nondeliberate willing in them.

Although the A-T psychologist and the behaviourist both pay lip service to evolution and growth, the A-T psychologist and the behaviourist both deny that selves are developed within some of the bodies which we know are evolved and grown. The A-T psychologist clings to his delusion of a Creation which he believes happened by way of the Creator's use of his will in his created laws, while the mortalistic behaviourist clings to his delusion of a Creation which he believes happened automatically by way of uncreated laws. Neither the A-T psychologist nor the mortalistic behaviourist realise that Nature has always instinctively used Its Will to continually evolve, grow, develop, deteriorate, and devolve bodies and continually generate selves within some of these bodies.

Stedman et al. write, '…, A-T realism does not limit our ability to determine truth to the scientific method…it is important to recognize that the scientific method is not "the gold standard", but rather the method that is best adapted to the investigation of the physical' (Stedman, Kostelecky, Spalding, & Gagné, 2016, p. 207).

Stedman et al. failed to realise that "the scientific method" to which they referred is actually a scientismistic quantitative technical method, not *the scientific qualitative selfological Style* which transcends technical quantitative methods as the practice of an "unmethodical" scientific approach which is really the approach best adapted to "the investigation of the physical". You see, we're only able to subjectively, not objectively, investigate Nature's unseen willing of Its evolving, growing, developing, deteriorating, and devolving of the physical. Consequently, a scientismist who investigates physical phenomena is indulging in myth, like the Creationist, because he or she has no way of investigating Nature's unseen willing, Nature's unseeable selves, or the ability of these unseeable selves to *feel* their instinctive nondeliberate as well as deliberate noninstinctive use of Nature's unseen Will in tandem with Nature's instinctive nondeliberate use of Its Will.

A self is able to realise that it exists by cognising that it exists its multicellular body, which proves to it, in turn, that it is existing its ability to recognise. This self learns through experience that it's using its ability of recognising to realise that it is real as well as that it exists because it is able to use the eyes of its body to observe its body. However, a self also knows that it exists by using its ability of Selfkinetics to activate its introspection and extrospection so that it's able to sense other realities.

The conclusion that it exists is based on a self's observation of its body because a self's observing of its body takes place in its body. But the self is only able to subjectively prove this conclusion is valid by deducing that it's using its ability of recognising to guide the motions in its body and the movements of its body in the environment by feeling its instinctive nondeliberate as well as deliberate noninstinctive use of Nature's Will to do so. Of course, the self doesn't know that it's using Nature's Will to activate motions in and movements of its sensable organism until it's subjectively proven that it's able to feel its use of Nature's willing so it realises that Nature has the only Will which Nature and Its selves are able to use in Freedom, rather than that selves have possession of their own "free wills".

Until this realisation occurs to a self, it may mistakenly believe that it's using its understanding to guide its body's motions and movements according to what it believes is its *own* will, rather than Nature's Will. When a self has realised that Nature has the only Will by meditating on Nature's Will, the self continually deepens its understanding of Nature by engaging its reasoning. Reasoning is an ontologist's means of synthesising information which has been gathered together by the ontologist's introspective philosophical research approach so that the ontologist's synthesis of this information results from the ontologist's knowledge which is the ontologist's realisation of the truth or falsity of this information.

In the introduction, I wrote the following words which I repeat here for your convenience:

'I define ontology as a self's phenomenology as well as a self's naturalism; therefore, ontology, phenomenology, and naturalism are a self's study of Reality, Phenomenon, or Nature, realities, phenomena, or natures, and real, phenomenal, or natural qualities for the purpose of indicating, describing, and explaining their relationships by using an extrospective scientific research Style and an introspective philosophical research approach in accord with the self's need to attain or deepen its wisdom.'

My phenomenological use of my stylistic *epoché* (the setting aside of assumptions so that a Reality, its context, and, perhaps, its overall Context may be indicated and described) and my stylistic use of *bracketing* (the setting aside of assumptions so that only the Reality may be indicated and described) helped me to assimilate the knowledge of the Evolver, Grower, Developer, Deteriorator, and Devolver, Its suefs and luefs, Its particles and bodies, and the selves who inhabit some of Its bodies and luefs. When an ontologist recognises that the Evolver, Grower, Developer, Deteriorator, and Devolver is the Reality, he remains focused on his Style of using epoché; however, he's not focused on his Style of using bracketing anymore because he's developed his knowledge of Reality as the absolute Context of his ontological approach and ontological Style.

The ontologist uses his ontological approach in harmony with his ontological Style. An ontologist's extrospective scientific research Style proceeds in accord with the following three steps:

(1) The ontologist selfkinetically activates his or her ability of extrospecting in anticipation of reaching conclusions about the qualities of the realities he or she will extrospectively sense.

(2) The ontologist tests his or her conclusions about how the realities he or she has extrospected are related by examining his or her memories of former conclusions he or she has developed about similar relationships.
(3) If his or her former and current conclusions are similar, the ontologist may consider them to be tentatively proven to be true or conclusively proven to be true depending on the range of experiences a conclusion explains. If his or her former conclusions don't hold true for his or her current conclusions, the ontologist will consider these conclusions true for only a small range of experiences or not true at all.

An ontologist's introspective philosophical research approach proceeds in accord with the following three steps:

(1) The ontologist integrates the knowledge he or she has gained from his or her extrospection of realities and his or her introspection as well as his or her extrospection of Reality.
(2) The ontologist introspects Reality as the Source of Will which developed him or her.
(3) The ontologist selfkinetically uses his or her faculty of cognition to introspect its source with his or her ability of knowing so he or she realises that the self is this source as well as that the combination of the self and its male or female sensable organism are validly referred to as "he" or "she" and "him" or "her", respectively.

The goal of the ontologist is to explain through the harmonising of his ontological approach and Style exactly how the realities of the outer world, which he has realistically extrospected, indicated, and described, and the realities of his inner world, which he has realistically introspected and explained, are related to Reality so he attains the wise realisation that "he" is not really "he" because the self is an "it", not a "he".

Understanding is a result of inferentially reasoning from experience based on the ontologist's knowing of his experience as his known; therefore, the A-T psychologist's contention that we know the truth a priori (before experience) is his delusion. In other words, the A-T psychologist's rationalism is his fiction, while an ontologist's empiricism is his or her realism because the ontologist knows Nature as the Reality or Phenomenon in which he exists.

The A-T psychologist doesn't realise that his love is his own, not God's, although he usually recognises that love is only experienced by dwelling in it so that it may be known. An ontologist knows Nature's harmonising of the Infiniverse by examining the way that the Infiniverse evolves, grows, develops, deteriorates, and devolves, while Nature's generating of selves is only known by examining the way that selves develop their selfological qualities, like their needs, so that the knowledge of how these selfological qualities are generated may be analogised to Nature's generating of selves.

Aristotle ignored the importance of needs. Aristotle's hylomorphic theory includes an account of "the four causes". Aristotle didn't understand that selves instinctively or deliberately cause by using Nature's Will in their needs; therefore, Cause is Nature's use of its Will, while cause is a self's use of Nature's Will. Consequently, there are only four needs related to selves which activate as well as respond to their four needs by using Nature's Will as their cause.

The first of our four *needs* is our condensation need (not Aristotle's material cause). Our condensation need is our need for Nature to condense Its portions into natured natures (condensed energies or materialised matters) and grow these natured natures into bodies. These bodies are then used by us to produce a thing, like a marble slab.

The second need is our structuring need (not Aristotle's formal cause), like the structure of Hermes sculpted into a marble slab by a self. The structuring need is what we use to specify how we will structure a thing.[11]

The third need is our efficient need (not Aristotle's efficient cause), like the sculptor's need to sculpt the likeness of Hermes out of the slab of marble. Our efficient need is our need to guide the changing activity (the thing), even if it seems to be resting, so that we're able to learn from the experience of such guidance; therefore, our efficient need is our need to develop wisdom.

The fourth need is our final need (not Aristotle's final cause). Our final need is the purpose which has motivated us to develop a goal for our purpose so that we're able to strive to fulfil this goal, like the sculptor's goal of honouring Hermes.

Nature's Will is the means of Nature's efficient need to guide changing activities (things); therefore, Nature's Will is the effective activation of change in Its suefs, luefs, particles, and bodies; however, Nature is unable to reason. Consequently, Nature is unable to use intelligent reasoning to discern.

---

[11] The example of the sculptor was originally Aristotle's example.

A self uses its disabling ability of ineffective cogitating to develop delusions, not understanding. A self develops its understanding by inferential reasoning, not by ineffective cogitating. Nature is unable to develop understanding because It has no ability to know and no ability to reason; therefore, Nature is unintelligent because Nature has no ability of reasoning to guide Its willing.

Even though an illusory reality contrasts with a physical reality, all illusions as well as all physicalities are natures of Nature. A-T psychologists are intrigued by the Greek word "phantasm" because it stands for an illusory apparition. "Phantasia" is a word which suggests it's possible for us to be misled by an illusory apparition if we mistake it for a physical appearance. Two common examples of such misleading phantasms are the mirages of an illusory oasis cast by an actual oasis and a bent stick cast by a straight stick shoved in a pool of water.

A mirage is just as real as the object from which it's reflected because it's sensed. The cast mirages of an actual oasis and a straight stick are real, despite their existence as phantasms, because only the real is sensed.

That images occur subjectively means that they aren't existent objectively in the environment because objective photons travel from the environment to our retinas and are translated into subjective suefs which are imaged by us as subjective photons in our imaginations; therefore, phantasms are as actual as organic bodies because objective photons are projected from actual phantasms as well as from actual organic bodies by Nature.

Phantasy and fantasy may be similar in pronunciation, but their similarity ends with their pronunciation, because we envision fantasies whereas we vision phantasms. A phantasm is converted by our *visioning* to an image in our imaginations; therefore, a phantasm is not the *envisioning* of an image in our imaginations.

A phantasm is a reality in the environment which is evolved by Nature. Objective photons are willed by Nature to travel from an objective phantasm to the rods and cones of their sensable organism's retinas for its inhabiting self's cognitive knowing. These objective photons are absorbed by the retinas' rods and cones resulting in the stimulation of sensations (subjective suefs) so that these sensations are transmitted via a quale's impulse along the sensable organism's optic nerves so this impulse is received by the occipital lobe of the its brain, again, for its inhabiting self's cognitive knowing.

Nature also instinctively wills in objective photons to reflect them from a physical tree so that they travel from the tree to the rods and cones of a sensable organism's retins to stimulate a sensation which will travel as an impulse in its optic nerves so that this impulse is also received by the occipital lobe of its brain. Then the self is able to sense a subjective phantasm in its visual faculty after having sensed subjective photons in its imagination which were converted from the objective photons it sensed in its occipital lobes.

Objective phantasms are real because they mislead us when we confuse them for physical realities.

For example, a parched man in the desert might mistake his sighting of a nearby mirage for its distant oasis so that he dies of thirst in his vain effort to reach the distant oasis because his vision of the mirage convinced him that the distant oasis was nearby.

The Aristotelian-Thomistic psychologist proposes four inner senses which he terms the "common sense", the "imagination", "memory" and "cogitation". Cogitation is also referred to as the "estimative sense" by the A-T psychologist. The A-T psychologist believes these senses are the senses of an ego's cognition.

The A-T psychologist believes the common sense is used to integrate an ego's different sensations as well as distinguish between them; however, a self uses Nature's Will to sense, then, perceive, and, finally, understand suefs and their qualia so that it may attend to, interpret, and assimilate the various colours, sounds, feelings, flavours, odours and their suefs. There is no integrating and distinguishing common sense because the inner senses are integrated and distinguished by a self who uses its inner senses. A self uses its ability of understanding (not its "common sense") to integrate and distinguish between its different sensations.

A self's attentive faculty of sensation, interpretive faculty of perception, and assimilative faculty of understanding contain the abilities it uses to distinguish between qualia and their suefs while its faculty of imagination contains the abilities of imagiting and imagining. Areas of a sensable organism's brain are only associated with its inhabiting self's faculty of imagination; therefore these areas of the materialised sensable organism's materialised brain aren't the immaterial self's immaterial faculty of imagination; however, they are *related* to the self's immaterial faculty of imagination by the self's usually instinctive nondeliberate use of Nature's Will.

Objective photons are willed by Nature to reflect from physical objects in the environment. Nature wills objective photons to interact with a sensable organism's retinas so that these objective photons are converted into subjective suefs by the combined willing of Nature and the sensable organism's inhabiting self. After these objective photons have been converted into subjective suefs, these subjective suefs are impulsed by Nature's instinctive nondeliberate willing and the self's instinctive nondeliberate use of Nature's Will to will these impulses from the sensable organism's retinas along its optic nerves to the association area of its lobe for its inhabiting self's cognitive knowing.

Nature's instinctive willing and the self's instinctive utilisation of Nature's Will in these subjective suefs stimulates the association area of the brain's occipital lobe where Nature instinctively assists the self's instinctive willing of waves (qualia) as inner visible light so that this visible light is shone through these subjective suefs and they are imaged as subjective photons by the self in its faculty of imagination. These subjective photons are then volitionally impulsed by the self to the prefrontal lobe of the brain where they are known by the self in it's immaterial faculty of intelligence and held by its materialised sensable organism's materialised brain's prefrontal lobe. The self then translates its knowing of these subjective photons into thoughts and notions. Then these thoughts and notions are translated into symbolic concepts and ideas by the self's use of its ability to think. Finally, these symbolic concepts and ideas are translated into symbolic hypotheses and theories by the self's use of its ability to reason.

The self's immaterial faculties of intuition, cognition, and recognition, its immaterial faculty of intelligence, and its immaterial disabling faculty of intellect are held by the self in its materialised brain. The self's immaterial faculties of intuition and cognition contain its immaterial ability of thinking, while its immaterial faculty of recognition contains its immaterial ability of reasoning. A self uses its immaterial faculty of intelligence to guide its immaterial reasoning, while it uses its immaterial disabling faculty of intellect to guide its immaterial disabling ability of cogitating. A self's immaterial abilities of thinking reasoning, and cogitating are associated with its materialised brain's prefrontal cortex in its materialised sensable organism, but the materialised brain is not the origin of these immaterial abilities. The materialised brain is only used by its inhabiting self to channel the self's thinking, reasoning, and cogitating when the self decides to activate them.

A self's immaterial faculty of intuition is associated with a its immaterial ability to attend to its immaterial thinking so that its immaterial thoughts and notions result. A self's immaterial faculty of cognition is associated with the self's immaterial ability to interpretively think with its immaterial thoughts and notions so that its immaterial concepts and ideas result. A self's immaterial faculty of recognition is associated with its immaterial ability to inferentially reason with its immaterial concepts and ideas so that immaterial hypotheses and theories result. The self uses its immaterial ability of thinking to develop and attend to its immaterial thoughts and notions as well as develop and interpret its immaterial concepts and ideas. Finally, the self uses its immaterial ability of reasoning to develop and explain its immaterial hypotheses and theories.

A self's immaterial sensory abilities are channelled in areas of its sensable organism's brain. These areas of its sensable organism's brain are related to the self's immaterial memory in much same way that the self's immaterial faculty of imagination is associated with its materialised areas of the brain. Subjective suefs in a sensable organism's area of its brain associated with its inhabiting self's immaterial memory are derived from the self's immaterial senses of seeing, hearing, feeling, smelling, and tasting so that it's able to evolve the immaterial or pure energies of colours, sounds, feelings, odours, and flavours in its immaterial visual, auditory, tactile, olfactory, and gustatory faculties. The self translates the electromagnetic patterns of these suefs into thoughts by way of its ability to immaterially think in relation to its immaterial sensing of the materialised atoms of these electromagnetic patterns.

Even A-T psychologists are guilty of treating their materialised brain as if it were a machine that uses feedback "mechanisms"; therefore, they believe an individual's memory is a materialised aspect of their materialised brain's feedback mechanism; however, an individual's immaterial remembering is actually its immaterial feedback *ability*; therefore, a materialised brain has no materialised feedback "mechanism". A self immaterially thinks and reasons with immaterial inner words (or immaterial inner ideograms) that it remembers from its immaterial memory so that its immaterial beliefs, delusions, theories, and understandings it has stored in its immaterial memory are immaterially fed back to it. The immaterial self is then able to immaterially think and reason with these immaterially remembered beliefs, delusions, theories, and understandings so it's able to work towards enlightenment.

An immaterial self holds its immaterial faculties, like its memory, in the materialised lobes of its materialised sensable organism's materialised brain; therefore, the materialised lobes of its materialised sensable organism's materialised brain aren't this materialised brain's materialised faculties because faculties—as well as abilities—can only exist as the immaterial inner aspects of a self's World. Unfortunately, a materialised sensable organism's aging materialised neurons composing this materialised sensable organism's materialised brain deteriorate and interfere with the self's immaterial ability to channel immaterial information so that the self's immaterial ability to feed its immaterialised memorised information to its immaterial cognition as well as its immaterial ability to store its newly developed immaterial information in its immaterial memory store are handicapped because its inhabitation of the materialised stem of the materialised reticular formation at the stem of its materialised sensable organism's materialised brain is lived "in-between" the immaterial self and its essential immaterial faculty of memory.

The self is centralised in the reticular formation of the brain stem it inhabits because it's from this area of the brain that the rest of the brain is activated which is why this area of the brain is known as the "reticular activating system"; however, the reticular formation is unable to activate the rest of the brain because the reticular formation has no abilities. Only a self has the ability to use Nature's Will; therefore, the self who inhabits its sensable organism's reticular formation activates the rest of its sensable organism's brain by its activation of the reticular formation.

The self's essential memory store surrounds its sensable organism's brain; therefore, the self's remembering of information contained in its memory store may be hampered by the damaged or impaired neurons of its sensable organism's brain. The self uses the damaged or impaired neurons of its sensable organism's brain in its attempt to channel information from its working memory and episodic memory stores surrounding its sensable organism's brain to this self's location at the center of its sensable organism's brain; therefore, the self has difficulty remembering information from these memory stores because its damaged or impaired neurons interfere with Nature's will waves in the informational energy it's attempting to transmit by way of these neurons.

The impulse of a sensation is conducted by Nature's Will from the peripheral nervous system's afferent nerves to the central nervous system's afferent nerves which are then used to conduct the impulse to the neurons of the lobe of the brain most suited to receive it. Sensations (subjective suefs) are motioned or impulsed by way of waves of will (qualia) to the lobe of the sensable organism's brain most suited to receive them. These suefs of sight, sound, feeling, odour, and flavour are impulsed to the prefrontal lobe so that the self may translate the electromagnetic patterns these suefs carry into thoughts and notions, translate these thoughts and notions into concepts and ideas, and translate these concepts and ideas into hypotheses and theories.

The A-T psychologist's inner "sense" of cogitation is not a sense because cogitation is not an ability of sensing. Cogitating is a disabling ability of the disabling faculty of intellect, not an ability of sensing, such as seeing. Cogitation is also not what A-T psychologists refer to as the "estimative sense" because we're unable to use a sense to estimate. A self uses its knowing to cogitate as its ability to estimate which is a self's disabling ability, not its ability to sense.

Conclusion

The Aristotelian-Thomistic immortalist approach to psychology is a more advanced scientism than the mortalistic behavioural approach to psychology because the A-T immortalist approach is more concerned with quality than it is with quantity. The mortalistic behavioural approach not only ignores qualities but denies that they are realities; however, despite its advancement on the mortalistic behavioural approach, the A-T immortalist approach is just as delusional an approach as the mortalistic behavioural approach because the A-T immortalist approach is based on the myth of the Creator.

The A-T immortalist approach and the mortalistic behavioural approach aren't conducive to understanding because uncreated laws are the superstitious delusions by which mortalistic behaviourists believe phenomena are created, while the mythical Creator's created laws are the superstitious delusions by which A-T immortalist psychologists believe the Creator creates "noumena" as well as phenomena.

The ego, the psyche, and the mind which underpin psychology are fictions. The self, the sensor, and the cognition of a Selfist are truths. The metaphysical approach of my selfology which is uncertain of whether a self is immortal or mortal is conducive to a self's understanding because it's based upon the reality of the Evolver, Grower, Developer, Deteriorator, and Devolver, not the Creator. I know that Nature's instinctive willing is the reality by which Nature evolves, grows, develops, deteriorates, and devolves phenomena.

Evolution has been shown by qualitative scientists' natural experience as well as by quantitative scientismists' artificial experiments to be the way that mineral, vegetable, and sensable species change; however, we're only able to subjectively prove that geological and biological evolution, growth and development are truths because we can only subjectively prove a truth is a truth and a falsity is a falsity. There is no objective proof of a truth or a falsity because objects have no ability to prove. Consequently, Creationists are free to spout their ridiculous theory of Creationism, despite all evidence to the contrary, because we're unable to use objective evidence to prove that their philosophy is superstitious.

Our increased understanding of genetics has made it very clear that mineral, vegetable, and sensable species of organisms aren't created. An ontologist understands that our need to instinctively as well as deliberately use Nature's Will is the basis of the rest of our needs. An ontologist understands that the falsehoods of commandments and laws (supposed to be the prerogatives of the Creator) aren't the basis of our needs. An ontologist understands that the Creator is a myth upon which the myth of Creation is based.

What must be stressed in this conclusion is that species aren't created by Natural Law as scientismists believe. Scientismists, like the late Albert Einstein, subscribe to objectivism; therefore, they mistakenly hypothesised that we're only the brains of sensable organisms. They also mistakenly hypothesise that invisible laws automatically govern mechanisms, like computer chips, as well as the organic neurons of our brains. Such invisible laws provide no means by which motions and movements occur which is why automatism is an absurd hypothesis.

Instead of searching for the means by which motions in and movements of sensable organisms, like a human body, actually happen, scientismists either ignore the obvious truth that there is no means by which a law could cause their motions and movements or they assert the absurd doctrine that motions and movements are only illusions. These scientismists also denounce the Will of Nature as the ability by which motions in and movements of bodies are activated because they don't want to admit that their laws are their delusions.

A hypocritical doctrine of scientismists is that Natural Law is an *invisible* truth, while Nature's Will is a falsehood *because it's invisible.*

Albert Einstein believed that Nature automatically functions by laws, instead of activates in accord with Its willing. Einstein believed that motion was an illusion; however, even if he had believed in the reality of motion, he would have believed that Nature mechanically motioned his finite universe by invisible laws. Einstein seemed to believe that his universe was a finite machine. Einstein didn't realise that he needed to ask a couple of obvious questions. One obvious question is, "Exactly how is a physical mechanism used to produce the illusion of movement?" The other obvious question is, "Exactly how is a physical mechanism used to produce movements which are actually occurring?"

In answer to the former question, the movement of a mechanical movie projector's film is usually too fast for a self to use the processes of its sensable organism's brain to distinguish between the frames of the film flashed on the movie screen because a brain's processes are too slow. The processing of electromagnetic patterns in a brain simply won't happen fast enough for the self who inhabits this brain to use its cognising to distinguish between the individual frames of the moving film. Consequently, the illusion of a moving picture is cognised by the self instead of the individual pictures which are really flashing on the movie screen.

In answer to the latter question, the movement of a machine, like a car, is not produced by invisible laws in the car's gasoline. The gas from the gasoline is not exploded in the car's cylinders by way of invisible laws in the spark plugs nor do the sparks from the spark plugs in the car's cylinders ignite the gas by way of invisible laws. The ignition of the gas occurs when the car's driver deliberately and noninstinctively uses Nature's Will in his fingers to turn the key in the car's starter thereby stimulating Nature to instinctively and nondeliberately will a wave of electricity from the car's battery to the car's spark plugs and vitalise a spark in the car's cylinders as Nature concurrently, instinctively as well as nondeliberately wills gas from the gasoline to enter the cylinders. Nature's quale or will wave combusts or ignites the spark so that the gas explodes and the cylinders begin pumping. The movement of the cylinders is transferred to the wheels of the car by Nature's instinctive nondeliberate use of Its Will in other mechanisms so that the wheels turn and the car moves.

Scientismists hypothesise that the tools we make, like a movie projector or a car, have invisible laws which govern their movements as well as the movements of organisms, like organic mineral rocks, organic vegetative petunias, and organic sensable lizards. Their hypothesis is absurd because our ability to make tools was the basis of our development of laws.

We developed laws to explain how tools work before we applied these laws to Nature. Historically, organisms preceded the tools that we learned to make;

therefore, we're not able to use invisible laws to explain how organisms are grown because organisms preceded our making of tools while our making of tools preceded our development of laws to explain how our tools work. The laws we developed came after our making of tools and our making of tools came after Nature's continual, immediate, instinctive, and deliberate willing of the evolution, growth, and development of organisms, like our sensable human organisms; therefore, organisms were not created by laws. Our modern scientismists are simply blind to the fact that these organisms are evolved, grown, and developed by the spontaneous instinctive nondeliberate Volition of Nature, not created according to the automatism of "natural" laws.

Organisms were activated by Nature before we developed laws; therefore, we're unable to use invisible laws to delineate how motions in organisms or the movements of organisms happen *because invisible laws are a hypothesis based on our ability of making, rather than on Nature's abilities of evolving, growing, developing, deteriorating, and devolving.* The mechanically oriented don't realise that organisms are natural because they've been evolved, grown, and developed in accord with Nature's ability of willing, while physical tools are derivatively natural because we felt the desire to make them. The mechanically oriented don't understand that we only need to use Nature's invisible will to make our tools, not invisible laws.

The consequence of these facts is the undeniable truth that the Infiniverse is not an infinite Machine run automatically by invisible laws. The Infiniverse is an open infinity of organic particles and organic bodies composed of organic particles which are activated by Nature's spontaneous instinctive nondeliberate willing.

The Infiniverse is not Newton's Machine because the Infiniverse is continually organised, disorganised, and reorganised by Nature, the Evolver, Grower, Developer, Deteriorator, and Devolver, not made, ordered, and disordered by the Creator. Nature is not the "Inventor", the "Maker" or the "Producer" any more than It's the Creator; however, human selves are inventors, makers, and producers (although, of course, they aren't creators); therefore, *Nature is unable to make tools*; only human selves are able to make tools.

The falsehoods of logic, ethical morality, mathematics, measurements, and Natural Law are the delusions in which most modern humans indulge. Ignorant scientismists, like the late Albert Einstein, are able to convince the ignorant layman or laywoman that there is no Will of Nature because these ignorant scientismists fail to understand the way in which their own motions and movements are effected.

My late beloved father, James Douglas Mowat, had a favourite expression which was, "Bullshit baffles brains!" By this expression, he meant that absurdities, like the falsehoods of Creation, logic, ethical morality, mathematics, measurements, and Natural Law, baffle the intelligence of scientismists and most philosophers, artists, and religionists. My father had a great respect for people who recognised the harmony of Nature because he knew the Freedom of his own harmony within Nature's harmony.

If you believe in the absurd falsehoods of Creation, logic, ethical morality, mathematics, measurements, and invisible Natural laws, you will attempt to keep your understanding from attaining wisdom because you will be reluctant to give up these beliefs and start knowing from a realistic basis. We evade our responsibility of attaining wisdom by irresponsibly clinging to the absurd. Either we choose to exist as responsible coordinating cooperative adults who have transcended the irresponsibility of childhood or we choose to remain irresponsible "adult children" who pray to a "Big Daddy in the sky" to be our "Authoritarian Leader". Many people are obsessed with the insane desire to uncooperatively compete so that they will not have to grow up and be responsible adults who guide by way of coordinated cooperating.

Your choice to mature so that you cease to develop and believe in superstitious absurdities means that you need to develop beyond the insanities of your own society, like its repressive religious, political, educational, judicial, and commercial institutions. Such a choice often results in sanctions. These sanctions are often illegally imposed on you by members of your society's institutions of justice (who are supposed to be above reproach). Consequently, the choice to grow out of absurdities, like ethics, morals, logic, etcetera, is a struggle which hardly seems worth the effort.

Fortunately, I'm able to tell you from experience that wisdom carries with it the understanding that helps you to withstand the undue enmity of people who share your society with you. The fact that your metaphysical orientation may be threatening to another (because he or she is none too sure of the "Truth" of his or her own metaphysical orientation) is only a problem if you attempt to *pressure* him or her to switch his or her metaphysical orientation to yours.

You need to resist the temptation to "save" another self by arrogantly attempting to convert this self to your metaphysics. Instead, you need to take an interest in what this self has to say about its metaphysics. Then you'll recognise the stage of understanding it's attained and you'll be able to help it attain more understanding. By this Style of approaching other selves, you don't arrogantly use conversion tactics, but considerately let them develop as they need to develop.

If you're wise, you'll feel no insane desire to pressure another self to give up its metaphysics since you have the knowledge that it will only change from believing in the absurdities of its metaphysics when it realises that its absurd beliefs aren't its understanding. Also, you would be wise to take an interest in another self's metaphysical views because this self might have more advanced knowledge in some of its views than you do. I know that I have been put in my place on more than a few occasions!

You're unable to attain true knowledge by memorising my writings or lectures about naturalism, ontology, or phenomenology. True knowledge is worked out by reasoning, inferentially, on your own about what you've experienced, while considering what you've heard and seen in regards to verifying your Truth, such as my lectures and writings. True knowledge is knowing your experience. Consequently, the more you acquaint the self you are with your immaterial thoughts, concepts, and hypotheses related to your own experience, rather than with your immaterial thoughts, concepts, and hypotheses based upon your faith in fictions that contradict your experience (like the fictions of Creation, logic, ethical morality, mathematics, measurements, and Natural Law, not to mention the fictions of eternity, time, and the Now), the more you're able to progress in your understanding and finally realise the Truth. You then need to *subjectively* prove that your Truth is *the* Truth because you're unable to "objectively" prove the Truth is the Truth.

That The Ultimate Truth of Freedom is only subjectively, not objectively, proven will be demonstrated by those who disagree with this Truth, despite my explanations in this book of why Freedom is The Ultimate Truth. That I'm unable to subjectively prove The Ultimate Truth of Freedom to any other self because I'm unable to use this self's subjective world to prove the Truth to it often resulted in my wanting to pull out my hair by the roots! Fortunately, I've attained enough wisdom that I'm able to laugh at this limitation, rather than lament it.

If you persevere in your quest for wisdom and attain it, you'll convulse with side-splitting laughter upon your attainment of it because you'll understand that wisdom is not the omniscience of your intelligence that you might have believed it was before you attained wisdom. You'll understand that there's always more to learn about Reality because your stupidity is much deeper than you'll ever be able to probe. With the attainment of wisdom, you'll realise that you'll never be able to use your ability of reasoning to fathom the depth of your stupidity to the bottom because your stupidity is boundless.

Those who are afraid of boredom in their immortality (that is, if selves really are immortal) haven't anything to fear because our stupidity is unbounded. We'll never be bored as immortals because we will always be challenged by our stupidity and our tendency to "slip" into expressing our emotion of hate, while ignoring, suppressing, or repressing our tendency to express our emotion of love.

Chapter Eight
The Character Types and Personality Roles of a Self

A self develops delusions, beliefs, theories, and understandings as characteristics of its various character types. A self uses Nature's Will to develop these characteristics with its intelligence and understanding as well as with its intellect and misunderstanding. A self's character types are developed by the self's ability to relate these characteristics to each other.

Each of us has five basic character types. We use our five basic character types to develop a basic personality role which corresponds to its respective character type. The late psychoanalyst and sociologist, Erich Fromm, analysed our social characters and classified them into five different types. Fromm described these social characters as our productive, receptive, marketing, hoarding, and exploitative character types. I've also classified by Fromm's productive character type as a developmental character type. I've discovered and classified five basic social roles, false selves, or personae of the personality which are related to and derived from Fromm's five character types.

Our five basic social roles are the adult player, the infantile victim, the childish authoritarian, the preadolescent trickster, and the adolescent hero which I've associated, respectively, with the productive-developmental character type, the receptive character type, the hoarding character type, the exploitative character type, and the marketing character type. We also have other roles which are subordinate to our personality's five basic roles.

A self uses a character type to develop a corresponding personality role in which the self has oriented its thinking and reasoning. A self's sane adult player role is derived from its productive-developmental character type. A self's sane adult player role has the developmental age of adult associated with it, although it may be expressed at any age. A self's four insane roles, derived from its four insane character types, each in a self's manifestation of them at a certain developmental age, although they may be activated at any other age as well.

The word "self" refers to the true self, while the words "role" and "persona" refer to a false self which is acted out by the true self; therefore, you aren't "yourself" because you're unable to own or possess the self you are. The self is you; therefore, "yourself" is a false self you're acting out. Only the self you are is genuine, sincere, and authentic, not "yourselves"; consequently, there is a clear distinction between you and "yourselves" because you aren't your pretensions, roles, personae, or false selves which you label "yourselves".

Your male, hermaphroditic, or female sensable organism and/or sensor are used as references of the self you are which is why your use of the terms "himself", "him-her-self", or "herself" to refer to a self who inhabits a male, hermaphroditic, or female sensable organism and/or sensor is not your use of these labels as your pretensions; however, they do not actually describe what you are either. You're really an "it" or a self without a sex, not a "he", a "he-she", or a "her", which are terms describing a sexless self's relating of the self it is in its sensable organism and/or sensor with a male, hermaphroditic, or female sex.

"Diagram 2: The Character Types and Personality Roles of a Self" illustrates a circle symbolising a self's productive-developmental character type (in white) squared by its four receptive, hoarding, exploitative, and marketing character types (in grey) which all appear in the foreground of this diagram. These character types are circled, in turn, by the self's player personality role (in white) squared by its four victim, authoritarian, trickster, and hero personality roles (in grey) which all appear in the background of this diagram. The five character types are in the foreground of Diagram 2, while the five personality roles are in the background of this diagram, because every personality role is derived from its corresponding character type.

Diagram 2: The Character Types and Personality Roles of a Self

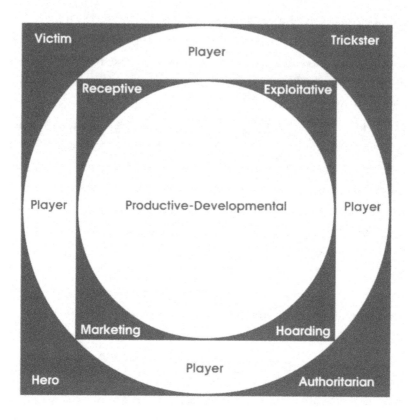

A self who uses its productive-developmental character type knows that it needs to guide its use of the artefacts it develops, such as its essential inner words, and the selfological qualities it expresses, such as its emotion of love. A wise self understands that its emotion of love is a means of its natural harmony within Nature's harmony.. The productive-developmental character type is used by a self to develop its adult player role. A self's orientation in the role of an adult player is that of the "guider", which means "a self who prepares the way"; however, its sane desire to act out its role of adult player is not its need because it needs to genuinely, sincerely, and authentically express its emotion of love from the core of its conscience without the artifice of playing a role.

A self who uses its receptive character type feels that the means to its natural harmony is existent outside of it; therefore, it attempts to suck Nature's harmony into it, not realising that Nature's harmony has always been within it as well as ubiquitously outside of it. The receptive character type is used by its inhabiting self to develop its infantile victim role. A self's orientation in the role of an infantile victim is that of the "sucker", which means "a self who is gullible and easily deceived".

A self who uses its hoarding character type feels the insane desire to possess what it is as well as what others are; therefore, it believes that, to feel harmonious, it not only has to attempt to command what it is, but also has to attempt to command other selves. The hoarding character type is used by its inhabiting self to develop its childish authoritarian role. A self's orientation in the role of a childish authoritarian is that of the "commander", which means "a self who dictates to others".

Like the self who uses its receptive character type, a self who uses its exploitative character type feels that the means to its harmony is existed outside of it; however, it takes what it insanely desires from others by using cunning in its attempt to feel harmonious. The exploitative character type is used by its inhabiting self to develop its preadolescent trickster role. A self's orientation in the role of a preadolescent trickster is that of the "manipulator", which means "a self who handles others".

The self who uses the marketing character type feels that its value is dependent on that for which it's exchanged; therefore, it thinks it needs to be in demand to feel harmonious. The marketing character type is used by its inhabiting self to develop its adolescent hero role.[12] A self's orientation in the role of an adolescent hero is that of the "saviour", which means "a self who rescues others".

Adulthood is associated with a self's productive-developmental character type and personality role of adult player, although the self's use of them is the sanity it's striving to actualise at any age. Infancy is associated with a self's character type of receptiveness and personality role of infantile victim. Childhood is associated with a self's character type of hoarding and personality role of childish authoritarian. Preadolescence is associated with a self's character type of exploitativeness and personality role of preadolescent trickster.

---

[12] Erich Fromme believed that the marketing character type was a fairly recent development in the history of humanity; however, the fact that the adolescent hero role has always been enacted by us as an insane role throughout history means that the marketing character type has always been an aspect of our arrogance.

Adolescence is associated with a self's character type of marketing and personality role of adolescent hero. A self is most susceptible to developing these character types and personality roles at these ages because its societal relations at these ages reinforce the self's tendency to develop these roles.

Infancy, childhood, preadolescence, adolescence and adulthood are descriptions of a self's selfological activity as well as descriptions of the age of a self's body; therefore, a man whose sensable male organism is at an adult age, may be inhabited by a self who is a selfological infant. The selfological infant's strongest tendency is to express its insane receptive character type, rather than its insane marketing, hoarding, and exploitative character types, while expressing its insane personality role of victim, concurrently, rather than expressing its insane personality roles of hero, authoritarian, and trickster. The selfological child's strongest tendency is to express its insane hoarding character type, rather than its insane receptive, marketing, and exploitative character types, while expressing its insane personality role of authoritarian, concurrently, rather than expressing its insane personality roles of victim, hero, and trickster. The selfological preadolescent's strongest tendency is to express its insane exploitative character type, rather than its insane receptive, marketing, and hoarding character types, while expressing its insane personality role of trickster, concurrently, rather than expressing its insane personality roles of victim, hero, and authoritarian. And, finally, the selfological adolescent's strongest tendency is to express its insane marketing character type, rather than its insane receptive, hoarding, and exploitative character types, while expressing its insane personality role of hero, concurrently, rather than expressing its insane personality roles of victim, authoritarian, and trickster.

Every self has an instinct to express its emotion of love so that the self is able to activate its instinct to play, just as every self has an instinct to express its emotion of hate and condition its expression of love so that it disables its instinct to play by activating its instinct to toy with other selves' emotions. These instincts wait in Potentiality to be activated in the self's expressions.

The expression of a self's benevolent desires as it plays results in its self-enjoyment (selfkomology), while the expression of the self's malevolent desires as it toys results in its self-suffering (selfpathology). A self is able to play, genuinely, sincerely, and authentically, without playing at its personality role of adult player or is able to play, ingenuinely, insincerely, and inauthentically, at this role, while it is also able to disable its instinct to play by toying, ingenuinely, insincerely, and inauthentically, in its personality roles of infantile victim, childish authoritarian, preadolescent trickster, and adolescent hero.

A self uses its productive-developmental character and its false self of adult player responsibly in arriving at its own choices, decisions, and selections as well as helps guide other selves back to their own sane desire to arrive at responsible choices, decisions, and selections so they can release their unnecessary anxiety; therefore, a self who is using its productive-developmental character and its false self of adult player is on its way to wisdom by way of its sanity. Unfortunately, a self who uses its four insane character types and four insane personality roles has the craving to use Nature's Will in its insane and irresponsible attempt to control the choices, decisions, and selections of other selves. Consequently, a self who uses its four insane character types and four insane personality roles is indulging in the insanity of stupidity in response to its fears and frustrations which tempt it to hate, rather than love.

A wise self tends to keep the insanity of its four insane character types and its four insane personality roles in its "background" (its memory). A wise self uses Nature's Will, intelligently, to activate the sanity of its productive-developmental character type and, through it, actualises the sanity of its sane adult player personality role in its "foreground" (its expressions). A stupid self keeps the sanity of its sane character type and the sanity of its sane adult personality role in its background. A stupid self often misuses Nature's Will by activating the insanity of all four of its insane character types and, through these character types, activates the insanity of all four of its insane personality roles in its foreground.

A wise self understands its doings because it's using Nature's Will to intelligently activate its sane productive-developmental character type, while concurrently activating its sane adult player personality role. A wise self often accords its sane adult player role to its sane productive-developmental character type so that its emotions aren't in conflict. A stupid self is confused about what it's doing because it intellectually misuses Nature's Will. It activates its insane receptive, marketing, hoarding, and exploitative character types, while concurrently actualising its insane personality roles of infantile victim, childish authoritarian, preadolescent trickster, and adolescent hero. Thus, a completely stupid self is a selfpath whose emotions are in continual conflict due to its conflicting insane desires which are stimulated by its intellectual use of Nature's Will in its four insane character types and its four insane personality roles.

The receptive character type and infantile victim personality role are usually in conflict with the hoarding character type and childish authoritarian personality role; however, they may also be in conflict with the marketing character type and adolescent hero personality role as well as with the exploitative character type and preadolescent personality trickster role. The hoarding character type and childish authoritarian personality role are usually in conflict with the receptive character type and infantile victim personality role; however, they may also be in conflict with the marketing character type and adolescent hero personality role as well as with the exploitative character type and preadolescent trickster personality role. The exploitative character type and preadolescent trickster personality role are usually in conflict with the marketing character type and adolescent hero personality role; however, they may also be in conflict with the receptive character type and infantile victim personality role as well as with the hoarding character type and childish authoritarian personality role. The marketing character type and adolescent hero personality role are usually in conflict with the exploitative character type and preadolescent trickster personality role; however, they may also be in conflict with the receptive character type and infantile victim personality role as well as with the hoarding character type and childish authoritarian personality role.

"Diagram 3: The Conflicting Relationships of a Self's Insane Personality Roles" has each of the four corners of its square symbolising one of the four insane personality roles of the self (i.e., infantile victim, childish authoritarian, preadolescent trickster, and adolescent hero) so the three directions of conflict for each of these four insane personality roles are symbolised by the arrows on each of the three lines leading away from each corner symbolising one of these roles.

Diagram 3: The Conflicting Relationships of a Self's Insane Personality Roles

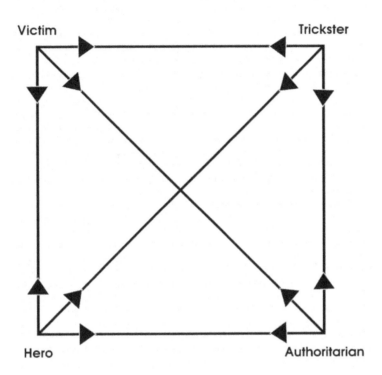

Unlike the stupid selfpath, the ignorant selfpath is in conflict because it concurrently uses all five of its character types and all five of its personality roles. The ignorant selfpath doesn't repress its sane productive-developmental character type or its sane adult player personality role, as the stupid selfpath does, which means that the ignorant selfpath has more subjective wellness than the stupid selfpath.

Examples of insanity in the conflicts between the four insane personality roles are seen in myths, where each insane personality role is personified.

For example, the Jewish fable of Adam and Eve is associated with the Christian fable of the Christ. In the Jewish fable of Adam and Eve, Adam and Eve are the personifications of infantile victims who are persecuted by Yahweh. Yahweh is the personification of the childish authoritarian. Yahweh is portrayed as a hoarder. Yahweh doesn't want to give up his possession of the fruits of the tree of the knowledge of good and evil or his possession of the fruits of the tree of life that are planted in the Garden of Eden. Yet Yahweh irresponsibly and covertly tempts Adam and Eve by keeping them in the Garden of Eden, while telling them not to eat the fruit of the tree of knowledge of good and evil. When the serpent, personifying the role of the preadolescent trickster in the Garden of Eden, irresponsibly and overtly tempts Adam and Eve, Yahweh childishly blames the serpent as well as Adam and Eve for his own irresponsible act of covertly tempting Adam and Eve as well as covertly tempting the serpent by not relocating the tree of knowledge of good and evil and the tree of life to another Garden.

Jews and Christians as well as Muslims and Baha'is attempt to rationalise Yahweh's covert temptation of Adam, Eve, and the serpent by saying that Yahweh was "testing", rather than tempting, them. Their excusing of Yahweh's behaviour is obviously their attempt to "sweep the childish dirtiness" of Yahweh's irrational logic "under the carpet".

After punishing the serpent by taking away its legs and punishing Adam and Eve by banishing them from the paradise of the Garden of Eden so they had to struggle and die, Yahweh (obviously feeling guilty) decided to send his "only begotten Son" to the humans on earth as the personification of the adolescent hero (the Christ) with the *unnecessary* goal of saving humans from perishing (The Gospel of John, 3:16). The perishing of a self is a myth or a fiction that Yahweh commanded his prophets to write so that readers of this myth would think of Yahweh as their authority. The goal of saving humans from perishing is only necessary in myths because a self *is unable to perish if it's immortal*. A self who inhabits an immortal body is imperishable. Only an immortal self's sensable organism would be perishable, not the immortal self.

Yahweh's guilty reconsideration of his condemnation of humanity in his myth of Adam and Eve shows he has a conscience, despite his authoritarianism.

Friedrich Nietzsche wrote, 'What does your conscience say?—"You shall become the person you are"' (Nietzsche, 1974, p. 219). But Nietzsche was mistaken. Your conscience doesn't say, "You shall become the person you are", because you are not a person. Your conscience says, "You shall accept what you're expressing".

Who you're expressing is often the person you're pretending you are because the person you're expressing is a persona (your "mask"), not your genuine, sincere, and authentic expression of you. *What you genuinely, sincerely, and authentically express is you, not your person, because your person is only your persona, your role, or your false self.* You and I aren't the person you and I are expressing. You and I are each a self who expresses the self it is as it is or expresses a false self it is not as it is not.

You and I are what we are. The energy you are is different from the energy I am, but the energy you are and the energy I am are developed from the same absolute Energy. Consequently, you're different from me, but you're not unique, because the energy you are is identical to the energy I am.

Conspicuously absent in the Christian myth of Adam and Eve is the personification of the adult player role because Christians refuse to believe that their wisdom is developed by them in response to playing this role. Christians don't believe that they're able to develop their own wisdom because they believe that they have to rely on the understanding of Yahweh. This is why Christians are subservient to Yahweh and obey the "Holy" Bible's Commandments.

Christians naively believe that Yahweh is the Creator because they believe Yahweh convinced his Hebrew prophets to write the Torah by proxy; therefore, Christians only want to believe in the words of the Bible, not become wise and independent. Their doctrine is that they should not rely on their own understanding because the Bible instructs them to have only a simple faith in "the Word" of their mythical "Creator".

Yahweh is only a self, not the Creator. The Bible is Yahweh's Bible, not Jesus' Bible. It was Yahweh who wrote his Bible by proxy (if Yahweh exists) because (if Yahweh exists) he is the irresponsible self who pretends to be the absolute Creator. Yahweh's Bible is not "holy" because the concept of the "holy" is delusional. There isn't anything holy in Reality, including Reality's harmony, because "holy" is just another nominal word (a word which doesn't refer to a referent).

As a consequence of their lack of understanding, Christians and other religionists who believe in the Creator, like Western Jews, Muslims, and Baha'i, fail to understand that their immortality isn't dependent on their delusion of an authoritarian Creator because Reality either develops immortal or mortal selves without the ability to "give" them their immortality or mortality. The absurd notion of a vengeful Creator (who supposedly has the ability to "bestow" the "gift" of immortality on those who had faith in his *adopted* Son, Jesus, and keep from bestowing it on those who disbelieve in this myth) was thought up by a selfpath who believes in retributive justice. Guess who this selfpath is.

If Nature develops us as centers of its invulnerable energy, then we're invulnerable, too. We'd inevitably exist as immortals if we're expressions of Nature's invulnerability because Nature has no ability of choosing to "grant" us invulnerability and immortality.

It's important to understand that a false self of adult player is a pretension because every false self is a role or a persona. The productive-developmental character type is a pretension because every character type is a caricature. Even your expression of your personality's sane adult player role is not genuinely, sincerely, and authentically expressed by you. Even a selfkomic self can occasionally, ingenuinely, insincerely, and inauthentically act and react as an adult player. You see, selfpathic selves often attempt to conflict a selfkomic self's thinking, irritate its sensor, as well as harm its body when the selfkomic self is expressing genuine, sincere, authentic thoughts because selfpathic selves disagree with the thoughts of selfkomic selves.

Carl G. Jung was Sigmund Freud's student. Jung broke away from Freud's school of thought called "psychoanalysis" to develop his own school of thought called "analytical psychology".

Jung called the various roles or false selves we act out and react to our expressions of "archetypes". Jung believed these archetypes were located in our genes and that these archetypes motivate us to express the various roles, false selves, or personae at which we toy or play with our own as well as other selves' emotions. Unlike Jung, I realised that our sane and insane desires, not "genetic archetypes", result in the character traits that motivate us to express our various roles, false selves, or personae. Our sane and insane desires are the source of our personae, not our DNA, because personae are transmitted by our volition in our desires, not by our volition in our DNA. We only use our DNA to develop our sensable organisms, not our cognitions. In other words, we learn how to act out our personae according to our cognised desires, not the genes of our DNA.

Jung identified twelve hypothetical ectypal personae that he believed were derived from his hypothesis of our sensable organisms' genetic archetypes which he hypothesised, in turn, were derived from his delusion of the "collective unconscious". These personae are the innocent, the sage, the lover, the explorer, the hero, the rebel, the magician, the jester, the orphan, the caregiver, the ruler, and the creator. Jung arrived at the number of twelve because he superstitiously believed that the constellations of the zodiac influence us. Jung didn't realise that his hypothesised genetic "archetypes" from which his twelve personae were derived were better described as genetic "ectypes" because the astrologers' delusion of twelve constellations were actually the source of Jung's hypothetical "genetic archetypes". Erich Fromm based his analysis of character types on the social characters we all express; however, Jung didn't base his archetypes on empirically gathered evidence. Instead, Jung based his belief in his archetypes on the fiction of astrological constellations as well as on his superstitious faith in the Creator.

Jung didn't really identify genetic archetypes. He only identified some of the personae we develop. Jung's twelve personae are existed, but they aren't basic. Instead, they're subordinate to my five basic roles with the exception of the hero because the infantile hero is one of my five basic roles.

Each of Jung's remaining eleven roles may be assigned as a subordinate persona to a persona of my five basic personae. Consequently, my persona of adult player has Jung's personae of sage, lover, and orphan as its subordinates, my persona of infantile victim has Jung's personae of innocent and caregiver as its subordinates, my persona of childish authoritarian has Jung's personae of creator and ruler as its subordinates, my persona of preadolescent trickster has Jung's personae of jester, magician, and rebel as its subordinates, and my persona of adolescent hero has Jung's persona of explorer as its subordinate.

Astrology is delusional because it's believed to be predictive. The premise that constellations allow for certainty of prophecy is a delusion of astrologers, just as the premise that measurements of probability allow for the certainty of prediction is a delusion of advocates for scientism.

You're only genuine, sincere, or authentic as what you are when you're not pretending to be a caricature and its derived persona which is why you need to decondition your thinking so you understand that your caricatures and personae are your pretensions. Only then are you able to choose when you will pretend to be a caricatured persona or express what you are, genuinely, sincerely, and authentically.

A self is only able to express what it is, genuinely, sincerely, and authentically, when it ceases to indulge in its use of caricatured personas; therefore, the self is only really what and how it is when it realises what the difference is between the self it is, its intelligence, and its intellect. These differences aren't hard to recognise. After all, the difference between a self and its intelligence is that it uses its intelligence to develop what it is, genuinely, sincerely, and authentically, while the difference between a self and its intellect is that it uses its intellect to develop who it isn't as its ingenuine, insincere, and inauthentic character types and personality roles.

Every self who concurrently activates the insanity (malevolence) of its four character types as it actualises the insanity of its four personality roles is dependent on the delusions of commandments and ethical morality. Even an atheist, who has ceased to believe—or has never believed—in the false idea of the Creator usually suffers from the misunderstanding that laws refer to realities.

A wise selfkom understands that laws don't refer to the regularities of Nature because the Creator and non-Existence are only falsehoods without a referent; therefore, the laws of these falsehoods have no referents either. Consequently, the regularities of Nature aren't the referents of an immortalistic Creationist's created laws or a mortalistic scientismist's uncreated laws because these laws are only their delusions.

Laws are developed because the self who develops them has a perverted desire to use laws in attempt to use its delusional belief that it can control its emotional hate which he or she doesn't understand is not possible because we're only able to guide our use Nature's Will to also guide, not control, our emotional hate. Our instinctive hate is stimulated by the application of laws to our behaviour because we hate restrictions on our actions and behaviours; therefore, we respond to laws with instinctive hate because we resent the conditioning of our actions and behaviours. We know "deep down" that we can only guide our behaviour by way of our wise conscientious use of love which stimulates our instinct to play or guide our behaviour by way of our unwise unconscientious use of hate.

A wise self understands that the regularities of Nature are the result of Nature's spontaneous instinctive nondeliberate use of Its Will, not the laws of a Creator. A wise self understands that the difference between a law and a need is that a law is associated with logical procedure, while a need is associated with motivation; therefore, our needs (as well as our sane desires derived from our needs) motivate us to act and react, reasonably, but our insane desires motivate us to act and react unreasonably by proceeding with our use of logic to justify our unjustifiable application of it to our reasoning simply because we want our reasoning to be "perfect" which is impossible.

Laws were not originally created by the Creator because the Creator only exists as a delusion; therefore, laws are developed by stupid selfpaths in the ethereal realms of the after-death (if these ethereal realms and the after-death exist) as well as by stupid selfpaths on Infiniversal planets because they want to be irresponsible. The stupid selfpaths who develop these laws fail to realise that laws are unnecessary because Nature's regularities only develop from Nature's need to express Its Will in Its phenomena as well as outside of Its phenomena; therefore, Nature's regularities don't obey laws because laws are delusions with which we attempt to control our impulsivity by impulsively using our intellects, rather than realise we only effectively guide our impulsivity by spontaneously using our intelligence.

Until we understand our need to conduct our behaviour in Freedom from moral as well as immoral laws of conduct, we'll suffer unnecessarily; therefore, we need to understand the truths of a self's *aethics* and *amorality*. Aethics is a self's study of amorality so it realises it has a need to develops it harmony and conscience in relation to its amorality, while a self's amorality is simply its realisation of and response to its needs.

An aethicist is a self who advocates for aethics. An amoralist is a self who advocates for amorality. A moralist is a self who advocates for morality. An immoralist is a self who advocates for immorality. An ethicist is a self who advocates for ethics. An ethical moralist and an unethical immoralist both act and react irresponsibly in discord with their needs by basing their behavioural conduct on laws.

An amoralist understands that he, he-she, or she needs to base his, his-her, or her conduct on Freedom so that he, he-she, or she may choose the needs he, he-she, or she will use to motivate his, his-her, or her behaviour. An amoralist also understands that his (his-her and her) ability to enjoy his behaviour depends on choosing his needs in harmony with his Freedom based on his conscientious integrity. The amoralist knows better than to base his behaviour on rules in an attempt to avoid developing an understanding of Reality. Therefore, I define amorality as:

'A self's activation of its actions and reactions while letting other selves decide how they'll act and react by focusing its knowing on fulfilling its amoral needs in relation to its undeniable Freedom.'

My definition of amorality is based on my definition of my coined word "aethics" which it was necessary to invent because ethics can't be used to study amorality. You see, amorality is not ethical; therefore, philosophers obviously can't use ethics to study or to define amorality because an ethical philosopher uses principles, rules, and laws to describe any subject or topic they're considering, instead of the harmony, conscience, and needs. Needs guide an amoralist's actions of cognitive knowing as well as his or her sensorial and sensable organic behaviours.

I searched for a word in English that describes the study of amorality but found to my consternation that no such word exists. I finally realised that I had to invent a word which described not only the study of amorality but also its transcendence which I immediately realized was easily done by distinguishing it from ethics in the same manner amorality was distinguished from morality and immorality—by simply placing the letter "a" in front of ethics with the Latin or Greek meaning of "not". In other words, my coined word "aethics" is literally meant to signify "not ethics".

I define aethics as follows:

'The study of amorality for the purpose of a self's realisation of the realism which is its harmony and responsibility in activating its conscientious actions and reactions by focusing its knowing on its actions and reactions of independently fulfilling its amoral needs in relation to its undeniable sovereignty and Freedom while concurrently letting other selves independently decide how they'll act and react without interfering with their decisions.'

Your understanding that you're an absolutely free self develops in accord with your understanding that you're absolutely free to select a need as your motivator or instinct in using Nature's Will to drive in this need. In other words, you aren't determined by your needs. You aren't even determined by Nature's spontaneous instinctive nondeliberate use of Its Will because you're absolutely free in your spontaneous or impulsive instinctive nondeliberate as well as deliberate noninstinctive use of Nature's Will, just as Nature is absolutely free in Its restriction of only spontaneously, instinctively, and nondeliberately using Its Will in you and around you.

Maturing is largely a matter of realising that you're absolutely free to choose which of your needs will motivate you. You're also able to choose not to choose which of your needs will motivate you. Your choice to not choose which of your needs will motivate you is your decision to let Nature's absolutely free willing in your needs establish which of your needs motivates you. Your choice to not choose which of your needs will motivate you lets Nature instinctively use Its Will within your needs unhindered by your use of Its Will. Nature's stimulation of your needs is a random act; however, you choose to let Nature randomly stimulate your needs.

Your belief that you don't choose is your delusion because, obviously, you have to make a choice not to choose, that is, once you've learned from experience that you have the ability to choose. Once you've learned that you have the ability to choose, there's no going back to the innocence of not knowing you choose because such unknowing only characterises the inner world of an infant.

You're not an infant self who doesn't realise yet that it chooses. You're an adult who realises that the ability to choose is yours; however, if you're absurdly denying your ability to choose, you're afraid of Freedom. In other words, you want to remain an unknowledgeable and unwise infant who has decided to let others choose for you, instead of choose to develop your own knowledgeable wisdom of how to choose. You don't want to choose because choice carries with it the responsibility to stop your stupidity of hating.

You're afraid to choose among your needs or choose to let Nature instinctively Will your needs to motivate you because you stupidly hate you, other people, and Reality. You're afraid of your need to choose because you instinctively know that you're responsible for you. You know that choosing in accord with your needs would mean that you'd have to learn to stop your insane desire of stupidly giving into your expression of hate.

Your Freedom is the harmonious core of your conscience. Only your choice to always act from this core is wise. To deny your Freedom is to deny your choice to always act from the harmonious core of your conscience. In other words, your denial of your Freedom to choose is not only your delusion, but also your affirmation of your selfpathy, because you're denying the harmonious core of your conscience.

Your denial of your ability to choose with Freedom is the result of your selfpathic denial of your need to dwell in your desired harmony and your need to share your expressions of love. Your denial of your ability to choose with freedom is also your selfpathic affirmation of your desire to wallow in hate and cast your emotionally energised expressions of hatred into the temperamental emotional energies of other selves.

We need to learn the difference between our needs, our sane desires, and our insane desires. Infants haven't yet learned whether a desire is sane (benevolent) and is okay to fulfil or is insane (malevolent) and is not okay to fulfil; therefore, the infant will attempt to fulfil his or her desire whether this desire is sane or insane. When the infant has developed into a child who has established his character types and personality roles, the child remains ignorant of the fact that his needs motivate his sane desires, while his insane desires are motivated by his feelings of *deprivation*, not by his needs; therefore, he doesn't yet have a choice in the selection of his character types and personality roles. An individual's feelings of need and feelings of deprivation are entirely different because an individual's feelings of need are accompanied by his or her insights into love whereas an individual who feels deprived is missing these insights.

Like an infantile victim, a childish authoritarian is unable to deliberately activate his productive-developmental character type because the childish authoritarian has yet to realise it can exist this character type; therefore, a childish authoritarian is also unable to deliberately use this character type to actualise its corresponding adult player personality role. Even more mature selves who realise that they have a choice in activating the productive-developmental character type and its corresponding adult player personality role often fail to realise that their infantile victim, childish authoritarian, preadolescent trickster, and adolescent hero personality roles are only insane personality roles developed from insane desires. Instead, they misunderstand the truth and distort the facts so that they think these insane personality roles are sane, like their sane adult player personality role. As a result, they fail to understand that the desires motivating these character types and personality roles are insane because they're motivated by feelings of deprivation.

Such ignorant selfpaths are motivated by their insane greed which is derived from the feeling of deprivation which is at the basis of all their insane desires, like their insane desires of lust and envy. Consequently, an ignorant selfpath tends to believe that all five basic character types and all five basic corresponding personality roles are sane because he or she may not yet understand how wisdom is related to stupidity.

A selfkom who activates the sanity of its productive-developmental character type and its corresponding adult player personality role has cognitive wellness because a selfkom has wellness of ego, wellness of self, and wellness of instinct. A wise selfkom is well because it's using Nature's Will to express its emotion of love in understanding. Understanding or intelligence is a selfkom's sane way of deliberately and noninstinctively playing.

Neither the ignorant selfpath nor the stupid selfpath understand that they activate the insanity of their four insane character types and the insanity of their corresponding four insane personality roles because they are unwell. Selfpaths become unwell because they are using Nature's Will to emote hatred by which they condition their emoting of love as their way of misunderstanding or intellectualising. Just as ignorant and stupid selfpaths fail to realise the nature of intellectualising, they fail to realise that intellectualising is a selfpath's insane way of deliberately and noninstinctively toying with the emotional energies of other selves.

Insane character types and the insane personality roles are developed by way of a selfpath's insane (malevolent) desires. The reality of an insane desire needs to be realised by the selfpath before it will become selfkomic and render this insane desire sterile. By acting sanely (benevolently), a selfkom renders its insane (malevolent) desires sterile because its expression of its emotion of love is based on need, not the drive of deprivation and the unneeded desires derived from it, such as greed.

Nature's spontaneous instinctive nondeliberate willing is neither sane nor insane. We develop our needs (which Non-Individual Nature doesn't have) from the individuality of our existence; therefore, our needs are neither sane nor insane because they're based on our existence as individuals, not our benevolence or malevolence.. But our desires are either sane or insane because the source of our desires is The Ultimate Freedom at our basis with which we conscientiously choose to express our sanity (benevolence) or unconscientiously choose to express our insanity (malevolence).

Our discontent arises from our emotions, like fear. Our discontent is the result of our insane desires. Fears are not needed because we only need courage to face a challenge. We use our fears to motivate our cowardly repression or suppression of love; however, we may also analyse a fear and, through this analysis, work up the courage to express our love, despite our fears.

When we have repressed or suppressed a need, we usually develop an insane desire as compensation for our inability to do what we need to do.

For example, you may allow your fear of your need to express your emotion of love motivate you because your parents have "taught" you that your expression of this emotion will meet with severe punishment. Consequently, your fear of punishment may keep you from expressing this emotion; however, as compensation for your inability to express your emotion of love, you may develop the insane desire to punish those who do feel free to express this emotion because you've learned this way of behaving from your parents or your own tendency of selfishness.

If a selfkom understands its knowledge of love as well as hate so that it expresses its love wisely, the selfkom is said to be "enlightened" as well as "lightened". An enlightened Selfkom understands that it has chosen the "light" over the "dark" which is a way of expressing, as a metaphor, its wisdom in choosing to develop its understanding of love and hate over its ignorance of these emotions. When we develop an understanding of our ability to love and hate, we're said to be "in the light" while we're said to be "in the dark" when we fail to develop such understanding.

An ignorant as well as a stupid selfpath's instincts reveal to them "deep down" that they have chosen "the dark over the light"; however, their choice is unknown to them because they choose to ignore the revelation of their instincts. Choosing the dark over the light is a way of expressing, as a metaphor, the selfpath's foregoing of its development of any understanding of its ability to love and hate because it's clinging to its ignorance (its darkness) of this ability. Ironically, the selfpath believes that a selfkom, who cherishes its ability to love, is unable to face "the hard facts of life"; however, the selfpath is afraid to face the hard facts of life, not the selfkom, because a selfkom know it's sane to cherish its ability to love.

The hard fact of any selfkom's knowledge so far as expressing its existence in living its life is that it knows it needs to be responsible in acting or reacting appropriately and effectively in relation to its needs so it's able to express what it genuinely, sincerely, and authentically is by considering the meaning of death. A selfkom also needs its knowledge of love and hat *before* it develops its ability to responsibly, independently, genuinely, sincerely, and authentically relate. A selfpath only relates dependently, not independently, because it's afraid to face the hard fact that it needs to develop its knowledge of love and hate as well as its responsibility, independence, and sanity.

A self must face the meaning of death. Death is defined by some philosophers as 'the cessation of life' (Blackburn, 1994, p. 89). Obviously, like these philosophers, some selves fail to understand that they might live their sensors forever. A naïve selfpath takes the philosopher's idea that death is the cessation of life for granted because these philosophers are thought by this naïve selfpath to be the authorities who have the "job" of doing its reasoning for it. A naïve selfpath conveniently believes that philosophers have this job because the naïve selfpath wants to remain naïve.

Naïve people don't want to do their own reasoning about death because they fear they'll die with their sensable organisms. As a result of their fear, they have a selfpathic desire to survive. These naïve people fail to realise that their sensable organisms only seem to have the ability to live; therefore, they also fail to realise that death might only indicate their sensable organisms' cessation, not their inner aspect of their World,, or their sensors. A naive selfpath doesn't want to know that it uses Nature's Will in its sensable organism or that its sensable organism doesn't use Nature's Will. A naïve selfpath doesn't want to know its sensable organism doesn't live because it merely an unalive organism that its inhabiting self exists to live; therefore, our belief that our sensable organisms live is our delusion, just as our belief that we die might simply be another of our delusions.

Selfpaths fail to realise that they might continue to use Nature's Volition in their objective large uncondensed energy forms after their multicellular sensable organisms die. This means that every self would be immortal.

Nature exists every self; however, every self exists its inner world. A self's sensable organism and sensor (objective large uncondensed energy form) have no ability to use Nature's Will; however, I'm able to use Nature's Will to live my sensable organism as well as my sensor. Death is the cessation of a mineral, vegetative, or sensable organism's processions which are the living of motions in them by Nature's spontaneous instinctive nondeliberate willing. Neither mineral nor vegetative organisms are inhabited by a self who would be able to exist in and live them. The processions of a sensable organism are lived by its inhabiting self as well as by Nature.

A self who inhabits its sensor and sensable organism instinctively and nondeliberately exists in and lives them: however, after its sensable organism dies, the self might generate suefs for its progressions as it continually lives its sensor. But a self is unable to generate particles for its processions as it continually lives its sensable organism. A self is only able to live the processes of its sensable organism, not generate new particles from Nature to replenish it; therefore, a sensable organism has to die because a self is unable to generate particles from its sensor as it uses its sensor to generate suefs. A self is only able to use its sensable organism to ingest (eat) organically bodied particles in its environment. Consequently, the self's sensable organism isn't immortal because the self is unable to generate particles to continually revitalise its sensable organism as it generates suefs in its sensor to continually revitalise it.

Just as the word "lightenment" is a metaphor for a selfkom's knowledge of its emotions of love and hate, the word "enlightenment" is a metaphor for the wisdom which is the understanding of this knowledge. Lightenment is not enlightenment because knowledge is not wisdom.

A self's understanding is the result of its inferential reasoning about its knowledge. A self uses its ability of reasoning about the qualities it knows to develop an understanding of these qualities so that it's not ignoring its knowing anymore. Experience is known by a knower (a self who knows). A self knows its experience as its known by way of its ability of cognising. Wisdom is a self's cognised understanding of how bits of knowledge are related to its basic pattern of knowledge which it developed as a product of its knowing of Reality and Its realities.

Just as the word "dark" is a metaphor for a selfpath's ignorance of its emotions of love and hate, the outer word "endarkenment" is a metaphor for a selfpath's stupidity which results from such ignorance. A darkenly endarkened (ignorantly stupid) selfpath misunderstands these emotions; however, a lightenly enlightened (knowledgeably wise) selfkom uses Nature's Will to express its knowledge of love because it understands that its emotion of love is its preference.

On one hand, a receptive infantile victim, a hoarding childish authoritarian, an exploitative preadolescent trickster, and a marketing adolescent hero are all characterologically typical and personality pretensioned as they are guided and expressed by a selfpath who misunderstands how its love and hate are to be known. On the other hand, a productive-developmental adult player is characterologically typical and personality pretensioned as its guided by a selfkom who understands how its love and hate are to be known.

A wise selfkom's crowning knowledge about its emotion of love is that it knows it has a sane preference to love a selfpath because every selfkom has a natural preference to express its emotion of love towards other selves, even though it occasionally expresses its emotion of hate towards a selfpath's malevolent behaviours. Our natural preference to express our emotion of love towards other selves necessitates that we care about each other, even if we're expressing hatred in relation to their cognitive actions and reactions and/or their sensorial and bodily behaviours, because our preference for love is a reflection of Nature's harmony of Freedom in our consciences. Ironically, Nature has no conscience of Its own.

It's possible for us develop a preference to express hatred but our preference to express this emotion is the result of conditioning, not Freedom, therefore this preference is pathological.

A knowledgeably wise selfkom realises that it's able to express its emotions of love and hate towards the center of Nature it is. I'm able to express my love and hate by introjecting these emotions, rather than projecting them; therefore, I'm able to express my emotions of love and hate towards what I am or away from what I am by using Nature's Will in my temperament.

I'm able to project these emotions away from me towards my intelligence or understanding as well as introject these emotions towards me from their stay in my temperament; however, it's not wise to identify what you are with these emotions because you're not these emotions. You are only able to project or introject an emotion, not be it.

People project their own sanity onto Nature; therefore, they interpret Nature's shining of the sun's rays as demonstrations of Nature's benevolence. They also project their own insanity onto Nature; therefore, they interpret the natural disasters they experience as demonstrations of Nature's malevolence. Their projection of their own benevolent and malevolent tendencies onto Nature results in their crazy delusion that Nature is benevolent and malevolent, like them.

Nature doesn't experience emotions because Nature is unable to emote. Nature has no emotions to intentionally express benevolent behaviours or malevolent behaviours. Nature is unable to identify phenomena, like emotions, or identify what It is with a label. Nature is not the Knower because Nature is unable to know; therefore, Nature is unable to identify.

A knowledgeably wise selfkom understands that it's a mistake to identify its realisation of what it is with anything. A knowledgeably wise selfkom identifies what it is because it identifies with the center of pure energy it is in and of Nature; therefore, you're able to identify with what you are because you're able to identify what you are with an identifier; however, you're unable to use your identifier of what you are to realise you as you are because you would be confusing your realisation of your identifier for your realisation of you.

When I write that I'm a center of Nature, the outer word "center" is my identifier of what I am; however, my identifier is *not* my realisation of what I am. When you need to realise what you are, you need to cease thinking, speaking, and writing about it with identifiers and take the drastic step of *insighting* that you exist in your sensable organism but aren't your sensable organism. You must step out of your identifications so that you develop the insight that you are. I don't mean that you're reasoning out what you are because insight is non-verbal self-actualisation. When you're insighting what you are, you also gain insight into how you are and how you aren't as well as who you are and who you aren't. You're able to play around forever in your attempt to describe the self you are in words; however, this will bring you no closer to self-actualisation.

People often take drastic measures to develop insight into what they are.

For example, some sad adolescent girls forlornly attempt to develop insight into what they are by cutting or slashing their arms and wrists so that the resulting pain will "wake them up" to what they are, although they don't understand that this is their motive for their abuse of their bodies.

You're only able to develop insight into what you really are by ceasing to identify what you are with outer words and paying attention to the truth that it's you who is experiencing everything you know. You finally gain insight into what you are when you realise that you're the knower of your experience who *inhabits* your body and that your body doesn't experience because you use the body for *your* experience. In other words, you are a self in a human body who experiences in your human body or your human thing.

Although you exist as the knower in your body, you are not the word "knower" any more than you are your body or the experiencing of your body because you exist beyond your words, your body—and your experience.

Conclusion

Our expression of love towards others is our expression of friendship in a genuine, sincere, and authentic way of existing which leads us to enjoy our ability to relate to other selves; however, our expression of hate towards other selves is our expression of enmity in an ingenuine, insincere, inauthentic way of existing which leads us to suffer. Our emotions are in harmony when we express enjoyment, but they conflict with each other when we suffer.

In attempting to resolve the conflict of sane desires with insane desires in a self, it's a necessity for the self to select its productive-developmental adult player as the means by which it resolves these conflicting desires because it's unable to use its receptive infantile victim, its hoarding childish authoritarian, its exploitative preadolescent trickster, and its marketing adolescent hero to resolve them. A selfpath who selects one of its insane typical roles to resolve its conflicts has yet to understand that its true challenge is its deluded belief that its emoting of love is not needed to resolve its conflicts because it mistakenly thinks that its emoting of hate is all that is necessary.

A selfpath chooses to express its emoting of hate over its emoting of love because it has chosen to avoid its knowledge of love and hate as well as its recognition of them. By ignoring this knowledge as well as its emotions, the selfpath will never have to make the effort to recognise how it needs to use inner words and outer words to relevantly reflect its knowing and knowledge of love and hate.

A selfpath is unable to de-conflict its malevolent desires until it realises why it has chosen to ignore its expressions of love and hate. Until the selfpath realises why it has chosen to ignore, rather than know, these emotions, it will never recognise the importance of gaining an understanding of them.

The only way for a selfpath to understand the importance of its knowledge concerning its emoting of love and hate is to confront the fear which terrifies it. Although it's tempting to blame a selfpath's fear of its own death as the cause of its ignorance, the true cause of its ignorance is its fear of responsibility.

A selfpath's fear of death motivates it to believe in its delusion that its understanding isn't very important because it either mistakenly believes in its mortality or its immortality without realising it will only know that it's immortal if it doesn't die with its sensable organism, while it will never know its mortal if it dies with its sensable organism since it wouldn't have any opportunity to know it was dead; therefore, it thinks that understanding isn't very important because it thinks its understanding as well as its knowledge dies with it.

If the self identifies with its sensable organism, it believes it's only a secondary characteristic (an epiphenomenon) of its sensable organism who will die with it. As a consequence, such a self refuses to believe that its intuiting of its own invulnerability is realistic because it simply refuses to acknowledge that it might be immortal.

A selfpath usually thinks it's not important enough for Nature to immortalise it, despite Nature's inability to intentionally—or unintentionally—develop anything as mortal or immortal. A selfpath also ignores its ability to emote the emotion of love because it feels its death has been ordained; therefore, it feels deprived of love. Ironically, the selfpath has accurately assessed that Nature doesn't love it—but has also inaccurately assessed that Nature hates it—because the selfpath assumes that Nature has condemned it to death.

A selfpath shrinks from examining the reality of death because, ironically, it thinks its examination of death will prove that it dies. A selfpath fears it will prove the "truth" of its death, even though it intuits in its depths that it might exist as an invulnerable and, thus, an immortal self. Until the selfpath develops the courage to face its own fear of death, it will remain ignorant of its probable immortality and its possible mortality. Its ignorance is unfortunate because the knowledge of its probabilities and possibilities would acquaint it with its desire to emote its emotion of love.

A cowardly selfpath who is afraid to face the meaning of death is also afraid to be independent. Because independence is necessary for a self to be truly spontaneous, a selfpath is also afraid of the responsibility inferred by its need to fairly assess the reality it is as well as other realities existing in and by way of Reality which is why it irresponsibly, rather than responsibly, chooses to activate its receptive infantile victim, its hoarding childish authoritarian, its exploitative preadolescent trickster, and its marketing adolescent hero roles, while confining its productive adult player role to memory.

Until a selfpath realises that its desire to obey arbitrary laws is an insane desire inspired by its fear of responsibility, it will suffer from this insane desire. A self who has yet to understand that there is no Creator who it thinks will take responsibility for it and save it from death will also fail to understand that it's either obeying the orders of selfpaths from realms in the after-death who are pretending to be the Creator (if these realms and the after-death exist), obeying the orders of telepathic selfpaths inhabiting sensable organisms on earth who are pretending to be the Creator (if telepathy and telekomy exist), or obeying the orders of its own projected hallucinatory images and/or voices issuing from its imagination and/or audition; therefore, such a selfpath will remain trapped by in its insane typical roles because it will only experience malevolent desires which are always in conflict.

A selfpath is tempted to settle for faith in its immortality; however, its faith in immortality is obviously dependent upon its doubts about its immortality; therefore, it's unable to use faith to dispel the anxiety it feels in relation to the doubts it has about its own immortality. A selfpath is unable to use faith to dispel its fear of death because its faith is based on its fear of death.

If a self has refused to cling to its fear of death, it won't mistakenly and pathologically cling to faith. Such a self would only have the sane desire to use its reasoning to prove its immortality is either a truth or a falsehood. Only by realising that its own death is either a truth or a falsehood does a self dispel its fear of death as well as its desire for faith because it realises that Nature is the Generator or Activator, not the Creator; however, a self has a need to base its knowledge that Nature is the Generator or Activator on its experience so that its knowledge is scientific, instead of a fantasy, an imagining, or a hallucination.

Yogis claim that the Chakras they identify are based on experience, not theory. People don't need to "go within" to experience their Chakras because they already are within; however, they need to pay attention to their Chakras with the Third Eye Chakra each of them is if they are ever to learn how to deal with life. The Third Eye Chakra is the "I" Chakra. The other six Chakras are the Root Chakra, the Sacral Chakra, the Navel Chakra, the Heart Chakra, the Throat Chakra, and the Crown Chakra. Each Chakra, with the exception of the Crown Chakra, is a center of energy. A self's emoting ability is the Heart Chakra. The self (the Third Eye Chakra) is responsible for working in harmonising with its Heart Chakra to express its emotions.

Unlike Yogis, my ontology is not based on identifying with the Crown Chakra because the Crown Chakra is a delusion of Yogis. Consciousness (The Crown Chakra) is thought by Yogis to be the reality, while they are supposedly only the "illusory" Third Eye Chakra. These Yogis are deluded because I am a reality (a self) who has and uses my cognition. Consciousness is falsely imagined. I identify with "I" because I *am* I. I am not consciousness because I know. I am a knower. My cognition is the faculty of my ability to know;

therefore, I am a knower who uses the knowing of my cognition to know my experience as my known. Consequently, The Crown Chakra is not a center of consciousness at the top of my head because "consciousness" is only a nominal word (a word without an actual, illusory, delusional, or hallucinatory referent).

We only have cognition, not consciousness. We aren't awareness and consciousness or unawareness and unconsciousness; rather, we are selves who intelligently use our knowing and cognisance to realise the realities each of us is or intellectually use our unknowing (ignoring) and incognisance to avoid realising the reality each of us is.

You have a need to learn. You are free to act on or ignore your need to learn. The choice is yours because your understanding is your own. A teacher is paid to indoctrinate you, not let you learn; therefore, I can only assist you with my relation of my understanding by sharing my understanding with you for your consideration while providing you with the caveat that you need to develop your own understanding (which will never be identical to that of any other self) by learning on your own and avoiding the temptation to submit to the teachings (prejudices or biases) of "teachers" who may be well-intentioned but are irresponsibly denying your need to be responsible for your own development of your understanding.

Unfortunately, you may want entities to "answer your prayers, instead of using your own understanding to greet your challenges. Your prayers to such entities for help is simply your way of ignoring your need to learn. Praying for assistance is not responsible because only entities from realms in the after-death who are not yet enlightened respond to your prayers (if these entities actually exist). Enlightened entities don't assist you because they know you have a need to "stand on your own two feet."

A wise entity (who might simply exist as your hallucination) usually lets you talk out your challenges and sends its emotion of love to your Heart Chakra to let you know that there is a realm of love beyond your realm of tears. A stupid entity (who also might simply exist as your hallucination) will often try to control you by raising anxiety in your Navel Chakra (your center of excitement, easiness, and anxiety) so you will be tempted to choose badly.

Fortunately, you're capable of learning how to deal with the anxiety a stupid entity raises in your center of excitement, easiness, and anxiety by emoting the emotion of love from your Heart Chakra to deal with this anxiety. Your expression of love to your Navel Chakra from your Heart Chakra dissipates the anxiety that the stupid entity raises in your Navel Chakra. You see, the anxiety a stupid entity raises in you is its own anxiety which it transfers to you for you to experience as "your" anxiety which, of course, was not originally yours. Likewise, the love you express to greet this anxiety not only dissipates the anxiety in you, it also dissipates the anxiety in the entity who is trying to control you *because this stupid entity is anxious about your actions and behaviour.*

Realising that a stupid entity is anxious is important because you learn that "evil" entities are only your fantasies. You learn that only anxious entities exist who don't know how to deal with their own anxiety. Anxious entities express their cognitions, maliciously, because they've experienced malicious treatment by other selves. A malicious entity is simply caught in a "dirty circle" of misunderstanding.

I was labelled with a psychiatric "disorder" known as "bipolar disorder" which is thought by psychiatrists to arise from a genetic disorganisation; therefore, psychiatrists thought I had a polygenetically aberrant sensable organism which was responsible for my fluctuating moods of mania and melancholia when I didn't know how to deal with my anxiety. DNA is used by a self to replicate genes from its sequence of tri-nucleotides; therefore, a self is responsible for the organisation of its sensable organism's genes by learning to use its sensable organism's DNA to guide its DNAs development of neurotransmitters. The DNA of the body is not responsible for organising the body's genes because DNA has no ability to respond. Rather, a self has to learn how to respond to its sensable organism's circumstances by learning how to affect its genes as well as its DNA.

The hypothesis of a mental genetic disorder or "mental illness" is obviously a myth because minds are our delusions. Only cognitions are existed by a self, not minds. Of course, cognitions are immaterial, not materialised.

Although trauma is responsible for anxiety, malicious selves from ethereal realms of the after-death (if ethereal realms of the after-death exist) also use Nature's willing in my DNA to change the chemistry of my body and effect changes to my sensable organism's anxiety, easiness, and excitement center by using my DNA to raise anxiety in my excitement center. These malicious entities used Nature's willing in the anxiety generated in my excitement center to affect my cognition so that my emoting of my emotions and moods, my use of my cognition to sense my circumstances, as well as my use of my understanding to understand my circumstances are affected.

I experienced disturbed emotions, disturbed moods from an extreme of mania to the extreme of melancholia, cognitive disturbances, and cognitive disruptions, like delusional misunderstandings of paranoid persecution and grandeur, because selfpathic entities from ethereal realms of the after-death or selfpathic telepaths on earth were attracted to my vulnerability or I was undermining my own needs by hallucinating images of selfpathic entities in my imagination. These entities maliciously attacked my already disturbed anxiety, satisfaction, and excitement center, my center of emoting, and my intelligence. I allowed these malicious entities to raise anxiety in me so that my cognition became disrupted, instead of simply disturbed, resulting in delusions which affected my ability to understand *because I didn't know that I, not these malicious entities, was raising anxiety in me.*

My experience has proven that the raising of anxiety in me is the cause of an increase in my tendency to develop dementia, not faulty DNA, just as a self's oversensitivity is due to its lack of knowledge of how to keep its calm and easy in the face of trouble. Oversensitivity is usually the result of a self's inability to handle its energetics; therefore, the self often experiences inner unease which leads to brain dis-ease (a disturbance in the chemistry of a self's brain). In other words, oversensitivity is a symptom of dementia, while dementia is a symptom of anxiety. Oversensitivity is often a symptom of a self who has yet to learn how to address its anxiety.

Psychotropic medications are only a "bandage". They cover up the anxiety which a self is responsible for raising in its anxiety, easiness, and excitement center, rather than enable the self to cope with this anxiety by learning how to deal with it. It's a self's degree of vulnerability which is the stimulus for attacks on it by selves from ethereal realms of the after-death, by telepathic selves on earth, or the vulnerable self's projection of hallucinatory selves in its imagination who are inspired by malicious intentions. Unfortunately, selves who realise that their vulnerability is the real issue often commit the mistake of defending against these malicious entities or "attacking back" rather than understanding that loving these malicious entities is the only way to deal with their vulnerability and anxiety.

Attack and defence are methods used by selves who are caught up in The Game of the Gods. There are three major Games at which we're able to lovingly play or anxiously toy. We're able to lovingly play or anxiously toy at The Game of Life which is our major Game of playing or toying at our own Game within The Game of the Gods because The Game of the Gods is the major Game of society at which we're only able to anxiously toy. We're also able to play or toy at the minor religious game of genuinely searching for truths about Reality, Nature, or the Phenomenon so we're able to progress towards playing or toying at metaphysics as a minor game.

Religion is a minor game. We're also able to play or toy at the major Game of striving for wisdom which is the Game of genuinely searching for the Truth of Nature by which Nature wills. The Game of Wisdom is our Game of overcoming our ignorance and stupidity by understanding the relationship of the three major Games to each other. Most of us continue to play The Game of Wisdom because it's usually refreshing and enjoyable to play this Game.

The Game of Wisdom is enjoyable to play because it necessitates that we have a profound understanding of the merits and demerits of all three of the major Games, such as the merit of playing with other selves and the demerit of toying with other selves. The Game of Wisdom also helps us to gain the understanding that wisdom is not a finale, but may be deepened forever; however, our ultimate goal is not to play and toy at The Game of Wisdom.

Our ultimate goal is to genuinely, sincerely, and authentically exist so we are able to play without playing a Game, not even The Game of Wisdom.
Nature instinctively develops us from It as Its immortal centers; *however, our immortality (if we are, indeed, immortal) isn't due to Nature's instinctive willing because Nature didn't grant Its own immortality.*

Nature instinctively evolves all things from It; however, unlike Nature, particles are instable; therefore, a particle evolved from Nature is mortal because its very instability results in its aging and deteriorating, then its decaying or disintegrating, and, finally, its decondensing or devolving so it blends with immortal Nature without any possibility of "resurrection" as the same thing again. In other words, there won't be a "final judgement" where "the faithful" have their bodies resurrected from "dust".

A system of laws are usually a part of all religions, but Selfism has no laws for its adherents to use, "obey", or "disobey". These laws are the basis of scientismists' technical quantitative methods. It's also this system of laws which comprise our false beliefs, such as the beliefs of Sigmund Freud about the ego.

An ontologist understands that a self uses its understanding as well as its misunderstanding to develop its character types. There is no ego nor is there a consciousness which is a trait of the ego, as Freud thought, because a self only has understanding and intelligence as well as misunderstanding and intellect.

Contrary to the opinion of philosophers, like Siddhartha Gautama, the self is not the intellectual "illusory" ego. A self is an intelligent center of Nature who uses its intelligence to compose its knowledge. A self uses its intellect to compose its beliefs and delusions, such as its delusional belief in the Creator's laws and his system of commandments.

An example of the insanity of an intellectual self is its desire to find ways to survive because it believes in time. Since it believes that it is limited by time, it believes that it has a "need" to search for ways to survive on earth. Such an intellectual self doesn't understand that the selfpathic *desire* to find ways to survive is its dilemma. If it realised it might exist immortally, it would know that a self's death might be impossible. It would feel selfkomologically contented, instead of selfpathologically discontented. It would also have the selfkomological desire to heal, rather than the selfpathological desire to kill.

A sane self doesn't want its multicellular body to die, but it doesn't want its body to survive either. A sane self simply desires enjoyment in what it's doing, whether it's working at a job, playing at a hobby, or simply "goofing off". Such a self is sane because it had the responsibility to face its fear that it might die with its multicellular sensable organism as well as its fear that its death might be impossible. This self is sane because it always works in or towards wisdom. It's sane because it knows that all the evidence demonstrates that it will probably continue to exist in an immortal form after the death of its body.

Although we are wise, we will never be perfect or imperfect which is demonstrated by our tendency to consistently guard against attacks. The Canadian anthem advises Canadian citizens to "stand on guard" in relation to the aggressive behaviours of foreign countries. Defending against imaginary attacks is unnecessary; therefore, our violent tendencies often take hold of us when we "stand on guard" (imagine an attack is forthcoming).

Paranoid people never relax because they are always standing on guard. Ironically, paranoid people attempt to rationalise their paranoid tendency *to attack others* by claiming that their tendency to attack is their defence against the attacks of others.

It takes courage and wisdom to release our guarding tendency and express benevolence; however, a self who feels the desire to express benevolence perfectly fails to realise that this desire is malevolent because it arises from the desire to control the reactions of the recipient of its benevolence. The courage to make mistakes is the stimulus for the wisdom required to prove to a self that its religious absolute and its metaphysics are appropriate because the courage to make mistakes is used to develop the tenacity with which to strive for wisdom. The development of wisdom takes a lot of work, but the results are worth all the effort a self puts into this quest.

A self understands that its hypothesis of dying with its sensable organism might be mistaken when it realises that it might exist as an immortal center of Nature who also exists as such an immortal center in Nature. Realising its own probability of immortality is so great a relief to a self that it experiences a release from its insane typical roles because these insane typical roles have been relegated to memory; therefore, the self has the experience of its sane productive-developmental adult player in Freedom from its insane typical roles. Before this experience, the self was only able to experience its sane productive-developmental adult player in conjunction with its insane typical roles; therefore, it acted out its sane productive-developmental adult player as it was concurrently trapped by its conflicting desires and, thus, its conflicting emotions.

The experience of Freedom from its insane typical roles is a selfkom's first experience of Freedom from conflicting desires and emotions (outside of its experience in the womb); therefore, this experience is the selfkom's first mature experience of true happiness. This initial experience of true happiness leads the selfkom to realise that the goal of its existing is to enjoy its existing. With this realisation, the selfkom is also released from its caricatured persona of productive-developmental adult player so that it's able to develop genuinely, sincerely, and authentically. Truists use the term "priming" to describe a self's initial realisation of its harmony with Nature. After priming, a Truist learns how to practice engagement. Engagement is a self's practice of continually harmonising with Nature and the natures of Nature.

A knowledgeably wise Truist continues to engage with its ability to freely deduce and induce (inferentially reason) after its priming experience so that it continues expand in its knowledge. A wise Truist realises that it doesn't have to judge other selves anymore and has squelched its insane desire to use logic in an insane attempt to judge a self's "righteousness" for the purpose of salvation or judge a self's "unrighteousness" for the purpose of condemnation. Such a knowledgeably wise Truist realises that righteousness is based on the laws of an ethical morality which are obsessively adhered to by "righteous" ethical moralists, while unrighteousness is based on the laws of an unethical immorality which are obsessively adhered to by "unrighteous" unethical immoralists.

A wise Truist has realised its need to distinguish between its sane and insane desires so it's able to maintain its use of its sane typical role of productive-developmental adult player, while relegating its insane typical roles of receptive infantile victim, hoarding childish authoritarian, exploitative preadolescent trickster, and marketing adolescent hero to memory. Because such a wise self focuses on its sane desire to discern, rather than on its insane desire to judge, it refuses to blame or praise another self because blame usually results in the other self's resentment, while praise usually results in its conceit.

Blaming is a method of those who judge and feel the insane desire to unfairly punish, rather than penalise, by applying fair consequences. Fair consequences usually don't result in the guilt and conceit in which punishments tend to result because fair consequences are the result of inferential reasoning, while punishments are unfair consequences which result from intellectualised cogitating, especially the formal intellectualising I call "logicising". It's no coincidence that a selfkom seldom feels guilty or conceited because it realises that the result of fair consequences is confidence, not fear inspired guilt or the conceit which is the result of a self's repression of its guilt. A selfkom also understands that fair consequences are delivered by it with its expression of love, while punishments are delivered with an expression of hate and the repression of love.

The book in which Erich Fromm discussed his five character types is entitled, *Man for Himself: An Inquiry into the Psychology of Ethics*. By reading "between the lines" of this book, I was able to ascertain that Fromm meant humanity's ethics was the study of the delineation of moral laws. Unfortunately, Fromm failed to understand that moral laws are the delusions of moralists because Fromm had a streak of moralism in him

Unfortunately, Fromm mistakenly thought that a self's conscience is based on needs and its needs are inspired by love, rather than based on Freedom and its need to continually attend to its integrity so it avoids the chicanery which results from its inattentiveness to its integrity. Fromm didn't understand that ethical morality sabotages our needs. A self's behaviours are *spontaneous* when sanely guided by its emotion of love, while the self's behaviours are *impulsive* when insanely guided by its emotion of hate. Fromm understood our desire for love, but he ignored the fact that ethical morality is our unnecessary reaction to our own impulsive tendencies.

Our spontaneous behaviours are amorally motivated by our need to genuinely, sincerely, and authentically express them. We don't have a need to express our behaviours with our typical role of productive-developmental adult player; however, we do have a spontaneous and sane desire to ingenuinely, insincerely, and inauthentically express our behaviours with this typical role based on our feelings of love. We also have an impulsive and insane desire to ingenuinely, insincerely, and inauthentically express our behaviours with our typical roles of receptive infantile victim, hoarding childish authoritarian, exploitative preadolescent trickster, and marketing adolescent hero based on our feelings of deprivation.

The fact that we're able to be impulsive, rather than spontaneous, prompted our ancestors to develop a morality which they used in their attempt to logically conduct their behaviours by way of laws, rather than allow their behaviours to be dangerously impulsive. Unfortunately, their morality also kept them from spontaneously enjoying life.

Fromm understood that we often assimilate an "authoritarian conscience" (a term coined by him) by assimilating the sanctioned moral laws of an authoritarian society. Fromm seemed to think an authoritarian conscience was a childish authoritarian *system of assimilated memories*. Fromm also thought that our "humanistic conscience" (a term also coined by him) was devoid of authoritarianism.

We're able to develop and memorise our own moral laws, just as we're able to memorise our societies' moral laws; therefore, Fromm's description of authoritarianism wasn't his fantasy, although he made the mistake of thinking that the authoritarian conscience was a reality, instead of just the authoritarian memory. Fromm didn't understand that the humanistic conscience he described didn't need to be labelled "humanistic" because the authoritarian "conscience" he described wasn't actually a conscience. There is no authoritarian conscience; therefore, there is no need for the conscience to carry the label of "humanistic" to distinguish it from Fromm's mistakenly hypothesised authoritarian conscience.

A self's intelligent ability to express and experience love as well as express and experience hate is prompted by its conscientious need to continue loving or take subjective action to alter its hating. Fromm understood that a self is conscientiously prompted by needs which are the ongoing activity of a self's knowledge existed by it in the activity called its "memory store". Unfortunately, Fromm didn't see the need to rid his thinking of moral laws.

Fromm mistakenly believed that an individual's conscience is based on its need to love and be loved because he thought that love is the central need of an individual's conscience; however, he didn't understand that only an individual's knowledge about this need is memorised, not this need; rather, this need is *continually realised* by a self so it knows and understands it and, thus, is subsequently able to memorise this knowledge. Unfortunately, Fromm mistakenly called our conscience, the "humanistic conscience" rather than the "humanistic memory" because he didn't understand that conscience is the ongoing need of a self to know whether or not it is expressing its integrity. Instead, he thought that conscience is our memory store of knowledge about the morality of love and the immorality of hate.

Sigmund Freud based his theory of conscience on the interaction of the ego, the id, and the superego. The superego was Freud's misunderstanding of conscience because he thought the superego was a constraint on the ego. Freud didn't understand that the intellect, not the ego, is used by a self as the self's arrogance. Freud also failed to understand that there is only a self's conscience, not an ego's superego. The emoting center is instinctive; therefore, it corresponds to Freud's id. However, the self doesn't correspond to Freud's concept of the ego because Freud's ego was supposedly developed from the body, while truth is that the ego is developed from and used by a self as its understanding; therefore, the self can use the ego to understand that it originated from unbounded Energy (the Ether or Nature). Freud didn't understand that the self in him might exist immortally which meant that his belief that he was mortal as well as his concepts of the ego, psyche, and mind were his delusions.

A self uses its understanding to intentionally harmonise with other people. Arrogance is self's use of its misunderstanding to disregard its intelligence with the intention of contending with other people. Wisdom is a self's ability to intelligently understand its knowledge, while stupidity is a self's cowardly disabling of its faculty of intelligence and its ability of reasoning because it experiences too much fear and anxiety in its attempts to develop wisdom by using its intelligence and reasoning to do so.

Freud and Fromm were both groping their way to the truth. Fromm was able to improve upon Freud's understanding. Unfortunately, Fromm failed to understand that we're only sane when we cease trying to conduct our behaviour by using our delusional immoral childish authoritarian memory or by using our delusional moral humanistic memory and, instead, conduct our behaviour by freely using our amoral need to understand.

We have a conscience which is guided by our preference to express our integrity to every self and our reluctance to express out chicanery. There is no need for a self to guide its behaviour by the morality of its humanistic memory or the immorality of its authoritarian memory.

Fromm believed that the productive character type was an expression of the humanistic "conscience". He believed that this character type was based on humanistic moral laws as well as love because Fromm missed the clue of absolute Freedom which demonstrates that amoral needs, rather than laws, are the motivators of action and behaviour. Fromm also believed that the hoarding character type was an expression of the immoral authoritarian conscience which he knew was based upon the emotion of hate. Fromm's humanistic morality was derived from his expression of his sane character type and sane personality role.

Unlike Fromm (on whose giant shoulders I am standing), I understand that memory is used by a selfpath to recall its personality's insane roles of infantile victim, childish authoritarian, preadolescent trickster, and adolescent hero (which I discovered). Then the selfpath immorally, ingenuinely, insincerely, and inauthentically expresses its roles in relation to their respective insane receptive, hoarding, exploitative, and marketing character types (which Fromm discovered). I also understand that memory is used by a selfkom to recall its personality's sane role of adult player (which I discovered). Then it morally, ingenuinely, insincerely, and inauthentically expresses this role in relation to its sane productive character type (which Fromm discovered). Unlike Fromm, I realised that a selfkom's sane productive character type (which Fromm discovered) is outwardly directed while its sane developmental character type (which I discovered) is inwardly directed. Unlike Fromm, I understand that a self uses its conscience to amorally, genuinely, sincerely, and authentically express who it is from what it is with its integrity without the sane desire or the insane desire to act out a role, a false self, or a persona.

Sadly, Fromm didn't experience priming because he didn't fully understand that morality is always a falsehood. Morality is based on the myth of the Creator and his mythical ability to create. Although Fromm was a Mortalist who renounced the Creator, he developed his own ethical system of morality and called it "the humanistic conscience".

Despite the fact that Fromm didn't experience the priming of wisdom, his contribution to our knowledge of love and hate was considerable as is demonstrated in two other books written by him entitled, *The Art of Loving* and *The Anatomy of Human Destructiveness*. Fromm was able to make such a contribution to our knowledge of these emotions because he was always in search of the wisdom which he thought he might develop by way of his interest in mysticism, particularly the mysticism he found in Zen Buddhism.

Fromm wrote about the relation of psychoanalysis to Zen Buddhism in a book he co-authored with Daisetz Teitaro Suzuki and Richard de Martino entitled, *Zen Buddhism and Psychoanalysis*. Unfortunately, Fromm was confused by the doctrines of Siddhartha Gautama, mistakenly referred to as "The Buddha" or "The Enlightened One". The basic doctrine of Siddhartha, which not only confused Fromm, but continues to confuse many other people, is the doctrine maintaining that there is no reality to be known as a self (the doctrine of "anatta") which also asserts that we're only empty illusions, rather than immortal or mortal selves.

Unfortunately, Fromm didn't understand that he was a center of absolute Activity; therefore, he failed to negate Siddhartha's contention that a self is only an empty illusion. Fromm agreed with Siddhartha's postulates because Fromm wasn't just an atheist, Fromm was a Mortalist, like Siddhartha. The fact that Fromm was also a *psycho*analyst is ironic because Fromm's search for knowledge of the psyche was dependent on his realisation of the reality of the self which would have revealed the truth that the psyche, like the anima and the soul, was only a delusion. Fromm likely has his own fair share of chagrin. After all, he is probably a current resident in his own realm of the after-death and where he would know he's an immortal.

Fromm was seduced by Siddhartha's doctrines because it was a doctrine of Siddhartha that, in death, we blend with "Emptiness" which he believed was our

Source. Suzuki referred to this Emptiness as "Unconsciousness". It's this Unconsciousness which Carl G. Jung referred to as our "collective unconscious".

Fromm was seduced by the Buddhists he met, like Suzuki, because they believed in compassion. Although Siddhartha had a great respect for love and kindness, he didn't refer to them as much as he referred to compassion. Siddhartha believed that we need to continually experience compassion so we're able to cope with our need to escape from suffering. Siddhartha believed that the only way to escape suffering was to cease existing as a projected illusion of Emptiness. Siddhartha called such cessation "Nirvana".

Supposedly, by attaining Nirvana, we cease to experience rebirth so that we return to the Emptiness which was supposed by Siddhartha to have projected us as its empty illusions; therefore, behind every Buddhist's compassion lies the insanity of sorrow because they believe that they must sooner or later cease to exist as even empty illusions. Ironically, Buddhists irrationally and irresponsibly long for immortality despite their irrational and irresponsible belief that they're mortal.

Siddhartha unknowingly intuited that his Buddhism was lacking realism which is why he predicted that Maitreya, the Buddha of love, would be reborn on earth, although he didn't know that his prediction was an admission of the inadequacy of his doctrines. Siddhartha prophesised that such a Buddha of love would come because he had unknowingly intuited that his emphasis on compassion was misplaced. Siddhartha knew that his philosophy was inadequate because he intuited (without cognising or recognising) that he had failed to emphasise love and joy.

I realised that reincarnation as well as rebirth are only myths. I realised that, as a self, I'm an established self who is unable to stop Nature from instinctively generating a new self in a spermatozoon It's merging with an egg; therefore, I'm unable to compel Nature to reincarnate the self I am in Nature's merging of a spermatozoon and an egg because Nature's instinct is to generate a new self, not reincarnate or incarnate a self who is already established.

I continued to strive for wisdom (as I saw it to be). I knew that wisdom wasn't just the activity of developing my knowledge concerning my emotion of love and my emotion of hate but was also the activity of developing my knowledge concerning these emotions so that I could relate all the bits of my knowledge together and understand them as my wisdom.

I developed the knowledge that Emptiness is not unknowingly imagining us as its empty illusions.

We aren't imaginings of Emptiness because we're real selves of Nature. Our sensable organisms are also real because they're evolved, grown, and developed by Nature from Nature. Nature is the Reality in which we exist as real selves, while we concurrently exist in our cognitions and live our sensors and sensable organisms. Our sensors and sensable organisms are real because they are composed of Reality (Energy, Matter, or Nature).

Like Siddhartha, Fromm failed to understand that if we cease to exist, we're realities given out by the Source which the Source is unable to generate again. Despite basing his psychoanalytic and sociological theories on the realistic promise of kindness, Fromm's belief in Siddhartha's unrealistic doctrines of compassion and Nirvana was an indication of his fear of probing into Reality on his own. Like Fromm, we find it extremely difficult to develop truths based on knowledge, such as the truth that we need to be kind, rather than compassionate.

Even though Erich Fromm was a psychoanalyst (an analyst of psyches) as well as a sociologist, he didn't give credence to immortal selves because he was "bamboozled" by the false belief of philosophers, like Siddhartha Gautama and David Hume, that a self is an illusion of a sensable organism's "epiphenomenal mind". Gautama and Hume both believed that selves are only our "illusions". Gautama and Hume both failed to understand that their description of selves as "illusions" was their misunderstanding. Gautama and Hume really meant that selves were our delusions, not our illusions, because illusions apparition in the environment; therefore, selves wouldn't be illusions if they weren't real. Rather, an unreal self would simply be a delusional thought. Ironically, Gautama and Hume didn't understand that they were deluded because they didn't know that they were each a self.

Many modern day philosophers are like their ancestors, Gautama and Hume, because they don't believe that we exist as immortal selves. Their absurd belief is that we are only mortal sensable organisms who project minds as the expressive epiphenomena of the brain with which each of use as the sensable organism each of us supposedly is. These philosophers fail to understand that only a self has needs, not its sensable organism; therefore, they fail to understand that only selves have intentionality. Sensable organisms have no needs at all which is a fact that these modern philosopher's intuit. This intuition eats away at these philosophers because they are denying their responsibility of realising that they are selves, that they have needs, that they might exist forever, and that their happiness depends on their recognition of their desire to dwell in love as well as share their expression of it with every self they meet.

Chapter Nine
The Implications of Naturalism for Society

We need to base our truths and falsehoods on empiricism; however, our empiricism is not the Truth because our empiricism is not our cognition. It's our *knowing* of our experience which reveals our truths and falsehoods to us, not our experience—however, our knowing and cognition are dependent on our experience because there isn't any knowing or cognition without experience. Our metaphysics depends on our truths and our falsehoods, just as our truths and falsehoods depend on our experience. Consequently, a metaphysician needs to change his metaphysics if his metaphysics conflicts with his experience; however, the metaphysician needs to know his experience if he is to know his metaphysics is in conflict with it.

Evolution, growth, development, deterioration, and devolution are processes objectively demonstrated in our environment by empirical evidence; therefore, any metaphysician who has a mythical doctrine of the Creator as his premise must change this doctrine to reflect the empirical evidence. Unfortunately, the metaphysical fictions which dominate the thinking of Western people are that the universe was created by way of the willing of a Creator in his created laws, like "The Three Laws of 'Motion'" (which Newton really meant as "Movement"), or that uncreated laws of Nature "automate" the universe, like the laws of quantum mechanics. Ironically, these scientismists believe they "discovered" their laws in Nature, not realising that they *wished* them in their cognition, because they have abandoned their need to know in favour of their desire for ignorance.

Creationists refuse to acknowledge that (if he exists) Yahweh lied to his Jewish prophets by telling them that he was the Creator. They also refuse to acknowledge Yahweh's inability to create; therefore, they cling to their belief that Yahweh created the moral laws of conduct which we insanely use to compel everyone's obedience to the authorities who imitate Yahweh and develop their own laws. A Creationist's insanity is his faith in his fictions of the Creator, Oneness, separability, connection, disconnection, attachment, detachment, authoritarianism, creation, ethics, moral laws, mathematics, justice, orders, obedience, obligation, duty, rights, and right and wrong based on his gullibility. His gullible faith keeps him from understanding what a self is, who it isn't and isn't, how it is and isn't, and why it is, rather than isn't. A Creationist's fictions reinforce his insane desire to compete for the attention of the "authorities" in his society's institutions who "sit in place" of his ultimate Authoritarian (his mythical Creator). The authorities in his institutions compete with each other for dominance because they all cling to the doctrines of their ancestors which resulted from their belief in the Creator myth.

The governments of our world have unwisely and irresponsibly made weapons of mass destruction as well as polluted our planet. We've reached a developmental crisis on our planet. We need to learn how to get along by expressing our love in kind cooperation or we'll destroy each other's sensable organisms and the planet by expressing our hatred in cruel competition.

To develop cooperation, we need to realise that selves in the after-death have conspired to toy and play at their own Game of Life within The Game of the Gods; therefore, Creationists need to eradicate their ancestral belief in the Creator myth as well as the fictions they've developed which correspond with the myth of the Creator and replace them with the knowledge of the Evolver, Grower, Developer, Deteriorator, and Devolver and Its corresponding truths, as outlined in this book. Seventeen basic facts of a Naturalist's knowledge are contrasted with seventeen fictions of a Creationist's myths in the table below entitled, "The Facts of Naturalists and the Fictions of Creationists".

The Facts of Naturalists and the Fictions of Creationists

The Facts of Naturalists	The Fictions of Creationists
1. Nature, the Activator	God, the Creator
2. Relatedness	Oneness
3. Isolation	Separability
4. Relatedness	Connection or Attachment
5. Unrelatedness	Disconnection or Detachment
6. Libertarianism	Authoritarianism
7. Activation	Creation
8. Conscience	Ethics
9. Needs Moral	Laws
10. Language	Mathematics
11. Habilitation	Justice
12. Requests	Orders
13. Negotiation	Obedience
14. Choices	
15. Hobbies	Duties
16. Freedoms	Rights
17. Proper and Improper	Right and Wrong

Before Yahweh's ascendance (if he exists), our ancestors were able to guide their use of Nature's Will in accord with their needs and sane desires. They experienced relatively little intrusion of their insane desires in their experience before Yahweh's interference as an actual entity in a realm of the after-death (or their hallucination). Unfortunately, when Yahweh lied to his prophets by saying he was the Creator and developed The Ten Commandments to authoritatively accompany his lie, we began to toy more often with our insane desires because this was the consequence of believing Yahweh's lie.

Instead of acting in accord with their preference for emoting and expressing love, Yahweh's "true believers" acted in discord with this preference by acting with their conditioned preference of emoting and expressing hate. They "fell from grace" because they lost touch with their desire to emote and express love. Instead of embracing love and recognising their sane desire for it, they learned to obey the authoritarian, Yahweh. They also learned to introject his childish authoritarianism.

Our uncooperative competitive governing tactics reflect our heritage. Our childish authoritarian ancestors (who believed Yahweh's lie) developed monarchies with childish authoritarian monarchs or "rulers" who were meant to reflect Yahweh's childish authoritarian rule in his realm of the after-death. Today, we have totalitarian theocratic governments, totalitarian communistic governments, as well as monarchies whose governing monarch is clinging to his or her totalitarian rule. Even our modern day democracies are clinging to totalitarian rule because they are based on the insane faith in the Creator myth and the fictions related to the Creator myth.

Our democratic governments are inadequate because they only pretend to uphold our need for liberty. Unfortunately, our democratic Constitutions are based on the Creator, Creation, principles, rules, laws, rights, authoritarianism, competing, and governing, rather than on the Activator, Activation, harmony, conscience, needs, Freedoms, libertarianism, cooperating, and allowing; therefore, our democracies are insane societies because democratic governments only offer uncooperative competition, not coordinated cooperation.

We've all experienced conditioning by Creationists who attempted to indoctrinate us with their belief in the Creator, Creation, principles, rules, laws, rights, authoritarianism, competition, and government. As a result of our conditioning, we elect capitalistically oriented receptive politicians who are irresponsible spendthrifts because they're sentimentally sensitive to the hardships of others or we elect capitalistically oriented hoarding politicians who are irresponsible misers because they're boorishly insensitive to the hardships of others.

We need to use our desire for love as our guide in developing a democratically coordinated cooperative based on the philosophy of anarchy. Then, we'll be able to generously express our love in an economic system that is democratically socialistic, not democratically capitalistic. We need to cease frivolously spending money and compulsively hoarding money as our contradictory capitalistic economic methods in Canada's free enterprise system.

It would be an interesting task to write a sane Constitution for a coordinated cooperative in which all philosophers, even authoritatively toxic philosophers, are given their Freedom of expression. We need to give authoritatively toxic philosophers the Freedom to express their philosophies so that we're able to talk them out of their toxicity. Like many theological philosophers, atheistic and agnostic philosophers are often authoritatively toxic; however, their atheistic and agnostic philosophies may also be based on love, despite their opinion that they're irreligious. Atheists and agnostics fail to understand that they're religious because religion is the absolute on which a self bases its metaphysics—even if this absolute is a nominal nothingness or, paradoxically, a relativity.

Canada's current Constitution needs to be changed because it's founded on "the rule of law" rather than our need for harmony. The rule of law in Canada's Constitution is derived from the belief in "the supremacy of God". Atheists and many agnostics disagree with this belief.

The insane preamble to Canada's Constitution is written as follows:

'Whereas Canada is founded upon principles that recognise the supremacy of God and the rule of law...' (Preamble to the Canadian Charter of Rights and Freedoms, Updated 11 May 2018 03:57 UTC).

Canada as a democratically coordinated cooperative would write the sane preamble for our Constitution as follows:

'Whereas Canada is newly founded on our understanding that we're guided by our need for harmony...'

Atheists usually think Nature is Reality. Agnostics "sit on the fence" because they think it's impossible to know whether God or Nature is Reality. Creationists think God is Reality. All thoughts need to be respected; therefore, a democratically coordinated cooperative would not include the absolutes of either God or Nature as a basis for its Constitution.

In a democratically coordinated cooperative, we would not have rights. Instead, we would only have *freedoms*. We need our freedoms expressed in Canada's Constitution. Our current Constitution is in discord with our needs because it advocates legal rights, instead of needed freedoms.

We need freedoms, not rights, because, contrary to the beliefs of our governing politicians, rights aren't necessary. Rights are unnecessary privileges. Canada's politicians uphold our rights, while only giving lip-service to our freedoms. Rights are restrictions on how we express our needs and sane desires. Consequently, rights are unnecessary.

Freedoms are necessary. Our insane desires aren't our freedoms because we express our insane desires with the goal of limiting our freedoms. Rights are the insane desires of governments because politicians reserve the "right" to limit our need for freedom of expression by focusing on their insane desire to enforce laws as their method of conditioning us to obey their orders.

Canadian conservatives are capitalistic "compellers" while Canadian liberals are capitalistic "libertines". Our Canadian conservatives attempt to gain more influence than they need by compelling us to behave according to their demands whereas our Canadian liberals attempt to gain more influence than they need by way of libertinism. These libertines and compellers both give us what we insanely desire, like titillating demonstrations of sex, instead of what we sanely desire, like sensual displays of love. A democratic libertarian, however, gives us the freedom to do what we need to do and sanely desire to do without any thought of gaining more influence, while restricting our behaviour if we abuse other people.

Our Canadian Liberal Party has perverted the meaning of the word "liberal" by associating it with the rights of a libertine capitalism. The rights of the Canadian Liberal Party's libertine capitalism are meant to appeal to our insane desires; however, the freedoms of the Canadian New Democratic Party are meant to appeal to our needs and sane desires, instead of appeal to the insane desires associated with rights. Unfortunately, even the members of the Canadian New Democratic Party have been bamboozled by Canada's capitalistic system so that they don't understand that rights are unnecessary, but freedoms are vital.

In a democratically coordinated cooperative's Constitution, our freedoms would be based on the truth that our conscience is our attentiveness to keeping our integrity and our avoidance of the inattentiveness which results in our chicanery. Of course, such a change in Constitution would require a subsequent change in the organisation and disorganisation of our society and its institutions.

For instance, we would not retain our institutions of justice, judgement, and retribution employing judges, lawyers, and police who punish by confining the judged in depressingly stark jails and prisons. Instead, we would have institutions of habilitation, discernment, and fairness employing discerners, motivators, and helpers who help dangerous people by confining them in appealing surroundings where they're able to learn to be responsible. These nurturers would understand that they are by no means anyone's authority; however, they would need to make it clear to their clients that they're responsible for confining or restraining them if they become dangerously and insanely irresponsible. Helpers would also have to make clear to dangerous selves that their confinement and restraints aren't punishments, but are necessary means implemented to help everyone remain safe as well as help everyone maintain their sanity, including the dangerous selves who are confined or restrained.

Penalties would be included in the philosophies of these nurturers. These penalties would be fair consequences that are agreed upon in advance by all participants. Situations would never necessitate "knee-jerk" punishments. Neither the staff nor dangerous selves are as tempted to act cruelly in habilitation centers as outside of them because they are safe in these habilitation centers. Consequences are "enfairments" (a word coined by me) because they've been worked out by all the parties concerned, including the people to whom these consequences are applied.

So far as the economic institutions of such a sane democratically coordinated cooperative are concerned, a minimum wage *and a maximum wage* would be established for its citizens. The businesses of this democratically coordinated cooperative would be free to prosper under the supervision of a Council, unlike the licentious enterprise system of uncooperative capitalistic competitors who have a strangle hold on politicians because their government is a democratic capitalism.

An example of the individualistic greed which has always driven democratic capitalists is the philosophy of the late Ayn Rand who wrote *The Virtue of Selfishness*. An example of the totalitarian greed which drives certain communistic capitalists is given in the philosophy of the late Vladimir Lenin. Lenin adjusted the philosophy of Karl Marx and Friedrich Engels for his own purpose of totalitarianism which was a demonstration of his greed for absolute control. *The Manifesto of the Communist Party* written by Marx and Engels emphasised influence. The goal of their communism was equal influence for every self, not the greed for absolute control.

Individuals in a democratically coordinated cooperative would be able to develop businesses but they would be subject to the cooperation of all individuals because these businesses would not be individual corporations for uncooperative capitalistic competitors in a society's democratic government nor would they be totalitarian institutions for uncooperative capitalistic competitors in a society's communistic government. Instead, the businesses of a democratically coordinated cooperative would be societal interests for coordinating co-operators in a society's organised anarchy, rather than individual corporations or totalitarian institutions in a society's government of orders.

In Canada's current economy, there is no reason why we needn't be satisfied with a minimum wage of, say, $200,000.00 per year and a maximum wage of, say, $1,000,000.00 per year with these wages indexed to inflation and deflation. There is also no reason why the handicapped and the disabled needn't be allowed to work at their own pace at a job they are able to do, rather than be forced to spend their day frivolously playing or destructively toying in meaningless activities because there is no work for them to do. All individuals, not just the disabled, would receive the minimum wage while they're helped to find a suitable job. In such an economy, there would be no problem of homelessness because it would be recognised by every self that all selves have a need for a home.

The maximum limit would apply to *any* self's ability to earn income in a year whether it was working for a business or another cooperative institution of society; therefore, there would be a surplus of capital which means that there would be no need for taxes. The Prime Coordinating Co-operators (instead of a Prime Minister or President) would be a Council responsible for the coordinated cooperation of this society.

The Prime Coordinating Co-operators would use their society's surplus of capital to maintain the democratically coordinated cooperative's ongoing organisation, such as paying employees, maintaining roads and highways, developing and maintaining energy resources, as well as developing and maintaining a diplomatic core meant to defuse the anger of people in foreign nations before they develop plans of attacking Canada. Of course, the vision of such a democratic coordinated cooperative would be world peace which is why its foreign relations would help foreign societies attain sanity.

The Realm of the Watchers is the realm of the after-death for Selfists (that is, if selves are immortal). The Realm of the Watchers (if it exists) is organised by a sane apolitical Council of Prime Coordinating Co-operators. Of course, the members of this Council aren't absolutely sane since the Potentiality in us will always include the activity of insanity. You will be a Selfist when you learn the meaning of coordinating cooperatively which is to accommodate what and how you are to what and how other people are without intervening or interfering in their affairs because you arrogantly think you know better than they do what they need.

This book is my attempt to convince those who aren't rigidly logicising inside a "box" of fictions that our only way to peace is to realise that Freedom is The Ultimate Truth; however, we need to develop a society where we're able to work towards or maintain our wisdom with Freedom, while helping the licentious develop and work towards attaining the goal of wisdom. I take great interest in your willingness, as a citizen of the world, to work towards changing the Constitution of Canada which is the proposition I am recommending in this chapter of my book.

A self's use of force to change the Constitution of Canada is contraindicated because a wise self has recognised the need of people to freely change from superstitiously trusting to wisely reasoning; therefore, I will only use my talent of writing to suggest by way of reason, not teach or indoctrinate, by way of logic, because my need is for my fellow citizens to freely decide whether or not they will change Canada's Constitution. Such a change is necessary if every self in Canada is to have the opportunity to become wise. This change needs to be developed by the people we elect, not by the force of rabble rousers who simply want to kill the sensable organisms of those people who don't want to change the Constitution.

We need to change our current dependency on the rule of law to our need for harmony by working within the rule of law to show that the rule of law is corrupt. Some people might advocate operating outside of the rule of law to force Canadian citizens to accept our need for harmony as our Constitutional axiom; however, such an undertaking would be unwise as well as corrupt because we would be using force to get our way, instead of listening to our need for harmony.

Unfortunately, coordinating co-operators are unable to work within a democracy's court system to prove that the rule of law is corrupt because our justice system is based on the rule of law. Our only recourse is the electoral system because coordinating co-operators will have to be elected before they will be able to revamp our justice system and change it into a habilitation system.

You might feel the need to change Canada's Constitution; however, you'll need to use a different talent than teaching to change the Canadian Constitution.

For example, your skill in changing the Canadian Constitution might be best expressed by running as an *apolitical* candidate with the platform of establishing a democratic coordinating cooperative. As an apolitical democratic coordinating co-operator, you would not be focused on toying uncooperatively with other selves' emotions by competing with them. You would be focused on playing in cooperation because you'd understand that the consent of the majority of Canadian citizens would be necessary to rewrite the Constitution.

As an apolitical candidate, your election promise would be to change the government and its ruling politician, the Prime Minister, into an apolitical democratically coordinated cooperative with its guiding Council of Prime Coordinating Co-operators. You would have the goal of seeking election as the first member of Canada's Council of Prime Coordinating Co-operators. You would not be the Prime Minister of such a Council because you would have no more ability to influence than any other member of this Council.

This is not an impossible goal of dreamers. It's a realistic goal of practical people because we'll only overcome our tendency to toy politically with the emotions of the citizens of Canada if we start to play apolitically with them, rather than toy politically with them. Unlike arrogant politicians, the apolitical Council of Prime Coordinating Co-operators will play apolitically with Canada's citizens because they'll understand that they, too, are citizens of Canada, not glorified rulers.

Good luck results from attaining wisdom. Wisdom is the result of your continual knowing of love and hate which habilitates or enables your knowledge of coordinated cooperation. It's not a coincidence that you receive good luck the more knowledge you have about coordinated cooperation because your good luck is derived from your unselfish actions and behaviours which you effect in accord with your knowledge so you don't have to "dutifully obey the rule of law". Dutifully obeying the rule of law brings only bad luck. *Good luck happens when you realise your need to conscientiously respect the needs of all selves.*

Good luck or good fortune is the consequence of a self's refusal to design an agenda to promote as its selfish, egotistical, ambitious bid for glory.

Nature doesn't have the ability to design; therefore, Nature doesn't designate Saviours or Messiahs. Jesus designed badly because he didn't know that his agenda to save us from suffering was his selfish, egotistical, ambitious bid for glory. Consequently, Jesus had the bad luck of crucifixion.

Final Note

I exist in a human body, like you do and Jesus of Nazareth did. I've demonstrated that Nature is the immortal "It" while there is no God or immortal "he". I've also demonstrated that I'm only a self, an immortal or a mortal "it", not a god or an immortal "he". I've demonstrated that Nature instinctively willed the activity I am in It from It by Its instinctive generation of the activity I am into a spermatozoon and an egg It was merging together. Nature instinctively completed my generation as an activity in my activated zygote after the merger of the spermatozoon and egg which resulted in my zygote. Nature and I then instinctively grew my resulting single-celled organism or zygote into my multicellular body. Nature also instinctively used Its Will to evolve my large uncondensed energy form or sensor which I use my cognition as my means to sense through my sensor.

My proof will never be objectively satisfactory because proof is never objective. "Objective proof" is the great falsity of scientism. A true scientist understands that proof is always and only subjective. A true scientist recognises that his (or her) science is founded on his nonverbal religion of because he recognises that his science is his verbal religion.

My religion is Selfism. After having read the nine chapters of my book, you'll have understood that Selfism is the religious basis of Naturalism. My Selfism and naturalism are both founded on philosophy—the love of wisdom—which is simply the art of intelligent loving which is why this book is my expression of my nonfictional philosophy of religion, not my expression of my religion of spiritual fiction.

We're able to act in love as well as react in love which means we're accountable for our actions as well as our reactions. In other words, we need to responsible for our desires of love and hate.

Responsibility is accountability for your reactions or responses of love and your reactions or impulses of hate because you choose your reactions or responses of love, just as you choose your reactions or impulses of hate. "Responsibility" is accountability for your spontaneous actions of love and your impulsive actions of hate because you cognisantly choose your actions of love, just as you cognisantly choose your actions of hate. There is no such thing as an unchosen action or reaction of cognisant spontaneity, nor is there such a thing as an unchosen action or reaction of cognisant impulsivity, although others may attempt to compel us to choose the way they want us to choose.

Nature is only spontaneous because Nature is free of needs and desires, like the need to choose and the desire of compulsion.

Wu-wei is the nonsensical notion of Taoists and Zenists that they're able to conduct their behaviours without choosing how they conduct them. Although Nature wills in us without choosing to do so or how it will do so, we're unable to borrow and cognizantly use Nature's Will without choosing how we'll use it. Consequently, Taoists and Zenists are irresponsible because they deny that they cognisantly choose how they use Nature's Will within them and ubiquitously around them to conduct their cognitive actions and their sensorial as well sensable organic behaviours.

Glossary

a posteriori: Refers to that which is existed by a self after experience.

a priori: Refers to that which is existed by a self before experience.

abstraction: A self's ability to use abstract things to relate its selfological world to it objective world.

Activationism: 1. Generationism. 2. The knowledge that Activity is the basis of existing, not stillness.

adolescent hero personality role: Nature's orientation in the role of an adolescent hero is that of the "saviour", which means "a self who rescues others".

adult player personality role: A self's orientation in the role of an adult player is that of the "guider", which means "a self who prepares the way".

aesthetics: The study of beauty.

Aethicist: A self who advocates for aethics.

aethics: The study of amorality for the purpose of a self's realisation of realism which is its harmony and responsibly in activating its conscientious actions and reactions by focusing its knowing on its actions and reactions of independently fulfilling its amoral needs in relation to its undeniable sovereignty and Freedom while concurrently letting other selves independently decide how they'll act and react without interfering with their decisions.

amoralist: A self who advocates for amorality.

amorality: A self's activation of its actions and reactions while letting other selves decide how they'll act and react by focusing its knowing on fulfilling its amoral needs in relation to its undeniable Freedom.

apparition: The stimulus for an image to be developed in the self's imagination for the self to see.

appearance: An observed objective phenomenon, like a mineral organic rock, a vegetative organic tree, or a sensable organic amphibian, which is converted and seen by a self as an observed subjective phenomenon..

arrogance: 1. A self's use of its misunderstanding to disregard its intelligence with the intention of contending with other people.

Arrow of Activity, Motion, and Movement: The Continuity or Progression of Nature's activities, motions, and movements.

Arrow of Time: The false belief that time exists and has directionality.

assimilating: A self's use of its intelligence to ably perceive or accurately interpret its feeling of an emotion or a sensation and absorb this feeling as its interpreted knowledge as well as use of its intellect to disable its able perceiving or accurate interpreting so it misperceives or misinterprets its feeling of them and absorbs this feeling as its interpreted illusion.

attention: The alertness with which a self uses its intelligence in its sensing or knowing.

automatism: A false philosophical doctrine which asserts that activity, motion, and movement are the result of mechanical "force", while volition in activity, motion, and movement is only an illusion.

autovolitional nervous system: Our spontaneous or impulsive instinctive nondeliberate use of Nature's Will in tandem with Nature's spontaneous instinctive nondeliberate us of It Will to initiate motions in this nervous system which are meant to harmonise certain behaviours in our organs, like digestion.

awakening: 1. A metaphor for realisation. 2. The start of enlightenment. 3. A self's realisation that it's an immortal or a mortal center of Nature.

beliefs: Our arrogant opinions about the validity of facts (hypotheses).

black hole: Supposedly, a singularity point with no volume and infinite density in bounded expanding space.

block universe theory: The theory that space is bounded and has three dimensions of length, height, and width as well as a fourth dimension of time in which the "block" of all things (the universe) happens.

character types: Erich Fromm's analysis of our social characters which he classified as five different types, the productive, receptive, marketing, hoarding, and exploitative character types.

childish authoritarian personality role: A self's orientation in the role of a childish authoritarian is that of the "commander", which means "a self who dictates to others".

choice: A self's deliberate noninstinctive use of Nature's Will in spontaneous harmony—or impulsive disharmony—with Nature's always instinctive nondeliberate use of Its Will as the self's Freedom to liberally act or react in accord and licentiously act or react in discord with Nature's nonliberated and nonlicentious Freedom from which Nature has no ability to choose, unlike the selves It generates.

cogitating: 1. A disabling ability used by a self to delineate the arrangement of inner formulas and inner equations as well as outer formulas and outer equations. 2. A disabling ability which unnecessarily blocks our ability to think and thus our ability to reason.

cognition: The faculty containing a self's ability of knowing.

common sense: Believed by A-T psychologists to be used by the mind to integrate the different sensations as well as distinguish between them.

compatibilism: The mistaken hypothesis that we're determined by the laws of Nature, but that "somehow" we have our own free wills and are able to use our free wills to choose between fate and Freedom.

conscience: A self's attentiveness, rather that its inattentiveness, to keeping its integrity intact so it avoids the chicanery which results from its inattentiveness.

Continuity: The ongoingness in and of its [Continuity's] Immediacy.

Continuity in Immediacy: The attribute of the Continuum by which Continuity is the ongoingness in and of the Continuum's Immediacy, while Immediacy is the carrier of the Continuum's Continuity.

Continuum: The unbounded *extent* of Activity.

Council of Prime Coordinating Co-operators: The apolitical Council of selves in the Selfists' realm of the after-death, The Realm of the Watchers (if it exists), as well as the apolitical Council which I have suggested would be a sane replacement for political governments on earth.

Creation: Bringing something into existence from nothing.

Creationism: 1. The doctrine that the universe and all matter and forms of being within it are the result not of evolution but of God's direct and instantaneous creation. 2. The mistaken hypothesis that stillness is the basis of Existence.

data: A self's outer signs existent in its environment.

death: The cessation of a mineral, vegetative, or sensable organism's processions which are the living of motions in them by Nature's spontaneous instinctive nondeliberate willing.

delusions: Our mistaken hypotheses (mistaken facts) which we fail to realise are mistaken.

departiclise: Nature's accidental spontaneous instinctive nondeliberate use of Its Will to decondense or dematerialise an unsettled particle.

derepression: A Satan's choice of releasing its Freedom from repression.

derivatively natural: Refers to our natural artefacts, like our natural artificial tools.

determinism: Fatalism. The mistaken hypothesis that events are fated to occur by way of the uncreated laws of Nature.

Doppler Effect: The Doppler Effect is the effect of the expansion or contraction of radio waves. A low pitched sound is heard when a sound source is moving away from the hearer, while a high pitched sound is heard when the sound source is moving towards the hearer. The Doppler Effect is also the effect of the expansion or contraction of light waves. The spectral lines of the light spectrum seen when a body is moving away from another body are redshifted, while the spectral lines of the light spectrum seen when a body is moving towards another body are blueshifted.

duration: 1. Supposedly, a section of the World line. 2. The mistaken hypothesis that our selfological activities, the motions in our sensable organisms and/or sensors, as well as the movements of our sensable organisms and/or sensors are illusions simply because scientismists believe that only static spans or lengths of time are real.

emoting: A selves' ability to express emotions.

Energy: Nature, Substance, Ether, etcetera.

engagement: A self's practice of continually harmonising with Nature and the natures of Nature.

enlightenment: A metaphor for wisdom.

envision: Your ability to fantasise, imagine, or hallucinate a subjective suef which you image by shining it as a subjective photon to see in your imagination.

Essence: The advancement of Nature's Existence as Activity.

eternal Now: The absolute Moment in which the Creator is believed to perpetuate; therefore, this absolute Moment is supposedly the Creator's absolute Time.

eternity: 1. The infinite Duration or Perpetuity of the Creator. 2. The simultaneous presence of the mythical Creator to all his created moments of time in bounded universal space. 3. The delusion that static Perpetuity or infinite Duration is the expanse of the Creator's absolute Now, Moment, or Time.

ethical naturalism: The theory of ethics which maintains that a self develops its ethics in relation to its experience.

ethical rationalism: A theory of ethics whose adherents believe that the laws of ethical morality are real in objective reality as well as subjective reality.

ethicist: A self who advocates for ethics

ethics: The study of morality and immorality.

event: An abrupt change which is supposed to occur in time.

Existence: The absolute Activity called "Nature" or "Thingness" which is the absolute Source of activation for the only Will that Nature or Thingness and Its relative sources or activities of activation called "selves" use in effecting immediately continual changing currents of Flow in the World, including the inner-outer World of these selves.
existing: Any nature, thing, phenomenon, or reality which Nature, Thingness, the Phenomenon, or Reality has generated or activated who is also able to use

Nature's Will to generate or activate immediately continual changing currents of Flow in the World, i.e., selves, like you and I.

experience: The known of a knower (a self).

exploitative character type: Like the self who uses its receptive character type, a self who uses its exploitative character type feels that the means to its harmony is existed outside of it; however, it takes what it insanely desires from others by using cunning in its attempt to feel harmonious. The exploitative character type is used by its inhabiting self to develop its preadolescent trickster role.

extrospection: Our ability to recognise realistic, natural, or phenomenal qualities existent in our sharable outer aspects of the World.

fatalism: The false belief that the Creator has created the events of the past, present, and future which we simply live through.

Flow: The absolute Continuity or Current of an object's changes in which the object's relative activities, motions, and movements occur.

General Theory of Relativity: The theory that a materialised matter (a particle) or a body composed of materialised matters is able to miraculously shape the bounded space-time of Einstein's finite universe so the shape of this bounded space-time is the gravity which these particles and bodies follow in their movements.

Generationism: 1. Activationism. 2. The truth that Nature is the absolute Generator or Activator and, thus, the absolute Origin of everything.

gravity-antigravity field: An interaction of Nature's spontaneous instinctive nondeliberate willing in gravitons and antigravitons.

happening: An activity which is existent in a situation and changes the circumstances of this situation by way of an activation of the activity of motions in and movements of the phenomena in this situation.

harmony: A self's acceptance of its need to use Nature's Will because it finally understands that its desire to end Its use of Nature's Will is impossible and, therefore, futile.

hoarding character type: A self who uses its hoarding character type feels the insane desire to possess what it is as well as what others are; therefore, it believes that, to feel harmonious, it not only has to attempt to command what it is, but also has to attempt to command other selves. The hoarding character type is used by its inhabiting self to develop its childish authoritarian role.

hypotheses: Our guesses about the truth of certain facts.
icon: A sign that resembles as well as stands for a reality, e.g., the word "buzz" resembles as well as stands for the sound a bee makes when it's flying.
Individuals are Inclusive while Communities are Exclusive

idealisations: A self's fantasising of illusions, delusions, and fictions by way of its unknowing which is its denial of its ability to know and its retreat from it into fantasy.

image: A subject's imagitive or imagined motion picture seen by the subject in its faculty of imagination.

imagining: Our ability to fantasise or hallucinate an image by way of envisioning.

imagiting: Our ability to translate a reality existent in the environment to our imaginations by way of visioning.

Immediacy: The carrier of Continuity.

immoralist: A self who advocates for immorality.

improper: The opposite of wrong, just as proper is the opposite of right. Improper is the opposite of wrong because wrong is based on a self's superstitious laws, while improper is based on a self's realistic needs.

indeterminism: 1. The lack of determinism. 2. Absolute Freedom.

index: Supposedly, a "symbol" that corresponds to a reality, but doesn't stand for the reality because it's only related to this reality.

inevitability: Refers to an occurrence in and of Nature which selves (generated by, from, and in Nature) are incapable of avoiding or evading, like the deaths of their sensable organisms; however, when such an occurrence will happen is unpredictable as well as unprophetic. **infantile victim personality role**: A self's orientation in the role of an infantile victim is that of the "sucker", which means "a self who is gullible and easily deceived".

infatalism: A word I've coined meaning "the lack of fate".

inferential reasoning: Developing conclusions by free deduction or induction based upon our needs, rather than upon unneeded logical laws which we're unable to use to reason.

infinity: The beginninglessness and endlessness of contents.

Infiniverse: The infinity of physicalities existing in and by way of the unboundedness of the Ether.

information: A self's composition of inner signs which the self exists in its cognition and memory store.

inner speech: 1. Our ability to think inner symbols as silent sounds for our inaudible listening in our cognitions.

insane desire: A self's unnecessary, unrealistic, delusional and greedy use of Nature's Will to drive for authoritarian control of Nature's Will.

insanity: 1. Unwellness in relating. 2. A self's expression of malevolence based on malevolent motivations, aims, intentions, or purposes which, in turn, reflect malevolent desires.

instinct: A self's spontaneously harmonised or impulsively disharmonised nondeliberate use of Nature's Will with or in isolation from Nature's spontaneously instinctive nondeliberate use of Its Will.

integrity: A self's respect of the Freedom of other selves to choose an action, actions, reaction, or reactions stimulated by their choice to fulfil their chosen need, needs, sane (benevolent) desire or desires without interference by this self's choice to act or react on its chosen insane (malevolent) desire or desires, unless, of course, these selves choose to act or react on their chosen insane desire or desires to interfere with the choice or choices of this self in which case its self-respect (its respect for its own Freedom) will inevitably result in conflict between it and these interfering selves.

intellect: 1. A self's disabling faculty of misunderstanding.

intellectualising: 1. Cogitating or idealising. 2. A self's disabling ability of cogitating or idealising its illusions as delusions and its delusions as fictions.

intelligence: 1. A self's faculty which it uses to guide its ability of reasoning in accord with its harmony within Nature's harmony.. 2. A self's ability of realising its knowledge as meanings and its meanings as facts. 3. A self's ability to gain insight into realities and understand these realities based on its ability to know or realise them.

interpretation: A self's use of its ability of perception to develop concepts as possible explanations of realities based on its ideas.

introspection: Our ability to recognise realistic, natural, or phenomenal qualities existent in our unsharable inner aspects of the World.

intuition: Our pure thinking or our thinking without using inner symbols in our thinking.

kinesiology: The study of the motions in and the movements of a human body as well as factors which effect and affect such motions and movements.

Kinesis: Nature's use of Its Will to activate absolute motion in and movement of bodies.

Kinetics: 1. The activity of Nature's Kinesis. 2. Nature's use of Its Will to activate absolute activities.

knowing: A self's ability of cognising an energy which is experienced by it in its faculty of cognition.

knowledge: 1. Known experience. 2. Our subjectively proven bits of knowledge organised into a continually changing structure.

laws: Delusions with which attempt to control our impulsivity by impulsively using our intellects, rather than realise we only effectively guide our impulsivity by spontaneously using our intelligence.

life: The ability to live.

limfs: See this Glossary's definitions of **luefs**.

living: 1. A means of a self's ability to exist. 2. The use of Nature's Will to activate the progressions of a sensor or the processions of a sensable.

logic: The study of applying laws to a self's cogitating so its cogitating is conditioned.

logical reasoning: A contradiction in terms because logic is not used to establish the activity of free reasoning.

logicising: 1. Conditioned cogitating. 2. Our "second guessing" of our inferential reasoning or our "formal intellectualising". 3. A judgement about the truth or falsity of our free inferential reasoning, instead of using our understanding to discern its truth or falsity. 4. A logician's application of laws to his activity of free reasoning which changes his activity of free reasoning into his absurd activity of conditioned cogitating.

luefs: An acronym standing for "large uncondensed energy forms" which is identical to the acronym, limfs, "large immaterial matter forms", because unbounded uncondensed Energy is identical to unbounded immaterial Matter.

marketing character type: A self who uses the marketing character type feels that its value is dependent on that for which it's exchanged; therefore, it thinks it needs to be in demand to feel harmonious. The marketing character type is used by its inhabiting self to develop its adolescent hero role.

materialism: The philosophical basis of scientism which is the proposition that immaterial phenomena are produced by materialised phenomena, rather than the proposition of immateriality, the philosophical basis of my sciences, selfology and TSQ kinesiology, which is that materialised phenomena are produced by immateriality, i.e., the Phenomenon.

Matter: Energy.

matters: Energies.

Maya: The outer word some Eastern philosophers use to describe our tendency to distort how we intuit as well as cognise realities and Reality so that our recognition of them is also distorted.

meaning: A self's assimilated feeling of an emotion or a sensation for the purpose of symbolising this emotion or sensation.

mechanics: Isaac Newton's word for the study of motion which actually meant the study of how to quantise movement.

metaethics: The knowledge of that beyond ethics.

metalogic: The knowledge of that beyond logic.

metaphysics: 1. The study of immaterial realities existent in and by way of immaterial Reality beyond the existence of materialised realities which are existent in and by way of immaterial Reality. 2. The knowledge of that beyond physics.

misperceiving: A self's disabling ability of intellectually as well as inaccurately assimilating Its feeling of an emotion or a sensation as its interpreted illusion.

moments: The idea that the present is divided into points which follow one another in succession.

moralist: A self who advocates for morality.

morality and immorality: A self's idealistic principle of ruling over its own and other selves' actions and reactions with moral and immoral laws in relation to its superstitions of theistic moral destiny and immoral fate or atheistic moral and immoral fate.

morals: Laws which are supposed to govern behavioural conduct.

motion: An unobservable effect of a self and /or Nature's willing in a particle or organism; therefore, motion only applies to the unobserved, such as the usually unobserved motion of blood cells in our sensable organisms' veins and arteries.

movement: An observable effect of a self and/or Nature's willing, such as the self and/or Nature's use of Its Will to move the arms and legs of this self's sensable organism.

natural: That which is evolved, grown, and developed from Nature by Nature.

natural harmony: The interaction of Nature's willing in Its natures.

Naturalism: S 1. My attempt to reconcile my understanding of Nature's spontaneous instinctive nondeliberate use of Its Will with my spontaneous or impulsive instinctive nondeliberate and deliberate noninstinctive use of Its Will based on my ability to realise the Freedom of my own harmony within Nature's harmony. 2. The metaphysics I've developed which is the basis of my understanding of science—and scientism. 3. The compilation of insights I've had which helped me to understand the importance of Nature's spontaneous instinctive nondeliberate willing in relating Kinetics to Kinesis as well as its importance and the importance of my spontaneous or impulsive instinctive nondeliberate and deliberate noninstinctive willing in relating Selfkinetics to Selfkinesis. 4. My ontology or phenomenology (a self's study of Reality, Phenomenon, oe Nature, realities, phenomena, or natures, and real phenomenal, or natural qualities for the purpose of indicating, describing, and explaining their relationships by using an extrospective scientific research Style and an introspective philosophical research approach in accord with the self's need to attain or deepen its wisdom).

nature: That which is composed of Nature.

Nature: 1. Reality, Activity, Ether, Reality, Quality, Energy, Matter, or Thingness. 2. The Source of everything.

need: A need is a realistic motivator, but a motivator is not necessarily a need, because a motivator is also existed as a sane or an insane desire.

noncognitivism: The theory of ethics which asserts that ethics is a delusion and that we only know our feelings, emotions, decisions, commitments, attitudes, and dispositions which we use delusional concepts, like "evil", "wrong" and "right", to vent.

Nothingness: Usually thought to be a "synonym" for non-Existence; however, nothingness isn't even a mistaken hypothesis or delusion of those who give it credence because it simply isn't existent. Nothingness isn't a synonym for "non-Existence" because the word "non-Existence" carries the connotation that nothingness is the "content" of non-Existence, whereas non-Existence carries the connotation that it's the "container" of nothingness.

noumenon: A delusion of idealists who suppose that a noumenon is a thing as it really is, while a reality is supposedly the noumenon's "unreal" appearance or "phenomenon"; however, a reality is a thing as it is because there are no ideal realities.

ontology: See Naturalism.

organics: The word I use for "the study of motion and movement", rather than Newton's unsuitable word "mechanics".

organism: An evolved, and developed mineral, vegetable, or sensable organic body.

particlise: Nature's spontaneous accidental instinctive nondelibrate use of Its Will to condense or materialise a portion of Its unbounded uncondensed Energy or unbounded immaterial Matter into a condensation or materialisation called a "particle".

perceiving: A self's ability of intelligently as well as accurately assimilating its feeling of emotions and sensations as its interpreted knowledge.

personality roles: Our five social selves, the adult player, the infantile victim, the childish authoritarian, the preadolescent trickster, and the adolescent hero which I have analysed and associated with their respective character types.

phantasia: A Greek word which suggests that it's possible for us to be misled by an appearance if we mistake an illusory appearance (a phantasm) for a physical appearance.

phenomenology: See ontology. The study of phenomena.

Phenomenon: Nature or Reality.

physicality: 1. An activity of realised realities, naturalised natures, condensed energies or materialised matters which are evolved, grown, and developed into the continually changing *structures* of mineral organisms or bodies, vegetable organisms or bodies, and sensable organisms or bodies. 2. A structure that is evolved, grown, and developed by having portions of Reality realised and structured by Reality, portions of Nature natured and structured by Nature, portions of Energy condensed and structured by Energy, or portions of Matter materialised and structured by Matter.

physis: Defined by Aristotle as 'the essence of things that have a source of movement within themselves' (Blackburn, 1994, p. 277).

Polyselfism: The knowledge that selves are either immortals or mortals who originate from and are accidentally generated or activated by Nature's spontaneous instinctive nondeliberate use of Its Will in a parental sensable organism's zygote or bud.

practical reasoning: Freely reasoning about a situation so that we're able to recognise what is happening in this situation and act to use this situation to our advantage.

Preadolescent trickster personality role: A self's orientation in the role of a preadolescent trickster is that of the "manipulator", which means "a self who handles others".

predeterminism: The mistaken hypothesis that the Creator has used his will to create laws by which he has planned our destinies as inevitable events.

priming: A self's initial realisation of its harmony with Nature.

productive-developmental character type: A self who uses its productive-developmental character type knows that it needs to guide its use of the artefacts it develops, such as its essential inner words, and the selfological qualities it expresses, such as its emotion of love. A wise self understands that its emotion of love is a means of its natural harmony within Nature's harmony. The productive-developmental character type is used by it's the self to develop its adult player role.

proper: The opposite of right, just as improper is the opposite of wrong. Proper is the opposite of right because right is based on a self's superstitious laws, while proper is based on a self's realistic needs.

quale: (Plural, "qualia"). A will wave, like a wave of gravity-antigravity, a wave of electromagnetism, or a wave of emoting.

rationalism: A self's superstitious belief that its knowledge is a supernatural a priori implant in its memory which the self thinks God is responsible for implanting.

realisation: A self's recognition of its knowledge, meanings, and facts by its use of its ability to know.

Reality: Nature or Phenomenon.

reasoning: An ability used by a self to explain the arrangement of inner sentences and outer sentences.

receptive character type: A self who uses its receptive character type feels that the means to its natural harmony is existent outside of it, not realising that Nature's harmony has always been within it as well as ubiquitously outside of it; therefore, it attempts to suck into it. The receptive character type is used by its inhabiting self to develop its infantile victim role.

recognitivism: A recognitivist's knowledge beyond ethics.

religion: 1. A self's verbal expression of its wisdom. 2. A self's exploration into the questions of what it is, who it's genuinely, sincerely and authentically expressing from what it is, instead of ingenuinely, insincerely, and inauthentically expressing roles, personae, or false selves from what it is, how it expresses who it is or isn't from what it is, and why it exists as an existent, rather than simply isn't existent.

salvation: The release from suffering you experience when you realise your harmony with Nature.

sane desire: A self's realistic motivating drive in relation to a need.

sanity: 1. Wellness in relating. 2. A self's expression of benevolence based on benevolent motivations, aims, intentions, or purposes which, in turn, reflect beneficial desires.

Schrödinger's cat paradox: A "mind" experiment in which a cat (a symbolisation of a "subatomic particle") is supposedly trapped in an air-tight box containing a radioactive atom with a fifty-fifty chance of decaying within the hour so that, if it decays, its radiation will trigger a relay that will cause a hammer to fall and break a glass container holding a sufficient amount of prussic acid to kill the cat.

science: The critical and suitable use of scientific conceptual terms based on the axioms or experiential truths of voluntarism, harmony, conscience, needs, Style, experience, qualification, participant-observation, description, and subjectivism.

scientism: The uncritical and unsuitable use of scientismistic conceptual terms based on the premises or hypothetical propositions of automatism, principles, rules, laws, technique, experimentation, quantification, measurement, delineation, and objectivism.

scientismist: An indifferent advocate of scientism.

scientimistic physics: A scientism of misunderstanding because its premise is that the motions of particles in bodies and the movements of bodies in the environment are governed by laws.

self: A center of pure immaterial energy inhabiting its sensor (its "me" or "aura") as well as its sensable organism or organic body's reticular formation located on its brain stem at the "foot" of its brain who instinctively and nondeliberately or deliberately and noninstinctively uses Nature's Will in harmony or disharmony with Nature's instinctive nondeliberate use of Its Will to activate the activity of its cognitive knowing, motions in and movements of its sensor, motions in its brain and, by way of its brain, motions in and movements of the rest of its sensable organism.

Selfism: My religion which is my understanding of Nature as the Origin of selves.

Selfkinesis: A self's use of Nature's Will to activate motions in and movements of its sensor and sensable organism as well as use the movements of sensable organism to move mineral vegetative, and sensable organisms in its environment.

Selfkinetics: A self's use of Nature's Will to activate its selfological qualitative activities, like Selfkinesis.

selfkom: 1. A self who enjoys its expression of who it's expressing and how it's expresses who it's expressing because it chooses to express harmonious actions and reactions. 2. A lightened or knowledgeable self as well as a lightenly enlightened or knowledgeably wise self. 3. A self who develops its ability to enjoy and help other selves enjoy.

selfkomology: The study of self's enjoyment.

selfkomy: The tendency of a self to enjoy.

selfological qualities: 1. A self's abstractions, like its needs, abilities, and faculties.

selfology: The ontological study of the self, its selfological qualities, how it uses its needs to activate its sensor, and how it uses its cognition to sense by way of its sensor.

selfpath: 1. A self who suffers from its expression of who and how it's pretending to be and leads others to suffer from its expressions of who and how it's pretending to be because it chooses to act on hate. 2. An ignorant self as well as a stupid self. 3. A self who suffers and hinders other selves by causing them to suffer.

selfpathology: The scientific study of a self's suffering or unease.

selfpathy: The tendency of a self to suffer.

sensable organism: 1. A self's sensibly sensed organic body which the self lives as well as inhabits. 2. A self's body of substance, body of procession, or body of energy impulses (sensations).

sensing: A self's ability of cognising a sensation (an impulse of energy) which is experienced by it in its body.

sensor: My emanation of pure energy from the center of pure energy I am as my cognitively as well as directly known "me" or "aura" through which I indirectly know the other inner aspects of my World, like my other inner faculties and abilities, and indirectly know, by sensing through this emanation, my sensable organism and other aspects of my outer World, like the mineral, vegetative, and sensable organisms which I share with the World's infinite selves who also inhabit their sensable organisms and/or emanations of pure energy.

simfs: An acronym standing for "small immaterial matter forms" which is identical to the acronym, suefs, "small uncondensed energy forms", because unbounded uncondensed Energy is identical to unbounded immaterial Matter.

singularity: Supposedly, a primordial particle with a mass smaller than a proton, but with almost infinite density, existing in bounded space-time.

situation: A continual changing of circumstances in relation to a self's needs, abilities, faculties, suefs, luefs, particles, and whole body.

Situation: The Reality in which all situations are existed.

Special Theory of Relativity: Albert Einstein's assumption that the movement of light is constant and may be used to measure simultaneous events in a frame of reference by using light as a means of measurement; however, Einstein also assumed that an observer in another frame of reference who uses light to measure the same events in the original frame of reference will find that these events aren't occurring simultaneously.

specious present: The duration of "the recent past".

stillness: A self's illusion resulting from its limited view of a situation because every situation is an unchanging activity, not an unchanging inactivity (an unchanging stillness).

stupidity: A self's cowardly disabling of its faculty of intelligence and its ability of reasoning because it experiences too much fear and anxiety in its attempts to develop its wisdom by using its intelligence and reasoning to do so.

Style: 1. My natural informal ability to watch what's happening as I interact with this happening by participating in it to intentionally change it to accord with my conscience. 2. My unique natural informal way of relating how I'm acting in accord with whom I'm genuinely, sincerely, and authentically expressing as me from what I am because I know why I exist, i.e., I'm an unplanned undesigned accident of Nature, not a planned designed necessity of God. 3. Continually dallying in my natural informal calmness and enjoying my pleasant emotions, so I'll experience my feelings of happiness as a by-product of my enjoyment, which results in my wellness of cognitive knowing and my sensorial and bodily health!

Substance: The activity of procession.

suefs: See this Glossary's definition of **simfs**.

symbol: An ideogram or a word that only refers to the reality for which it stands, without corresponding to or resembling that reality, e.g., the reality from which I drink is called a "cup", but the word "cup", as a symbol, only stands for the reality and doesn't correspond to or resemble the reality from which I am drinking.

Synconcurrency: The meaningful co-incidence of concurrent situations happening together in Immediacy.

synonyms: The mistaken hypotheses or delusions of linquists who fail to appreciate that every word has certain dissimilar as well as similar connotations which denote a slightly, moderately, or drastically different actuality, illusion, delusion, or hallucination that they've referred to as having exactly the same meaning as other words whose different connotations they're ignoring.

take. "That which applies to the proper, accurate, and appropriate" is another connotation for the word "take"; therefore, a take is the complement of a mistake because a mistake is that which applies to the improper, inaccurate, and inappropriate.

The Big Bang Theory of the Universe: The theory that the universe started from the explosion of an extremely massive particle called a "singularity", which was "somehow" created by the Creator or by non-Existence, to start the Existence of space-time which, in turn, supposedly expanded with the explosion of this extremely massive particle.

The Game of Life: An individual's way of using Nature's Will to lovingly play or anxiously toy at his (or her) own Game within his society's variation of The Game of the Gods.

The Game of the Gods: 1. An uncooperative competing for supremacy. 2. The Game of striving for authority over people who have been indoctrinated with the doctrine that law and order are necessary. 3. A self's attempt to gain more and more influence by continually increasing its rank, privileges, monetary wealth, or fame so gullible people will be impressed by these fleeting illusions and worship them, instead of wisely develop their integrity by paying attention to their consciences.

The Game of Wisdom: Our Game of overcoming our ignorance and stupidity by understanding the relationship of the three major Games to each other.

The Primary Truth of Selfism: Nature's Will.

The Reality of the Harmonious Infiniverse: Nature's way of spontaneous instinctive nondeliberate willing in Its continual evolving, growing, developing, deteriorating, and devolving of an infinity of particles and bodies in Its harmonious and ongoing organisation-disorganisation-reorganisation of them.

The Realm of the Watchers: The realm of the after-death for Selfists (that is, if selves are immortal).

The Secondary Truth of Selfism: Nature's harmony.

The Steady State Theory of the Universe: The theory that the infinite Universe exists in a steady state of "continuous creation" instead of a harmony of organisation-disorganisation-reorganisation; therefore, The Steady State Universe is a myth because this theory is dependent on the falsehoods of Creationism and the steadiness or stability of the Universe.

theology: The delusional study of a fictitious Supreme Being called "God".

theoretical selfological qualitative kinesiology (TSQ kinesiology): The study of the self, its effecting of motions in and movements of its human body, and factors which affect such motions and movements.

theories: Our arrangement of hypotheses (facts) into an organised as well as continually changing structure.

The Ultimate Truth: Freedom.

thing: 1. A composition of Thingness. 2. A nature of Nature or a reality of Reality.

thinking: 1. An ability used by a self to indicate and describe the arrangement of inner sentences and outer sentences 2. The ability of attending to and interpreting realities.

time: The delusional belief that space exists, is static, and is divided so that infinitesimal points in this stasis called "moments" are created and lengths, stretches, or spans of this stasis exist between these points as "durations", such as the past, the present, and the future.

Truism: A Truist's (a Selfist's) word for his or her practice of meditation which is based on the Truist's (the Selfist's) realisation that he, he-she, or she is an expression of the self who inhabits its male, hermaphroditic, or female sensable organism and/or sensor.

Truist: A member of the religion of Selfism (a Selfist) who subscribes to the meditative practice of Selfists called "Truism".

unboundedness (boundlessness): Beginningless and endless extension.

universe: All phenomena taken collectively or all phenomena combined into one.

unknowing: 1. A knower's denial of its need to know. 2. A self's inability to know because the self is ignoring its ability to know.

unlearning: A Satan's activity of replacing its prejudicial conditioning of its activities and behaviours by its irrational belief in destiny or fate with its unprejudiced as well as unbiased realisation of its basis of Freedom.

unsettlement: The final stage of a particle's existence since the particle has become so "brittle" with age that it's inevitably returned to the unbounded uncondensed Energy or unbounded immaterial Matter from which it was first accidentally condensed or materialised by Nature's spontaneous instinctive nondeliberate use of Its Will so that Nature's continued accidental willing in it results in the brittlely aged particle's decondensation or dematerialisation whereupon it ceases to exist as an individual particle.

use: A self's free spontaneous liberal or free impulsive licentious instinctive nondeliberate or deliberate noninstinctive borrowing and expressing of Nature's Will in harmony or disharmony with Nature's free spontaneous instinctive nondeliberate possession and expression of Its Will which, simply put, is a self and Nature's free application or employment of Its Will.

usury: A self's licentious use of Nature's Will.

validity: Our ability to subjectively prove a bit of knowledge as a truth.

valuability: The knowledge of values which is our true guide.

value: Our appreciation of the varying worth of phenomenal qualities as well as our knowledge that every phenomenal self is equal in worth to every other phenomenal self.

vision: Your ability to image a subjective suef you have received from the environment by shining it as a subjective photon to see in your imagination without fantasising, imagining or hallucinating this image.

Volition: Nature's spontaneous instinctive nondeliberate use of Its Will and a self's spontaneous or impulsive instinctive nondeliberate or deliberate noninstinctive use of Nature's Will.

voluntarism: The realisation of the truth that Volition is the ability of Nature which Nature uses to activate natures, like selves, who can use Nature's Will to activate natures (which are not selves) in the nature every self is.

Will: 1. Nature's ability to activate. 2. Nature's factor of relatedness.

wisdom: 1. A self's understanding of its religion. 2. A self's cognition and knowing of its experience of harmony within Nature's harmony, 3. Our cognition by which we continually assimilate new bits of knowledge to our structure of knowledge about Reality and Its realities so our structure of knowledge is always changing to accommodate new bits of knowledge.

Zen: A Zen Buddhist's word for meditation.

References

8 Standard Computer Components and What They Do. (n.d.). Houk Consulting, Web. Accessed 1 Aug 2019.

Airaksinen, T. (2017) 'A Philosophical and Rhetorical Theory of BDSM', *The Journal of Mind and Behavior*, **38**, 1, 53-74.

Algorithm (2019) 'Wikipedia, The Free Encyclopedia', *Wikipedia Foundation*, Inc. Web. Accessed 10 Aug 2019.

Alvele, B. (2018) *Exactly What is Time? Word Press & The WP Theme*, Web, Accessed 12 June 2018.

Audi, R. (1995) *The Cambridge Dictionary of Philosophy, 2nd Edition*, Audi, R. (ed.) Cambridge, United Kingdom: Cambridge University Press.

Babcock, W. (1883) *Jung-Hesse-Harold: A Spiritual Psychology*, New York, New York: Distributed by Dodd, Mead & Company.

Baggott, J. (2018) 'What Einstein meant by 'God does not play dice', *Cosmos*, Web, Accessed 6 Jan 2019.

Basmajian, J. (1970) *Primary Anatomy, Sixth Edition*, Baltimore, Maryland: The Williams & Wilkins Company.

Becker, E. (1973) *The Denial of Death*, New York, New York: The Free Press.

Berne, E. (1961) *T/A: Transactional Analysis in Psychotherapy*, New York, New York: Ballantine Books.

Berne, E. (1964) *Games People Play*, New York, New York: Ballantine Books.

Berg, B.L. (1998) *Qualitative Research Methods for the Social Sciences, 3rd Edition*, Needham Heights, Massachusetts: Allyn & Bacon.

Bettelheim, B. (1950) *Love is not Enough*, New York, New York: The Free Press.

Bevilacqua, L. and Goldman, D. (2011) 'Genetics of Emotion', *National Center for Biotechnology Information*, Web. Accessed 18 Nov 2018.

Binder, V., Binder, A. and Rimland, B. (1976) *Modern Therapies*, Englewood Cliffs, New Jersey: Prentice-Hall, Inc.

Blackburn, S. (1994) *Oxford Dictionary of Philosophy*, Oxford, New York: Oxford University Press.

Boynton, D. (2016) 'Science and Sympathy: "Intuition" and the Ethics of Human Judgement', *The Journal of Mind and Behaviour*, **37**, 2, 141-62

Breger, L. (1974) *From Instinct to Identity: The Development of Personality*, Englewood Cliffs, New Jersey: Prentice Hall, Inc.

Bruno, F. J. (1977) *Human Adjustment and Personal Growth: Seven Pathways*, New York, New York: John Wiley and Sons, Inc.

Buber, M. (1947) *Between Man and Man. Glasgow*, Great Britain: William Collins Sons & Co., Ltd.

Buber, M. (1958) *I and Thou*, New York, New York: Charles Schribner's Sons.

Campbell, A. (1974) *Seven States of Consciousness: A Vision of Possibilities Suggested by the Teachings of Maharishi Mahesh Yogi*, New York, New York: Harper & Row, Publishers.

Campbell, J. (1968) *Creative Mythology: The Masks of God*, New York, New York: Penguin Books.

Campbell, J. and Moyers, B. (1988) *The Power of Myth*, New York, New York: Anchor Books, Doubleday.

Clayman, C. (1991) *The Brain and Nervous System*, New York, New York: Reader's Digest Association, Inc.

Clegg, B. (2003) *A Brief History of Infinity: The Quest to Think the Unthinkable*, Croydon, Great Britain: CPI Group (UK) Ltd.

Cohen, A. and Bradford, D. (1990) *Influence without Authority*, New York, New York: John Wiley & Sons.

Crummett, W. and Western, A. (1994) *University Physics: Models and Applications*, Dubuque, Indiana: Wm. C. Brown Publishers.

Death: The Greatest Teacher. Melvin Mcleod: Editor-in-Chief. (2017, November). Lion's Roar: Buddhist Wisdom for Our Time, pp. 1-88.

Descartes, R., Spinoza, B. and Leibniz, G. W. (1960) *The Rationalists*, New York, New York: Anchor Books.

Diamond, M. L. (1974) *Contemporary Philosophy and Religious Thought: An Introduction to the Philosophy of Religion*, New York, New York: McGraw-Hill, Inc.

Doidge, N. (2007) *The Brain that Changes Itself: Stories of Personal Triumph from the Frontiers of Brain Science'*, New York, New York: Penguin Group, Inc.

Ellenberger, H. F. (1970) *The Discovery of the Unconscious: The History and Evolution of Dynamic Psychiatry*, New York, New York: Basic Books Inc., Publishers.

Extance, A. (The Royal Society of Chemistry. 20 Feb 2017). Do hydrogen bonds have covalent character? Chemistryworld, Web. Accessed 9 Dec 2018.

Feifel, H. (1959) *The Meaning of Death*, Feifel, H. (ed.) New York, New York: McGraw-Hill Book Company.

Five Basic Components of Computer System. (n.d.). byte-notes, Web. Accessed 1 Aug 2019.

Freshwater, D. (2006) *Mental Health and Illness: Questions and answers for counsellors and therapists*, Chichester, West Sussex, England: Whurr Publishers Limited.

Freud, S. (1961) *Civilisation and Its Discontents*, New York, New York: W. W. Norton & Company.

Fromm, E. (1947) *Man for Himself: An Inquiry into the Psychology of Ethics*, Greenwich Connecticut: Fawcett Publications, Inc.

Fromm, E. (1950) *Psychoanalysis and Religion*, New Haven, Connecticut: Yale University Press.

Fromm, E. (1956) *The Art of Loving*, New York, New York: Harper & Row, Publishers.

Fromm, E. (1962) *Beyond the Chains of Illusion: My Encounter with Marx and Freud*, New York, New York: Simon and Schuster.

Fromm, E. (1964) *The Heart of Man: Its Genius for Good and Evil*, New York, New York: Harper & Row, Publishers.

Fromm, E. (1969) *Escape from Freedom*, New York, New York: Avon Books.

Fromm, E. (1970) *The Crisis of Psychoanalysis: Essays on Fred, Marx, and Social Psychology*, New York, New York: Holt, Rinehart, and Winston.

Fromm, E. and Xirau, R. (1968) *The Nature of Man. E. Fromm & R. Xirau* (eds.), New York, New York: MacMillan Publishing Co., Inc.

Fromme, E. (1955). *The Dogma of Christ: And Other Essays on Religion, Psychology, and Culture*, New York, New York: Holt Rinehart and Winston.

Fromme, E. (1973) *The Anatomy of Human Destructiveness*, Greenwich Connecticut: Fawcett, Publications.

Garfield, C. (1977) *Rediscovery of the Body*, New York, New York: Dell Publishing Co., Inc.

Genes and thinking skills. (No update). AgeUK, Web. Accessed 18 Nov 2018.

Glasser, W. (1965) *Reality Therapy: A New Approach to Psychiatry*, New York, New York: Harper & Row, Publishers.

Goddard, D. (1938) (ed.) *A Buddhist Bible. D. Goddard*, Boston, Massachusetts: Beacon Press Books.

Goffman, E. (1959) *The Presentation of Self in Everyday Life*, Garden City, New York: Doubleday & Company, Inc.

Golden, C. (No update) 'The 12 Common Archetypes', *Tree of Life*, Web. Accessed 22 June 2021.

Greenberger, D. and Padesky, C. (1995) *Mind Over Mood*, New York, New York : The Guilford Press.

Gregory, R. (1966) *Eye and Brain: the psychology of seeing*, New York, New York: McGraw-Hill Book Company.

Gribbin, J. (1996) *Companion to the Cosmos*, New York, New York: Little, Brown and Company.

Gruber, R. P. and Block, R. A. (2013) 'The Flow of Time as a Perceptual Illusion', *The Journal of Mind and Behavior*, **34**, 1, 91-100.

Hall, C. S. (1979) *A Primer of Freudian Psychology*, New York, New York: A Mentor Book.

Hanh, T. N. (2017) 'See the Universe in a Sunflower', *Melvin Mcleod: Editor-in-Chief, Lion's Roar: Buddhist Wisdom for Our Time*, 36-45.

Happold, F. C. (1963) *Mysticism: A Study and an Anthology*, Harmondsworth, Middlesex, United Kingdom: Pelican Books.

Hard Disc Data Encoding and Decoding. (n.d.). Angelfire, Web. Accessed 1 Aug 2019.

Harpur, T. (2004) *The Pagan Christ: Recovering the Lost Light*, Toronto, Ontario: Thomas Allen Publishers.

Harris, T. (1967) *I'm OK-You're OK*, New York, New York: Harper & Row Publishers, Inc.

Hasanoglu, K. (2018) *Accounting for the Specious Present*, The Journal of Mind and Behavior, **39**, 3, 181-204.

Hawkins, D. R. (1995) *Power vs Force: The Hidden Determinants of Human Behaviour*, Carlsbad, California: Hay House, Inc.

Hayakawa, S. (1943) *The Use and Misuse of Language*, New York, New York: Fawcett World Library.

Hayakawa, S. I. (1963) *Language in Thought and Action*, New York, New York: Harcourt Brace Jovanovich, Inc.

Henderson (Jr.), C. P. (1946) *God and Science: The Death and Rebirth of Theism*, Atlanta Georgia: John Knox Press.

Hendricks, S. (2017) 'Did Einstein Pray? What the Great Genius Thought about God', *Big Think*, Web. Accessed 6 Jan 2019.

Herrigel, E. (1953) *Zen in the Art of Archery*, New York, New York: Vintage Books.

Herrigel, E. (1960) *The Method of Zen*, New York, New York: Vintage Books.

(2019) 'How do digital images work?', *Bitesize*, Web. Accessed 3 Aug 2019.

Humphreys, C. (1951) *Buddhism*, Harmondsworth, Middlesex, United Kingdom: Penguin Books, Inc.

Hurley, S. (2015) 'The Steady State Theory', *Explaining Science*, Web. Accessed 14 May 2021.

(2018) 'Hydrogen Bonding', *Chemistry Libre Texts*, Web. Accessed 9 Dec 2018.

Jung, C. (1938) *Psychology and Religion*, Binghamton, New York: The Vail-Ballou Press, Inc.

Jung, C. (1957) *The Undiscovered Self*, New York, New York: The New American Library, Inc.

Jung, C. (1971) *The Portable Jung*, Campbell, J. (ed.) Harmondsworth, Middlesex, England: Penguin Books.

Jung, C. G. (1959) *The Basic Writings of C. G. Jung*, de Laszlo, V. S. (ed.) New York, New York: The Modern Library.

Kaku, M. and Thompson, J. (1987) *Beyond Einstein: The Cosmic Quest for the Theory of the Universe*, New York, New York: Anchor Books, Doubleday.

Kant, I. (1949) *Fundamental Principles of the Metaphysics of Morals*, Indianapolis, Indiana: Bobbs-Merrill Educational Publishing.

Kaplan, L. J. (1978) *Oneness and Separateness: From Infant to Individual*, New York, New York: Simon and Schuster.

Kapleau, P. (1965) *The Three Pillars of Zen*, New York, New York: Beacon Press.

Kapleau, P. (1978) *Zen: Dawn in the West*, New York, New York: Anchor Books.

Koestler, A. (1972) *The Roots of Coincidence*, London, England: Hutchinson & Co., Ltd.

Koterski, J. W. (2009) *An Introduction to Medieval Philosophy: Basic Concepts*, Chichester, West Sussex, United Kingdom: John Wiley & Sons, Ltd.

Krellenstein, M. (2017) 'Moral Nihilism and its Implications', *The Journal of Mind and Behavior*, **38**, 1, 75-90.

Kübler-Ross, E. (1975) *Death: The Final Stage of Growth*, Englewood Cliffs, New Jersey: Prentice-Hall, Inc.

Laing, R. D. (1960) *The Divided Self: An Existential Study in Sanity and Madness*, Harmondsworth, Middlesex, United Kingdom: Penguin Books, Inc.

Laing, R. D. (1961) *Self and Others*, Harmondsworth, Middlesex, United Kingdom: Penguin Books, Inc.

Laing, R. D. (1967) *The Politics of Experience and the Bird of Paradise*, Harmondsworth, Middlesex, United Kingdom: Penguin Books, Inc.

Laing, R. D. (1970) *Knots*, Harmondsworth, Middlesex, United Kingdom: Penguin Books, Inc.

Laing, R. D. and Esterson, A. (1964) *Sanity, Madness and the Family*, Harmondsworth, Middlesex, United Kingdom: Penguin Books, Inc.

Landau, S. I. (1968) *Standard College Dictionary*, Landau, S. I. (Editor in Chief) New York, New York: Funk & Wagnalls.

Lazarus, R. S. and Lazarus, B. N. (1994) *Passion and Reason: Making Sense of Our Emotions*, Oxford, New York: Oxford University Press.

LeShan, L. (1976) *Alternate Realities: The Search for the Full Human Being*, New York, New York: Ballantine Books.

LeShan, L. and Margenau, H. (1982) *Einstein's Space & Van Gogh's Sky: Physical Reality and Beyond*, New York, New York: MacMillan Publishing Co., Inc.

Lock, J., Berkley, G. and Hume, D. (1961) *The Empiricists*, New York, New York: Anchor Books.

Lowen, A. (1975) *Bioenergetics*, Harmondsworth, Middlesex, England: Penguin Books, Ltd.

MacLachlan, J. (1988) *Children of Prometheus: A History of Science and Technology*, Collegiate Edition, Toronto, Ontario: Wall & Emerson, Inc.

Manser, A. (1966) *Sartre: A Philosophic Study*, Oxford, New York: Oxford University Press.

Marx, K. and Engels, F. (1986) *The Manifesto of the Communist Party*, In McLellan, D. *The Essential, Marx-Engels-Lenin-Mao: Five Texts on the Principles of Socialism*, 7-99, Second Edition. McLellan, D. (ed.) Boston, Massachusetts: Unwin Hyman Ltd.

Moore, J. (2016) 'Behaviour Analytic Pragmatism', *The Journal of Mind and Behavior*, **37**, 3 and 4, 219-46.

Moore, J. (2017) 'John B. Watson's Classical S-R Behaviorism', *The Journal of Mind and Behaviour*, **38**, 1, 1-34.

Murchland, B. (1976) *The Meaning of the Death of God*, New York, New York: Vintage Books.

Needleman, J. (1970) *The New Religions: The Teachings of the East-their special meaning for young Americans*, Richmond Hill, Ontario: Simon & Schuster of Canada, Ltd.

Newberg, A. and Waldman, M. (2016) *How Enlightenment Changes Your Brain: The New Science of Transformation*, New York, New York: Penguin Random House.

Nietzsche, F. (1966) *Beyond Good and Evil*, New York, New York: Vintage Books.

Nietzsche, F. (1967) *On the Genealogy of Morals*, New York, New York: Vintage Books.

Nietzsche, F. (1974) *The Gay Science*, New York, New York: Random House, Inc.

Northrops, F. S. (1946) *The Meeting of the East and West: An Inquiry Concerning World Understanding*, New York, New York: The MacMillan Company.

Numbers, R. L. (2009) *Galileo Goes to Jail and Other Myths about Science and Religion*, Cambridge, Massachusetts: Harvard University Press.

O'Connell, A. L. and Gardner, E. B. (1972) *Understanding the Scientific Bases of Human Movement*, Baltimore, Maryland: The Williams & Wilkins Company.

Pagels, E. (1995) *The Origin of Satan*, New York, New York: Vintage Books.

Parker, D. H. (1928) *Schopenhauer: Selections*, Parker, D. H. (ed.) New York, New York: Charles Scribner's Sons.

Parker, J. and Stanton, J. (2003) *Mythologica: A Treasury of World Myths and Legends*, Parker, J. and Stanton, J. (ed.) Vancouver, British Columbia: Raincoast Books.

Patanjali, B. S. (1938) *Aphorisms of Yoga*, London, England: Faber and Faber Limited.

Pearson, C. (2011) *Albert Einstein: "There Is Neither Evolution Nor Destiny; Only Being"*, TM BLOG, Web. Accessed 6 Jan 2019.

People also ask. (No update). Wikipedia: The Free Encyclopaedia (in relation to Wikipedia's feedback on genetics), Web. Accessed 18 Nov 2018.

Peri Phuseôs: Physics, Physicists, and Phusis in Aristotle (2nd draft). (No update.). Academia, Web. Accessed 16 Dec 2017.

Perls, F. (1969) *In and Out the Garbage Pail*, New York, New York: Bantam Books, Inc.

Perls, F., Hefferline, R. and Goodman, P. (1951) *Gestalt Therapy*, New York, New York: Crown Publishers, Inc.

Pinker, S. (1997) *How the Mind Works*, New York, New York: Norton & Company.

Pinker, S. (2007) *The Stuff of Thought: Language as a Window into Human Nature*, New York, New York: Penguin Group, Inc.

Pirsig, R. M. (1974) *Zen and the Art of Motorcycle Maintenance: An Inquiry into Values*, New York, New York: Bantam Books.

Polk, T. (2016) *The Aging Brain*, Chantilly, Virginia: The Great Courses.

Preamble to the Canadian Charter of Rights and Freedoms. (Updated 11 May 2018 03:57 UTC). Wikipedia: The Free Encyclopaedia, Wikipedia Foundation, Inc. Web. Accessed 18 May 2018.

Purines and Pyrimidines. (No update). Diffen, Web. Accessed 9 Dec 2018.

Putney, S. and Putney, G. (1964) *The Adjusted American: Normal Neuroses in the Individual and Society*, New York, New York: Harper & Row, Publishers.

Rand, A. (1961) *The Virtue of Selfishness*, New York, New York: New American Library.

Randall, L. (2005) *Warped Passages: Unravelling the Mysteries of the Universe's Hidden Dimensions*, New York, New York: HarperCollins Publishers.

Renou, L. (1961) *Hinduism*, Renou, L. (ed.) New York, New York: George Braziller, Inc.

Rinpoche, S. (1993) *The Tibetan Book of Living and Dying*, New York, New York: Harper San Francisco.

Rohr, R. (2019) *The Universal Christ: How a Forgotten Reality Can Change Everything We See, Hope for, and Believe*, New York, New York: Convergent Books.

Sahakian, W. S. (1965) *Psychology of Personality: Readings in Theory*, 2nd Edition. Chicago, Illinois: Rand McNally College Publishing Company.

Sartre, J. (1953) 'Being and Nothingness', *Washington Square Press Edition*, New York, New York: Pocket Books.

Sartre, J. (1963) *Search for a Method*, New York, New York: Vintage Books.

Sedgwick, P. (1971) *R. D. Laing: Self, Symptom and Society*, In Boyers, R. and Orrill, R. *R. D. Laing & Anti-Psychiatry*, 1-50, New York, New York: Harper & Row, Publishers.

Seeley, R., Stevens, T. and Tate, P. (1989) *Anatomy and Physiology*, St Louis, Missouri: Times Mirror/Mosby College Publishing.

Shippee, S. (2017) *The Real Meaning of Original Sin*, Mcleod, M. (ed.) *Lion's Roar: Buddhist Wisdom for Our Time*, 13-4.

Smith, H. (1986) *The Religions of Man*, New York, New York: Harper & Row, Publishers.

Smith, T. V. (1934) *Philosophers Speak for Themselves: From Aristotle to Plotinus*, Smith, T. V. (ed.) Chicago, Illinois: The University of Chicago Press.

Smoot, G. and Davidson, K. (1993) *Wrinkles in Time*, New York, New York: Avon Books.

Snelling, J. (1991) *The Buddhist Handbook: The Complete Guide to Buddhist Schools, Teaching, Practice, and History*, Rochester, Vermont: Inner Traditions International.

Stedman, J. M., Kostelecky, M., Spalding, T. L. and Gagné, C. L. (2016) 'Scientific Realism, Psychological Realism, and Aristotelian-Thomistic', *Realism. The Journal of Mind and Behavior*, **37**, 3 and 4, 199-218.

Stedman, J. M., Kostelecky, M., Spalding, T. L. and Gagné, C. L. (2017) 'Animal Cognition: An Aristotelian-Thomistic Perspective', *The Journal of Mind and Behavior*, **38**, 3 and 4, 193-214.

Stevens, J. (1975) *gestalt is*, Stevens, J. O (ed.) Moab, Utah: Real People Press.

Suzuki, D. T. (1969) *The Zen Doctrine of No Mind*, London, England: Rider Pocket Edition.

Suzuki, D. T., Fromm, E. and DeMartino, R. (1960) *Zen Buddhism and Psychoanalysis*, New York, New York: Grove Press, Inc.

Tegchock, K. J. (2012) *Insight into Emptiness*, Boston Massachusetts: Wisdom Publications.

The Genetic Code. (No update). Khan Academy, Web. Accessed 9 Dec 2018.

The role of the genetic code in protein synthesis. (6 Nov 2014, 16:55). Animal Research, Info, Web. Accessed 9 Dec 2018.

Thurman, R. A. (1995) *Essential Tibetan Buddhism*, Edison, New Jersey: Castle Books.

Tillich, P. (1952) *The Courage to Be*. Glasgow, Great Britain: William Collins Sons & Co., Ltd.

Tolkien, J. (1990) *The Lord of the Rings*, Hammersmith, London: HarperCollins Publishers.

Transcription, Translation, and Replication. (No update). atdbio, Web. Accessed 9 Dec 2018.

Vardley, L. (1995) *God in All Worlds: An Anthology of Contemporary Spiritual Writing*, Vardley, L. (ed.). Toronto, Ontario: Vintage Canada.

Varnon, C. and Abramson, C. (2018) 'The Propeller Experiment Controller: Automation for the Comparative Analysis of Behavior in Research and Teaching', *The Journal of Mind and Behaviour*, **39**, 1 and 2.

Watson, J. D. (1968) *The Double Helix*, New York, New York: The New American Library.

Watson, W. (No update) *"Notes to Pages 83-84": The Lost Second Book of Aristotle's Poetics*, University of Chicago Press, Web. Accessed 17 Dec 2017.

Watts, A. (1957) *The Way of Zen*, New York, New York: Vintage Books.

Watts, A. (1958) *This is it*, London, England: John Murray.

Watts, A. (1966) *The Book: On the Taboo Against Knowing Who You Are*, New York, New York: Vintage Books.

Wegner, D. (2002) *The Illusion of Conscious Will*, Cambridge, Massachusetts: MIT Press.

What Baha'is Believe. (No update). The Baha'i Faith, Web. Accessed 19 Oct 2017.

White, M. (2001) *Tolkien: A Biography*, London, England: Abascus (Time Warner Book Group UK).

Whiting, D. (2016) 'On the Appearance and Reality of Mind', *The Journal of Mind and Behavior*, **37**, 1, 47-70.

Wittgenstein, L. (2009) *Philosophical Investigations*, Hacker, P. and Schulte, J. (4th ed.) Chichester, West Sussex, United Kingdom: Wiley-Blackwell.

Wood, E. (1957). *Zen Dictionary*, Harmondsworth, Middlesex, United Kingdom: Penguin Books.

Woollams, S. and Brown, M. (1979) *TA: The Total Handbook of Transactional Analysis*, Englewood Cliffs, New Jersey: Prentice-Hall, Inc.

Zimmer, C. (2004) *Soul Made Flesh: The Discovery of the Brain and How It Changed the World*, New York, New York: Free Press.

Zukav, G. (1979) *The Dancing Wu Li Masters: An Overview of the New Physics*, New York, New York: Bantam Books.

Zweig, C. and Abrams, J. E. (1991) *Meeting the Shadow: The Hidden Power of the Dark Side of Human Nature*, New York, New York: C.P. Putnam's Sons.

Printed in the USA
CPSIA information can be obtained
at www.ICGtesting.com
LVHW010811260524
780465LV00009B/22